PRAISE FOR *FLY FISHING WITH DARTH VADER* AND MATT LABASH

"Matt Labash's book rocks. He is Hunter S. Thompson on acid."
—P.J. O'Rourke

"I started reading Matt Labash because I was beginning to be afraid that the devil had all the best tunes: now it's the tunes themselves by which I am seduced."
—Christopher Hitchens

"Matt Labash is, simply put, one of the best journalists in the country. He's a brilliant writer—hilarious, profound and sharp as an X-Acto. His prose can do the impossible—even humanize Dick Cheney."
—A. J. Jacobs

"Every now and then, a collection of remarkable stories from a magazine writer has the effect of unleashing a significant new voice on an unsuspecting public. Tom Wolfe's *Kandy-Kolored Tangerine-Flake Streamline Baby* comes to mind. And so it is with Matt Labash's wonderful *Fly Fishing with Darth Vader*."
—Mark Warren, *Esquire*

"In a just world, Matt Labash would be celebrated as the heir to Tom Wolfe, Hunter Thompson and other writers in the 1960s and 1970s who were corralled under the rubric of 'new journalism'. . . . Mr. Labash inhabits a story so thoroughly that readers feel as if they're at his side, seeing events with his sharp eye, privy to his wisecracks, savoring moments when he reels in what feels like the truth."
—Mark Lasswell, *The Wall Street Journal*

"Consistently one of the best magazine writers in the country."
—David Brooks, *The New York Times*

"The funniest thing I'll read all year. . . . Labash has an innate sympathy for scoundrels, and he brings them to life like no other journalist today. . . . Take a stand for great journalism and buy it."
—Jeffrey Goldberg, *The Atlantic*

"Mr. Labash is known as the king of hang time, insinuating himself into a subject's world—remember immersion journalism?—and then writing those encounters up in all their rococo glory."
—David Carr, *The New York Times*

"Labash takes readers to the fringes in his portraits of people and places outside the mainstream and, very often, beyond our ken. His subjects are outlandish and unforgettable. . . . [He] gives readers a real glimpse at the strangeness and silliness that suffuse American political life."
—*Publishers Weekly*

"Go buy Matt's book, which has been dubbed 'the funniest book of the year' by multiple *Atlantic* blogs, including this one."
—Joshua Green, *The Atlantic*

"[Labash is] an excellent word slinger. . . . The best stuff is the unexpected, and *Fly Fishing* is packed with it."
—Martin Zimmerman, *The San Diego Union Tribune*

"Whatever their politics, readers will appreciate Labash's energetic style and biting insights."
—*Booklist*

"By targeting his sensibilities on the fringe figures of American politics, Labash performs a valuable public service even as he establishes himself as one of the top writers of his generation."
—David Blum, *First Things*

"Labash makes a worthy case for entry into the canon of gonzo journalism elites."
—Daniel Newhauser, *Roll Call*

FLY FISHING

WITH DARTH VADER

And Other Adventures with Evangelical Wrestlers,
Political Hitmen, and Jewish Cowboys

MATT LABASH

SIMON & SCHUSTER PAPERBACKS
NEW YORK   LONDON   TORONTO   SYDNEY

Simon & Schuster Paperbacks
A Division of Simon & Schuster, Inc.
1230 Avenue of the Americas
New York, NY 10020

First Simon & Schuster trade paperback edition February 2011

SIMON & SCHUSTER PAPERBACKS and colophon are registered
trademarks of Simon & Schuster, Inc.

For information about special discounts for bulk purchases,
please contact Simon & Schuster Special Sales at
1-866-506-1949 or business@simonandschuster.com.

The Simon & Schuster Speakers Bureau can bring authors
to your live event. For more information or to book an event,
contact the Simon & Schuster Speakers Bureau at
1-866-248-3049 or visit our website at www.simonspeakers.com.

Designed by Esther Paradelo

Manufactured in the United States of America

10 9 8 7 6 5 4 3 2 1

The Library of Congress has cataloged the hardcover edition as follows:

Labash, Matt.
Fly fishing with Darth Vader : and other adventures with evangelical wrestlers, political
hitmen, and Jewish cowboys / Matt Labash.
p. cm.
1. United States—Civilization—1970—Anecdotes. 2. United States—Politics and
government—2001–2009—Anecdotes. 3. United States—Politics and government—1993–2001—Anecdotes. 4. United States—Social conditions—1980—Anecdotes. 5. Politicians—United States—Anecdotes. 6. Celebrities—United States—Anecdotes. 7. Political corruption—United States—Anecdotes. 8. Political culture—United
States—Anecdotes. 9. Labash, Matt—Anecdotes. 10. Journalists—United States—Biography—Anecdotes. I. Weekly standard (New York, N.Y.) II. Title.
E169.12.L25   2010
973.9—dc22   2009033330

ISBN 978-1-4391-5997-2
ISBN 978-1-4391-5998-9 (pbk)
ISBN 978-1-4391-7010-6 (ebook)

To Alana

"No one likes a fellow who is all rogue, but we'll forgive him almost anything if there is warmth of human sympathy underneath his rogueries. The immortal types of comedy are just such men."

—W.C. Fields

"I will be a model prisoner, as I have been a model citizen."

—Edwin Edwards

CONTENTS

INTRODUCTION

Within minutes of finishing reading this book, I predict you'll be writing a check ($19.95, plus S&H) for your charter membership in the Matt Labash Fan Club. The writing is that good. But let's say you're short on time and instead of actually reading every chapter, you simply want to know what the author is like. Fair enough. Let me sum him up for you:

Midway through 2003, the voters of California tired of their drab, inept governor and decided to trade him for an entertaining and inept version. For journalists, the idea of Arnold Schwarzenegger running a state was too much to resist, so Matt and I flew to Los Angeles to cover the story. On election night, we headed to the ballroom of the Century Plaza Hotel to watch Arnold declare victory.

Like most political events, it was a disappointment. The room was cavernous and hot, packed shoulder to shoulder with frustrated reporters and camera crews, none of whom could get within six sheriff's deputies of the new governor. I shifted from foot to foot, sweating and scribbling in my notebook, desperately trying to find some color in a surprisingly colorless night.

Schwarzenegger was doing the winner's dance at the front of the room. Behind him stood a set of risers populated with what appeared to be his wife's entire extended family, rows and rows of Kennedys, each with the same chin and teeth, an Irish Catholic version of the Boys from Brazil. In the middle of this sea of familiar jawlines stood a lone man in an Italian suit with a glass of bourbon in his hand. It was Matt Labash. He was staring down at Arnold's bald spot and grinning. A purloined Secret Service pin glittered in his lapel.

To this day I have no idea where he got the pin or how he wound up on stage. (Trade secrets.) But I wasn't surprised that he did. Nobody gets closer to the story than Matt Labash. And nobody has a better time doing it.

Matt doesn't write for the most widely read publication in America; he's unlikely to win a Pulitzer Prize for a nine-part series on congressional earmark reform. He doesn't care, and it's not his beat. His subject is the individual, and that's what he writes about, more deeply than anyone I know.

To see him report is to watch a man in a kind of purposeful trance. Nothing distracts him from the goal of knowing more. I once saw him walk alone, without hesitation or even a flashlight, into the darkened, fetid, and dangerous New Orleans Convention Center after Hurricane Katrina, something cops with riot guns were unwilling to do. (In fairness to the police, I didn't follow him in, either.) When the second war in Iraq broke out, some journalists embedded with the military and many others covered the action from their camera positions in Qatar. Matt entered the country overland by Jeep, armed only with a half-drunk Christopher Hitchens.

I'll never forget walking past Matt's office at the *Weekly Standard* one afternoon in the late 1990s. He was on the phone with a reluctant source, an old friend of Bill Clinton's from Arkansas, as I remember. Matt's side of the conversation went like this:

"Look, you're uncomfortable talking. I understand. No shame in that. But I think you know it's the right thing to do. Don't take my word for it. Let's bring this to a higher authority. Let's pray about it."

At this point, phone to his ear, he fell to his knees on the floor of his office.

By the time I returned with a cup of coffee from the break room, he had the story.

It dawns on me that what I just wrote might make Matt sound like an ordinary sleazeball reporter, someone willing to say anything to make the sale. Not so. In order to be slick you have to be shallow. Matt, by contrast, immerses himself so completely in the worlds of his subjects that he almost always winds up empathetic. Anyone can write the Al-Sharpton-is-a-pudgy-race-baiting-phony piece, for instance, and many have. But the caricature is only partly accurate. No man is the sum of his press conferences. There's more, and it's almost always fascinating. Matt has the tenacity to capture all dimensions.

Being a magazine writer specializing in profiles is a little like serial monogamy: You enter into a series of intense, passionate relationships that at a certain point ends abruptly. Hurt feelings are inevitable. Yet Matt is the rare literary womanizer who has left behind a trail of affection. Years later, people he once wrote about still call him for advice.

It's not that he was so kind to them in print. Often he wasn't. It's that he understood them. And likely entertained them.

Matt Labash is the single wittiest person I have ever met in a life devoted to seeking out amusing people. This collection speaks for itself, and I don't want to spoil it. But let me put it this way: Anyone who can, off the top of his head, sum up Canadians as "a docile, Zamboni-driving people who subsist on seal casserole and Molson" is worth having dinner with. I recommend it if you ever get the chance.

—Tucker Carlson

FLY FISHING WITH DARTH VADER

DETROIT

The City Where the Sirens Never Sleep

This is the place where bad times get sent to make them belong to somebody else, thus, it seems easy to agree about Detroit because the city embodies everything the rest of the country wants to get over.
— Jerry Herron, *AfterCulture: Detroit and the Humiliation of History* (1993)

Detroit

My plane hadn't even finished descending through the snow-drizzly sheets of December gray when already, I heard someone crack on it. "Ladies and gentlemen," a Northwest flight attendant announced, "welcome to lovely Detroit, the one and only home of the Detroit auto worker of America. Happiness is a way of travel, not a destination."

The lawyer sitting next to me sniggered. He was only buzzing in for a day or so, but knowing I was a reporter, come to write a story on the city, he asked, "How long are you in for?"

"About a week," I responded.

"Good luck with that," he said, piteously shaking his head. "It sucks."

Before I'd left, I'd asked an acquaintance if he was from Detroit. "Indeed I am," he said. "Give me all your fucking money." Another colleague, always mindful of my desire for maximum material, suggested, "You should go when it's warm, you'd have a better chance of getting hurt."

Somewhere along the way, Detroit became our national ashtray, a safe place for everyone to stub out the butt of their jokes. This was never more evident than at the recent congressional hearings featuring the heads of the Big Three automakers, now more often called the Detroit Three, as that sounds more synonymous with failure. Yes, they have been feckless and tone-deaf in the past, and now look like stalkers trying to make people love them with desperation moves such as Ford breaking the "Taurus" name out of mothballs, or Chrysler steering a herd of cattle through downtown Detroit for an auto show (some of the longhorns started humping each other in front of reporters, giving new meaning to the "Dodge Ram," which they were intended to advertise).

But with millions of jobs on the line, including their own, the Detroit Three honchos went to Washington to endure the kabuki theater, first in their private jets, then in their sad little hybrids. All to get their slats kicked in by Congress (and who has been more profligate than they?) in order to secure a bridge loan to withstand an economy wrecked by others who'd secured no-strings bailouts before them. The absurdist spectacle was best summed up by car aficionado Jay Leno: "People who are trillions of dollars in debt, yelling at people who are billions of dollars in debt."

It happens, though, when you're from Detroit. In the popular imagination, the Motor City has gone from being the Arsenal of Democracy, so named for their converting auto factories to make the weapons that helped us win World War II, and the incubator of the middle class (now leading the nation in foreclosure rates, Detroit once had the highest rate of home ownership in the country) to being Dysfunction Junction. To Detroit's credit, they've earned it.

Before arriving, I conducted an exhaustive survey, reading everything I could about Detroit, including and especially the journalistic labor of the diligent if shell-shocked scribes of the *Detroit News* and the *Detroit Free Press.* How bad is Detroit? Let's review:

Its recently resigned mayor, Kwame Kilpatrick, he of the Kangol hats and five-button suits, now wears jailhouse orange, as he's currently serving a four-month sentence as part of a plea agreement for perjuring himself regarding an extramarital affair with his chief of staff, which yielded soupy love-daddy text messages that would make Barry White yak in his grave. Those in Detroit who are neither recipients of sweetheart contracts nor Kilpatrick family members on the city payroll at inflated salaries think he got off easy. Because what led to the perjury was concealing an $8.4 million payout from city coffers to settle a whistleblower suit brought by cops who'd been fired for investigating, among other things, the murder of a stripper named Strawberry who, prior to her death, was allegedly beat up by Kilpatrick's wife when she caught her entertaining her husband.

In a city often known as the nation's murder capital, with over ten thousand unsolved murders dating back to 1960, the police are in shambles through cutbacks and corruption trials. (They have a profitable sideline, though, as one of the nation's largest gun dealers, having sold fourteen tons of used weapons out-of-state.) Their response times are legendarily slow. Their crime lab is so inept that it has been closed. One Detroit man found police so unresponsive when trying to turn himself in for murder that he hopped a bus to Toledo and confessed there instead.

Detroit schools haven't ordered new textbooks in nineteen years. Students have reported having to bring their own toilet paper. Teachers have reported bringing hammers to class for protection. Declining enrollment has forced sixty-seven school closures since 2005 (more than a quarter of the city's schools). The graduation rate is 24.9 percent, the lowest of any large school district in the country. Not for nothing did one frustrated activist start pelting school board members with grapes during a meeting. She probably should've reached for something heavier.

An internal audit, which was fourteen months late, estimates next year's city deficit to be as high as $200 million (helped along by $335,000 embezzled from the Department of Health and Wellness Promotion). With a dwindling tax base—even the city's three once-profitable casinos are seeing a downturn in revenues (the Greektown Casino is in bankruptcy)—the city has kicked around every moneymaking scheme from selling off ownership rights to the tunnel it shares with neighboring Windsor, Canada, to a fast-food tax. It's perhaps unsurprising that Detroit now has the most speed traps in the nation.

It also has one of the highest property tax rates in Michigan, yet has over sixty thousand vacant dwellings (a guesstimate—nobody keeps official count), meaning real estate values are in the toilet. Over the summer of 2008, the *Detroit News* sent a headline around the world about a Detroit house that was for sale for one dollar. But it's not even that uncommon. As of this writing, there are at least five one-dollar homes for sale in Detroit.

The city council has been such a joke that one former member demanded seventeen pounds of sausages as part of her $150,000 bribe. Its prognosis for respectability hasn't grown stronger with Monica Conyers, wife of congressman John Conyers, taking the helm. She has managed to get in a barroom brawl, threatened to shoot a mayoral staffer as well as have him beaten up, and twice called a burly and bald fellow council member "Shrek" during a public hearing. But with all the problems facing the city, the council still found time to pass a non-binding resolution supporting the impeachment of George W. Bush.

How bad is Detroit? It once gave the keys to the city to Saddam Hussein.

Over the past several years, it has ranked as the most murderous city, the poorest city, the most segregated city, as the city with the highest auto insurance rates, with the bleakest outlook for workers in their twenties and thirties, and as the place with the most heart attacks, slowest income growth, and fewest sunny days. It is a city without a single national grocery store chain. It has been deemed the most stressful metropolitan area in America. Likewise, it has ranked last in numerous studies: in new employment growth, in environmental indicators, in the rate of immunization of two-year-olds, and, among big cities, in the number of high school and college graduates.

Men's Fitness magazine christened Detroit America's fattest city, while *Men's Health* called it America's sexual disease capital. Should the editors of these two metrosexual magazines be concerned for their safety after slagging the citizens of a city that has won the "most dangerous" title for five of the past ten years? Probably not: 47 percent of Detroit adults are functionally illiterate.

On the upside, Detroit ranks as the nation's foremost consumer of Slurpees and of baked beans on Labor Day. And as if all of this isn't humiliating enough, the Detroit Lions are 0-14.

The best description of the feel of the place came to me from Jason Vines: "We're all Kwame-fatigued, the economy is crap, and the Lions suck. We're tired." A former executive with both Ford and Chrysler, Vines spun me around the decimated, half-abandoned neighborhood of Highland Park, which Chrysler left in the early nineties for the greener pastures of Auburn Hills. It's hard to fault them, he notes, since bullets used to occasionally whiz into the Chrysler buildings from the surrounding neighborhood.

Like many Detroiters (he lives in a posh suburb, where houses on his block have remained unsold for six years), he's bracing for one or all of the Big Three to go down. He predicts millions will be thrown out of work, right down to the diner owner in Utah who serves lunch to the people who produce the screws that are bought by the widget manufacturers who produce a component that goes into a seat of a Ford automobile. The diner owner thought he wasn't in the auto business. "But he was," says Vines. "He just didn't know it."

Precisely what caused all this mess is perhaps best left to historians. Locals' ideas for how it happened could keep one pinned to a barstool for weeks: auto companies failing or pushing out to the suburbs and beyond, white flight caused by the '67 riots and busing orders, the twenty-year reign of Mayor Coleman Young, who scared additional middle-class whites off with statements such as "The only way to handle discrimination is to reverse it," freeways destroying mass transit infrastructure, ineptitude, corruption, Japanese cars— take your pick.

What's clear, though, is that Detroit has failed, that it's broken and cracked. It is dying. But it's not yet dead. Although it has lost over half its population since 1950, nine hundred thousand people still live there. I went to Detroit to experience a cross section of those who live between its cracks, who either choose or are stuck with living among the ruins.

For many, Detroit is identified with cars or soul music, with the novels of Elmore Leonard or the architecture of Albert Kahn. If they really hate Detroit, they might recall that its suburbs coughed up Madonna. But for me, Detroit has become synonymous with one man: Charlie LeDuff.

Currently a metro reporter at the *Detroit News,* Charlie crossed my path in 2003 when he was a hotshot national correspondent for the *New York Times.* Stuck on a press bus trailing Arnold Schwarzenegger in the last days before the recall election, I spied a madman a few rows ahead banging on the window as a jubilant crowd in Bakersfield mistook ours for the candidate's bus. Pounding away, Charlie fed back their mistaken adulation. "I'M THE MEDIA! YOU LOVE THE MEDIA!" he bellowed.

I errantly asked someone what motorcycle magazine he worked for, thinking him an out-of-work biker/pirate since he looked like the bastard spawn of Sonny Barger and Jean Lafitte—I described him at the time as "a leathered scribe with bandito facial hair." Part Cajun, part Native American (he says his Indian name is "White Boy"), Charlie was as much performer as reporter, walking around in sleeveless *New York Post* baseball jerseys, once breaking a wineglass on his head to keep campaign staffers off balance. "It's a trick," he told me quietly, "the glass is thin up at the top."

But Charlie was also writing some of the best newspaper feature stories in the country. His beat involved covering what he calls "the hole," forgotten people in forgotten places. He smuggled himself over the Mexican border with coyote-guided migrants and manned the lobster shift with a Burger King drive-thru attendant trying to support her two kids on $252 a week (before taxes). He won a Pulitzer with a piece in which he went to work in a North Carolina slaughterhouse. His editors pulled him out after a month, though he wanted to stay for six. He still thinks he'd have gotten a better ending, since he's convinced somebody on the killing floor would've gotten stabbed.

Charlie grew up in Livonia, a working-class suburb of Detroit, wanting to be a forest ranger. His stepfather had a quick fist and a big ring. The aggression that bred might explain how Charlie could start at nose tackle in high school (nickname: "the Missile") weighing 130 pounds. Feeling adrift after attending the University of Michigan, he took two years off to roam the world. He rode the Trans-Mongolian Railway and slept in the Gobi Desert. He was a bartender in Australia, a baker in Denmark, and worked at a cannery in Alaska, where he lived in a treehouse after chasing the woman who would become his wife up north. (Upon seeing her trip at a party, bump her head on a stove, and lie sprawled on the floor laughing, he thought, "What an ass. I love her!")

Still drifting, he ran into a friend at a party who said he was going to journalism school. "Not trying to paint myself as a rube," says Charlie, "but I'd never heard of journalism school. I never thought I was a genius, but I'm not stupid. This looked good." He applied to Berkeley and got in, though he at first missed the acceptance letter on account of living in the treehouse. As a journalism student, he applied everywhere for internships with clips he picked up at the *Alaska Fisherman's Journal*. Nobody was interested except for one paper: the *New York Times*. "Luck counts too, doggie," he says.

The internship turned into a trial, the trial turned into a marquee gig, in which he got to write a bar column called "Bending Elbows" and a roaming column called "American Album." Charlie also did a participatory documentary series on the *Times*'s Discovery Channel in which he might, for instance, ride a bull in a gay rodeo or get clobbered in an Oakland fight club. "I had whiplash for six months," he says.

But even though he became a fully made man over his decade at the *Times,* it was always a trial of a sort in that politicized meat-grinder. "My stomach hurt every morning," he says. It had been happening for a while, but by 2006, in real estate bubble-wrapped America with no recession in sight, Charlie felt himself having to fight to get his kind of stories into a paper where they were once welcomed. So he walked.

The bubble burst shortly thereafter. Charlie didn't get as much money out of his overpriced L.A. house as he'd assumed, but he wrote a book, played Mr. Mom to his infant daughter, and did some top-shelf magazine work, such as traveling to China for *Vanity Fair* with legendary eighty-four-year-old photographer Robert Frank, who nearly died in Charlie's arms in a soup shop.

But earlier this year, as the nation was roiling and the Detroiti-fication of America was set to explode with the mortgage crisis and massive layoffs, Charlie moved home to work for the *Detroit News.* "I chose them because they chose me. They let me do human," he says. At first, I felt sorry for him. After all, who goes back to Detroit willingly to find work these days? There was a notes-from-Siberia feel to the whole enterprise. When I talked to Charlie on the phone, passing on an idle bit of media gossip, then insisting it stay in the cone of silence, he'd say, "Who am I going to tell, Matt? I'm in Detroit."

But I stopped feeling sorry for him when his pieces started arriving in my inbox like a steady drip. Charlie was back in the hole with a vengeance.

He rode around with a near-suicidal Jack Kevorkian in Kevorkian's new egg-shaped electric car. Fresh from prison, Dr. Death now lived in a dumpy apartment, wore Salvation Army clothes, and told Charlie he wished he'd never been born. He hung with Dead Squad cops, who told stories of how more Detroiters get killed before Christmas so the murderers can avoid buying Christmas gifts, while puzzling that one murder victim had her feet removed ("Why did they take the feet? We can't use the feet").

He profiled a repo man who, with business now booming in the economic downturn, was suddenly able to remodel his bathroom, send his child to private school, and shop for vacation property. While everyone has done the white-flight story, and a few more have done the black-flight story, Charlie did "The Flight of the Dead." He got the idea while putting around the streets of Detroit in his 1973 Checker Cab ("made in Kalamazoo," he says proudly), cruising past a cemetery where someone was getting disinterred. Turns out, a lot of people were. Charlie found out that Detroit has now gotten so sketchy that for every thirty living human beings who leave Detroit, a dead one is brought along too.

I go see Charlie at the paper and find him standing in the freezing weather outside the building, having a smoke. He's in his traditional winter wear: Carhartt jacket, slouchy ski hat, motorcycle boots, and leather work gloves. He looks less like a newspaperman than like an undercover narcotics cop in one of those seventies Sidney Lumet movies: the guy who's been on the street too long, whom the desk sarge can't reel back into HQ.

Charlie moves abruptly and fast, like he's being chased by something, and maybe he is. He admits he was affected by the scenes he witnessed after 9/11, when he covered the firehouses of Manhattan for weeks. It seems to have sped up his metabolism. "I have a short wick. I don't eat much. I smoke a lot," he says. "Then I crash. Then I get up and go again. I don't think I'm going to have a long time. It's just the speed of my organism."

The *New York Times* may have recently had to mortgage its building, but it is obvious that the *Detroit News* is no longer the big leagues. Charlie shows me a big screen in the lobby on which a scenes-from-Iraq loop has been repeating itself endlessly, tormenting the front-desk guy. "Nobody can figure out how to change it," says Charlie. "The guy who did it before took another job. NPR, I think. Everyone's jealous," he jokes. "He got out!"

But Charlie's stomach doesn't hurt anymore, and he almost seems to glory in being back in the minors. He shows me his desk, surrounded by empty cubicles, colleagues now gone from buyouts. Unlike in his *Times* days, his cell phone has no international service. His desk phone has only one line. His chair is broken. But he seems strangely energized, ricocheting around the halls like a pinball.

He talks to a woman in an elevator, saying he should've taken the stairs, but he just wants to ride it one last time before the paper has to sell it off. He also calls dibs on a historic plate honoring the service of Detroit newsmen in World War II. He barks at a newsroom television screen flashing the Detroit Three congressional hearings, saying,

"Just give them the money or don't! Why are we your kickin' boy?" His outburst earns tepid applause from colleagues, who mostly mind their knitting in a newsroom as quiet as a public library.

A week or so later, there will be an announcement that the *Detroit News* will curtail home delivery to just two days a week. Like all reporters these days, Charlie knows that the American auto industry isn't the only one that's dying. He barges into the deputy managing editor's office to introduce me. "Leaner and meaner, eh?" says Charlie, of the changes that are coming. "Leaner, anyway," shrugs his editor.

Despite the monumentally low morale in journalism at the moment (Gannett whacked two thousand jobs the week I was in Detroit, and the Tribune Company filed for bankruptcy), Charlie believes in reinvention through a simple mantra: "Don't be boring." Along with his shooter/videographer, Max Ortiz, he makes himself a double threat on the *News*'s website, not only hosting a show called *Hold the Onions* out of the American Coney Island diner downtown, but also doing video pieces that stretch the definition of by-the-numbers journalism.

When councilwoman Monica Conyers got in hot water for calling her colleague "Shrek," Charlie arranged to have her sit down on camera for an interrogation by a group of middle schoolers. She proceeded to get a condemnatory lecture on how to behave like an adult from the kids. Charlie then interviewed her, convincing her to recite lines from the infamous Shrek-ish city council meeting, with him playing the part of her, in her sassiest Detroit voice. ("You know you not my daddy!" he said.)

It was a good stunt, as evidenced by its getting picked up (without attribution) by a number of national media outlets. But then he turned around and wrote a wrenching story on the girl who schooled Conyers—a thirteen-year-old who is ashamed to be poor, whose parents sell candy out of the trunk of a rattletrap Cadillac, who is not allowed to bring her books home from school because there aren't enough, and who dreams of escaping this city.

One night over dinner, Charlie admits that he knows most people think he's gone back to a dying newspaper in a dying town. But he feels he has work to do here. Not the kind of work that makes Gawker. Real work. He's always wanted to write about "my people," as he calls them—Detroiters in the hole—but he wasn't ready before. Now he is. He sneers at books like Thomas Frank's *What's the Matter with Kansas?*, which treat human beings like electoral blocs to be extrapolated from. "We're not stupid," he says. "We do count, you know. All those statistics you're going to lay out? Fine. But we know how to make shit. We know how to fix shit. We do know how to read. Saved the union a couple of times, you know what I mean?"

He says there has to be room for the kind of journalism "where it's not a fetish, where it's not blaxploitation, where you are actually a human being with a point of view. The city is full of good people, living next to shit." But most media types don't bother to ask since they view those people as "dumb, uneducated, toothless rednecks. They're ghetto-dwelling blacks. Right? They're poor Mexicans. They're a concept, not a people."

Regardless of media-industry misfortunes, work lies before him. "God gave me something to do, and I'm not turning my back on it. I'm trying really hard. Maybe I'm not great. I'm always nervous, never sure if it's any good. But I'm just trying. What's wrong with trying?"

Detroit has always been a city of fire. Nearly all of it was destroyed by fire in 1805, more of it burned in the Detroit Race Riot of 1863, and over two thousand buildings were consumed in the Twelfth Street Riot of 1967. Even its flag contains fire; its Latin motto translates as "We hope for better things; it shall rise from the ashes."

About a week before I left for Detroit, I got a message from Charlie, in which he was laughing, saying he was supposed to be at a big media day for firemen. "We were gonna put out some fake fires," he said, "but had to call it off because the fire simulator's broken. Good metaphor." A day later, he left another message, but this time he wasn't laughing.

One of the most popular firemen in the ranks of the Detroit Fire Department, Walter Harris—a biker, minister, and mean firehouse cook—had died that night fighting an arson fire in a house that had burned before but had yet to be knocked down by the city. Walt had gone upstairs looking for victims, since empty houses in Detroit are often occupied—by everyone from drug addicts to homeless families. The roof collapsed on him, ending a nineteen-year-career and leaving his six children (one of whom he adopted out of the ghetto as a teenager and who has become a firefighter himself) fatherless.

Back in April, Charlie had done a story and video about the men of Squad 3/Engine 23, which included Walt. It was more of an angry cry than a piece. The details of what the firemen endured in this dysfunctional city were nearly unbelievable. Charlie relayed how the average Detroit fireman faces twice as many fires as his New York counterpart, but in much more adverse conditions. In a city of looters, these firefighters once went out on a call in the middle of dinner, only to find upon returning that their meal had been stolen, as had the truck of one of the men. In fact, after one deranged woman set fire to a house, she tried to drive away in their fire truck as they were putting out the blaze.

The city is so cash-strapped that firefighters have to purchase their own toilet paper and cleaning supplies. Their aging bunker gear is coated in carbon, "making them the equivalent of walking matchsticks." The firehouses' brass poles have been removed and sold off by the city.

When I get to town, Charlie wants me to meet his new friends. Even after his story, he kept stopping by the firehouse regularly, chancing to hear Walt's final prayer on the last day of his life. Being a minister, Walt often said premeal prayers. During his last one, Charlie disrupted it with laughter, he says, as the television above Walt's head incongruously showed a "cheerleader with budding nipples coming through a chiffon dress" while the big man was asking Jesus to bless the food.

We take off in the newspaper's pool car, a Plymouth Neon, and Charlie drives me through blighted neighborhood after blighted neighborhood. I suggest I'm prepared for this, as I watched the Eminem film *8 Mile* before coming. Charlie, mistakenly convinced he's better than Eminem, decides to freestyle by ticking off the scenery before us: "Liquor store / Liquor store / Nail salon / Pawn shop / Car parts / Get your Jesus on."

We tear through the ravaged east side—not to be confused with the ravaged west side. When he was growing up, Charlie's mom had a flower shop down here, but there are almost no signs of commerce now. In my line of work, I've seen plenty of inner cities, but I've never seen anything in a non–third world country like the east side of Detroit. Maybe the Ninth Ward of New Orleans after Katrina. But New Orleans had the storm as an excuse. Here, the storm has been raging for fifty years, starting with the closing of the hulking Albert Kahn–designed Packard Plant in 1956, which a half century later, still stands like a disgraced monument to lost grandeur.

There is block after block of boarded windows and missing doors, structures tilting like the town drunk after a vicious bender. Some houses have buckled roofs, some have blue tarps, some have no roof at all. Which is not to say nobody lives in them. A mail carrier I see on the street says desperate squatters will frequently take up residence, even switching house numbers as it suits them. Not all fires are started maliciously. With no utilities, they'll often make warming fires on the floor. At one point, we stop the car just to count how many burned-out houses we can see without moving. We count six, all from different fires.

We enter the firehouse of Squad 3/Engine 23, or the "Brothers on the Boulevard," as they are nicknamed. It looks like a very orderly frat house. There is Dalmatian statuary in lieu of a real dog, a mounted swordfish, a photo of Walt holding a giant sub on the bulletin board. It is ordinarily a place filled with mirthful gregariousness, a place where new recruits might get dropped to their knees with buckets of water, or where middle-aged men play air guitar to Thin Lizzy solos coming from radio speakers.

But today, nobody's in the mood to smile. In a 90 percent black city, a firehouse is one of the only truly integrated places. The photo that ran with Charlie's April story contained white Sergeant Mike Nevin, smoking one of his ever-lit Swisher Sweets, clapping black Walt on the shoulder. They looked like ebony and ivory, living together in perfect harmony. They faced death together every day. When they call each other "brother" around here, they mean it.

Several wear shirts memorializing their fallen brother. A black wreath commemorates him on one wall. Charlie and I hang out for the better part of a day, and the stories come fast and furious. Firemen tell me that the safest time to be here now is Devil's Night, the infamous night before Halloween for which Detroit earned its title as the arson capital of the world. With Angel's Night counterprogramming, which sees more cops and neighborhood patrols on the street, they've managed to whittle the over eight hundred fires they suffered in 1984 down to sixty-five fires this October 30. Only in Detroit could sixty-five arsons in one night be considered a success.

They tell me of getting their ladders stolen off trucks, and then sold for scrap, how 90 percent of the fires are in vacant homes, which the city takes at least a year to tear down, if they ever do tear them down. They tell how they have even walked up on people having wakes for dead loved ones in which they deliberately burn abandoned houses in a "Detroit-style campfire." I hear from one firefighter, Wes Rawls, that he actually had his car stolen from outside the church at Walt's wake. He didn't really sweat it, since it was the fourth time his car has been stolen. (The third time it happened, he was conveniently coming out of anger management class.)

When Mike Nevin walks in, Charlie suggests I call him Sgt. Mullet since he sports one. "I'm a hockey player first, fireman second," explains Nevin. Charlie tells me, "Look at this shit," pointing to Nevin's gear. Ordinarily, cities might replace a fireman's turnout gear every six months or so. Nevin's had his for nearly a year and a half, and it looks like it. There are random rips. The white outlines of his harness straps are evident from where flames have licked around them. There is a hole in his crotch, which could theoretically leave his chestnuts roasting on an open fire.

The station fire bell is itself a Rube Goldberg absurdity. When the house gets a call, it comes by way of fax from the central office. The printer paper comes out and pushes a door hinge, which then falls onto a screw that's wired to an alarm. They had to rig it themselves.

I ask how this could be, where is their funding? "I'll tell you what happened to our funding," Nevin says, stomping over to pick up a newspaper with a picture of Kwame's mistress copping a plea. "Kwame Kilpatrick, who is a fucking retard. There's twenty years of Coleman Young, who is a fucking retard." He doesn't limit it to black Detroit politicians. He suggests that Congressman Sandy Levin, who represents most of Detroit's northeastern suburbs, "can suck my nuts." Nevin is furious. His friend is dead. He's tired of do-nothing politicians who cuddle up to firemen like kewpie dolls during election time, then underfund them and fail to demolish the thousands and thousands of structures that burn again and again. The surprise isn't that Walt's dead, it's that more of them aren't. (When I ask Nevin later if he wants to exhibit such candor, he reconsiders. "You'd better have Levin kiss my balls," he says, much more gingerly.)

Charlie and I later meet up with Nevin at the house where Walt perished. Nevin leads us up a rickety, charcoaled staircase, and we stand atop what's left of the second floor in the frigid wind. Nevin shows us the spot where the flimsy roof crushed his friend, his boot pawing the ash-caked floorboards with bitter regret. He doesn't care if his complaints sound impolitic. "We're doing the fucking job," he says. "We're scoring the touchdowns. We're the guys running down the sidelines with shitty gear, okay? Not them."

Nevin loves what he does. He bleeds for his city, even if he had to move out of it a few years back because he was worried for his family's safety. Being a fireman on the east side, what the boys call "the old third battalion," involves more than just putting out fires. Nevin calls his men "urban soldiers," and says, "I swear to God, I feel like our helmets should be light blue with 'U.N.' on the side." Detroit police are so outmanned that many citizens call in fires when they have other problems, such as domestic disturbances. The bad guys "hear these big chariots coming, man, they're out of there."

Aside from the troublemakers and firebugs, there is an odd kind of trust between the firemen and the neighborhoods they are paid to protect. "These people love us, and we love them too," Nevin says. When Walt died, well-wishers streamed in with baked goods and covered dishes. Old women came by in church hats out of respect.

Children often stop in so firemen can pump up their bike tires. One boy showed up in his underwear, complaining that his mom was getting beat up by her boyfriend again. "We put him in fire clothes," says Nevin. "You're safe, man," they told the child. "As long as you wear this sweatshirt. You show them that." They visited his mom, telling her, "'You need to get out of this neighborhood, quit dealing with this asshole, and move.' She did. She got away."

Nevin told me they recently fought a fire resulting from a man illegally siphoning gas with a rubber hose. He blew up an entire block. "They had kids in the street, glass sticking out of their head," he says. But, as horrible as it was, he says, "The guy's got four kids. And there's no jobs. And you know, he's got to keep the kids warm. So they come out, and they cut the gas off. Everybody looks to Dad. 'Hey, Dad, I'm cold. Hey, Dad, I'm hungry.' It breaks your fucking heart, man. You're Dad. You're Superman. So what do you do? 'I've got to pull something by hook or crook, man.' You know, it's like everybody is just trying to get by right now."

Nevin says that the contained redevelopment in the downtown area is well and good, but everyone can't work at the Hard Rock Cafe or pour beer at Ford Field. As the car companies moved outside the city, Nevin says, he watched the east side wither. The tool and die shops went away. The mom and pop groceries all folded. He has no soft spot for the Big Three, who he thinks abandoned Detroit in order "to chase the sun."

But what he really hates, what makes him seethe, is the misman-agement of what's left, the fact that all these "mousetraps," as he calls all the wrecked, abandoned homes that dot the city like tombstones, are not taken down. That the house that killed Walt is still standing now. "Hear the sirens?" Nevin asks. "Someone is going to a fire. That's all day long. This is a city where the sirens never stop."

This place, he says, "It's like a forgotten secret. It's like a lost city. And they never really talk about the fucking truth about what is going on with this town." Of the house we stand on, he says, "We want it down. It symbolizes nothing. It symbolizes failure. We lost one of the best men this job will ever have or see. And yet, this car-cass still sits here. Arson is done. This is not a crime scene anymore. There's no tape. There's no one watching it. It just sits there to remind us that the city we work for has failed."

The city's ombudsman, a good, honest woman named Durene Brown, who is a regular thorn in the side of those who wish to turn a blind eye to the city's problems, shows me the figures. In 2005–2006, the city demolished 909 structures, but they're proposing only 522 in 2008–2009. Be it ineptitude, lack of funds, environmental disposal considerations, concern over lawsuits, you name it, there is always an excuse. Meanwhile, Detroit keeps burning, and Nevin and the Broth-ers on the Boulevard have to keep risking their hides in mousetrap infernos. The firemen need this house to come down, and Charlie has promised to help them.

There is something about the unsettledness of Detroit that forces its inhabitants to confront it. Therefore, many of them tend to have the most vivid of worldviews. Take political consultant Adolph Mongo.

He is one of Charlie's regulars, both in print and on his web show. This is no easy feat for Charlie, since Mongo's favorite word, one he uses every five sentences or so, is "motherfucker." A large black man who favors Versace glasses adorned with gemstones, he's known as the local flamethrower, unafraid to compare his opponents to Hitler or to run anti-lynching ads in support of his client, Kwame Kilpat-rick, who sources say owes Mongo money that he'll never see.

Still, throwing a curveball, Mongo wishes me to know he's practi-cally a conservative and asks for a column at my magazine. "I'm for low taxes, kicking people in the ass, tough on crime, and don't bail out motherfuckers. No welfare state. We need to destroy the school district," he says, advocating "charters, vouchers, everything. My wife [a former public school teacher] is going to die if she reads this shit."

Mongo says he has black clients and he has white clients. "I'm not a bigot, I'm a pro." He worked for Kilpatrick, of whom he once was a fierce critic. Kilpatrick offered to hire him because "I beat his ass for two years." And he's worked for some of the people who put Kilpatrick in jail as well. "People ask me what I do," says Mongo. "I fuck with people. I know how to debate. You've got to know both sides of the issue. I can be for you. I can be against you. I'm like a prostitute in the night. Nobody wants to admit that they've been with me, but they come seek me out."

Suckled in the Coleman Young machine, Mongo freely admits to playing the politics of race, because in Detroit, that's the way it works. "Black people stick together," he says, while he admits the downside: "We accept mediocrity." Those politics are played against Detroit all the time too, he wishes me to know. And not just from white suburbs. Look what's happening now, he says, with the Big Three congressional hearings.

When white politicians want to get elected around here, explains Mongo, "They don't say 'nigger' anymore, they say 'Detroit.'" And so, while the Big Three have been running away from Detroit for years, they "got a rude awakening when they went to D.C." Mongo holds that when congressmen associate automakers with Detroit, what they're intending to associate them with are all the inept black people who come from there. Or as he puts it, when they say "Detroit," "they really said, 'They the new niggers.' Welcome to the club."

Charlie then takes me to see L. Brooks Patterson at the Mesquite Creek steakhouse in Clarkston, outside the city. He's another of Charlie's regulars, whom Charlie introduces as "the head honky in charge." Patterson, who looks like everybody's best golfing buddy, is the longtime executive of Oakland County, Michigan, which contains Detroit's affluent northern suburbs. A pro-sprawl Republican who used to regularly buck up against Coleman Young when he worked as a prosecutor, Patterson has suggested that the dysfunctional members of the city council belonged in the Detroit Zoo, causing one of them to refer to him as "the Grand Dragon of Oakland County."

Patterson laughs at the charge. He's not a racist, and doesn't hate

Detroiters. He is a Detroiter. He grew up in the city, and he's friends with Mongo (two sides of the same coin, Charlie calls them "Dee and Dum"). The problem, Patterson says, is his county is "tired of being Detroit's ATM machine." If Detroit's repeatedly disastrous decisions hurt his taxpayers, he will oppose them. "Once you understand that, everything I do and say makes sense."

The demographics of his own county are changing with black flight from Detroit, and he understands why people can't wait to leave. When automotive parts supplier BorgWarner was deciding whether to relocate from Chicago to Auburn Hills, Patterson says, "We had to send what I would call grief counselors over to convince them it ain't that bad. We actually did videos saying, 'You are not going into the war zone. You are not going into the deluge. You are coming to Oakland County.' "Patterson adds, "I would love to see the city come back for a lot of reasons. It would make my job easier. But nothing works."

As the night wears on, Charlie grows defensive, and almost defiant, about Detroit. He recounts everything it's done for the country, insists the city still matters and won't disappear, speculates about the potential for it to become a major port since "water is the new oil," and insists that Henry Ford is more important to history than Jesus Christ, since "even Muslims drive Toyotas." At this, Patterson, a good Catholic boy, leans in to my tape recorder. "That was Charlie. When I go home tonight, I will make the sign of the cross and pray to Henry Ford."

Charlie heads for the restroom, and Patterson grows philosophical: "Detroit's history has gone the way of Rome and Athens and Constantinople. It is what history does. History moves on. And history has moved away from the Babylonian Empire. It moved away from Egypt. It be what it be. I think Detroit sees itself in its rearview mirror. But Detroit will never again be where those other cities were, including Detroit."

Later, I ask Charlie why he was pushing so hard, aside from his blood-alcohol content. After all, Patterson didn't say anything that Charlie hasn't said to me about his city. He explains it thus: "Living in Detroit is like having a retarded brother. You are allowed to make jokes, but once anybody else does, you are allowed to light them the fuck on fire, man."

Despite all the ugliness during my week in Detroit, I discover pockets of grace. The first finds me in the backseat of a black Crown Victoria.

Former Motown superstar and current city councilwoman Martha Reeves, of Martha and the Vandellas, sits in the front seat. Maxine Powell, a crisp eighty-four-year-old, sits beside me. She now works in Reeves's office but used to be Motown's finishing instructor, teaching poise classes for two hours a day. She showed the entire Motown stable how to do everything from walk to dress. "Class, style, and refinement turned the heads of kings and queens," she informs me. Reeves's driver is Ulysses, who has two gold teeth and wears a coat that must've meant the end for an entire mink ranch. (He promises me that if any PETA members throw ketchup on him, they won't be around to throw it on anyone else.)

I've talked Reeves into showing me around Hitsville USA, Motown's first headquarters and now a museum. Along the way, she does her part as civic booster. Ulysses drives us through a shiny new town-house complex that used to be a housing project. All the streets are named after Motown stars. Reeves is a little cross that hers is abbreviated "M. Reeves." Ulysses says her full name would be too long. "No longer than the Temptations," she huffs. The rest of the drive is through the typical blight. Reeves admits it's affected her too. Recently, someone broke into her late father's old east side house, a house where the doors never used to be locked, unless she didn't make it home by midnight, in which case her father locked the doors on her. The thief boosted a hundred thousand dollars' worth of recording equipment, which she hasn't managed to replace.

Then there was the time three decades ago when she'd just returned to Detroit from Los Angeles. While she was getting out of a Mercedes and going into a house, a mugger grabbed her purse, the strap of which was wrapped tightly around her hand. He dragged her for five hundred yards. I ask if she was hurt. "Scratched up knees, torn stockings, and my pride was just killed," she says.

Hitsville sits next to a funeral home. We cover every inch of the museum. She knows every drummer and backup singer and secretary in every photo. She tells of the '62 tour in a broken-down bus with no toilet, in which Little Stevie Wonder wouldn't let anybody sleep. She sings into the trademark Motown echo chamber that provided much of its fabled sound. She dances and harmonizes to every other song playing over the speakers, songs by Smokey and Marvin and Shorty Long with that walking bass line beckoning us to his "Function at the Junction."

She takes me into the studio, where the floor has heel damage be-hind the soundboards from long-ago engineers, now "gone to heaven" in her words, who were keeping time with the music. She shows me the exact mike where she sang behind Marvin Gaye, whom she'd flirted with.

As she tells me these stories, she attracts a small crowd, all of them white people, who periodically sing along with her. A woman who left the city long ago—though she still wears a Red Wings jer-sey—tells me she misses it while getting an autograph from Reeves. "It was once a great town," she says.

Reeves is sixty-seven years old, but as we walk the halls, about forty of those years fall away. "You see the pride and happiness I have coming in here," she tells me. Ulysses chauffeurs us back to my truck, parked behind the Coleman Young Municipal Center downtown. As we ride up on it, we see the Spirit of Detroit, the Marshall Fredericks monument in which a seated man holds a gilt bronze sphere that emanates rays meant to symbolize God.

Or at least we see its silhouette. Night has fallen, and, this being Detroit, the lights are off. "He's out in the dark," says a puzzled Reeves. "Ain't he scared?"

"He's got a ball in his hand," says Ulysses. "He awright. He got people with him. He's cool."

The second pocket I discover by accident. Charlie once quoted Sam Riddle, a local political warhorse, as saying that the only difference between Detroit and the Third World, corruption-wise, is that "there are no goats in the streets in Detroit."

Actually, there are. With so much empty space these days in De-troit, "urban farming" has taken off—vegetable patches right in the middle of the city. And I'm told someone keeps goats a few blocks away from my hotel, the gleaming MotorCity Casino Hotel, which sits in a downwardly mobile neighborhood with businesses like Goodwill Industries, a sewing machine repair shop, and liquor stores.

While combing the streets of the North Corktown neighbor-hood, unable to find the goats, I see a black man carrying a box. I stop to ask directions. He offers to show me, so I tell him to hop in my truck. I take him for a construction worker or mover or something, but he's homeless.

His name is Wayne Williams, and he has a gentle spirit. We get to talking, and I quickly lose interest in the goats. He says he moved to Detroit two years ago. He was a gravedigger back in Alabama, and he came here to get a better job.

"You came to Detroit to get a better job?" I ask.

"Yeah," he says, smiling. "I know better now."

He says he's tried to get a job in over a hundred places, everything from construction to fast food to gravedigging again, but hasn't managed. The box he is carrying is full of clothes that he got out of a dumpster. He walks the empty streets waiting for passersby, seeing if they want to buy any. His own clothes are all from charity, which might explain why he wears snowboots that look like they belong to a ten-year-old boy.

I ask him where he lives, and he shows me. He lives beneath a Rosa Parks Boulevard underpass, in the shadow of Tiger Stadium, which has been mostly torn down, though the preservationists are trying to save the last of it. The Tigers now play at Comerica Park, though the company the park is named for has fled to Dallas.

He shows me his lean-to boxes and blankets, and a Bible sitting on a bridge girder as though it were his bookshelf. I ask how he could sleep, it's so incredibly noisy. He's used to it, he says, and he wants the traffic. That's why he's there. He figures there's less chance of getting killed if he sleeps where motorists can see him. A few months ago, he was robbed and thrown off an overpass. He shows me his still-swollen thumb and the scars on his head and back. "I feel safe under the bridge," Wayne says.

We go back to my truck. He asks me for nothing. But I tell him I'll give him a lift to wherever he's going since he's been a good guide, and also slide him twenty bucks. He offers me a breast cancer awareness pin. He found a bunch of them in a dumpster and is going to try to sell them, but thinks I should have one for free.

We talk local politics a little. With time on his hands, he reads all the newspapers he finds. He's disappointed in Kwame: "Great leaders take care of their people." He says he would make a good one because "I love the human race." He prays for them, as well as for Detroit, he says, which he worries about. I ask him if he gets lonely out here. He says yes, he does, but a red-tailed fox sometimes comes to visit him, though it's too scared to approach, so he'll roll food down the overpass embankment to it. Plus, he talks to God a lot. He calls him "my partner."

"All I want to do is live to be an old man," Wayne says. "That's what I ask my partner for."

I ask Wayne if he has a substance abuse problem. He says he's never been drunk in his life. And even if he was a drunk, he adds, he couldn't afford to be one out here, in case he has to defend himself. But he does admit he smokes pot "about five times a year." Recently, he says, he was scoring some weed at a nearby drug house. What he saw there, he says, he'll never, ever forget, no matter how hard he tries.

"What?" I ask.

He's extremely reluctant to tell. He breaks eye contact, and looks to the sky in pain. "I can't believe the things I've seen," he says. "Some are hard to talk about." I prompt him some more, and the details start tumbling forth. He says he saw a young woman there: very attractive, nice body. There were about nine men there as well. For their benefit, or maybe for the benefit of their drugs, says Wayne, "She was having sex with a pit bull."

I stop writing. "C'mon," I say in disbelief.

Wayne looks at me as though he's hurt that I'd doubt his story and shoves the twenty-dollar bill I gave him back at me. "Take this if you don't believe me," he insists. I shove the money back at him. "If I'm lying," he says, "then God is gay. And I know He ain't gay, cause He's my partner."

He shakes my hand, starts to get out of the truck, then shakes my hand again. "I have a hard time saying goodbye to people I like," he says. "That's what I don't like about the human race. You meet people you like, then there's no way of seeing their face again."

He asks me if I'd stop by to bid him farewell before I leave. I say I will. "What time?" he asks. I tell him I have a lot of appointments, so I can't predict, and I don't want to hold up his schedule. "Okay," he says. "If I'm not there, just leave a note in my Bible." He gets out and shuffles off to White Castle, but after about thirty yards, he turns around again and waves.

The last pocket is found by exploring Detroit with Randy Wilcox, a photographer and artist who combs the ruins of Detroit and posts his riveting studies of the city on detroitfunk.com. He knows every inch of Detroit, from underground tunnels and abandoned auto factories to the empty skyscrapers that make the skyline at night look like what he calls "a smile with broken teeth."

He comes from a Big Three auto family, and so wearing a bomber jacket and a plaid stocking hat, he dutifully drives us around in a Ford Taurus with a crack all the way across its windshield because, he says, "I can't afford a Honda." We park his car far away from the buildings we crash, to avoid detection by police (not that we ever see any). We hit the hot spots, such as the old Packard Plant, which he calls a "whore" ("a building that everybody has had"), and the beautiful ruins of the once-magnificent beaux arts Michigan Central Station, which saw its last train in 1988 and which from afar looks like a porous cheesecloth.

He ticks off all the injuries he's gotten exploring, from scratches to sprains to nails through the shoe. He gives me the taxonomy of who he runs into, from drug addicts to scrappers to historians to foreign tourists to ghetto dogs to "Vikings," troublemakers who just come to break things more than they're already broken.

Wilcox is the opposite of a Viking. He is an aesthete and amateur historian with an appreciation of architectural detail and a story for every street corner. As we walk through various ruins, seeing old commodes and junked files and discarded boats, we run into no trouble, though we hear Vikings on the prowl here and there. Most don't want a confrontation and make their escape like specters.

Wilcox walks me all around the poorly lit edifices, except for where the roof is missing and snow drifts in, pointing out curios like discarded "whore bags"—condom-filled duffels that prostitutes use to ply their trade. I have notebook pages filled with descriptions of what we saw, but reading it now, all the wreckage runs together.

Wilcox drives me all over the city, pointing out missed urban planning opportunities and eyesores. He takes me downtown to what the locals call "Skyscraper Graveyard," where the clock seems to have stopped in the Art Deco period and high-rise after high-rise sits empty. He points out the landmark Book Tower, a thirty-eight-story building finished in 1926, which he says is now vacant except for Bookies Tavern on the first floor. Wilcox's lawyer told him he'd been "the last tenant there. He had to downsize. People are too broke to sue people. He's now switching to bankruptcy law to try to save his house."

I come to think of Wilcox as the curator of a museum that's been overturned and looted. The prize of his collection, or what could have been his collection, is the detailed production notes he found written in Marvin Gaye's own hand for the legendary *What's Going On* album. He found them, along with other treasures from artist itineraries to expense accounts, in the Motown Center, which housed the label, then sat empty for thirty years until it was knocked down in 2006 to make way for Super Bowl parking. Wilcox witnessed the demolition, which was typical of Detroit's callous disregard for its own history: "Motown letterhead was blowing down the road."

When NPR did a story on Wilcox's find, the phone calls started flooding in, plenty from people trying to muscle him for the rights to the production notes. His solution? He gave them to the Detroit Public Library. When I ask him why on earth he didn't keep them or flip them on eBay, he says it's because he made two decisions: One, that he didn't want to get sued. The other, "that I am not a looter." "I am a steward," he says. "I am just in possession of stuff until it gets where it is supposed to be."

I ask him if he ever feels that in spending so much time among the ruins, he's feeding off a carcass. "No," he says. "I'm part of the carcass."

On a sunny, cold morning, we all stand in front of the house where Walt Harris died: two of Walt's sons and Mike Nevin and the Brothers on the Boulevard and a few city council members and reporters and neighbors and more firefighters and the Axemen, the motorcycle group Walt rode with. Charlie LeDuff is there too, which is only fitting, since he's pretty much the reason we all came: to watch this mousetrap inferno get crushed like charred Lincoln Logs.

Charlie had gone to New York for Thanksgiving but promised Nevin that if that house was still standing when he got back, he'd start rattling cages and kicking in doors. The house was standing, and that "monument to failure," as Nevin called it, would've kept standing, as sixty thousand others do, for infinity, because the city is too poor, too concerned about procedures and lawsuits, too inept to knock them down.

Charlie started working the phones and, after runarounds and dead ends, found a sympathetic city councilwoman, Sheila Cockrel, who fast-tracked the demolition at his behest, as a favor to the mourning firefighters.

Still wearing his ever-present ski hat, Charlie has shed the Carhartt work jacket and today has on his three-quarter-length brown dress leathers. It's a special occasion. There's not even a notebook in sight. He doesn't want to write. He just wants to take it in, as there are not a lot of days of similar triumph working for a dying newspaper in a dying town.

As we watch the wrecker take the house down, I'm struck by the fact that rather than sadness, there is almost a note of celebration. How could anyone with eyes celebrate? Just looking around this very block, I count five or six similar houses, mousetraps that Nevin and his gladiators will inevitably be revisiting, piling off their chariots, swinging their axes, hoping the roof doesn't come down on their heads.

I stand next to Charlie as he toasts up a Winston. I put the question to him: How could these guys celebrate? Just look at what surrounds them.

He exhales a funnel of smoke, shaking his head in assent. But he corrects me. "No one's going to cover this place in chrome tomorrow, or anything. But you've got to let the people have some hope. It matters."

With the house now in a heap, the grateful firefighters are hugging it out. They hug everybody. Each other. Charlie. Me. Since his wife dropped him off, Charlie asks me if he can bum a ride back to the newspaper. As we start heading to my truck, he catches a black man and woman on the porch across from the house that killed Walt. He'd interviewed them previously and had apparently made promises to more than just Mike Nevin and the men of Squad 3/Engine 23.

"Merry Christmas," Charlie bellows, pointing at them. "I told you we'd get that house knocked down."

The black man rises and starts toward Charlie, beaming and nodding his head. "Thank you," he says. "Thank you."

Then he comes to a stop, and his smile fades as he surveys the wreckage around him. "But what about the rest of it?" he asks.

On the way to the airport, I have one last stop to make: to bid farewell to my homeless guide, Wayne Williams, as promised. I park my truck near what's left of Tiger Stadium and make my way down to the bridge overpass that Wayne calls home. I can see his boot prints in the light snow, heading out from underneath it. He's not home, nor is the Bible he instructed me to leave a note in.

His blankets and boxes are still there, however. So I place on them a book I bought for him the day before. Wayne seemed to be into the religious material, so I bought him a slim volume called *God's*

Promises: Bible extracts, the good parts without all the genealogies and oxen sacrifice. It breaks verses out by subject, for occasions such as when you're afraid or lonesome. I mark a passage for him from Psalms:

> The Lord is my light and my salvation—whom shall I fear? The Lord is the stronghold of my life—of whom shall I be afraid? Though an army besiege me, my heart will not fear, though war break out against me, even then will I be confident.

I wait around a few minutes, but he doesn't return, and I have to make a flight. Maybe he's at White Castle. Maybe he's out peddling breast cancer awareness pins. But it is Sunday. So he could be in church, talking to his partner about the human race or Detroit.

Detroit should hope so. Wayne's partner is the only one who can save it now.

ROGER STONE, POLITICAL ANIMAL

New York/Miami

Being a skilled confidence man is both a blessing and a curse. If you truly excel at the long con, raising it to a form of art, marks will never know they've been taken. But if you become renowned for such artistry, when it is synonymous with your very name, people never believe you're off the grift, even when you're playing straight.

Such is the life of Roger Stone, political operative, Nixon-era dirty trickster, professional lord of mischief. It's hard to assume he's not up to something, because he always is. He once said of himself, "If it rains, it was Stone." For that's the view most people take of him. Three years ago, everyone from the DNC's Terry McAuliffe to the left-wing blogosphere blamed him for leaking George W. Bush's forged Air National Guard records, the ones that looked like they would damn Bush, but ultimately blew up Dan Rather's career. It's preposterous, he says, a triple bank shot that no one could ever have conceived of. "I get blamed for things I have nothing to do with," he says, somewhat wounded. But when asked about all the things he doesn't get blamed for that he does have something to do with, he thinks a bit, then shrugs. "It does balance itself out," he says.

Naïfs might say he's a cancer on the body politic, everything that is wrong with today's system. But maybe he is just its purest distillation: Politics is war, and he is one of its fiercest warriors, with the battle scars to prove it.

The first time I laid eyes on Roger Stone, he was standing poolside at a press conference on the roof of the L'Ermitage hotel in Beverly Hills. With a horseshoe pinkie ring refracting rays from the California sun and a gangster chalk-stripe suit that looked like it had been exhumed from the crypt of Frank Costello, Stone was there to help his friend and longtime client Donald Trump explore a Reform Party presidential candidacy in 2000.

Actually, it was more complicated than that. After having

recruited Pat Buchanan to seek the nod ("You have to beat some-body," Stone says), he pushed Trump into the race. Trump relentlessly attacked Buchanan as having "a love affair with Adolf Hitler," but ended up folding. A weakened Buchanan went on to help the Reform Party implode, and Republicans suffered no real third-party threat, as they had in 1992, thus helping Stone accomplish his objective. If, in fact, that was his objective. These things are often hard to keep track of with Roger Stone.

Trump's short-lived campaign provided lots of memorable Stone moments. There was the scene on the roof, where Stone, a dandy by disposition who boasts of having not bought off-the-rack since he was seventeen—he's now fifty-six—taught reporters how to achieve perfect double dimples underneath their tie knots, while providing them hand sanitizers should they want to shake hands with the ger-mophobe Trump. Then there were the hardball negotiations he drove backstage at *The Tonight Show*, where he promised access to the dress-ing room, but only if we refrained from "making fun of Mr. Trump's hair" in print.

But the moment that has most stuck with me came after report-ers had just watched Trump dispense invaluable life tips at a Tony Robbins seminar ("Get even. When somebody screws you, screw 'em back—but a lot harder"). Stone mounted the bus, which in Trumpian fashion was named "A Touch of Class," and announced, "I'm here. Who needs to be spun?"

It was a throwaway line, not even one of the serially quotable Stone's best, but the naked cynicism at the heart of it might be why his fans in the press corps over the years have called him things like "a state-of-the-art sleazeball," "an extreme right-wing sleazeball," and the "boastful black prince of Republican sleaze" (the sleaze theme is popular). Color me contrarian, but I will say something I don't believe another Washington reporter has ever admitted publicly: I like Roger Stone.

Over the years, we've had our ups and downs: the occasional threats of litigation over some piece I was writing about one of his clients, his playful stabs at blackmail over fabricated infractions (once accusing me of hitting on his wife at a Reform Party convention by giving her my cell phone number, at a time when I had neither met her nor acquired a cell phone). He doesn't actually mean any of this, of course—he's just keeping in game shape.

That's why I find sentiments like "Who needs to be spun?" strangely refreshing. Unlike most political hacks, who are bloodless participants in a pageant that turns almost entirely on artifice, Stone acknowledges the game and his exploitation of it. He often sets his pronouncements off with the utterance "Stone's Rules," signifying to listeners that one of his shot-glass commandments is coming down, a pithy dictate uttered with the unbending certitude one usually associates with the Book of Deuteronomy. Some original, some borrowed, Stone's Rules address everything from fashion to food to how to screw people. And one of his favorite Stone's Rules is "Unless you can fake sincerity, you'll get nowhere in this business." He is honest about his dishonesty. "Politics with me isn't theater," he admits. "It's performance art. Sometimes for its own sake."

He has dabbled in at least eight presidential campaigns, everything from working for Nixon's Committee to Reelect the President (CREEP) in 1972, to helping stage the infamous 2000 Brooks Brothers Riot in Miami, where angry Republicans in loud madras shorts and pinstripe suits helped shut down the Miami recount. (Stone was directing traffic by walkie-talkie from a nearby van.)

He made his bones as a principal in the Reagan era lobbying firm Black, Manafort & Stone. Stone's bread is now primarily buttered by his strategizing for corporate clients, everything from casino interests to the sugar industry, but his love of the action ensures that he is usually waging at least one exotic war on the political periphery.

For instance, after Trump, he went on to advise the gubernatorial campaign of New York billionaire Tom Golisano. It can be regarded as a revenge fantasy against George Pataki, whom Stone considers a counterfeit conservative, and whose lobbying commission dinged Stone and Trump for a $250,000 settlement—Trump paid—the largest in state history, for not filing lobbying reports about radio ads attacking the expansion of Indian casino interests. It chafes Stone to this day. He is adamant that the settlement contained no admission of wrongdoing, and says it wasn't his call, joking that Trump settled because "he's a pussy."

Stone exacted a little revenge by causing headaches for Pataki, who won the 2002 general election but was aced out of the desired Independence Party nomination by Golisano. This was partly due to tried-and-true Stone ploys such as mailing voters official-looking envelopes inscribed with "Important Property Tax Notice," while the message inside informed voters that since George "Patakifeller" had been governor, "property taxes in your county have increased by nearly 48.9 percent."

In Stone capers, revenge is a powerful motivator. His friend Jeffrey Bell had Stone run his failed bid for New Jersey senator in 1982. Bell says that Stone was so agitated at losing the Republican primary to the dearly beloved, pipe-smoking septuagenarian Millicent Fenwick that Stone packed Bell's pollsters off to her Democratic opponent, Frank Lautenberg, and they persuaded his campaign to attack her on age grounds. Lautenberg narrowly won. Bell, who'd resisted the tactic, recalls hearing Stone saying something to the effect of "I am going to kill that woman." "He's a lord of mischief," laughs Bell. "He likes money, and has made plenty of it, but that's not the prime mover. I don't think he's that ideological. He's a political junkie. He loves to be in the middle of it."

Shortly after Golisano's defeat, Stone got involved in advising Al Sharpton's 2004 presidential campaign. Many cast Sharpton as the Trojan horse Stone was trying to ride into the enemy camp. Stone doesn't deny that it was great fun watching Sharpton take the piss out of Howard Dean for not employing minorities—which he did at Stone's prompting. But he dismisses any grand conspiracy: "I love the game. I'm a kibitzer. I couldn't resist giving him good advice. He followed some, he ignored most." Though as Sharpton's campaign manager, Charles Halloran, an old Stone crony, told me during the South Carolina primary in 2004, "If Roger found some ants in an anthill that he thought he could divide and get pissed off with each other, he'd be in his backyard right now with a magnifying glass."

I hadn't had dealings with Stone since the Sharpton campaign but became convinced we needed to renew our acquaintance in August. Stone had been retained in June 2007, for twenty thousand dollars a month, to help demoralized New York State Republicans gain ground from the caped-crusader/governor Eliot Spitzer (whom many, including Spitzer, seem to regard as some sort of cross between Robert Kennedy and Jesus). Stone and a loose collection of coconspirators began battering the governor for his administration's numerous ethical lapses. (When I called Stone for this story, he asked if I'd gotten all the anti-Spitzer e-mails. I told him I wasn't sure; it seemed like

I'd been receiving five a day for months from all sorts of mysteriously named accounts. "Good," he said. "It's working.")

In July, Spitzer took a major hit when the state's Democratic attorney general, Andrew Cuomo, chastised the governor's office for asking the state police to keep tabs on Republican state senate leader Joseph Bruno (Stone's client) and for peddling travel documents to the press to try and create a "Choppergate" scandal. Bruno was cleared of misusing the state's air fleet, and Stone and his associates have kept up a relentless anti-Spitzer e-mail blitz. (One of their recent Spitzer missives showed Osama bin Laden driving a New York City cab, referring to Spitzer's boneheaded play of allowing illegal immigrants to obtain driver's licenses without proof of citizenship.)

Stone seemed more interested, however, in refocusing attention on an old scandal that had been wheezing along: a more complicated story, but one he regarded as having possible criminal repercussions thanks to a shady tangle of loans. Stone believes in waging multifront wars, and his philosophy on the subject is one of the most sacred of Stone's Rules, right up there with "Don't order fish at a steakhouse," "White shirt + tan face = confidence," and "Undertakers and chauffeurs are the only people who should be allowed by law to wear black suits." It goes like this: "Hit it from every angle. Open multiple fronts on your enemy. He must be confused, and feel besieged on every side."

At issue is a $5 million campaign loan given to Spitzer by his multimillionaire father, Bernard, during the 1998 race for attorney general. During that campaign, Spitzer claimed that he'd secured the loan by mortgaging apartments given to him by his real estate developer father. He appears to have lied, however, having later admitted that his father was essentially financing the campaign by paying off the loan—a possible violation of campaign law. The story wasn't nearly as sexy as Choppergate until the Spitzer camp announced that on Monday, August 6, the eighty-three-year-old Bernard Spitzer had received a message from a phone traced to Roger Stone's Central Park South apartment. A voice that appeared to be Stone's said:

> This is a message for Bernard Spitzer. You will be subpoenaed to testify before the senate committee on investigations on your shady campaign loans. You will be compelled by the senate sergeant at arms. If you resist this subpoena, you will be arrested and brought

to Albany—and there's not a goddamn thing your phony, psycho, piece of shit son can do about it. Bernie, your phony loans are about to catch up with you. You will be forced to tell the truth. The fact that your son is a pathological liar will be known to all.

Stone denied it was him. Bruno didn't take a position but threw Stone overboard anyway, terminating his contract. And everyone I know who knows Roger Stone had the same reaction: Of course he did it. I didn't even need to hear the tape (which pretty much cinches it) before coming to this conclusion. The speech is absent his sparkling wit, but the rest of the touches are his: the B-movie-gangster intimidation, the high-wire dramatics, the swinging song-of-the-street cadences à la Sinatra abusing an underling after a couple of Jacks on the rocks.

Over the next week, Stone offered an array of exotic alibis, almost as though he were joking. Possibly, he was. (He did, after all, in the middle of the hubbub, get Richard Nixon's head tattooed on his back at the Ink Monkey in Venice Beach and sent a photo of it to reporters, just out of puckish spite.) He initially claimed it couldn't have been him, since at the time of the call in question, he'd been attending the play *Frost/Nixon*. Reporters unearthed a small inconsistency: There'd been no performance that night. Stone posted a review of the play on his Stonezone website anyway, recommending it to Spitzer, since "it underlines the dangers of hubris and the inexorable web a public official tangles himself in when he tells a lie." He admitted, however, that he'd confused the dates—an honest mistake. He may be a dirty trickster, but he's not a philistine; he knows the theaters are dark on Mondays.

From there, the story only got stranger. Various other alibis had Stone suggesting somebody used "spoofing" technology to make the phone call look as if it had originated from his apartment. He also offered the possibility that a disgruntled former colleague—and stand-up comedian/impressionist—named Randy Credico, impersonated Stone to sandbag him. Credico denied it, telling the *Washington Post,* "That's hilarious." Stone also floated the theory that the landlord of his Central Park South building, H. Dale Hemmerdinger, who is a Spitzer supporter and his pick to head the Metropolitan Transit Authority, might have allowed someone into Stone's apartment to make the call.

Later, Stone made public a two-page apology he'd written to Hemmerdinger. He said that he regretted "any inconvenience or distress my initial comments may have caused . . . despite our political differences, I must say that 40 Central Park South is an excellent building that is extremely professionally operated by capable employees at all levels." Then came the cherry on top: "I am certain that you will render great public service to the MTA."

On its face, the letter appears to be your standard inoculation against potential litigation, but rereading it I get chills. For me, red flags are flapping every which way, as they would for anyone who knows one of the most sacrosanct of Stone's Rules: "Always praise 'em before you hit 'em."

I arrange to see Stone in Manhattan, where he spends roughly one day each week, and Miami, where he lives. But beforehand, he threatens to take me to Ukraine, where the local press has outed him as being involved in the parliamentary campaign of Volodymyr Lytvyn, an Orange Revolutionary alum who's been mentioned as a future president. Like many American political consultants, Stone does the odd election overseas, though he likes to keep it quiet, since it often causes a local furor because "Americans are now hated everywhere in the world—thank you, George W. Bush."

"I don't particularly want to go," he says. "Our lives will be in danger. We will have bodyguards. Plus, the food sucks." On the upside, he says, we'll have a buxom translator named Svetlana, and "we can stop over in Amsterdam on the way home, for all the obvious reasons." It turns out we don't need to go; his guys on the ground have it covered. But it's a constant struggle, he says: "The Russians love intrigue." As though he doesn't.

He is in perpetual dispute with Lytvyn's local advisers, whom he calls the Politburo. They deliberately mistranslate his ads to reflect their own clunky slogans, and he resents their interference, since what could they know about winning free and fair elections, being recently converted Commies and all. The atmosphere is charged enough that he has now taken to sending secret messages directly to the candidate, nicknamed "Mister." Since his team assumes all their communications are monitored, they use code names such as "Buckwheat" and "Beetle." Stone's is "Mr. Pajamas," the same one used by ur–Nixon dirty trickster Murray Chotiner, one of his personal heroes and mentors. (Lytvyn's party was successful in the elections.)

I ask Stone how the Spitzer phone call story played over there. He says it's been a boon. Whether he did it or not—and he reminds me he didn't—"they thought it was great." He adopts a thick Ukrainian accent: "We like this. It shows Stone is not a pussy." "It means you have balls and aren't afraid to mix it up," he explains of the call, which if he had made it, it should be noted, was perfectly legal. Things over there tend to be a little more bare-knuckle. It is a place, after all, where a politician occasionally gets poisoned by dioxin. "They do say to me, 'Why did they get rid of Nixon, we don't understand?' I say, well, his guys broke into the headquarters of the opposition. 'Yeah, so—that's a reason to get rid of him?'"

From his speech to his dress, Stone's an old-school guy with old-school rhythms and tends to prefer old-school haunts, like Gallagher's and the '21' Club. A chronic workaholic, he will nearly always drop what he's doing to eat elaborate sit-down meals. Our first night, we tuck in at Sparks Steak House, which is all dark woods and white tablecloths and rich history. Gambino boss Paul Castellano was whacked on the sidewalk outside on John Gotti's orders.

It's a bit nerve-racking figuring how to properly dress for a Stone engagement. His longtime tailor is Alan Flusser, author of the sartorial bible *Style and the Man,* and one of Flusser's associates tells me Stone knows enough to work there. Sitting across from him is a bit like sitting across from Mr. Blackwell: Suppose you accidentally went with a single-vent jacket rather than side vents, which Stone finds unthinkable ("I'm not a heathen"), or if you wore trendy flat-front suit trousers instead of ones with properly draped pleats ("Pants today are like a little church in the valley—no ballroom").

I read once that he has three hundred solid-silver wedding ties. He says it's an exaggeration—he only has about a hundred. But to give an idea of his obsessiveness, he owns so many suits that there are one hundred in storage alone. His closets are meticulously ordered— even his jeans are organized "by jeaniness." He will launch into learned disquisitions on the differences among pencil, chalk, pin, and beaded stripes. He even has strict Stone's Rules about his cuff links: "Large hubcap types are for mafia dons from Jersey and Las Vegas lounge singers. Cuff links should be small, understated, and tasteful. No coffee grinders, no jet planes, no large stones."

Stone makes the scene in a navy double-breasted peaked lapel suit of blue Shantung silk, a white Windsor collar over a blue and white striped shirt, white roll-back cuffs (he never says "French cuffs"), a blue patterned Flusser tie, and high-shine black slip-ons by C. J. Cleverly from London's Burlington Arcade.

Though it's unseasonably hot for September, I decide to break out a gray flannel three-button I'm particularly fond of, throwing caution to the wind. It's one of Stone's Rules: "Be bold. The more you tell, the more you sell," courtesy of advertising guru David Ogilvy. (Stone keeps numerous copies of Ogilvy's *Confessions of an Advertising Man* in his office to dispense to friends.) He says my suit's weight passes muster. It's a relief.

The guy at the table behind us doesn't fare quite as well. Stone says he wants to remove the guy's glasses and "stomp on them." At first, I think they know each other and the guy owes him money. But no, it is just that the guy's eighties-style oversize tortoiseshells are "an affront to good taste." This happens frequently while I'm in Stone's company. Western-wear with suits drives him particularly bananas: "What do hemorrhoids and cowboy boots have in common?" he asks. "Every asshole eventually gets them."

As we order the first round of drinks, he launches into his life story. Half Italian, half Hungarian, he grew up in Lewisboro, New York. His mom was a small-town reporter, his dad a well driller. It was a fairly lonely childhood. There were no kids around in his rural surroundings, so sports weren't on the menu.

His dad left for work at 6:00 A.M., got home at 9:00 P.M., ate dinner, and dropped into bed. "You're not playing catch with your old man," he says. "My guess is he hated his job. But he never complained a day in his life. That's what it took to put food on the table." His folks still aren't entirely sure what he does and wonder why Stone didn't become "a plumber or an electrician or any of those guys who make good money." But, when he was working on Ronald Reagan's campaign in 1979, Stone introduced his dad to the candidate, which he calls "the proudest moment of my whole life. Reagan was great. He said, 'Your son works very hard for us.' Of course, he had no idea what I did."

Stone was bitten by the political bug early. In first grade, he supported John F. Kennedy, because he was Catholic, like Stone, and "he had better hair than Nixon." During a mock election at school,

Stone told classmates that if Nixon won, he'd make kids go to school on Saturdays. "Kennedy swept the election," he says proudly, "because of disinformation I spread about Nixon. It was kind of a first experience."

His liberal convictions didn't last long. After being given *Conscience of a Conservative* by a neighbor, he became a Goldwater zealot and rode his bike down to the local Republican headquarters each day to lick envelopes. While Stone considers himself a staunch Reaganite, with a libertarian twist that doesn't want the government "telling me what to do in the boardroom or the bedroom," he has mixed feelings today about his Goldwater infatuation. "It's like he was trying to lose. Going to Tennessee and coming out against the Tennessee Valley Authority? These were suicidal acts." As he developed his political worldview, he realized that Richard Nixon was "more pragmatic, more interested in winning than proving a point." He took a Stone's Rule from Nixon: "Losers don't legislate."

Becoming a student of political history, Stone deduced that Nixon "had been fucked out of the presidency in 1960, thanks to Joe Kennedy and our mob friends." He wrote a letter to Nixon, then practicing law on Wall Street, to that effect, telling him he should run again. Nixon wrote back, thanking Stone, saying he had no plans to run again, but that if he ever did, he'd be in touch. "Even then, he had full plans to run again," says Stone.

Stone was a student at George Washington University, in Washington, D.C., when Nixon was running for reelection in 1972. Stone invited the deputy director of the Committee to Reelect the President, Jeb Magruder, to speak at the university's Young Republican Club. "There are a bunch of hippie-type, left-wing, pinko degenerates that attend and harass him, but he handles it okay," recalls Stone. "He had highly polished shoes, I remember that very distinctly." Afterward, Stone hit him up for a job and got one. "My academic studies went right into the toilet. I could read about it, or do it for real. I'd rather do it for real." Though he was extremely junior, Nixon's old hands—"the UCLA ratfuckers" Stone calls them—had him getting into all sorts of hijinks, such as contributing money to a possible Nixon rival in the name of the Young Socialists Alliance, then leaking the receipt to the *Manchester Union Leader*.

By day, Stone says, he was working as a scheduler for Nixon surrogates. "By night, I'm trafficking in the black arts. Nixon's people were obsessed with intelligence." So at one point, Stone placed a mole in the Hubert Humphrey campaign, who ended up becoming Humphrey's driver. His source reported back all kinds of information—mostly libelous—which Stone kicked up the chain.

Stone speaks of this time nostalgically, but also with some distaste. A lot of what Nixon's henchmen were doing was "ineffective and relatively stupid. Typical of the mentality of the Nixon people, who were about to beat McGovern by twenty points." It goes against Stone's beliefs to do risky things for no reason. Though he has represented many casino interests, he doesn't gamble. "I never play games with my own money where the odds are stacked against you," he says.

Stone went to work for the Office of Economic Opportunity, which managed most of LBJ's War on Poverty programs. Bob Haldeman's "charge to us was to dismantle, replace, and fire everybody." After Nixon resigned, Stone spent the rest of the 1970s getting his Republican ticket punched. He worked for Senator Bob Dole (and was fired, after Jack Anderson reported he'd been a Nixon dirty trickster), worked for the Reagan campaign in 1976, and was national chairman of the Young Republicans in 1977. He and his first wife honeymooned by serving as camp counselors at the Teenage Republican Leadership Conference.

Around the time he became northeast chairman of Reagan's 1980 campaign, he had another awakening when he started working with the notorious lawyer Roy Cohn, former McCarthy henchman and also a Reagan supporter. "I'm still kind of a neophyte," Stone admits, "still kind of thinking everything's on the level. 'Cause the truth is, nothing's on the level." At a 1979 meeting at Cohn's Manhattan town house, he was introduced to major mobster and Cohn client "Fat Tony" Salerno. "Roy says to Tony, 'You know, Tony, everything's fixed. Everything can be handled.' Tony says, 'Roy, the Supreme Court?' Roy says, 'Cost a few more dollars.'" Stone loved Cohn: "He didn't give a shit what people thought, as long as he was able to wield power. He worked the gossip columnists in this city like an organ."

Stone, who going back to his class elections in high school has been a proponent of recruiting patsy candidates to split the other guy's support, remembers suggesting to Cohn that if they could figure out a way to make John Anderson the Liberal Party nominee in New York, with Jimmy Carter picking up the Democratic nod, Reagan might win the state in a three-way race. "Roy says, 'Let me look into it.'" Cohn then told him, "'You need to go visit this lawyer'—a lawyer who shall remain nameless—'and see what his number is.' I said, 'Roy, I don't understand.' Roy says, 'How much cash he wants, dumbfuck.'" Stone balked when he found out the guy wanted $125,000 in cash to grease the skids, and Cohn wanted to know what the problem was. Stone told him he didn't have $125,000, and Cohn said, "That's not the problem. How does he want it?"

Cohn sent Stone on an errand a few days later. "There's a suitcase," Stone says. "I don't look in the suitcase . . . I don't even know what was in the suitcase . . . I take the suitcase to the law office. I drop it off. Two days later, they have a convention. Liberals decide they're endorsing John Anderson for president. It's a three-way race now in New York State. Reagan wins with 46 percent of the vote. I paid his law firm. Legal fees. I don't know what he did for the money, but whatever it was, the Liberal Party reached its right conclusion out of a matter of principle."

I ask him how he feels about this in retrospect. He seems to feel pretty good—now that certain statutes of limitations are up. He cites one of Stone's Rules, by way of Malcolm X, his "brother under the skin": "By any means necessary." "Reagan got the electoral votes in New York State, we saved the country," Stone says with characteristic understatement. "[More] Carter would've been an unmitigated disaster."

In the 1980s, Stone and his old friends Charles Black and Paul Manafort hung out their shingle—later to be joined by other skilled knife-fighters like the late Lee Atwater. Stone was often rivals with Atwater, though he affectionately cites his rules: "'Lie low, play dumb, and keep moving.' As opposed to mine, which are 'Admit nothing, deny everything, launch counterattack.' Often called the Three Corollaries."

While Black, Manafort & Stone did work on behalf of blue-chip companies and boutique right-wing causes from the Contras to Angola's UNITA rebels, what they really did was advise presidential candidates. They worked on so many campaigns that in 1986 (when Stone was working with Jack Kemp), a congressional aide remarked to a *Time* reporter, "Why have primaries for the nomination? Why not have the candidates go over to Black, Manafort & Stone and argue it out?"

At this point Stone was operating comfortably in the main-stream—collecting high-six-figure fees, having fashion stories written about him in *GQ* and *Penthouse,* throwing society-page annual birthday celebrations for Calvin Coolidge ("a great do-nothing president")—but even then he demonstrated his self-destructive tendencies. In the thick of the 1988 election season, he called his colleague Lee Atwater's client George H. W. Bush a "weenie" in print. Stone has a knack for alienating and says that the people who like him like him, and those who don't never will anyway.

He seems to think he moves faster alone. (Stone's Rules: "Nobody ever built a statue to a committee.") "I'm not good at brown-nosing. Unlike Atwater, I wasn't willing to tell George Bush he's the smartest guy in the world, 'cause he's not. It's probably not very bright on my part. But I kind of call them like I see them. So I tell *Newsweek* Bush is a weenie. I also tell them if you elect him as president, he'll serve one term and drive the party to its knees, and he serves one term and drives the party to its knees. How do you lose to Bill Clinton? Guy's a fuckin' hillbilly. It's tough."

Stone's time-bomb tendencies brought a major life change for him in 1996, effectively ending his career in mainstream presidential politics. While Stone was serving as an unpaid adviser to Bob Dole, the tabloids got hold of photos of Stone and his second wife, Nydia, striking come-hither poses in swingers ads, putting out the call for bedroom playmates with exacting specifications: "No smokers or fats please."

His denials were adamant, his alibis elaborate. There was lots of talk about disgruntled employees and frame-ups and credit card fraud. When I bring this up to Stone, he looks pained. He says the revelations really hurt his wife, which is what bothers him the most. As for the alibis, he shrugs, "I did the best with what I had—which wasn't much."

As I earlier stated, Stone is honest about his dishonesty. I figure in this case, it's partly due to the drinks I ply him with at dinner. (Labash's Rules: "Without alcohol, people tell you what they want to say. With alcohol, they tell you what you want to hear.") But Stone comes clean on this too. Though he appears to knock down each drink I order him, it turns out he has had only one. He greased the waiter in advance, telling him to bring only olives and water in his martini glass after the first one. He didn't want me to have the edge, in case I was there to whack him like Paul Castellano. It's a trick he borrowed from Lyndon Johnson, who used to down iced tea in highball glasses to gain the advantage over dimwitted reporters who were slugging back the real thing.

Over the course of the week that I spend with Stone, we talk a lot about movies. He's a film buff, and particularly likes the gangster/con-artist/caper genre. We agree on our favorite film: *Miller's Crossing,* the 1990 Coen Brothers flick about underworld ethics. The film is filled with straight-razor repartee not unlike that often uttered by Stone—typical line: "It's a wrong situation. It's getting so a business-man can't expect no return from a fixed fight. Now if you can't trust a fix, what can you trust?"—and chock full of crosses and double-crosses. Characters' motivations are constantly shifting or in question. Nothing is as it initially appears.

It gets me thinking about Stone's own little Bernie Spitzer caper. When I outright accuse him of lying about it, he denies it, but barely: "Even if I did do this, which, like O.J., I didn't, it's not in my interest to cop to something I didn't do." But why would he do it? One of Stone's Rules is "Avoid obviousness." And nothing could be more obvious than this phone call, unless he just wanted it to look that way. Even his political rivals know that he is not a stupid man. When I tell a left-leaning political hand who himself frequently operates in the shadows that I'm doing a piece on Stone, he smiles wickedly and says: "Whatever people think of Stone and his scandals, he is an absolute artist. He doesn't feel useful if his knife is in the sheath."

Stone's business card features an elegant white-gloved man in top hat and evening clothes from a 1930s *Esquire* ad. He gave the card to a boy once who looked at it and said, "Are you a magician?" His response: "Sometimes, kid." One gets the sense with Stone, a showman above all else, that he has both the vanity and the frustration of the professional illusionist. The trick is only fun to pull so long as some-one knows he's pulling it.

Theories abound as to what the trick might be. I float some of them by Stone. Perhaps it was a calculated risk. Make the call to Bernard Spitzer, knowing they'll leak it. It regenerates headlines and gives the loan scandal new life. Sure, Stone takes a hit, and even appears to lose money when Bruno throws him under the bus, but

Roger Stone doesn't have to worry about sacrificing respectability, as he hasn't been considered respectable in some time.

Meanwhile, he can fall back into the shadows where he does his best work, perhaps even start a 527 in the form of a concerned-citizens front group to raise money from the throngs of wingnuts and Wall Street types who bear grudges against Spitzer. A group like, say, the Citizens Committee for Checks and Balances, whose fund-raising letter I obtained, and who, among other things, wants to "expose the illegal activities of the Spitzer administration." A group like that could not only pay one's salary, but could also help one carry out the missionary work of blast mailings, e-mail blitzes, and deep research that might eventually screw Spitzer to the wall (Spitzer's poll numbers are currently at an all-time low). When I run this thought past Stone, he won't confirm anything other than to say, "Shrewd theory."

Once you cross over into Stone Zone psychology, it feels as though you've been dropped in the middle of a David Mamet script. No matter what's been in the papers, nothing seems beyond the realm of possibility. I think about Randy Credico, the "master impressionist" whom Stone has accused of impersonating him on Bernard Spitzer's answering machine—the two have been sniping in the press. I suggest to Stone that the whole thing is a setup. Kooky and implausible as the alibi was, he and Credico are probably in on this together and are just pretending to fight, professional wrestling style. "Anything is possible," Stone says, giving the air of someone with whom it's fine if you believe the worst, since even if it's not true, it just feeds the lore and keeps everyone else confused.

I become so suspicious of Stone's deception maneuvers that I begin to suspect foul play everywhere. After lunch one day, he ditches me when I've been in a restroom too long, instructing a colleague to wait for me. When I catch up with him, I give him the third degree, asking him what that was all about, thinking he was trying to force me into conversation with his guy to casually plant something Stone didn't want to tell me himself. "Once in a while—very rarely—things are benign," Stone says. "Frankly, you were taking too much time in the john. I wanted to get back."

But most of the time, things aren't benign. One afternoon, it seems as though we are just walking the streets of Manhattan. Stone walks everywhere, abhorring cabs because they have lousy air-conditioning and "sweating through a suit—that is the worst thing in the world." His brisk gait is interrupted, however, in front of the Harmonie Club on East 60th Street. He stares at it for a while, then smiles.

He tells me that this place could soon become famous. In fact, it sort of already is. One of the city's oldest Jewish gentlemen's clubs, it's had a rash of bad headlines in recent years. Some New Yorkers consider it racist because of a lack of black or Hispanic members. Mayor Bloomberg saw fit to end his membership there in 2001, before his first mayoral run. And Barack Obama recently canceled a fund-raiser there on the same grounds.

A little bird has told Stone that Eliot Spitzer's father, Bernard, is a member. Additionally, so is Dale Hemmerdinger, the landlord Stone profusely apologized to who also happens to be Spitzer's choice for chairman of the Metropolitan Transit Authority. It strikes Stone that a lot of blacks and Hispanics take public transit in New York, and he wonders how it would play if it were to become known that the governor's pick belongs to a club that excludes them from membership. It seems like the sort of thing that might be troubling at a Hemmerdinger confirmation hearing. And it might be hard for Spitzer to walk away from his nominee, considering his own father belongs to the same club. Maybe nothing will come of it. But it's weird sometimes, how the news can be going one way, then take a funny bounce.

A month later, it does. Brooklyn assemblyman Hakeem Jeffries writes a letter to Eliot Spitzer, urging him to pull Hemmerdinger's nomination because he belongs to a predominantly white club, which "sends the wrong signal to the minority community." At his confirmation hearing, Hemmerdinger defends his Harmonie membership, but just a day later, he resigns from the club faster than you can cite the most apt of Stone's Rules: "Never do anything till you're ready to do it."

He is confirmed, but the issue won't die. Assemblyman Adam Clayton Powell IV charges Hemmerdinger lied during the senate committee hearing by representing that he'd actively recruited minorities while president of the Harmonie Club twenty years earlier, "unless he can show one [minority] person who was a member at the time, as he claimed." Just a week later, it comes out that Bernard Spitzer has been a member of the exclusively white club for thirty years, an inconvenient aside that the governor's aides neglected to mention when defending Hemmerdinger's association with the Harmonie.

As all this unfolds, I ask Stone how he thinks his prophecy was fulfilled. "Shit happens," he says.

I am being chauffeured around Miami in one of Stone's five Jaguars. At the wheel is A-Mill, his twenty-three-year-old driver/computer whiz/all-around Boy Friday. A-Mill looks like he'd fight as a featherweight, but Stone says looks can be deceiving. One late night, when they were walking across a strip club parking lot together, two large gentlemen tried to mug them. A-Mill reached into his boot, pulled out a blade, and slashed one of them across the face, causing both assailants to run. "Watch this guy," says Stone. "He's a killer."

A-Mill wears a porkpie hat of his own choosing, but with suits, he takes direction from Stone. When he first came to work for him, Stone took him to a haberdashery in Cleveland and lent him the money to buy four suits and some black Peal cap-toe lace-ups. "We deduct fifty dollars from his paycheck each week to pay me back," says Stone. If you want to roll with Stone, you have to look good. (Stone's Rules: "Look good = feel good.")

As we head north of South Beach to Stone's home on Biscayne Bay, Stone reviews his morning itinerary. He will try to outwit some of his rivals in the Ukrainian campaign, dictate a threatening letter to an online magazine that he says has defamed him, and put out a few Stonezone pieces maligning one Spitzer crony or another. Stone is like a U.S. Army of treachery: He screws more people before 9 A.M. than most people do in a whole day.

Stone has a nice life in Miami. He gets out to kayak quite a bit, enjoying the year-round good weather. He and Nydia have five grandchildren. A power law firm based in Fort Lauderdale, Rothstein Rosenfeldt Adler, recently brought him on to head their burgeoning public affairs side. The firm's head, Scott Rothstein, is a pit bull litigator with a taste for Bentleys and $150,000 watches. He shares Stone's operating philosophy, telling me that he tells all his lawyers, "Get into the game, or get the fuck out of the way."

Except for a poster of a stripper he picked up in Amsterdam and a photo of him standing poolside with porn star Nina Hartley—she thrusting her glistening glutei at the camera, Stone peddling his own wares with his oiled-up frame packed into a banana hammock—his office is a Hall of Nixonia. There are photos, posters, and letters from Nixon at every stage of his career. I ask Stone, whose politics more closely adhere to Reagan's, why he is such a Nixon fetishist. "It's about resilience," he tells me. "That's the whole point of Nixon. Coming back from adversity. Coming back from defeat. Coming back from setbacks. It's persistence. Obviously, he was tragically flawed in a number of ways. Aren't we all?" (It's hard to tell when Stone stops talking about Nixon and starts talking about himself.)

One of Stone's friends, who has known him professionally for a decade, tells me: "What I find interesting about Roger is how committed to the joke he is. He moons the establishment for the sheer pleasure of it, with no thought to whether it helps him. Obviously most of the time it doesn't, and maybe he cares—I'll bet he has mixed feelings—but he doesn't stop. Notice how he's willfully, self-consciously downmarket: Trump, Sharpton, the dyed hair and horse-shoe pinky ring. There's an ironic quality to all of it.

"He could have made a lot more money being Mike Deaver. It's not like he's not smart enough to have joined Cassidy and landed Microsoft as a client, like a thousand other semitalented former consultants. Instead, he's nearing sixty and still wallowing in the small-time sleaziness of New York State politics. And he doesn't even live there. There's no master plan with Roger. He just follows the most subversive, amusing course available to him at the time. I sort of respect that."

Stone, for his part, resists attempts to get him to wax maudlin about missed opportunities. But one night as we are having dinner at the Bal Harbour Palm, he talks about the swingers tabloid scandal that effectively chased him out of Washington—a place he says he detests and doesn't miss. The hardest thing wasn't the story, he says. It was the day he left. The moving van was in front of his house, and he was ready to go. But his beloved Yorkshire terrier, Pee Wee, ran out the door into the street, was struck by a car, and killed right in front of Stone and his wife. "It was like a final kick in the balls," he says. "I had a hard time getting over that. It's the single worst thing that's ever happened. Pee Wee was an extraordinary dog with a unique level of intelligence and personality. He's just a great dog, even still. And I really miss him."

I don't know what to say. I've never seen this level of vulnerability and human emotion from Stone. It makes me uncomfortable. I ask him what color the dog was. He seems mildly perturbed. "Brown and black—like all Yorkies," he snaps. Wanting the Stone I know to return—I hate to watch men cry—I bait him by telling him I didn't know that, since I usually have man-dogs, not cat-dogs. He glares at me. "Fuck you," he says. "They were bred to hunt and kill rats. They are not pussy dogs. Tonight, I'll sic my five on you, and see how you do. They will eat your ass alive." It's good to have him back.

His disclosure, however, fosters a new level of understanding and trust. I order us another round of drinks, then go to the restroom. When I return, a tall martini is sitting in front of him. I eye it suspiciously. "What are you looking at?" he asks. "Your drink—what is it?" I inquire. "A martini, obviously," he replies. I ask him to slide it to me, which he reluctantly does. I taste it. I thought we were just a couple of pals a couple drinks into the evening, but I'd forgotten one of Stone's Rules: "Always keep the advantage." It was nothing more than water and olives.

DOWN WITH FACEBOOK!

Look at the outer shell—the parachute pants, the piano key tie, the fake tuxedo T-shirt—and you might mistake me for a slave to fashion. Do not be deceived. Early adoption isn't my thing. I much prefer late adoption, that moment when the trend-worshipping sheeple who have early-adopted drive the unsustainable way of life I so stubbornly cling to ever so close to the edge of obsolescence, that I've no choice but to follow. This explains why I bought cassette tapes until 1999, why I wouldn't purchase a DVD player until Blockbuster cashiered their VHS stock. Toothpaste? I use it now that it's clear it's here to stay.

So I'm not inflexible. But there is one promise I've made to myself. And that is that no matter how long I live, no matter how much pressure is exerted, no matter how socially isolated I become, I will never, ever join Facebook, the omnipresent online social-networking site that like so many things that have menaced our country (the Unabomber, *Love Story,* David Gergen) came to us from Harvard but has now worked its insidious hooks into every crevice of society.

For the five or six Amish shut-ins who may not yet have heard of this scourge (your tenacious ignorance is to be admired, and I'd immediately friend you if I was into Facebook and you had electricity), Facebook is an online community where colleagues, friends, long-lost acquaintances, friends of friends or long-lost acquaintances, and perfect strangers find and "friend" one another based on their real or perceived affinity. They then have access to one another's web pages, and consequently to one another's lives, quirks, photos, jottings, oversharings, and mental disorders, as well as to those of the ever-expanding universe of their friends' circles, thus increasing the likelihood that you will either embarrass yourself or be embarrassed by someone whose life would never otherwise intersect with yours. (Right about now, a Facetard is ginning up an angry letter to the editor saying this would not be the case if you knew how to control your privacy settings. Save the geek speech for your Facebook friends, Facetard, I already got my eight hours' sleep.)

Why the resistance? There are many factors. But mainly, it's Farhad Manjoo. He's the technology columnist at *Slate,* an online magazine I regularly read and a place where I have several real friends, as opposed to the fake friends you collect on Facebook. I've not met Manjoo, who strikes me as a perfectly pleasant fellow even if his ilk is destroying America. A few weeks back, I received an e-mail from a California lawyer friend of mine. A proud skeptic and nonjoiner by temperament, he had downed a shot of Kool-Aid and was now asking me to clasp hands and join him in his journey to the new fantasyland of Facebook. Attached to his invitation, intended to shame me out of nonparticipation ("Resistance is futile, join the Borg," he wrote), was a link to a piece Manjoo had just written, tauntingly titled "You Have No Friends—Everyone else is on Facebook. Why aren't you?"

Manjoo cited all the statistics: Facebook had just added its 150 millionth member and, since last August, is signing up 374,000 people each day. It has achieved absolute critical mass, thus compounding its utility and effectiveness. Not joining now is an affectation in itself, like refusing to own a cell phone or rejecting the social lubricant of antiperspirant. "Facebook is now at the same point," he wrote. "Whether or not you intend it, you're saying something by staying away."

How right you are, Mr. Manjoo. I am indeed saying something, and it is this: I hate Facebook and everyone on it, including my friends, whom I like. My wife just joined it, and I dearly love her. But scratch that. I hate her too. After all, right is right. Sometimes, we courageous few must make a stand.

One by one, my nonjoiner friends have succumbed. As one reluctantly joined the world of "poking" and getting "poked" by people he already talked to, people he had no interest in talking to, or people he didn't know at all—all conducted under the suspect rubric of "friendship" so that they can look at one another's photos and write dreary "status updates" on their "walls" (brief squibs about what you are doing at that exact moment, usually with emoticons and inappropriate quotation marks: "Matt Labash is wondering how long to marinate human flesh to get out that 'gamey taste' ☺")—he was almost apologetic about it. Within two days of his birth on Facebook, he said, "I have 198 friends. I have never heard of most of them. This is so dorky, I hate myself for doing it."

Being a true friend, I didn't allay his guilt. I told him he was a very sad man, that collecting Facebook friends is the equivalent of being a cat lady, collecting numerous Himalayans, which you have neither the time nor the inclination to feed. "You have obviously never been on Facebook," he said. "It's so much worse than collecting cats." By this week, however, he'd lost all ironic distance. When I told him that he now took it all way too seriously, that I liked the old, conflicted him better, and that he should take a hard look at himself, he sloughed me off. He was now just another friend-whore: "I don't need to look at myself. I have 614 Facebook friends to do the looking for me."

Another longtime friend, the host of Fox's *Red Eye*, Greg Gutfeld, tells me he has 3,200 Facebook friends: "I know maybe fifty of them." To Gutfeld's credit, he is ashamed. He concedes that Facebook is a place that turns adults into teenage girls. "Instead of making things," he says, "We're telling people how great *Gossip Girl* is. Would your grandfather go on Facebook? Probably not. I think we've become a country thirsting for attention—Facebook is basically Googling yourself for people who don't have enough hits to warrant it." Being a television personality, Gutfeld will go on for the occasional ego stroke, but admits, "It's all pointless. A Facebook friend won't shave your back."

The hardest to watch fall, however, has been my wife. I'll call her "Alana," since that's her name (but note to Facetards: Don't try to friend her to heckle me, she will not receive you). A few months back, she became a hard-core Facebook addict, as our late-thirties age group has become the fastest-growing Facebook segment (thirty-five- to fifty-four-year-olds have increased 276.4 percent to nearly seven million users in just the past six months). There are worse things she could become, I suppose: a Meth dealer, a UPS delivery-man groupie, a Twitterer. Still, it's unsettling.

In our house, there have always been clearly defined roles. I procrastinate, shirk responsibilities, and spend much time peppering a fairly wide circle of friends with an incessant barrage of individually tailored e-mails, many of them lengthy (as opposed to the abbreviated, promiscuously generic, group-blog-like messages left on Facebook). I tell myself it keeps me in game-shape, writing-wise, like a baseball player taking cuts in the batting cage. Alana isn't an Internet dawdler by nature, but rather, a doer, a model of graceful efficiency. She is Felix to my Oscar.

But slowly, I noticed things taking a turn. The cosmetic stuff, like her immaculate appearance and hygiene, stayed the same. Nor did I see her do anything too creepy or severe, such as sending pictures of her feet at the request of a new Facebook friend or running out to some hot-sheets motel to get worked like a farm implement by an old high school flame who'd renewed contact (which happens with some frequency on Facebook). But I did notice a general distracted-ness, a vacantness, a thousand-yard stare. She seemed to notice it too. In the old days, she'd check her e-mail maybe once or twice a day. Now, she was hitting her laptop like a rat hits a lever for pellets in a Skinner box.

"I hate myself," she'd say.

"Why?" I'd ask.

"Because I'm becoming you," she said.

A regular complaint around here is that I ignore her when con-sumed in e-mail correspondence. But now, as I tried to relate a story to her from my day, she'd humor me, dutifully nodding. I would see only the top of her head, since her nose was buried in her computer. She pretended to listen, but was really just acquiring more Facebook friends or picking a piece of "flair" to put on her message board as if she were a waitress at T.G.I. Friday's or perhaps contemplating whether to hit someone with a "yellow snowball" (a Facebook ap-plication seemingly intended for six-year-olds, in which you can hit a friend with a snowball, leaving them with the knotty moral dilemma of whether to hit you back, though snow, of course, never actually changes hands). Or maybe she'd just be uploading pictures of herself, or worse, of me and the kids and Moses, our Bernese mountain dog, a presumptuous act. Without our consent, she was incorporating us in her new career as a flasher. It was harmless enough for now: unauthorized photos of me fly fishing, or sitting on the porch with our sons. But with the creeping exhibitionism that takes over most Facebook users, it seemed only a matter of time before she started posting the nudes, some shots I took when I was trying to break into Washington journalism (I was young and needed the money).

Normally a crisp woman who tackles tasks with speed and aplomb, she had a new slackness to her. All the things she usu-ally takes care of without my even being much aware (paying bills, making dinner, etc.) would slide, as she was now filling out the endless Facebook busywork questionnaires people constantly send to one another like dippy substitute teachers who don't know what assignment to give. As she filled out the now ubiquitous "25 Random Things About Me" list shooting around Facebook circles, near perfect strangers could come to know things it took me years to find out ("I hate when people talk without clearing their throats. . . . I tend to like those with an easy smile") and things I hadn't even yet discovered ("I wish I had more opportunities to shoot a gun").

I had earned this knowledge by taking the time to get to know her. But now, she was slutting it out for free. And not just to old high school chums who seemed to migrate to Facebook en masse almost instantaneously. Alana accepted friendship from people she knew, people she barely knew, and people who said they knew her but whom she couldn't pick out of a police lineup. With some of her new friends, it might come down to that.

One recent afternoon, my sister-in-law came over, carrying the local paper and informing Alana and me that a distant acquaintance from their childhood was on the front page for getting in a bar fight and holding a knife to a guy's neck, leaving a superficial wound. "That's a crazy coincidence," said Alana. "I have a friend request sitting from him in my inbox right now!" I read the story aloud, but Alana went straight to her inbox, looked up the knife-wielder in question, and hit "accept." On his Facebook page, he bragged of owning the "friggin' cemetery on Ward Road," while his profile photo featured him holding a fork at an odd angle, not unlike an angle at which you'd hold a knife against a guy's neck.

"What are you doing?" I asked, incredulous.

"Oh, c'mon," Alana said, shooing me off. "He's just a Facebook friend. It's not like we're having him over to the house for dinner."

Time magazine recently declared Facebook more popular than porn. But who are they kidding? Facebook is porn. With porn, you watch other people take off their clothes and abase themselves in public. On Facebook, where there's technically an anti-nudity policy (thus defeating the whole purpose of the Internet), you get to figuratively do the same.

By now, the horror stories are legion. It's a place where anorexics have been caught giving one another new ways to purge, where the

Uruguayan interior minister posted pictures of herself in the shower, where a site was set up where young men could boast of hitting prostitutes with doughnuts and hot chocolate. It's a place where a Swedish nurse got in trouble for posting photos of the brain from a brain surgery she was assisting with, where marauding bands of teenage thugs intercepted birthday party logistics so they could crash a home, leaving it in ruins and the dog comatose, and where a husband ended up hacking his wife to death with a meat cleaver after noticing she'd changed her Facebook status to "single."

It's a place with so many superficial friend hoarders that one guy vowed to eat all twelve McDonald's value meals in one sitting (including the fries) if one hundred thousand people friended him. They did, and he gave it a go, but somewhere short of the Filet-O-Fish, he ended up violently hurling in the parking lot. It's a place where friendship is so devoid of honor or value that it can be shown up by a cynical burger joint advertising stunt. Burger King, in their "Whopper Sacrifice" campaign, started a Facebook application that would reward you with a free hamburger when you sacrificed ten Facebook friends. Burger King would then send alerts to the jettisoned ones, effectively notifying the newly defriended that they were worth only a tenth of a flame-broiled Whopper. Facebook ended up disabling the application, but not before 233,906 friends were sacrificed.

As if all of this isn't embarrassing enough for Facebook devotees, the most cloying writer in the world, *West Wing* creator Aaron Sorkin, signed on, promising/threatening to write a Facebook movie.

But it isn't for all the aforementioned reasons you should join me in hating Facebook. Far from it. For after going onto my wife's account to know what I'm not missing, I would have been happy to run into some meat-cleaving husbands, showering Uruguayan ministers, or even Aaron Sorkin (actually, I'd take the McDonald's hurler over Sorkin). That, at least, would've been interesting.

No, the reason to hate Facebook is because of the stultifying mind-numbing inanity of it all, the sheer boredom. If Facebook helps put together streakers with voyeurs, the streakers, for the most part, after shedding their trench coats, seem to be running around not with taut and tanned hard-bodies, but in stained granny panties with dark socks. They have a reality-show star's unquenchable thirst for broadcasting all the details of their lives, no matter how unexceptional those details are. They do so in the steady, Chinese water torture drip of status updates. The very fact that they are on the air (or rather, on Facebook) has convinced them that every facet of their lives must be inherently interesting enough to alert everyone to its importance.

These are all actual status updates (with name changes): "Maria is eating Girl Scout cookies. . . . Tom is glad it's the weekend. . . . Jacinda is longing for some sleep, pillow come to momma! . . . Dan is going to get something to eat. . . . Anne is taking Tyler to daycare. . . . Amber loves to dip. I can dip almost any food in blue cheese, ranch dressing, honey mustard, sour cream, mayonnaise, ketchup. Well, I think you get the point." Yes. Uncle. Please make it stop. For the love of God, we get the point.

Then, of course, there is the crushing anticlimax of people reentering your life who might've fallen away into your past, because in each other's past is where you mutually belong. Perhaps you haven't seen them in twenty years. Perhaps she was the cheerleader whose shapely legs fired your imagination in geometry class, whose smile could heat the gymnasium, whose jojoba-enriched hair you smelled when you broke into her locker and pulled some strands from her brush, dropping it in a Ziploc baggie, taking it home to fashion an effigy for your hair-doll shrine.

Now you're left on Facebook, desperately trying to recapture the magic by paging through photos of her freckly kids at Busch Gardens, stalking her like some kind of weirdo. She's fifteen pounds heavier now. But that's okay, next to her husband, a red-faced orb who used to be a hale three-sport athlete, whose only physical exertion now appears to be curling gin-and-tonics and power carb-loading. But her words are still a caress, as even pixels carry the melodious lilt of a voice that perfumes the air like April birdsong, when she status-updates you and 738 of her closest friends with: "Madison ate bad clams last night. Boy, does her tummy hurt!!! ☹"

Last week, my wife logged onto Facebook, took it in for about three minutes, shook her head, snapped her laptop shut, and sighed.

"What's wrong?" I asked.

"I don't know, it's not the same," Alana said. "I was into it at first. But then I realized, there's no longer any wonder, any intrigue. Everything's out there, on display. For years, you wondered, 'Whatever happened to so-and-so?' And now you know. All questions get answered. There's no more mystery."

She reminded me of a line from F. Scott Fitzgerald's "The

Crack-Up": "It is sadder to find the past again and find it inadequate to the present than it is to have it elude you and remain forever a harmonious conception of memory."

Alana put on a winter coat, leashed up Moses, and walked out into the February cold, returning to the land of the living. I was glad to have her back. Maybe I could even learn to love her again, after her torrid Facebook affair. I could stop worrying about her now and get back to more important things, like my personal e-mail, where I could service my own circle in earnest, devoid of faux interlopers. Where I could experience human complexity: rivalry, and thinly veiled insults, and petty jealousies and imagined slights. Who needs Facebook friends? That's what real friends are for.

FLY FISHING WITH DARTH VADER

*I fish because I love to . . . because, in a world where most men seem
to spend their lives doing things they hate, my fishing is at once an
endless source of delight and an act of small rebellion; because trout do
not lie or cheat and cannot be bought or bribed or impressed by power,
but respond only to quietude and humility and endless patience . . .
because only in the woods can one find solitude without loneliness;
because bourbon out of an old tin cup tastes better out there; because
maybe someday I will catch a mermaid; and, finally, not because I
regard fishing as being so terribly important but because I suspect that
so many of the other concerns of men are equally unimportant—and
not nearly so much fun.*

—Robert Traver, *Anatomy of a Fisherman* (1964)

Jackson, Wyoming

At the risk of being publicly ridiculed, quarantined, or stoned, I'll just
say it straightaway: I really like Dick Cheney. Don't get me wrong, I
feel sick about it.

Not because I've ever held anything against the guy personally. In
fact, many of the parts of Cheney's public persona that repel others, I
rather enjoy. I've always liked his ruthless unsentimentality in an age
of lip-biters and tear-squirters. I like that you're never apt to hear him
invoke "the children" as a reason for peddling some unrelated initiative. ("I'm not a baby kisser," he once said on the campaign trail.) I
like that he doesn't seem to care about being liked, which is lucky for
him, since his approval rating hovers at 18 percent. But let's just say I
haven't cared for many of his signature projects as vice president. It is
not for nothing that the wags suggest that Cheney keeps George W.
Bush one heartbeat away from the presidency.

But Cheney is also known as a fisherman, and I am a fishing slut
with little or no moral center.

Last September, I attended a book party on the roof of the

Hay-Adams Hotel in Washington, D.C., which Cheney was to attend. I showed up early and, seeing there were two open bars, availed myself of both. By the time Cheney arrived, I had a bellyful of truth serum.

I made a beeline for him, squared up, looked him in the eye, and said, "I understand you're an avid fly fisherman."

"Yes," he replied.

"So am I," I responded.

From there, we were off. We might've talked five minutes or we might've talked five hours. It's hard to recall now. Fishing-related happenings tend to occur outside of time. Herbert Hoover, a noted fly fisherman, was fond of quoting an Assyrian proverb that went, "The gods do not subtract from the allotted span of men's lives the hours spent fishing." I believe the same is true of talking about fishing.

Cheney, a surprisingly attentive listener, asked as much as he answered. He was fascinated by an experiment I'd been conducting for some time: catching catfish on a fly. This isn't typically done, since catfish most often reject artificials. Many fly fishermen recoil at such an ambition, since telling trout purists you're chasing lowly catfish with a fly rod is tantamount to telling Heidi Klum that what you're really attracted to is bearded women with no teeth. But Cheney evidenced genuine curiosity. Perhaps he sensed a kindred spirit. Remaking the Middle East as a Western democracy versus chasing catfish on a fly—each of us is addicted to some pet implausibility.

He asked where I fish, and, when I gave generalities, he pressed for specifics. So much so that I was worried I might show up the next day to find the vice president taking largemouth in my favorite spot. So I lied slightly about the locales. You can't be too careful about such things.

As we talked, my wife sidled up to me, elbowing my ribs for an introduction. I told Cheney this was my fishing widow. He said hello to her and that he had one too. We immediately resumed the fish talk and ignored her. I was in good standing and hoping for an invite to fish his home river, the majestic Snake in Wyoming—an invitation I was convinced was forthcoming but which never materialized after Cheney was interrupted and pulled away.

After our conversation, second thoughts started nagging. Maybe Cheney was misunderstood. Maybe he wasn't BeelzeDick or Darth Vader, as his critics would have it. How could someone who spends so much time seeking out beautiful creatures in beautiful places not have the sensitivity of a naturalist and the soul of a poet? (As I said, there were two open bars.)

A year after the book party, with time running out on the Bush administration, I took another crack at Cheney and proposed to his people that I go fishing with him on his preferred home water near his Wyoming residence, which turns out to be the South Fork of the Snake River. Though Cheney grants few interviews, his people were uncharacteristically agreeable. Perhaps it's because after eight years, they were just weary of saying no. Perhaps it's because of the heartfelt piscatorial nature of the request.

While fishing doesn't occupy Cheney's every waking moment—according to his estimates, he only spends about ten to twelve days a year on the water because of his job—it still takes up plenty of space in his consciousness. This I learn from visiting the library at his official residence at the Naval Observatory.

The shelves of his library contain the art books, histories, literature, and presidential and vice presidential material (including the complete works of Dan Quayle) that one would expect. But many of these are shelved high and out of reach. Most accessible, on the shelves above the television, is a fly fishing library within a library, books on every subject from entomology to minor tactics of the chalk stream to practical dry fly fishing.

All the greats are represented—Lee Wulff, Izaak Walton, G. E. M. Skues, Lefty Kreh, Roderick Haig-Brown—and the not-so-greats as well. There are lush leather and gilt-edged collectibles with gorgeous frontispieces of men in tweeds casting bamboo rods on placid streams, and dog-eared paperbacks intended not for decoration, but to acquire hard-core fishing knowledge.

When I pull down an old volume of Ernest Schwiebert's classic *Trout,* I find discarded Hershey's mini–candy bar wrappers behind where the book sits, perhaps from surreptitious snacking during a less health-conscious time in the now trim Cheney's life (friends say he's lost around twenty-five pounds in the past year). In all, there are thirty-seven fishing books on the shelves, and forty-three more in stacks. This doesn't include whatever books he has in Wyoming or at his weekend place on Maryland's Eastern Shore. You can say many things about Dick Cheney that have no chance of leaving a mark. But say he fishes thoughtlessly, and you might wound him irreparably.

I learn from current and former aides just how obsessed the man whose Secret Service handle is "Angler" actually is. One directs me to a passage in Bob Woodward's *The Commanders,* which tells how when Cheney was being confirmed for secretary of defense, he told his vetters in the first Bush administration that they should be aware of some "youthful indiscretions." He was referring not just to two drunk-driving arrests from over twenty-five years prior, but also to the time he'd been fined for fishing out of season. Not a catch-and-release man back then (he tells me he hasn't killed a fish on purpose in roughly fifteen years), "the twenty-five-dollar fine was not the worst part," he said. "They took my fucking fish."

Another aide tells me that early on, those in the administration wishing to cut through the clutter of Cheney's daily barrage of mail would take to sticking flies in the envelopes, knowing his staff would make sure he received them. I am told how he fishes in rain and snow, and how once his mind is set on fishing, he will not be deterred, even by bloodletting.

Former aide Brian McCormack, now special assistant to the president for strategic initiatives and external affairs, says several years ago Cheney took him fishing on a drift boat on the Snake River. Relatively new to the sport at the time, McCormack, trying to adjust his cast on a windy day, ended up hooking the vice president. "The hook did not set," says McCormack. "But it smacked him on the back of the neck. I don't know how exactly one describes a vice presidential yelp. He let out a 'yoooooowwww.' The trees came alive with Secret Service. He leaned forward with a grimace, like he got stung by an enormous bee. I'm in the back of the boat saying, 'What the hell did I just do?' He turned around and looked at me. I said, 'Sir, I am reeeaallly sorry.' He said, 'Don't worry. I've gotten it in the ear before.' And he just went on fishing."

According to those who fish with him, Cheney is also quite competitive on the river. When I ask his daughter Liz about this, she downplays it, speaking of his grandfatherly attributes: his teaching members of the family to fish so they can enjoy "the magnificent beauty of the places you get to do it," showing the grandchildren how to cast, rig their lines, and remove their hooks. "I can't imagine a better, more patient guide or teacher."

His friends take an earthier view. "Is he competitive?" laughs Dick Scarlett, one of Cheney's closest friends and chairman of Wells Fargo,

Wyoming. "Oh, I think so." Scarlett heads up a group of eight friends, including Cheney, who for over a decade have annually put in two days on the Bighorn River in Montana before coming back to Jackson for a few more, and then a two-day float down the South Fork, while camping overnight in the canyon.

The group calls itself "The Great Release," though Jay Kemmerer, a member and owner of the Jackson Hole Mountain Resort, originally pushed for "The Rainbow Coalition" (after rainbow trout, of course). The camp, nicknamed the South Fork Hilton, is hardly roughing it. On some of the most productive dry fly trout water in the west, the camp contains wall tents, cots, fresh linens and towels. There is wine and whiskey (Cheney is a Johnnie Walker Red man, though these days he rarely drinks more than a glass of wine). The Great Release even imports its own personal chef.

Everyone calls the vice president "Dick"—even the guides. Current events are often discussed, though there are no prosecutorial arguments, as his friends reason Cheney gets roughed up enough in the outside world. And there is lots of entertainment. In fact, there is an entertainment committee. While what goes on at the South Fork Hilton is supposedly cloaked under a code of silence, a few details are forthcoming.

There are skits, Kemmerer tells me, often with elaborate props. "We clearly tell the Secret Service what we're doing," says Kemmerer, "because some of it—well, they might shoot us." Cheney laughs readily as an observer at this campfire Friar's Roast/Gridiron Dinner and is open to the same ribbing as everybody else. Kemmerer says there have been hanging chads strewn about the grounds, and that he personally has played John Kerry and John Edwards.

Rich Santore, an orthopedic surgeon and chief of staff at Sharp Memorial Hospital in San Diego, became a member of the group after replacing Scarlett's hips. As one of the unofficial heads of the entertainment committee, he takes it even further. A couple of years ago, he had to buy a whole bunch of dresses, bras, panties, and such for skit time at the South Fork Hilton. At the checkout line, after asking the clerk what dress size would be right for him, he felt compelled to tell her, "It's not what you think." ("That's what they all say," said the clerk.) When I ask who on earth was being portrayed, Santore says he'd better not disclose. "Janet Reno?" I ask him, figuring she has even odds if drag is involved. "Well," he says reluctantly, "that was one."

But these are all sideshows to the competitive main event: the daily Big Fish contest. Members ante up ten bucks a day, and the biggest fish takes the pot (Cheney used to pay by check, but since Scarlett kept one as a souvenir, refusing to cash it, Cheney will now pay only in cash). According to the estimates I gather from friends and guides, Cheney is the pot winner anywhere from one-quarter to one-half of the time. Scarlett, who is equally competitive, and who has been fly fishing since he was a small child, does not mince praise for the man who is often his boatmate.

"Dick Cheney is an excellent fisherman," he says. "He throws a mean dry fly. He goes in where the big fish are in the most difficult places. He can place a fly from forty to fifty feet out, into shrubbery, in between bushes where the big fish lie. Where most people are fishing two or three feet away from the bushes so they don't hook up, Dick can place a fly on a saucer at forty feet. He is very, very good.

"The guides will tell you he's one of the best fishermen they guide on the river," Scarlett continues, and indeed, several do. "Other than myself," Scarlett hastens to add, ever the competitor.

While his friends say Cheney isn't a trash-talker like some, they concur that he takes the Big Fish contest very seriously. Cheney later admits to me that, one year, "I had a picture taken of a brown trout I caught up here, blown up, life-size, and sent it to [Kemmerer], as a reminder of who caught the big fish that year."

Sensing my work is cut out for me, I head out west a day early to fish solo with a guide and acclimate myself to the South Fork, presumably lessening the vice president's chances of outfishing me. I drive about an hour outside of Jackson, through the switchbacks of the Targhee National Forest, to Irwin, Idaho. There I will launch with the same outfit that we will be using the following day (and that Cheney has been using for years), the pristine Lodge at Palisades Creek.

All knotty pine and rustic cabins (decades ago, the laundry building used to be a house of prostitution servicing the itinerant workers who helped build nearby Palisades Dam), the lodge serves up gourmet meals and single malts in its Liar's Den restaurant, and there's a full-service fly shop on the grounds.

My guide for the day is Jaason Pruett, a thirty-four-year-old former college hoops player, who is not some delicate Orvis-catalog-issue trout teapot, but a take-no-prisoners river rat. The bed of his pickup truck is littered with Twisted Tea and Budweiser empties. His dashboard is carpeted and stuck with many of his sentimental-favorite flies. He wears a denim bucket hat from a car dealership, an "Abercrabby and Fish" T-shirt, a red swimsuit, and green Crocs for wet-wading.

The South Fork of the Snake is a tailwater that runs fast and cold out of the Palisades Reservoir. The guides here double as rowers for the ClackaCraft drift boats, which, in addition to the middle bench for the oarsman, have swivel chairs for two fishermen in the bow and stern, along with leg brackets so you can stand and cast without falling into the drink, as the river is often rough. (Pruett says he's saved drowning people multiple times, and that less-adept civilian rowers see the river eating about four boats a season.)

We do a ten-mile float through what is truly God's country. It is wallpapered with wildflowers and golden willows, mountain maples and cottonwood forests, populated by bobcats, moose, and black bears. Red-tailed hawks and bald eagles patrol the skies overhead.

More important, however, the river is thick with trout—browns and cutthroats, rainbows and hybrid cutbows—about seven thousand fish per mile. These aren't the SNITs (standard nine-inch trout) I'm accustomed to back east either. There, the relative scarcity of good water means that our overpressured streams hold fish that are bombed with so many flies they ought to be issued hard hats. On the South Fork of the Snake, trout are fifteen to seventeen inches on average, with twenty-inchers not out of the question. They feed aggressively, and they are slutty for dries (flies that sit atop the water, which make fish rise so you can see the take). It makes perfect sense that this is one of Cheney's favorite runs.

As Pruett rows and sets me up on fish, he speaks of the hazards of being a guide: of the yuppies who spend all this money to come out and avail themselves of his services, but who then spend all afternoon telling him how to catch fish in his own backyard. Sometimes he has to teach them a lesson, such as the know-it-all "who thought he was the cat's meow. So I cut the hook off his fly, and he didn't know it. After about the sixth fish in a row that he missed, I said, 'Man, I thought you were good—why aren't you getting these fish?' He's like, 'Jaason, what am I doing wrong?' I said, 'Do you wanna listen to me? Let me change your fly out.' He listened."

Pruett and his guides have no such problems with Cheney. There are inconveniences, to be sure, such as having to sweep his truck and boat clean of any mysterious herbal substances and leave behind his gun, which he otherwise likes to pack on the river—just in case—in order to pass muster with the Secret Service. But Pruett says the guides regard Cheney as a gentleman without pretense, who's a pleasure to row.

Cheney isn't some fussy streamside entomologist, either, sifting water with a cheesecloth to see if he can match the hatch. But he knows his stuff, and when he doesn't know something, says Pruett, he is eminently coachable and invariably polite, even if he's not renowned for his small talk. He takes both fishing and solitude seriously, and the river is his place to escape. Other drift-boaters will often float by, having no idea that they just passed the vice president of the United States. ("We don't have a sign on him," Dick Scarlett tells me.)

Pruett says that the sight of Cheney on the river is so unexpected to some that, once, he even saw a young man who worked for Idaho Fish and Game who was checking fishing licenses, "but in sneaky spots," head out of the brush, walk right up to Cheney, ask to see his license, and still never put together to whom he was talking. "Clueless," says Pruett.

Pruett is not just a guide, it turns out. He is a stalker of fish. If trout had access to the courts, they'd hit him with a restraining order. He knows their names and unlisted addresses, and he constantly says things like "We're gonna get out of the boat here, I have to check on this fish." He puts me on to many. I catch a smattering of cutthroats, browns, and rainbows, along with several whitefish (which the locals derisively call "Rocky Mountain bonefish"). But I'm slow on the trigger today and miss many more.

Blessed with X-ray vision, Pruett even has me cast to a pet brown he's been stalking that I can't see, a twenty-four-inch monster laid up against the head of an island. I float a hopper over him, he explodes on it, then books down-current with line screaming off my reel behind him. Trying to slow him, I'm forced to follow on foot, as he's too strong to reel. He finally snaps off after nearly finishing my twiglike 4-weight rod. My expletives would curl his gills if he were still around to hear them.

Pruett is generous about the few fish I catch that come off as he's about to net them. "It counts," he assures, "you had control." I tell him he would say that. It's probably in the Fishing Guide Rulebook to always give the fisherman the benefit of the doubt. "Of course," he admits. "Is that a twenty-inch fish, or twenty-six? That's twenty-six. What's six inches between friends?"

But he tells it straight when I ask him how he thinks I'll do against Cheney. "First of all, he gets the front of the boat," says Pruett, meaning Cheney's fly gets first pass at all the fish. "Second, this is pretty much his backyard. I could candy-coat it, but I'd be lying. He's going to smoke your ass."

Back in Jackson the next morning, I drive to Cheney's house in the golf course community of Teton Pines. It is not a "ranch," as is often misstated (his neighbors are close enough to hit him with a rock), but rather a tastefully unostentatious place in a zip code where captains of industry often pay for extras like heated driveways so that their car tires never suffer the inconvenience of snowfall.

Cheney is dressed in zip-off cargo pants and a fly fishing shirt given to him by one of the lodges where he fishes. (It has "Vice President Dick Cheney" stitched above a breast pocket.) I take a backseat with him in a black Suburban. For the next hour plus, his motorcade will retrace the trek I made the day before.

Many had warned me of Cheney's lust for silence on the river. Ken Adelman once wrote, "Despite pleas over the years, [Cheney] adamantly refused to take me fly fishing in Wyoming. When pressed, he finally explained, 'You talk too much to go fly fishing.'"

With an unavoidable stretch of conversation before us (though Cheney did bring two books, which worries me until he tells me they are for the ride home), I probably should have gone the responsible-journalist route and grilled Cheney on matters of electoral politics and world affairs. But all either of us really wanted to talk about was fishing. So we did.

It was a lightning round of fishing talk. Cheney could even have passed as excitable. Though even on excitable, his voice doesn't vary much from the low hum of a room dehumidifier. I ask him if he's worried that our fishing trip will infringe on his getting back in time to watch that night's festivities at the Democratic convention. He smiles an unregretful smile and says, "It's been my good fortune to go fishing at crucial times in my career."

One of those times was before the vice presidential debate in 2004, when he and his debate prepper, Rob Portman, decided, in Cheney's words, "to hell with it," and instead went fishing on the South Fork. "The most important thing you can do before one of those debates is to be relaxed. I couldn't think of a better way to relax than to just tune it all out and go spend a day on the river." (Cheney also skipped the 1996 Republican convention, because he was, in his own words, "probably fishing.")

Cheney inherited a love of angling from his family. His grandfather "was a nut on going after catfish . . . one of these guys who was a great believer in stinky, smelly bait." He mixed his own, says Cheney: "Chicken guts marinated in blood for a week, or something like that." Once, his grandfather took a trip someplace and left his bait mix locked in his old Buick. "He took the keys with him, and we couldn't get it out. The whole neighborhood was rank by the time we got through."

Both of his parents were avid "worm fishermen." His dad, he says, "propagated nightcrawlers. He had—probably dangerous as hell, but he did it—a copper rod that was wired to an electric cord, which you could stick into the socket and a rubber hand line. He'd jam it down to the ground, and nightcrawlers would just pop out."

Cheney first fly fished when he was sixteen years old. Just before football season started, he and three friends threw their bedrolls into a 1948 Ford and took off for a week to the Middle Fork of Wyoming's Powder River, which cuts through a deep canyon. He went down to the hardware store, picked out a fiberglass rod and a half dozen flies, made the steep descent, and set about "catching trout in this deep canyon. I couldn't even get into it today. But it's a beautiful stream."

Years later, as a congressman, he became much more serious about fly fishing. According to my colleague Stephen F. Hayes's recent biography of Cheney, one day the congressman was interviewing Merritt Benson for a state rep's job in his office. Benson had worked for *Outdoor Life* magazine before taking a Wyoming Department of Fish and Wildlife job. Cheney glanced at his résumé and got down to real vetting.

Cheney: "I bet you know a few fishing holes in this state."
Benson: "Yeah, I do."
Cheney: "Well, I never travel anywhere without my pole in the trunk."

The job was Benson's without delay ("He had some special qualifications," Cheney told me). Under the tutelage of Benson, Cheney started fly fishing with conviction. Benson introduced him to the legendary guide Don Daughenbaugh, a former ranger at both Yellowstone and Grand Teton national parks. Daughenbaugh used to guide

Jimmy Carter, and up until this year, still rowed Cheney when he hit the Bighorn, though Daughenbaugh is now in his eighties.

I ask Cheney if fishing was ever a consideration in selecting his "undisclosed locations."

"No," he says. "But I have my regular schedule. Your undisclosed location could be a secure facility someplace, or it could be a cornfield in South Dakota where you're hunting, or the South Fork of the Snake."

Being the second most powerful person in the free world has its drawbacks, and work does tend to make its way to the river. His people ask me not to reveal security specifics, but I beg off when I'm told there are divers in trailer boats, as they could interfere with our fishing. I ask him if they're there to sweep the river for possible explosives. He's amused by the paranoia. They're rescue swimmers, he tells me, "in case I fall out of the boat."

His friends say that even on the South Fork Hilton trip, Cheney digests intelligence and wakes up before the rest of the camp to make secure calls back to Washington, never telling them of what transpired before he shows up to breakfast. Cheney admits, "I was over here on the South Fork when the Russians invaded Georgia, so I got word on the river that day. I've always got a communicator with me. We actually carry a satellite dish with us so we can pull over and set up on the sandbar. Stuff happens. Especially in August."

Because of his workload, Cheney can't fish nearly as much as he'd like. He has gotten out with the president in Crawford. "We fish for bass on his pond down there. It goes fine," Cheney says with the air of a man itching for faster, more interesting water. Cheney stays on the fly rod, while Bush chucks "bubba bait," as Cheney calls it, not so masterfully suppressing a fly fisherman's elitism. I ask Cheney who outfishes whom, and he looks slightly insulted. "He catches more fish out of his pond than I do. Because it's his pond."

Cheney sticks with a fly rod at all times (he has so many, he's lost count), because "to do it well, you have to concentrate. It's a way, when you get out there on the river, to sort of cleanse your mind of whatever other cares or concerns you've got. It's a place I [can] go and totally relax, set aside whatever issues I'm working on at the time and just focus on fishing."

He speaks wistfully of fishing for sea-run browns in Tierra del

Fuego and taking a rickety cargo helicopter, with benches for seats and all the luggage piled in the middle of the floor, to pull salmon out of the remote and untouched Ponoi River in Russia. There, with the sun not setting north of the Arctic Circle, a fisherman can put in a good, clean sixteen-hour day.

But it's steelheading in British Columbia that is his absolute favorite. He likes the challenge—you have to work, and you can go all day without a strike. "It's basically a sea-run rainbow trout," Cheney says. "I have a lot of respect for the fish, the acrobatics—a ten- or twelve-pound steelhead tailwalking down the water, taking out all your line. Catch them, and you're a serious fisherman." He used to fish the Babine River for a week every year with a group of friends who live in the northwest. The place they go is reachable only by air. "They've got about twenty-five or thirty miles of the river all to themselves," he says. He's been unable to join them for years, but "they're still saving my slot," he says, chomping at the bit.

Our convoy reaches the South Fork, where we put in next to what feels like a wind tunnel right beneath Palisades Dam. Cheney changes into his chest waders, hauls all of his own gear and rigs his own rods, one of which is a fine Sage 6-weight, with an ivory inlaid trout on its reel seat. His Abel reel too is a thing of art, decorated with the colored spots of a brown trout.

"What do you fish?" he asks curiously.

I tend to go with the ghetto setup: dull black, retro-looking twenty-dollar Pflueger Medalist reels—turned backward because I'm too lazy to switch them from right-hand to left-hand retrieve—and my beat-up L.L.Bean 6-weight, which has plumber's tape secured around a hairline crack under one ferrule. "I'm low-tech," I tell him, by which I mean I'm cheap—though the fish don't seem to know the difference.

He winces when I pull my tape recorder out of my chest-wader pouch. "I don't want to be on all day," he says. And he suspiciously eyes my beyond-raggedy lucky fishing cap, which I have on backward. "They ever offer to buy you a new hat, Matt?" Staying on the theme of my employers, he adds, "You know the only reason I agreed to this? I wanted to see what kind of reporter had the cojones to convince his editors to pay for him to come fish the South Fork."

Our guide, Pat Kelly, shoves us off into the chop, and despite all the forewarnings of sacrosanct Cheney silence on the river, he keeps up a steady patter over the next eight hours. He inquires about my kids and asks Kelly about his off-season employment. He tells me what he likes to read (*Fly Fisherman, Gray's Sporting Journal, The Economist,* raw intelligence), as well as what he doesn't (the blogs). "I don't blog," he says, as if clearing up a misconception. In April, though, the blogosphere was obsessed over a photo of Cheney fishing on the Snake. Many held that a reflection in Cheney's sunglasses revealed not a hand casting a fly rod, but a naked woman. When I ask Cheney about it, he breaks into a troublemaking grin. "I had a great guide that day."

He also offers several candid, and often funny, impressions of current political figures. Then immediately puts them off the record. Trying to drag them back on the record, as I attempt to do several times, proves futile. When I suggest to him that such secrecy and circumspection is precisely why his media image is in the crapper, he is unconcerned. "If I was interested in servicing my image," he says, "I wouldn't have become vice president. I had a good job."

That much-discussed job was one he was offered after impressing Halliburton executives while chewing the fat with them in the mid-nineties at a fly fishing camp. Loyal to his friends—some say to a fault—he gives a spirited defense of how unfairly his former colleagues have been publicly denigrated because of their association with him. But he doesn't want me going into the particulars. "I didn't come out here to piss and moan," he says. "I came out here to fish."

And fish he does. Kelly feeds us many different flies throughout the day, but the money setup seems to be a Rainy's hopper pattern on topwater with a lightning-bug nymph dropper dangling beneath it. (Pruett calls this the "Coors Light Can," as its red and silver sheen looks like every college girl's favorite beer.)

Cheney is a good fisherman. A really good fisherman. We're not in the water ten minutes before he's already had two hookups, while the only things I've caught in the same duration are a stick that I mistook for a whitefish and the vice president's line.

As I'm in the back of the boat, it's my job to time his backcasts so that we keep firing like alternating pistons—a rhythm that takes some getting used to in such tight quarters, especially since he is a fast and frequent caster. There are no catastrophes, à la the hook in the neck, unless you count my wrapping a fly around the guide's glasses. (No skin was touched.) Another time, trying to set the hook on a fish and missing—something Cheney rarely does—his Copper Bob rubber-banded out of the water and came within inches of my face before wrapping around my rod as I was trying to get out a tangle, nearly turning me into the fly fishing equivalent of Harry Whittington, Cheney's less fortunate hunting partner.

I go fishless all morning, as Cheney hits for the cycle: browns and rainbows, cutties and hybrids. It makes me nostalgic for the day before, when I had the front of the boat. I remind Cheney and Kelly that I'd had a fifteen-fish outing on their river just yesterday. Nobody seems remotely impressed.

As we break for a fried chicken boxed lunch on a gravel bar, I start feeling desperate and am thinking about turning to my big gun: the Pistol Pete, a woolly buggerlike fly that effectively mimics baitfish but has a little extra action with a propeller on front. I picked a brownie up near this spot on it the day before. I ask Cheney what he thinks and if he'd ever fish it. "If I had fished every other fly in my box, and none of them worked, then maybe," he says, as though I was defiling his water by chucking the equivalent of bubba bait.

Shamed, I still break out of Kelly's recommendation cycle and pick a green Thompson's Hopper of my own, all foam and hackle and rubber legs. I immediately take a cutthroat out of a riffle as Cheney is still finishing his lunch. "I'm back," I say to nobody in particular, as if I'd been there before.

But I wasn't back. Cheney goes back to catching fish, I go back to getting skunked. While Cheney is not a braggart in the least, he is a proud fisherman, and so he appreciates the White House photographer, David Bohrer, following behind in a trailer boat, taking snaps of his catches before he cuts them loose. "Where's David?" he says after one cutthroat. "He's bored, he's off taking pictures of flowers," offers Kelly. "You can tell he's a short-timer," shrugs Cheney.

When Bohrer isn't present, I step into the White House photographer role with my CVS disposable camera ("Let Matt get a picture of this," Cheney takes to telling Kelly) and start a loud patter of belly-aching about my bad turn of luck (refraining from the usual string of expletives, out of deference to Cheney's office). "You've got the same hoppers on that he does," Kelly offers, perhaps still stung that I briefly went outside his advised patterns or still ruffled that I almost blinded him in one eye. But I am beginning to see how it works: Cheney doesn't need to talk trash. He has people to do that for him.

Not that he doesn't talk any smack. At one point, when Kelly is netting one of Cheney's fish and about to cut it loose, Cheney says, "Wait a minute, do you want to let Matt get a look at that so he can see what he's missing?"

The fish deficit is starting to grow ridiculous.

I have time to think of all the reasons Cheney is outcatching me. For one, my drifts are getting screwed up by the oar and Cheney casting at too high an angle into my water, forcing my flies to drag more often than they should. For another, the guide seems to be setting him up on all the fish when the boat holds position. Then there is the front-of-the-boat problem. If it doesn't matter where you sit, why does he always take the front? When I mention this to Scarlett, he welcomes me to the back-of-the-boat club. Cheney's friends let him have the front of the boat since he's the vice president of the United States. "But he's got about four months left," says Scarlett. "Then he can do time in the back like everybody else."

But there is another reason, of course, that Cheney is outfishing me. It's probably the more important reason: He's a lot better fisherman. He is a fierce caster. He has pinpoint precision with his fly, throwing sliders under branches, lopping flies over tree limbs, dropping his hopper just off the bank's edge, making it look extra susceptible to a trout mugging, like a drunk falling off a curb.

As Kelly rows us alongside a steep rockface, with tiny crevices at the bottom where the current swirls by and fish are likely holding, Cheney perfectly sidearms a cast right into the pocket. His fly is inhaled by a greedy rainbow. It's like watching a mailman throw a letter through a door slot from thirty feet away. Even Kelly, who is no purveyor of flattery, says, "Now that was a cast."

We hit the end of our twelve-mile float and exit the boat onto the ramp. Cheney does not count his fish, though I do, obsessively (I've caught 869 so far this year, back when I used to catch fish). I tell him what the damage is:

Dick Cheney: twenty.

Me: two.

He doesn't give me that stingy, trademark lopsided grin that looks like a broken egg sliding off a rock. His is the full-on smile of an ebullient child. He shows back-molars and dental work, everything. In several decades of watching him, I've never seen him smile this big.

I ask him how much I should tip the guide, but he's already laid one hundred bucks or so on him. "It's all right, I got him," he says. I try to get the vice president back, but he won't have it. "It's okay, I can afford it," he says. Plus, he adds, "It's a small price to pay for bragging rights." We bid each other adieu. He's off to home and says that he has some pressing business there: He has to e-mail my friends that he beat me twenty to two.

The next day, I have lunch with Jack Dennis, a longtime friend and fishing guide of Cheney's. ("Don't believe anything he tells you," Cheney offered when finding out where I was headed.) Dennis is a bit of a local legend. He has introduced fly fishing to everyone from Harrison Ford to Arnold Palmer. He authors books, hosts fly fishing shows, and lectures on the sport worldwide.

Some speculate that the reason Cheney gets along so famously with Dennis is that Dennis does all the talking. Cheney doesn't have to fill in any spaces. And though Dennis is indeed a verbal firehose of stories, recollections, and trivia, he also has a melancholic streak. His office in Jackson, which is adorned with everything from letters of thanks from baseball legend Ted Williams—who was impressed by his fly tying—to landing nets with presidential seals, has a placard on his shelf inscribed with the words of Henry David Thoreau: "Many men go fishing all of their lives without knowing it is not fish they are after."

Dennis has fished with Cheney often over the years and has seen him at some peculiar times. There was the day not long before September 11, when Dennis was rowing Cheney and his daughter Liz, and a passenger jet flew close overhead on the way to the airport. Liz, says Dennis, asked her father if he was ever worried about a plane like that coming to hit him. "He looked at her and said, 'Why would they want to do that? All those people on that plane wanna live.'"

Dennis, who is a committed environmentalist, says Cheney has gotten a bad rap as a despoiler of the land, since he has often quietly worked behind the scenes, doing things like torpedoing prospective mines in Wyoming that would pollute treasured cutthroat fisheries. Once, when fishing, Dennis says, Cheney asked him, "How do you think fly fishermen view me?" Dennis replied: "'I don't think they view you very well, as a lot of people don't. It's not because of your fishing ability or anything, I think it's just because of the mood of the country.' He said, 'Well, I understand that.' I said, 'If they all went fishing with you, that would be a different story.'"

Perhaps the strangest moment for Dennis, however, was one afternoon on the river, just days after Cheney had a heart defibrillator implanted. Dennis says Cheney was reclining in the boat with "his head leaned back—he'd never done anything like that. I went back to look and see if he was breathing." Cheney popped open one eye and asked, "What are you doing?"

"I'm checking to see if you're breathing," Dennis said.

"Well so what?" Cheney snapped back. "What would happen if I wasn't? Will you just not worry about me? Leave me alone and whatever happens happens. I can't think of a better place to die than right here."

I wrap up with Dennis and realize I have a few hours left of daylight, so I ask him where I should fish. He grabs my notebook and draws a map to an unmarked creek in Grand Teton National Park. I ask him what flies I should bring. "Just go," he says. "You're losing time."

The directions are confusing, and I get lost several times. Even the park rangers don't know where Dennis's spot is. But I finally find it, after my car nearly plows into a black bear loafing off into the woods. After driving six miles down a dirt path and descending on foot down a steep embankment, which nearly causes a rockslide, I find a huge, slow eddying pool that feeds a faster creek, which itself feeds into the Snake about half a mile away. Sneaking up in the tall grass along the banks, I see a large cutthroat holding in the lazy current. But my first cast spooks him, as his shadow shoots downstream. I jump into the pool and wade down slowly, firing a fifty-foot cast to drift a hopper past some downed limbs near the pool's tailout. A cutthroat explodes on it, and moments later I am holding this gleaming, brilliant orange-hued fish in my hand, as the setting sun crowns the Tetons above me.

The fish has to be a nineteen-incher, though since I'm the only witness, I'm going to call it twenty. It's the biggest trout I take during my trip by far, and it's enough of a fish to wipe yesterday's humiliation off the books. As I place the cutthroat back in the cool water, watching it dart away as it realizes it's regained its freedom, I'm reminded of all the Cheney haters, who hope to God that when his stint ends in four months he permanently hangs out his GONE FISHING sign. I'm not sure Cheney and his critics won't finally find some agreement.

There are worse things to wish on a man.

YIPPIE KAY OY VEY

Kinky Friedman Runs for Governor

We are wayfaring, wandering gypsies alone
Looks like looking for is where we'll always be
Cursed to be born as serious souls
No one will take seriously

> —Billy Joe Shaver, country singer and
> spiritual adviser to Kinky Friedman

All Across Texas

When it comes to black, Kinky Friedman picks up where Johnny Cash left off. He wears a black bull-rider hat, black boots, and a black belt with a buckle the size of a Mini Cooper hubcap. Over his black pearl-button shirt, he mixes things up a bit. He'll wear either the black leather vest, given to him by Waylon Jennings, or the black "preachin' coat," cut by Manuel, the famed former head tailor of Nudie's in Nashville.

In the airy, pastel atrium of the Ambassador Hotel in Amarillo, Ma and Pa Frontporch do double takes at the breakfast buffet, pausing by the Froot Loops dispenser, saying, "Isn't that . . ." when they spy the dark rider with bandito facial hair hunched over his omelet, skimming the newspaper. Kinky looks less like a Texas gubernatorial candidate than like a desperado fortifying himself to knock over a stagecoach.

As I join his table, he welcomes me warmly. I've read a stack of Kinky stories on the plane, so I know how it works: Kinky is a shtick tommy gun, so if you tape eight hours of interviews with him but are looking for original material, you know you'll have to throw seven out right off the top. Most of it will already have traveled several times around the world. He's pro-recycling: He calls it "rotating the crops." And so I try to peel the onion a bit, getting right down to his raw, vital essence—not political, but musical.

Kinky (so named for his "Jew-fro," as the ladies at Supercuts call it) is most famous these days for trying to become the first independent governor of Texas since Sam Houston in 1859. For two decades prior, he was known for his seventeen well-reviewed comic mystery novels, with himself cast as the protagonist ("I'm not afraid of anything, just that I may have to stop talking about myself for five minutes," he's said). But it was as head cheese-maker in Kinky Friedman and the Texas Jewboys that he first entered public consciousness.

Before that, Kinky did a two-year Peace Corps stint in Borneo, where he introduced the locals to Frisbee while they introduced him to betel nut and hallucinogenic rice wine. Perhaps under the influence of it, he conceived the Jewboys. When Kinky got back to Texas in the early seventies, Austin had become a hothouse for outlaw country heroes who'd said *adios* to the slick sounds of Nashville in order to do some honest-to-God songwriting. Cosmic Cowboys and gypsy troubadours like Michael Martin Murphey, Jerry Jeff Walker, Billy Joe Shaver, and other guys with two first names walked the land.

Kinky and the Texas Jewboys served as the court jesters of the movement, though they were no redneck Weird Al Yankovics. There was much more going on. Kinky lampooned bigotry by assuming the role of the bigot in songs like "They Ain't Makin' Jews Like Jesus Anymore" and "Proud to Be an Asshole from El Paso." He could also pull off grim weepers, like "Ride 'Em Jewboy," undoubtedly the most haunting country song ever written about the Holocaust, even if it's the only one. "Anything worth crying can be smiled," he sang.

Because of his place in this universe, he has played, gotten drunk, or played drunk with nearly every musical hero of mine, from Levon Helm to Kris Kristofferson to the late, great Townes Van Zandt. Lyle Lovett is on his speed dial. He has gotten baked on the secondhand smoke of Willie Nelson. Bob Dylan ate barbecue at his late parents' ranch. ("Thanks, Mrs. Friedman," said Dylan. "You must be very proud of your son.") When I ask him about hanging out with Tom Waits and Chuck E. Weiss on the Bukowski side of Los Angeles in the early seventies, he lights up: "You know Chuck E. and the Goddamn Liars [Weiss's band]!!? Have you ever heard his 'Bad Jews in Malibu'? It's fucking great!"

The musical revelry hits a speed bump when we start talking about his close friend Willie Nelson, whom he calls the "hillbilly Dalai Lama," and with whom he currently has a double-or-nothing wager. Willie took him for a grand on how the Iraq War would turn out (Kinky thought Bush and Blair would be "heroes"). Kinky now stands to win two grand if Joe Lieberman beats Ned Lamont—eight thousand if you count his Lieberman side bets with other suckers. Kinky's an inveterate gambler who takes "fact-finding trips to Vegas," though "these days, I'm bettin' on Texas." Still, of Lieberman, he says, "That fucker better win."

I ask him if he's heard *Teatro,* some of the most achingly beautiful music Nelson ever recorded. He hasn't. So I take the CD out of my bag and try to give it to him. "It won't get listened to," he says. "I don't listen to music anymore. I think it stems from having been in so many dance halls and bars—I'm just pretty averse to it. Personally, I'd rather watch Fox News," he says. "Though I keep it muted most of the time."

Just then, a voter approaches and takes a seat at our table as if she were an old friend. Her name is Kelly Wages, and she's voted for Republican incumbent Rick Perry in the past, but now she's undecided, like much of Texas. Perry leads the pack of four candidates, but with an anemic 35 percent, meaning that he's hemorrhaging even Republican support. "Why should I vote for you?" she asks Kinky.

Most politicians would take this as a cue to begin sucking up. But Kinky shoots me a get-a-load-of-her look and goes the reverse-psychology route. "Because I have no political experience whatsoever." (This is only partly true. In 1986, he ran for justice of the peace in his Hill Country district, promising to lower the speed limit to 54.95. He lost.)

Wages says that's precisely what she's worried about. Kinky says she shouldn't be too worried. The other candidates have eighty-nine years of political experience between them, and Texas is fiftieth in education, health care coverage, and care for the elderly, while being first in executions, toll roads, property taxes, and dropouts, thus illustrating one of his campaign slogans: "Kinky Friedman: Why the Hell Not?" When I bring up a recent *Dallas Morning News* story taking issue with many of Kinky's figures, he says, "Oh fuck that lady! We're forty-third, not fiftieth—yaaayyyyy!" Wages starts laughing.

I ask Wages if he has her; I can feel her teetering. "Well," she says, "he talks some sense." She says Perry is too bullish on executions, and too negligent on health care. A little less indulgent of Wages since I'm not running for office and she's interrupted my interview, I point out that the two positions are complementary, that the more people are executed, the fewer will need health care. "That's a good point," Kinky allows.

He continues in the hard-to-get vein. If Wages doesn't want him, he doesn't want her. As a reformer, he wants to "get the money changers out of the temple," one of his frequent Jesus references. ("I'm washed in the same blood you are, brother," he tells me. "I'm a Judeo-Christian. Jesus and Moses are in my heart, two good Jewish boys who got in a little trouble with the government.") If Wages can't tell the difference between him and the other candidates, if she "thinks my style's too rough, and you prefer a dignified, self-important, pompous-ass politician," then maybe she should vote for someone else. Wages looks hurt, but intrigued. Kinky says the other candidates will try to sink him, like they do everybody, because that's what these cockroaches do. That's why someone like her, who's generally a good person, won't run for office. "They know what you've done," I assist. "It's a walk-in closet, isn't it?" asks Kinky.

After ten more minutes of this, Wages nearly has her pants charmed off. Kinky finally asks for her vote. "I'm an unemployed youth," he begs, "I need the job." (He's sixty-one, though "I read at a sixty-three-year-old level.") She says he's got it, and bids adieu with a lingering hug. After she leaves, he turns to me, mouthing his unlit and ever present Montecristo No. 2 cigar. "She ain't votin' for us. C'mon, let's go find some place I can smoke. There could be a guy running around here in a Hitler suit, and all they'd care about is the guy who's smoking."

Smoking is one of many ways Kinky proves himself politically incorrect, a trait he takes great pride in since the obverse has contributed to the "wussification" of Texas. I ask him what other behaviors are "wussified."

"Doing interviews with *The Weekly Standard*," he replies.

One of the reasons it's great fun campaigning with Kinky is that he's in on the joke. Which joke, you might ask? All of them, pretty much. He fundamentally understands how absurd it is to spend two years of your life begging people to love you, to secure a job in which half the population at any given time will hate you. I get the sense it's made him an action junkie, though he insists if he loses, he'll "retire in a petulant snit" to a life of quiet contemplation.

I ask why he does it. Because he loves Texas and hates what's happened to her, he says. And because "I'm a dealer in hope. That's a great thing to be, the next best thing to being a mender of destinies, which is harder." Watching his rapport with people, who mob him everywhere we go, I offer that he gives people "happiness injections." He mulls it over. "Happiness injections—that's a good line," he says. "Take it," I offer. "Ehh," he says, having second thoughts, "it's kind of gay."

After two years of banging away, he's finally convinced the press that his candidacy is serious, though he sometimes confuses them, such as when he says, "Fuck 'em if they can't take a joke." Or such as when he suggests Willie Nelson will helm his new Commission on Energy, which will champion biodiesel farmers' co-ops. (When critics raise Nelson's frequent pot-related brushes with the law, Kinky protests, "He's not heading the DEA.") Or such as when he lays out his Five Mexican Generals border plan (paying Mexican generals to keep illegals on their side, withdrawing money from their accounts when illegals make it through). "It's a joke," he says, "but a joke that's a good idea."

If the line is blurred, it always has been for Kinky. As he once wrote, "There is a fine line between fiction and nonfiction, and I believe Jimmy Buffett and I snorted it in 1976." (He's been off the "Peruvian marching powder" since 1985, he says, when he left New York and came back to the Texas Hill Country, which he calls "my hospital.") It might be a measure of the artifice of politics that many Texans regard Kinky, an ersatz cowboy who prefers to ride "two-legged animals" over horses, as the most authentic candidate in the race. "Rick Perry's a comedian too," says the only candidate who's been nominated this year for the Thurber Prize for American Humor, "he just doesn't know it."

As we traverse Texas, it becomes clear how uninterested Kinky Friedman is in appealing to delicate sensibilities. For instance, our driver, who is also his former keyboard player and current Bundini to his Ali, is named Little Jewford. "He's Jewish, and he drives a Ford," Kinky explains to audiences. The two, who have known each other since they were children at summer camp, are by now like an old married couple. Kinky has never married. He lives with his five dogs, "the Friedmans," and sixty or so others at his nearby Utopia Animal Rescue—he is always taking in strays, of both the canine and human variety (his current Kato is a Katrina evacuee, a street preacher and musician named Reverend Goat Carson). But he is emphatically heterosexual, saying, "I don't kiss babies, I kiss their mothers."

On their endless road trips, Kinky and Jewford feel no pressure to fill long silences. At campaign stops, Jewford keeps up an arch patter in a booming FM DJ voice, saying things to confuse voters, such as "I'm not laughing at you, I'm laughing through you," all while wearing a shimmery test-pattern sportsjacket that Kinky says is made of "Elvis's shower curtain." When challenged on his name, Jewford, a classically trained pianist, is not averse to showing doubters his Little Jewford Visa card as proof, a card he regularly whips out to pick up checks. Says Laura Stromberg, Kinky's press secretary who is also Jewish, of Jewford's lack of tightness, "He's a big disappointment to the Jewish community."

The campaign also proves unconventional in the journalists it attracts. Kinky and company are often followed by a documentary crew, Jeremy Cohen and Gopal Bidari, two talented young auteurs who work for hotshot producers out of Hollywood. They are so ever present that Kinky took to calling them Rosencrantz and Guildenstern. He then grew bored with that, deciding Cohen, who is Jewish, should be named "Jihad," while Bidari, who is Indian, should be "Macaca," in solidarity with the Senator George Allen scandal. He's even taken to introducing them at campaign speeches as such, saying they're making a documentary on him for Al Jazeera. Jihad and Macaca have taken to their parts. They now wear nametags at Kinky's fund-raisers.

In Texas, the smart money holds that Kinky has the Jewish cowboy vote sewn up. After those three voters, nobody's positive where he stands. Kinky's currently clustered about fifteen points behind Perry, along with the deadly dull Democrat, Chris Bell, who has said he "could be a corpse" and still get the straight Democratic vote, a theory he seems to be putting to the test. With them is fellow independent Carole "Grandma" Strayhorn, whose two big claims to fame are being former Bush spokesman Scott McClellan's mom and being a grandma. As most people who've ever suffered through a McClellan press conference would, she emphasizes the latter.

Such polling, however, registers only likely voters. And with two independent insurgencies, a big turnout could mean lots of unlikely voters making an appearance at the voting booth. "They ain't gonna come out to help Perry," says Kinky. Dean Barkley, Kinky's campaign manager, who masterminded Jesse Ventura's victory in

1998, says Ventura was languishing at precisely the same place Kinky is (around 20 percent) at the same point in the election, and that the pollsters were caught napping because of their likely voter fetish. For contradictory evidence, the campaign will hand you a sheaf of statewide call-in and Internet polls, contests Kinky walks away with most of the time. As even *Texas Monthly* has stated, if every eligible voter in Texas were required to cast a ballot, "Rick Perry would be out of a job and Kinky Friedman would be governor of Texas."

With such undercurrents swirling about, it's small wonder that Bell, "a serious man with a serious plan," in his words, privately called Kinky to ask him to step aside so that the anti-Perry vote wouldn't be fractured. Kinky publicly rebuked him, saying, "We will not negotiate with terrorists."

To sop up some of these unlikely voters, we go from Amarillo to Lubbock to Austin, hitting many universities along the way. At his college gigs, Kinky comes off like your favorite crusty uncle—the one who pretends to have a heart of stone, but who'll slide you candy or a dollar or a sip of beer when no one's looking.

On the way to the stage, he keeps loose with a steady patter of Kinksterisms. He'll ask the local student body representative, "How long will this ordeal last?" or "Has there ever been a candidate suicide?" As reporters leave him to take their seats, he'll say with utter solemnity, "Good luck out there," and he periodically revs himself up with reverse fist pumps, as though he is starting a weed-eater.

Politically, he says he's like Frank Sinatra: "I started left, and moved right." Consequently, Kinky is still fairly liberal on social issues—he's reluctantly pro-choice, and he's for gay marriage ("they have every right to be just as miserable as the rest of us"). Otherwise, he does a fairly convincing impression of a Republican from ten years ago, back when they still had principles: tough on illegal immigration and crime, anti-tax and pro–fiscal responsibility.

But his performances are less stump-speech, more period-piece/ one-man show. Just as Hal Holbrook plays Mark Twain, Kinky Friedman plays Kinky Friedman—offering a fruit platter of Twain and Will Rogers and Uncle Earl Long, all sliced and diced and stuck in a Cuisinart. He stalks the stage, punctuating the air with his cigar, spraying the glossolalial audience with a hail of one-liners: "I'm sixty-one years old, too young for Medicare and too old for women to care. . . . Once enough people can get biodiesel, I will trade in my own Yom Kippur Clipper. That's a Jewish Cadillac—it stops on a dime and picks it up, basically. . . . Musicians can better run this state than politicians. We won't get a lot done in the morning, but we'll work late. . . . Trust me, I'll hire good people."

After the show, as you come to think of it, the kids often stand a few hundred deep, wanting everything signed, from their shirts to their chemistry lab books—even though most of them don't know his writing or his music. He signs every last autograph at every stop—fan etiquette he learned from Willie Nelson. "I've seen him do it in the rain," Kinky says.

The university circuit, like the rest of the campaign trail, is a grind. But Kinky says the young people charge him and give him spark—they are the "wind beneath his knees," as Jewford says. He feeds on them like a hillbilly Nosferatu, giving them his phone number, telling them he needs their energy in his administration, promising them patronage jobs, as he does to Southwest Airlines ticket agents and hotel bellhops: "You'll be on Easy Street!" he says. "It's a big street," Jewford dryly confides.

As we hurtle over the flat plains of North Texas—"wandering through the raw poetry of time," as Kinky calls it—he expounds on why his outsider ethos isn't just some silly gimmick. "Common sense, common honesty—that's all it takes. That's all I've got. And sometimes I'm not sure about common sense." He mentions the Buddy Holly sound, which came right out of Lubbock. "He didn't read blogs, or see all these TV channels, or hear much different kinds of music other than R&B out of Shreveport. As a result, he came up with a really original sound. And that's because of the aching emptiness. Just the fact that he was surrounded by so much emptiness. Sometimes an original thought comes out of great expanses. Not just geographical, but spiritual as well." It's the "cowboy way," what Texas used to be about, says Kinky, "spiritual elbow room."

After our Lubbock stand, he starts thinking about the kids again. They always promise they'll vote but tend not to make it to the polls if, say, their favorite *South Park* rerun is on. He turns to me in the backseat, his black hat slung over his knee as he exhales cigar smoke. "You know, I think the young people will probably fuck us. They fuck everybody else, right?" I'm astounded and impressed by his candor.

Later, I find out he gave the same line in the same place to the London *Spectator* two months ago.

It's two days before the only gubernatorial debate, and Kinky is highly agitated. Not because Perry has agreed to only one of six proposed debates. Or because his campaign had to fight the other campaigns in a Texas death match for Kinky to be able to wear his cowboy hat during the broadcast. "He was born with that hat," protested Barkley, who won.

Kinky is fuming because the blogosphere and his opponents are tarring him as a racist. It's a bad rap for a guy who was a member of Students for a Democratic Society, who picketed segregation, who spent his entire irreverent music career making sport of the kind of yahoos they're suggesting he is. At issue is Kinky's calling bowling balls "nigger eggs" in a club performance twenty-six years ago and, more recently, his blaming Katrina evacuees for a spike in the murder rate in Houston, calling them "thugs and crackheads."

He has refused to apologize for any of it, saying the first charge is preposterous on its face, since he was playing a racist in his performance, and the second charge is true, but it has nothing to do with race, and this is precisely the kind of scared-of-your-own-shadow political correctness that keeps Texans from addressing real problems, like the border crisis. "If you ain't offending somebody," he says, "you ain't getting anything done."

In a debate prep session at his Austin headquarters, Kinky's staff throw all manner of questions at him, trying to trip him with the names of obscure Texas agencies, making him explain how a bill becomes a law. It's something he says he doesn't need to concern himself with since the institutionally weak Texas governor's gig means he'd basically be less of a legislative animal, more the "most powerful judge at the chili cook-off."

And anyway, all Kinky really wants to talk about is race. As his staff drills him on issues like health care and college tuition, Kinky finally explodes, "Ask me the nuclear question about the nigger eggs!" He has the single-minded obsessiveness of the man who has been unjustly accused.

He is so bothered that he is still chewing this cud when we move on to Dallas. At the Hotel Adolphus bar, drinks flow freely enough that I, who usually lead the charge in such matters, am given the nickname "Mr. Sip-Sip" when Dean Barkley decides I'm not drinking fast enough. Kinky ratifies it, and employs it liberally ("Sip-Sip, what do you think?"). But he is still stewing, swearing blood oaths that Perry better not tangle with him on this issue. "Fact is, you're going to call the only guy with a social conscience a racist—I'm going to nail your fucking ass."

He announces a new line he'll employ in the debate when given the chance: "There you go again, Governor, playing the race card against me. And I never played the gay card against you." Perry, who is married, has suffered unsubstantiated rumors that he is gay, enough so that he has seen fit to swat the rumors down in interviews with mainstream news reporters.

The next day, at a stop at the University of Texas at Dallas, Kinky is still discussing the idea with me and a few others. Taking off my journalist's hat, I tell him that while I'm always pro-entertainment, it's a bad political play. At the very least, he has to soften "the gay card" with a jokier term like "the Liberace card." He likes it. But he's not sure if "Liberace" is the right word. He calls for a strategy session. He wants suggestions, which come fast and furious: Butt Pirate, Pillow Biter, Twinkie, Teapot. Mr. Sip-Sip (that hurts). He abandons the idea—it wouldn't be the Cowboy Way. "There's no mud on the high road," he says.

The debate is at a Dallas television station later that night. Nobody wins, and nobody loses. It is uneventful and safe. The other three candidates come off as competently blow-dried, freeze-dried, and mummified, respectively. Kinky suffers a few perfunctory scoldings on the race issue, without resorting to calling anyone a Sip-Sip. He hangs in there and doesn't embarrass himself, but he is tentative and nervous, without fire. His best line comes in the press room afterward, when he says, "I stood toe to toe . . . and I feel good. Right now, I'm still voting for myself."

Later that night, we adjourn to the hotel bar with staffers, Kinky's girlfriend just in from England, and Jihad and Macaca, who are grateful for the free drinks. Kinky admits to me that he couldn't find his rhythm. "I did all right, but it was my C game." It's too bad the voters of Texas couldn't see his A game, as I had several hours before.

We make a stop at the Reading and Radio Resource Center, an audio reading service for the blind. Kinky takes his place in a studio, while Jihad, Macaca, and I watch him through the glass of the control room. He is a guest on the *Eyes of North Texas* show, hosted by an eighty-three-year-old volunteer named Adell Campbell. She is spunky and spry and gives him a workout. She mentions that he likes to refer to himself as "the Good Shepherd," and wants to know if he's equating the voters of Texas to sheep. He smiles appreciatively with cigar clenched in teeth, recognizing a kindred spirit. "Well, if this is a flock of sheep," he says, "we certainly hope they turn out November 7th."

Adell asks him to read something he's written, and he picks an essay he wrote for *Texas Monthly,* now collected in his book *Texas Hold 'Em: How I Was Born in a Manger, Died in the Saddle, and Came Back as a Horny Toad.* In print, Kinky shticks it up as much as he does on the stage, but he is a fine writer nonetheless. When he does a real piece of work, as opposed to, say, a chapter on Texas prison slang, he turns a beautiful phrase, gets in and gets out, and doesn't stop for smoke breaks.

The essay is titled "The Hummingbird Man." It's about his father, who taught him most of what he knows, from how to belch to how to always "treat children like adults, and adults like children." His dad, whom Kinky calls "Tom," ran a summer camp for kids on the ranch called Echo Hill where Kinky still lives. He died a few years ago.

The piece starts off with advice from one of their dishwashers, a guy named Slim who "wore a Rainbow Bread cap" and "drank warm Jax beer in infinite quantities." He told Kinky, "You're born alone and you die alone, so you might as well get used to it."

He didn't think much of it when he was a kid, but he's come to reconsider:

> I live alone now in the lodge where my late parents once lived, and I'm getting used to it. . . . Sooner or later, fate will pluck us all up by our pretty little necks. If you have a family of your own, maybe you won't feel it quite as much. Or maybe you will. I'm married to the wind, and my children are my animals and the books I've written, and I love them all. I don't play favorites, but I miss my mom and dad.

After a reminiscence about how he and his father used to tend the hummingbird feeder, watching as the population of birds exploded, he drops the hammer:

Now, on bright cold mornings, I stand in front of the old lodge, squinting into the brittle Hill Country sunlight, hoping, I suppose, for an impossible glimpse of a hummingbird or of my mother or my father. . . . And I still see my dad sitting under the dead juniper tree, only the tree doesn't seem dead, and neither does he. It takes a big man to sit there with a little hummingbird book, taking the time to talk to a group of small boys. He is telling them that there are more than three hundred species of hummingbird. They are the smallest of all birds, he says, and also the fastest. They're also, he tells the kids, the only birds who can fly backward. The little boys seem very excited about the notion of flying backward. They'd like to try that themselves, they say. So would I.

Adell chokes up, and ends her show early. "You put me in tears, Kinky," she says. He waves her off with a line he used to dispatch hecklers when they threatened to lynch him and worse: "If we can just reach one person . . ." I'm not far behind Adell, spared only by the ridiculousness of witnessing this scene in a room with two guys nicknamed Jihad and Macaca.

After a week on the road with Kinky Friedman, I'm starting to think that the rodeo clown of the gubernatorial election has some intangibles that won't show up in likely voter polls. He has a heart like a lion, "one eye laughin', one eye cryin'," as he says. Maybe the voters of Texas still have time to see that, and respond accordingly.

Or maybe they'll respond for other reasons, I think as I watch Kinky and Adell in the hallway afterward, him flirting with her, promising she can be the hostess of the governor's mansion, and then she'll be on Easy Street. Maybe they, like him, just need a job.

THE SANE FRINGE CANDIDATE

Los Angeles

When you have a name like John Cox—a plain vanilla name, an achromatic name, a name that people with more distinctive names would choose if they'd committed a heinous crime and needed to start afresh on the lam—it's easy to feel like everyman and no man. Switchboard.com, the online directory, says that there are 1,979 John Coxes throughout the land. But there is only one John H. Cox. Actually, there are sixty-six of them. But there's only one who is running to be president of the United States of America.

That John Cox, the Chicago millionaire who was the first declared Republican candidate (as of March 2006), called our offices a few weeks ago. He sounded vexed. He sounded desperate. He sounded like a man who was tired of screaming into the void. He needed something that any self-assured, self-contained, well-adjusted person who enters the political arena needs: He needed the validation of people he'd never met.

A good Reaganite conservative, Cox has tried to be self-sufficient, financing his campaign thus far to the tune of $800,000. After twenty trips, he's been to all ninety-nine counties in Iowa. He's been to New Hampshire fourteen times, and South Carolina, ten. He's won a Republican straw poll outright in Aiken County, South Carolina, and finished fifth in total votes among all Republican contenders when three other counties were totaled. And yet he's lucky if he ever gets mentioned in mainstream media candidate roundups. Meanwhile, doing interviews with the *Small Government Times* just isn't putting him over the top.

I'm not going to lie, I felt sorry for John Cox. He needed some media attention, and last time I checked my lapsed 2002 congressional press pass, I was a member of the media. I decided to redress this injustice and go see John Cox. I've spent a fair amount of time around fringe candidates, but he didn't seem like the others. He doesn't own a sandwich board or a megaphone. He never says "blood for oil" when critiquing the war in Iraq. His suits fit, and he has no tendrils of out-of-control ear hair.

By no means is he humorless, but he seems like a serious person. Let him tell it: "I'm a serious person." Born poor on Chicago's South Side to a mother who was raped by a father who split shortly thereafter (he points to his very existence as the reason he's adamantly against abortion), Cox, fifty-one, is a self-made man. He finished college in two and a half years "because I was paying for it," he says, adding, "My daughter finished in five years—because I was paying for it." He later went on to start several businesses: a law/accounting firm, an investment advisory firm, a real estate management company, and a venture capital firm. In the midnineties, he led a group that purchased the Jays Foods potato chip manufacturer, sparing more than six hundred local jobs and taking it from a $17 million loss to a $3 million profit in less than a year.

In the red flag department, he has run unsuccessfully for office in Illinois three times: in congressional, senatorial, and Cook County recorder of deeds races. But even in his most recent loss, in 2004, his high principle was in evidence. He spent around $200,000 of his own money running for the recorder's job on the promise to eliminate the position as wasteful spending if he won—the kind of idea that used to fire up conservatives back when they were, how to put it, conservative.

Still, if you're not an elected official or a celebrity, there is no surer way for a serious person to come to be considered unserious than to run for president. When I informed a colleague that I was going to write a piece on a sane fringe candidate, he looked at me disbelievingly: "Isn't that an oxymoron?"

The advantage of writing about someone who has absolutely no chance of winning is that you get to dictate terms. I agreed to see John Cox but told him there'd be some conditions. I would not be manhandled or warded off at crucial junctures by any punk press secretaries. Also, I would be granted exclusive access. He told me nobody wanted access, so that wouldn't be a problem. He added that I'd better get out there shortly, he was having an important press conference on Monday. That would mean I'd have to fly to Chicago on Sunday. But it was perfect weather outside, and I wanted to get some fishing in over the weekend. "Can you bump it to Tuesday?" I asked. "I don't see why not," he said.

In Chicago, we meet up at a trendy Asian fusion restaurant. In tow are his twenty-five-year-old daughter (he has three others, including a two-year-old) and his attractive second wife, Sarah, who is eleven years his junior. His first marriage broke up, he says, "because she didn't love me anymore." Sarah is partly responsible for his presidential run. Tired of seeing him barking at the television, at the corrupt and profligate Republican leadership as well as at the feckless president (Cox supported the war but calls its mismanagement "nothing short of an absolute disaster—Iraqis are pumping less oil today than they were before we invaded"), Sarah told him, "Why don't you do something about it?"

They were supposed to go on a trip the next day, but Cox stayed up all night. Waking early the next morning, Sarah found him sitting in the living room at 6:00 A.M., reading a Reagan book. "He said, 'Honey, I'm going to run for president.'" Her first reaction: "Oh. My. God." Her second reaction: "I said, 'Well, if you want to do it, go ahead.' He's got a lot of energy."

Cox feels that none of the current crop of Republicans is actually carrying the leadership mantle of Ronald Reagan. And it's not, he wishes you to know, as if he's one of those weirdo Reagan fetishists. Reagan had plenty of faults. "It's not that he was some giant," Cox says. "It's just that he stood head and shoulders above all the other midgets."

Cox feels he can do the same, given the faux conservative "Rudy McRomney" midgets currently in the on-deck circle. He says he doesn't even necessarily want to be president—he has a great life—he just wants to see the job done properly. "I'm pissed, because I expected something better out of a conservative Republican president. On everything—Iraq, immigration, spending." And many true conservatives he meets feel the same, which is how a no-name like him can win a South Carolina straw poll, a feat he mentions at the slightest prompting, or at none.

The next morning, I arrive early at the Intercontinental Hotel to get a good seat for Cox's brace-yourself announcement—that he has paid his $25,000 registration fee, and is on the South Carolina ballot. I needn't have bothered. There's nobody around, except for some California Closet Company conventioneers. When I ask the concierge where the John Cox press conference is, he says, "John who?" Cox's amiable press secretary, Dan Herren, a South Carolina political hand who's a RE/MAX realtor on the side, tells me this isn't out of the norm. When Cox tells strangers he's running for president, a common reaction is "President of what?"

I find my way to the proper room. A JLS FOODS INC. sign is still in the placard bracket from an event the day before. Only two reporters are there—a guy from a radio wire service and me. Cox, who is silver-haired and trim, immaculately tailored in a charcoal suit with a blue pinstripe, looks disappointed but not surprised. He muses that it doesn't help that the nationwide May Day immigrant-rights rallies are taking place the same day. Not only are illegals taking our jobs, they're taking our publicity.

Still, even while he makes plenty of noise about the need to seal our borders, the corrupt Mexican government, and a crackdown on businesses that hire illegals, he will not set his hair on fire by becoming a pandering immigrant-basher—he points to fellow GOP hopeful Tom Tancredo as an example. "I refuse to lower myself," says Cox. "I'm a businessman. I've got clients. I'm not going to make myself out to be a buffoon."

Cox eyes us two journalists, then says, "No need to go there," nodding at the podium. Instead, he pulls up a chair next to us. "It's much more intimate this way," I say, trying to make him feel better. "Most of my gatherings are pretty intimate," he says, with a pained smile. He tells us he is on the South Carolina ballot, and hits the highlights of his platform: how he wants to eliminate the IRS and our disastrous, confusing, punitive tax system and go to a "fair tax" (a consumption tax), how he's pro-life and pro–Social Security reform, how he's anti-spending and anti-corruption. I can't speak for the radio reporter, but to me it sounds pretty good. Though he didn't have to go into all those details. He had me at "eliminate the IRS."

Later, Cox, Herren, and I adjourn to his well-appointed Gold Coast apartment, which stands sentry over Lake Michigan, on the forty-fifth floor of a high-rise. His mahogany-paneled office evidences how different he would be from Bush, who has bragged that he is undistracted by reading newspapers. Cox, by contrast, has three TV monitors on the wall beaming nonstop news, and has eight postal bins filled with newspapers. He reads five or so a day during his morning workout on a recumbent bike. Since he and Sarah spend four months a year at their place in Naples, Florida, he's accumulated a backlog—the papers in the bins—which he intends to go through to make sure he hasn't missed anything.

But it is not current events Cox has on the brain. Or rather, it is only one current event—the Republican debate at the Ronald Reagan Library in Simi Valley. It's going off in two days, and all Republican candidates have been invited to participate. All, that is, except Cox. It makes him feel like the only kid left out of the class birthday party, and it's taking a psychic toll. He gets Joanne Drake on the phone from the library, which is organizing the debate along with MSNBC and Politico.com.

He is extremely courteous: "Hello, Joanne, my name is John Cox, and believe me, I understand you are probably running around like a maniac." He tells her he feels he should be included, but understands that he isn't. He tells her that he won a straw poll in South Carolina, and got more votes in other straw polls than many of the better-known candidates.

He tells her, "It's so ironic that this is at the Reagan Library, because I love Ronald Reagan. I've been to your library three or four times. You know who [supply-side guru] Arthur Laffer is? He's written that he fundamentally agrees with everything about my book"—his new 220-page book, *Politics, Inc.*, that sets out his ideas. (As a novice, Cox is under the mistaken impression that presidential campaigns are about ideas.) If they won't let him debate, the least she can do, pretty please, is to let him plead his case to the media in the spin room. She says she'll run it up the flagpole and get back to him. She never does.

It doesn't matter, though. John Cox is a true conservative, and he doesn't wait for others to make his good fortune—he makes his own. So Cox, Herren, and I, along with his wife, two-year-old daughter, and nanny, fly out to Los Angeles anyway. Cox hasn't exactly worked out what he's going to do. Herren had suggested perhaps hiring Lincoln and Reagan impersonators to stage a debate about why Cox should be included. But they decide against—wouldn't be very presidential.

He tries all morning to call various MSNBC executives and is extra irate because at the last second, CNBC cancels a much-needed television appearance he was supposed to make on *Squawk Box*. "I have a feeling I'm causing ripples up and down MSNBC—they want me to go away," he tells me. "Wasn't I personable? Rational? Courteous? There's a fine line here. I don't want people thinking I'm a crazy man, calling and threatening. I'm just a believer in the U.S.

Constitution. In the Soviet Union, they blackball candidates. Let the public decide if I'm crazy or legitimate."

As we arrive at LAX and Cox is loading his luggage in a rented Highlander, he finally gets NBC News senior vice president Phil Griffin on the phone: "I don't want to make trouble, all I want to do is see America get better. I'm not a kook. I'm a substantial person. I won a straw poll." He asks Griffin to let him in the spin room. Griffin says he'll make some calls and get back to him. He never does.

The debate is the next day, so Cox wants to run out to the library to scout out its penetrability. We drive an hour and a half in rush hour traffic from our Santa Monica hotel to get there at closing time. Cox enters the atrium of the library and asks to see his old nemesis Joanne Drake. He looks official, so security starts to get her on the phone, asking if he has an appointment. Cox, who is nothing if not honest, says he doesn't, but he's a presidential candidate. The formerly friendly security guards start to exchange nervous looks. When Cox spots a media rep and tries to corner her to again make his spin-room pitch, we are all asked to leave the grounds immediately.

I had suspected this would be our reception. So I'd made some backup plans. Before joining up with Cox, I'd told him that I was credentialed for the debate, so he should get someone from his campaign to apply to be my photographer, which Herren had done. The next day—debate day—we arrive early at the press credentialing table. I pick up my lammie, and Dan picks up his, giving it to Cox. Cox and I board the media shuttle bus at the bottom of a hill that runs us up to the Reagan Library. Cox, it appears, will have his day in the spin room.

But he is unhappy about the whole arrangement. It demeans him, he feels. I tell him to get with the program. His look is all wrong. For one thing, he's wearing American eagle suspenders over a crisp white dress shirt. If he wants to pass for a journalist, he can't go around looking patriotic. "Put on your suit jacket," I tell him. As we arrive at the library and walk through its gates, I give him more pointers on how to pass for a reporter. "If you see anything free, especially a drink, take it," I say. I hand him a prop reporter's notebook, and tell him if anyone asks why he's not holding a camera, since he's supposed to be my photographer, tell them he's taking mental pictures.

As I leave him at a courtyard buffet table, where journalists are inhaling raspberry sugar cookies and iced tea (the bar doesn't open until later), I turn to interview some elderly docents, who give me details on the library's architecture and vegetation. I watch out of the corner of my eye as Cox, on his cell phone, walks across the lawn. He might as well be wearing a neon IMPOSTER sign: His posture is too good, his clothes are too pressed, he is way too distinguished-looking and silver-haired, like Blake Carrington out for a stroll—really un-journalist-like. He disappears from my radar. Minutes later, when I find him again, he is standing next to a burly security goon outside the gate. I ask him what happened. "Umm, the guy came over and found out who I am." I ask how that could've happened. Not a single person had recognized him since we'd been there. "I told him," Cox says unapologetically. "I'm not going to lie to anybody."

We are bounced from the debate before it even begins. As we ride past the fringesters on the curb—Ron Paul supporters wearing dolphin suits to illustrate Mitt Romney's flip flops, guys in "Stop Chemtrails" hats, etc.—Cox grows reflective:

"Am I an anarchist? What have I done to merit the treatment I'm getting here? This country needs leadership, leadership from people who've actually accomplished something in their lives. What you saw demonstrated today is the real problem. Who, with any level of achievement, would want to get involved in this nonsense? If you've achieved something, created value and wealth in a business world where intelligence and skill and inventiveness are rewarded, is it going to be attractive to go into politics where you've got to steal a press pass to get heard?

"And so what do we end up with for leadership? We end up with the sons of former presidents who put us in a war and botch the whole thing up. We end up with politicians who make deals for bridges to nowhere. Is that what we want? Someone who's been in public office their whole life? Will that prepare them for solving problems? What prepares you to solve problems, I would submit, is a life spent actually solving problems. Actually doing something. Am I wrong?"

Cox will have his debate one way or another. So we go back to our hotel on Santa Monica beach. A good fiscal conservative, Herren's sought out a cheap wedding videographer instead of an expensive L.A. film crew to show up with a camera. Since the hotel room doesn't get MSNBC, Cox's wife mans the live Internet debate feed, waiting for questions to be asked, then hitting the mute button so

Cox can answer for the benefit of the video camera and eventually a YouTube audience. He wants to show America what they missed. He rips for ninety minutes straight, taking all questions, sometimes taking them twice, when the same question is batted around to multiple candidates who are actually at the debate.

His isn't a performance for the ages, but it's surprisingly good. I expected a clown show. But there are no gaffes. He is fluid and calm, optimistic without seeming Pollyanna-ish, critical without seeming a crank, at ease with all issues—a man who knows his own mind and isn't afraid to speak it. After his one-man debate, as he sits down at a desk, he seems reinvigorated.

"What's frustrating," he says, "is that I know I could've done well up there. But they won't let me off the bench. Actually, they won't even let me in the stadium to sit on the bench. So I guess I'm making my own stadium." And he is, too. A week later, he sues Fox News to force them to let him into their televised debate. As the *New York Sun* reported, "During his announcement at the News Corp. building in Midtown yesterday, Mr. Cox had to compete with red-spandex-clad cheerleaders for the New Jersey Nets who had arrived at the same spot to promote the team. While dozens stopped to gawk at the women, few paid attention to Mr. Cox."

It doesn't matter, though—he's used to being overshadowed. Presidential campaigns are a marathon, not a sprint. He will stick to the end. Or his name isn't John Cox.

DODGEBALL, THE NEW PHYS ED, AND THE WUSSIFICATION OF AMERICA

Of all the perplexing issues that have been brought to our attention by the *Journal of Physical Education, Recreation & Dance*—besides the fact that there *is* such a thing as the *Journal of Physical Education, Recreation & Dance*—none has been so puzzling as the question *JOPERD* chewed over in its April symposium: "Is there a place for dodgeball in physical education?"

In most adult memories of P.E., dodgeball at its best represented a test of skill and derring-do, requiring speed, agility, and accurate throwing in the face of barely controlled chaos. At its worst, it meant a red rubber ball fired into your goo-loos or glasses, a minor indignity filed away with all the other petty humiliations of growing up, like forgetting your homework, or being forced to wear those itchy Christmas corduroys that Aunt Bea sent along with the pecan roll.

But the debate has rocked the community of dodgeball scholars right to its foundations. While plenty of educators still believe dodgeball is a harmless exhibition of physical prowess and cunning, not to mention fun, the sport's naysayers have banded together with the moral fervor of the Abolitionists. Already, their movement has succeeded in having dodgeball banned in school districts in at least eight states.

In the *JOPERD* symposium, Jeff Byrd, a graduate student at Delta State University, urged that the "chance for injury is too great." Robert Kraft, a University of Delaware professor, worried that even with today's "nerf or foam balls that are often used for safety . . . the intent remains—to hit another person with an object." David Kahan, an assistant professor in the Department of Exercise and Nutritional Sciences at San Diego State University, employed no empirical data to denigrate dodgeball, but he did offer that his wife "dreaded dodgeball days in physical education class because she couldn't throw and was almost always the victim of a hard-thrown ball." Kahan found dodgeball guilty of "leaving a lone winner amid a multitude of losers" while providing "coeducational inequity, high risk for injury, and wounded psyches."

While the U.S. Consumer Product Safety Commission keeps no data on wounded psyches, it does catalog just about every other sort of injury. Despite the protestations of assistant professors from third-tier universities, dodgeball's injury rate is lower than that of nearly any other sport. In 1999, the CPSC's national estimate for dodgeball injuries, none of which required hospitalization, was 2,926—about the same as caused by electric corn poppers and considerably fewer than caused by key chains. As for comparable sports, bowling had eight times as many injuries as dodgeball, golf had sixteen times as many injuries, and inline skating (a noncombative, noncompetitive staple of P.E. programs designed by forward-thinking education-ists) produced thirty-three times as many injuries. According to the CPSC numbers, watching "murderball" (as detractors deem it) could be more dangerous than playing it, since bleachers cause eight times as many injuries as the game itself.

An academic debate, of course, is no place for hard evidence. So among flame-fanning alarmists, dodgeball and, more important, the dodgeball ethos—which prizes competitiveness, and starkly delin-eates a winner while eliminating losers—is the greatest threat to our children since Alar-lacquered apples. Even though most now play the game with a spongy gator-skin ball, school districts are wary.

A few years ago, New York filmmaker Art Jones jokingly made a faux documentary titled *Dodgeball*, in which his characters recounted their gym class horror stories. "I saw the best minds of my generation lost to that game," said one. But proving once again that it is nearly impossible to parody the education establishment, a Michigan physi-cal education association in 1997 released a no-joke documentary, *No More Dodgeball: A New Beginning*. In the film, overweight teachers recover painful gym class memories, as a reenactment flashes of a 1950s-style gym teacher making children perform unspeakable tasks like push-ups, sit-ups, and jumping jacks before he informs them with blood-curdling severity, "Okay, boys and girls, today we're gonna play a game called dodgeball." From there, it is all movie-of-the-week music swells, moist-eyed testimonials, and oblique-angled montages of pink, milk-fed children getting doinked with red rubber balls.

If one were forced to pick the single person most responsible for the anti-dodgeball hysteria, it would be Neil Williams, a professor in the

Department of Health and Physical Education at Eastern Connecticut State University. In the early nineties, Williams authored the first of a series of articles for *JOPERD* in which he set up the "Physical Education Hall of Shame." These articles masqueraded as scholarship—his references ranged from "Dear Abby" columns to *JOPERD* articles like "Premeditated Murder: Let's Bump Off Killer Ball"—but they read like the rants of a man who had suffered too many gym-class headshots.

In his series, Williams vilified not only dodgeball, but any game he deemed antithetical to good physical education teaching. These included games that "are patently dangerous, have minimal participation by the majority of students, have limited physical activity, require little . . . pedagogical skill to teach . . . or single students out for potential embarrassment." Dodgeball, he reasoned, "may have done our profession more harm than any other single factor." In Williams's telling, the game Duck, Duck, Goose sounds like Chinese water torture: "Children are forced to sit still while having their heads 'tapped.'" Kickball puts "the batter on display for embarrassment in front of all of the rest of the class." Failing to find a seat during Musical Chairs is the equivalent of being "embarrassed and punished." Steal the Bacon is reminiscent of a "Roman gladiator contest," and Simon Says employs "teacher deception."

More important, said Williams, the sports curriculum that has served as the backbone of our country's physical education system (basketball, soccer, volleyball, etc.) caters mostly to athletes, when as adults more people end up participating in what educators call "lifetime physical activities" than in team sports. Citing a National Sporting Goods Association list of the top fourteen sport-oriented leisure activities, Williams indicted our schools for not taking into account pursuits such as fishing, dart-throwing, and motor-boating.

Dart-throwing and motor-boating? To produce physically fit kids? When I ask Williams if he can possibly be serious, he squirms. "I know a lot of the activities that adults do happen to coincide with drinking beer," he admits. But he says he wanted to cite the complete NGSA list. Williams takes his own classes of aspiring P.E. teachers on exotic noncompetitive excursions like "walking through a river." Apparently they love it. He was just named Eastern Connecticut State's "distinguished faculty member of the year." For that matter, with the recent resurgence of dodgeball publicity, he is perhaps the only *JOPERD* contributor to have been on the *Today* show—twice in the last month.

At first blush, the entire dodgeball skirmish might seem a mere footnote to the larger story, the Wussification of America. Ours is becoming a childproofed nation, where playgrounds have been shut down because of sharp-edged jungle gyms, where legislatures pass anti-bullying measures, where students are no longer sent home with suspension notices, but are sent instead to peer mediation and conflict resolution classes. It's a place where—as a friend who coaches his son's T-ball team reports from Arlington, Virginia—"All players bat every inning, nobody who's thrown out has to leave the bases, no score is kept, nobody loses, and everybody gets a trophy."

But Neil Williams and his ilk aren't simply a late-innings curiosity, a paragraph or two in a News-of-the-Weird roundup. They are the future. For no longer is it sufficient for our mollycoddled children, raised like hothouse orchids, to attend school for mere academic instruction. They must also learn how to salve their self-esteem, to stay with the group in cooperative learning, to set the bar low, then throw themselves a party for clearing it. Nowhere will they learn this more effectively than in the New P.E.

From the beginning, different cultures have employed physical education for aims beyond pure health. In ancient Greece, the war-mongering Spartans used physical instruction to help them withstand the rigors of military life, while the Athenians emphasized not only physical well-being, but the body beautiful, conducting their gymnastic sessions in the nude (unthinkable in the New P.E., where showering may be an affront to a child's dignity).

By the mid-twentieth century, Americans not only had copped the British system of teaching motor skills and fitness through competitive sports, but also saw physical education as a chance to perpetuate the Brits' towel-snapping vigor. As John F. Kennedy said in 1962, in language that today would see him impeached, "There is nothing, I think, more unfortunate than to have soft, chubby, fat-looking children who go to watch their school play basketball every Saturday and regard that as their week's exercise." Just a few years before, the President's Council on Youth Fitness had been created to encourage kids to stay fit in the event Communists needed to be killed. It also sought to impart intangible benefits—that oddly enough did not include the enhancement of self-esteem.

The *Physical Education Handbook,* a fifties-era text, praised competitive sports for instilling sportsmanship, which the authors defined as "being humble in victory and gracious in defeat." Sports should teach the participant to "take hard knocks," to "subdue emotional outbursts for the good of the common cause," and to "adapt himself to constantly changing conditions of the game, just as he must in the game of life." "In real life," say the authors, "not all gain first place, not all win first prize, not all receive the acclaim and renown of the hero. So it is that sports are an ideal laboratory for education for living."

This quaint notion was generally subscribed to by the underemployed football coach types who often doubled as the P.E. teachers of yore. But over the past several decades, master's degree–holding P.E. teachers have become an avowedly sensitive lot, mindful that their status in the education hierarchy rests somewhere above the shop teacher's and below the cafeteria lady's. As Virginia Tech's George Graham, who crystallized much New P.E. theory in the late eighties, quoted Woody Allen as saying, "Those who can, do. Those who can't, teach. Those who can't teach, teach physical education."

To correct this perception, academics launched an image overhaul in the mid-1960s. They started by doing what academics do best—making the simple complex. As outlined in the textbook *Foundations of Physical Education and Sport,* an academic named Franklin Henry sounded a clarion in 1964 for the "organization and study of the academic discipline herein called physical education." From there, it was off to the races. Physical education subdisciplines sprouted like kudzu. While some of these, such as sports medicine and physiology, derived from the hard sciences, P.E. majors could now wade into the much murkier bogs of "sport philosophy" and "sport pedagogy"—allowing them to introduce humanism, personal growth, and self-actualization into curricula that had been concerned with making kids run laps and climb gym ropes.

These forefathers of the New P.E. were so relieved to be excused from the children's table at their universities that many even pushed to rename the discipline "kinesiology," which is the study of human movement. By some counts, there are now over 150 names—everything from "human biodynamics" to "leisure science"—for what used to be "physical education." In the decades that followed, an entire corpus of New P.E. literature was born. (Here, the term "literature" is used loosely, to include such works as "Changers and the Changed: Moral Aspects of Coming Out in Physical Education"—an examination of that time-honored stock character, the lesbian gym teacher.)

The fundamental tenet of New P.E. philosophy was distilled by Terry Orlick, a sports psychologist at the University of Ottawa, who authored *The Cooperative Sports & Games Book—Challenge Without Competition* in 1978 and a follow-up book four years later. In Orlick's world of cooperative games, "Everybody wins and nobody loses. . . . These games eliminate the fear of failure and the feeling of failure." Granted, there are plenty of New P.E. moderates who believe that competition used correctly is an effective learning tool. As Dan Midura and Donald Glover write in *The Competition-Cooperation Link: Games for Developing Respectful Competitors,* "Neither competition nor cooperation is inherently good or evil. It is how we deal with competition and cooperation that can allow for effective or ineffective results."

But a great many practitioners of New P.E. are in the Orlick camp—and what a camp it is. Instead of the dreaded Musical Chairs, for instance, Orlick espouses Cooperative Musical Hugs (when the music stops, children hug one another). King of the Mountain is now People of the Mountain. To level the field for less athletically inclined children, he suggests playing with imaginary equipment (racketless tennis) or completely overhauling the rules, as in "strike-outless baseball" ("Who said, 'Three strikes and you're out,' anyway? I don't think it was God. So why not just eliminate the possibility?"). Traveling the world to find cooperative games, Orlick imported some real crowd-pleasers, like Helping to Harvest the Land from the ever-cooperative Chinese. And when he went to study the Inuit Eskimos, he learned the most important lesson: Never keep score, unless it's a collective score. "When the Inuit batted inflated seal bladders back and forth centuries ago," wrote Orlick, "the aim was to have fun trying to keep the ball up."

While Orlick writes as if he's eaten some bad seal in the Canadian Arctic, his themes are still being echoed. Marianne Torbert, who oversees the Leonard Gordon Institute for Human Development Through Play at Temple University, is obsessed with "movement activities" instead of athletics. Under this thinking, a child cannot burp without developing a new "skill." Laboring under the motto "It's not just a game. It's a developmental experience," Torbert suggests playing a nonelimination variant of Simon Says called Birds Fly, in which kids try not to get caught flapping their wings when a teacher names a nonflying creature. If they screw up, they stay in the game. And a good thing too, what with all the benefits Torbert says the players experience. Though few would argue that even the original version of Simon Says provides many fitness benefits, Torbert claims that Birds Fly not only utilizes everything from self-control to "thinking processes," but also contributes to "shoulder girdle development."

Middle school P.E. teacher John Hichwa pushed the new approach even further in his recent *Right Fielders Are People Too*. Quoting the likes of Peter, Paul and Mary and Leo Buscaglia, Hichwa writes that even more important than teaching physical skills is "nurturing pro-social behavior." To that end, Hichwa advocates eliminating "human-target games," using whistles only when refereeing, having students use make-believe jump ropes ("Everyone succeeds and no one ever misses!"), letting the students choose all their own activities, and allowing children to help grade themselves. Hichwa, it should be noted, was rated the middle school teacher of the year by the National Association for Sport & Physical Education (NASPE) in 1993. Or maybe, in keeping with his teaching philosophy, they let him rate himself.

By now, the spreading of gooey layers of social science pap over formerly simple curricula has become a distinguishing mark of the field of P.E. Six years ago, NASPE—representing more than eighteen thousand gym teachers and professors—released its ideal "content" standards, the closest thing the diffuse discipline has to a bible. Of the seven standards, only four related directly to physical fitness, while the other three involved what the experts call psycho-social elements, such as understanding that P.E. activities provide an outlet for self-expression.

But while the New P.E. theorists bend over backward to shave the hard edge off competitive activities and make the activities conform to the student instead of expecting the student to master required skills, they are neglecting one of the oldest tenets of social psychology. Studies dating back to the nineteenth century support the concept of social facilitation, which holds that in any activity, from winding fishing reels to riding bikes, people try harder, and thus are often driven to perform better, when they're in competition with someone else.

One of the most common canards of the New P.E. is that traditional P.E. classes—supposedly rife with rope-climbing humiliations and bloody dodgeball battles—turned an entire generation of adults off lifetime fitness. But this isn't supported even by the New P.E. advocates' own data. A NASPE survey showed that nearly half of all adults polled "strongly agreed" that participating in P.E. as a child helped them to become active, healthy adults. Likewise, shielding children from the competition of team sports seems to be a losing battle, since 67 percent of adults and 69 percent of teens believed strongly that "participation in team sports helps children learn lessons about discipline and teamwork that are important and will help them in the future."

But one thing that nobody disputes about our children is that they are fat. According to the Centers for Disease Control, the number of young people who are overweight has more than doubled in the past thirty years. This is hardly surprising, since adults have gotten fatter too. So sedentary is our nation that even our pets are considered overweight (30 percent of them, to be precise). While New P.E. theorists speculate that our out-of-shape children are staying that way because they have disengaged from a system focused on competitive sports, these authorities seem to discount the more likely explanation: that our children are chips off the old blobs, little lipid factories programmed for maximum caloric input and minimal aerobic output.

Some New P.E. programs can fairly be said to address these problems. Madison Junior High in Naperville, Illinois—which features an amalgam of old and new activities—has students wear heart rate monitors while participating in everything from cardio machine workouts to touch football to rollerblading. But more New P.E. programs seem to feature a let-the-students-decide menu allowing kids to emulate the narcissism of their parents when it comes to basic fitness. Much as Mom and Dad have forsaken running on treadmills to dabble in more expressive fare like candlelight yoga or bellydancing classes, kids can now participate in activities that have only slightly more cardiovascular benefit than dart throwing or motorboating.

Combing stacks of news articles that unblinkingly congratulate the New P.E., one sees kids doing everything from tap dancing to white-water rafting to playing mini golf. There's also hacky sack, unicycling, bow hunting, tai chi, and, at one Illinois school, playing with yo-yos. While New P.E. teachers take a bow for figuring out how to minimize embarrassing performance-oriented competition, it's not clear that for a thirteen-year-old boy, doing the Electric Slide or chasing somebody around the gym with a rubber chicken in a new form of tag is less humiliating than shimmying up a climbing rope in tight polyester shorts. As one Wichita teenager told a reporter after he was done holding hands with classmates during a "social position" exercise: "I'm not gay."

Recently, I conducted my own field comparison between dodgeball-playing old P.E. and New P.E.–influenced classes. At Windy Hill Elementary School in Owings, Maryland, I fall in with Letty McNulty's fifth-graders. Without a D.A.R.E. shirt or cargo shorts, and with my hundred-pound weight advantage, I find it difficult to pass. No matter. I haven't come to make friends, but to participate in a dodgeball exhibition as the prototypical bully. I plan to whoop and holler, to intimidate and scourge. If memory serves, and I still possess the true aim, catlike reflexes, and bloodlust I believe I had as an eleven-year-old, I will stalk the basketball court perimeter and peg these little punks like human Lite-Brites.

But before we get down to business, we have a symposium on the gym floor. McNulty, though she has a "no whining" sign posted on her office window, is not completely averse to New P.E. ideas. She believes that her youngest students (first- and second-graders) are best served by practicing noncompetitive skill-building exercises, such as learning how to kick and throw. "But you will find," she adds, that even in first grade, "they try to keep score with anything. Even at low-level throwing stations, they'll say, 'We got forty-nine koosh balls in the basket!'"

As I address McNulty's class, I speak in the slow, patronizing tones of one not used to conversing with children. I explain how some adults want to do away with games where there are winners and losers, or where you might have to sit out. "Yeah," says one youngster already hip to the lingo, "you mean elimination games." I ask the kids how they feel about this. "Not good," says a boy named John. "It's good to have elimination games, 'cause you can compete against people." "But isn't competition bad?" I ask, adopting the tone of a New P.E. theorist. Won't there be damaged self-esteem? Wouldn't you rather measure yourself against your own personal best? Don't the girls get pushed around by the boys?

The children look at me like I've escaped from Special Ed. "We're tougher than the boys!" says a petite towhead named Stephanie, adjusting her hair kerchief. "I lose a lot of games, but it's still fun for me," volunteers a large student named Eric. "We've been playing these games almost all our lives," says a world-weary sprite named C.J. "We already know what our goals are, how good we are, how bad we play. [It's more fun to play] against other kids." Besides, adds a shy little girl named Julia, "you can train yourself to get better."

McNulty tells me that a few years ago, Julia avoided gym class like the bubonic plague, crying every time she attended. At this, Julia's eyes well with tears, and I fear we're headed for a New P.E. moment. "Don't cry, Julia," commands one of the boys. But the hard-fought tears of accomplishment flow anyway. After years of McNulty's working with her to develop her skills, and Julia's participating in extracurricular sports, she's now one of the best athletes in the class. As the teacher brags on Julia, the same boy slaps her a high five.

McNulty informs the class that today we'll be playing several variations of dodgeball. Since she's in a retro mood, McNulty announces that we're using an old-fashioned rubber playground ball, instead of the usual spongier gator-skin. The children convulse in enthusiastic titters, as if it had just been announced they'd be receiving cigarettes and skin magazines.

They seem excited to be playing a no-holds-barred game. In recent years, school administrators have shackled them at every turn. The boys tell me they are no longer allowed to play football during recess—not even touch—because of possible danger. Instead of using a softball, they are forced to play with a "rag ball" that looks like a stuffed dog toy. During kickball, says a tall girl named Carolyn, they are now forbidden to throw batters out by pegging them with the ball, even though at home, she says, "I roll the ball in the mud, then throw them out." "What's left to do at recess?" I ask. "Sometimes," says C.J., "We just relax."

As we take our positions around the court, I try to adopt a look of menace, bouncing one of two red rubber balls as McNulty explains the rules. Today's game is Greek Dodgeball, one of about fifty variations of the versatile sport. In this version, two teams line up on either side of the court, with a "goalkeeper" stationed behind each one. The goalkeeper is actually an opposing player who tries to pick off the team nearest him, while his team does the same from the opposite court, creating a crossfire. As people are hit, they get eliminated, but they're not really out of the game. Instead, they line the perimeter and become throwers themselves, until nobody on one team remains on the court.

As we play to the finish, the gym fills with gales of laughter. I'm surprised not to hear any wailing or gnashing of teeth—not even when a high heater I aim at young Carolyn's torso takes off and grazes her cheek. "You hit me in the face," she says, fixing me with an icy stare. "Are you okay?" I ask apologetically. "Of course," she says, as if shooing a fly, before she fells another of my teammates in retribution.

In our next game, we switch to Pin Dodgeball, in which two teams bean each other, sending players to a penalty box for one minute every time they are hit. The object is to clear opponents out of the way while you knock down two of their duckpins that sit at the far end of the court. For this round, I announce that my team needs a name. The kids kick around the "Blue Afros" and the "Crystals" (after the glue-on crystal Stephanie sports on her cheek). But we settle on "Sisqó," for the singer who brought us "The Thong Song." During this contest, I turn into the loudmouthed, bullying, win-at-all-costs dick-weed that New P.E. teachers so fear, just to see if I can make the weak cower.

We have switched to a softer gator-skin ball (though earlier, the children voted 12–8 to keep the red rubber one). It is lighter and takes off in unpredictable trajectories every time the gym's air conditioner blinks on. Dodgeball detractors like to say the sport is poor exercise because the weak are culled earliest, and they're the ones who need the action most. But as any ten-year-old strategist knows, it is wise to take out the good throwing arms first, in the interest of self-preservation. After firing up my troops—"C'mon Sisqó!"—I direct a steady stream of smack talk at the opposing team's best sniper, a rangy all-around jock named Colin, who nonchalantly makes me pay every time he takes aim.

All around me, the Sisqós are taking casualties, and our pin-keepers are getting the worst of it. With only one pin left and my team down to its nub, I take leave of the one-minute elimination box thirty seconds early (the kids do full stints, on their honor, but when it comes to dodgeball, I have none). As Colin drills another of our pin-keepers, I scurry to grab the ball that's just shanked off the leg of my fallen comrade. I prepare to unleash a hell-for-leather fury in the name of all that is good and right, all that is Sisqó. But as I coil into my ball-cradling windup, I feel the unmistakable ping of a gator-skin ball between my shoulder blades. I turn around to face my assassin and see Carolyn wearing the cherubic, cathartic smile that all but says, "Take that, you galoot."

Though dodgeball detractors say the game provides too little movement, you could have fooled us. After all the throwing and dodging and sprinting, we emit the dank human musk of a spent fifth-grade gym class. I'm now convinced that dodgeball, played properly, is as good a means of exercise as any. But don't take my word for it. Take that of Dr. Brad Strand, chairman of the Department of Health, Physical Education and Recreation at North Dakota State University.

Strand is a dodgeball opponent who set out several years ago to prove that the sport was deficient in securing cardiovascular fitness. After running a rigorous study using a middle school gym class in North Park, Utah, however, he found precisely the opposite to be true. Hooking students of all fitness and skill levels up to heart-rate monitors during several rounds of elimination dodgeball, Strand discovered that players stayed above a moderate heart rate of 140 beats per minute for a greater percentage of the time than they did playing most other team sports. Even more amazing, nearly half the class had a higher heart rate playing dodgeball than they did when they were sent on a nine-minute fitness run immediately afterward.

When I first contacted Strand to obtain his study, he sounded nervous, as if someone were trying to make the case that he was a child pornographer or Holocaust denier. "I'm a little leery of letting it out," he said. "I'm not a proponent of dodgeball . . . but the thing I haven't liked is people coming out and saying something is inherently bad without having any research to back it up." So intense is the current academic pressure against dodgeball that when Strand submitted his study to one prestigious journal, "they said they wouldn't even read it, it had 'dodgeball' in the title." Strand changed his study's title to the less offensive "The Effect of Class Size and Number of Balls on Heart Rate Intensity During a Throwing Game Activity." It was published in the rather unprestigious *Nebraska Journal of Health, Physical Education, Recreation, & Dance*. As far as Strand knows, it's never been cited.

A few days later, I'm off to Monocacy Elementary School in Dickerson, Maryland, where a student stands a better chance of winning Pimlico's Pick Six than getting beaned with a dodgeball in P.E. The gym teacher, Debbie Summers, is a New P.E. disciple, and she has the costume to prove it. Today she is sporting a safari hat, golf club earrings, and a ski map shirt. Her apparel is supposed to evoke the "skill themes" that her students have learned throughout the year, associated with the Amazon rain forest, the Olympics, a golf course, and a Winter Wonderland. Where most people look at the gym and see a basketball court, Summers sees a land of make-believe.

The gymnasium looks like the New P.E. equivalent of the Marine Crucible on Parris Island. Scattered around the court are about twenty-five stations where Summers's fifth graders will revisit the movement concepts they've been learning all year. Festive, magic-markered laminated placards identify the stations and highlight the aforementioned themes. From an even vaster array of activities, the stations set up today were voted on by the school's student government, since, Summers says, "It didn't seem fair for me to choose."

As the children enter the gym to the boom box strains of a jazzy "Jingle Bells" (in keeping with the Winter Wonderland theme—*not* Christmas, Summers assures me), she announces to the kids that they will be traveling to all their stations on sit-down gym floor scooters—seats on wheels, with side handles—which she calls "jeeps, sleds, golf carts, or whatever you pretend them to be." After a quick review, the students are unleashed. They mount their scooters, and I follow three of them to the Howler Monkey Howl station.

"What do you do here?" I ask. "You have to howl like a monkey," one girl deadpans. According to the posted instructions, it's a little more complicated than that. Students must "bend knees slightly, lean the body forward, hang arms at sides, touch fingers to the ground at each step, stop now, and then beat chest in monkey fashion." I ask Summers what "lifetime physical activity" this addresses. "Well, if you look," she explains, "they're shifting their weight a little bit."

From the monkey station, I catch up with a boy named Charles. He is tall and athletic and is sporting a blood blister on his lip that he got from playing basketball (not in Summers's class). As Charles sets about his task at the Blizzard station (in which children sit on their scooters while kicking tennis balls helter skelter), I ask him if he ever feels silly doing things like the Howler Monkey Howl. "Yes," he readily admits. "Because one, you don't do that stuff in real life. And two, it's not really a physical education activity."

There are, at several of Summers's stations, impressive displays of coordination, though the activities don't look as taxing as, say, a vigorous round of dodgeball. At a juggling station, it seems every student can at least keep up scarves, if not balls or pins. Most seem capable of making it partway up a climbing rope, which they're supposed to imagine runs through the four layers of the rain forest, though, as

Summers emphasizes, "They don't have to climb, they can just hang—there's no competition."

But most of the rest of the stations would have a fifties-era gym coach scratching his Vitalis-slicked head in puzzlement. At the Javelin Throw, kids toss pool noodles through a hula hoop. Over at the Coke Bear Dance, the students aren't getting a fraction of the exercise enjoyed by the hockey-playing polar bears that decorate the station's sign. Instead, they pull empty Coke cans out of a baby wading pool and use them to build pyramids.

Perhaps the most ridiculous stop is the Build a Snowman station, where students are asked to build snowmen from soccer balls stacked between rubber doughnuts. "What's the point here?" I ask Summers. She smiles, wiggling her fingers. "It develops fine motor skills." So does scratching your ear, of course, but most people don't expect to get an "A" for it in physical education.

In another corner of the gym—perhaps the busiest corner—sits the Gold Medal Stand. While students mount a crate and play a jambox that blasts the national anthem, they haggle over who'll get to drape themselves with a gold medal labeled "Winner," which they've earned for doing absolutely nothing. As a fifth-grader named Holly is taking her turn in the limelight, another student named Miles approaches her. "I want an award!" he demands impetuously. Holly tells him he'll have to wait. "You must worship me," she says. While Summers insists her kids don't perform any activities for which they're not cognizant of the attendant skill, it's hard to see what's being honed at the Gold Medal Stand. Maybe their self-indulgent-little-twit skills.

Over in the Snow Plow Zone, Cordelia and Julie sit on their scooters while picking up foam balls with their feet, which they then drop into a milk crate. Trying to impress them with my New P.E. buzzwords, I ask if this is one of those "lifetime physical activities" that will be so useful to them when they are adults. "Nope," says Cordelia matter-of-factly, before reconsidering. "Well, maybe if you have two broken arms." I ask the girls if they can think of anything that would promote physical fitness more effectively than the Snow Plow Zone. Their faces light up. They can. There's this one game that involves a lot of running. It's more fun, and they assure me that it's much "better exercise." It's called dodgeball.

WELCOME TO CANADA,
THE GREAT WHITE WASTE OF TIME

If the national mental illness of the United States is megalomania, that of Canada is paranoid schizophrenia.
                                    —Margaret Atwood, Canadian writer

Vancouver, British Columbia

Whenever I think of Canada . . . strike that. I'm an American, therefore I tend not to think of Canada. On the rare occasion when I have considered the country that Fleet Streeters call "the Great White Waste of Time," I've regarded it, as most Americans do, as North America's attic, a mildewy recess that adds little value to the house, but serves as an excellent dead space for stashing Nazi war criminals, drawing-room socialists, and hockey goons.

Henry David Thoreau nicely summed up Americans' indifference toward our country's little buddy when he wrote, "I fear that I have not got much to say about Canada. . . . What I got by going to Canada was a cold." For the most part, Canadians occupy little disk space on our collective hard drive. Not for nothing did MTV have a game show that made contestants identify washed-up celebrities under the category "Dead or Canadian?"

If we have bothered forming opinions at all about Canadians, they've tended toward easy pickings: that they are a docile, Zamboni-driving people who subsist on seal casserole and Molson. Their hobbies include wearing flannel, obsessing over American hegemony, exporting deadly mad cow disease and even deadlier Gordon Lightfoot and Nickelback albums. You can tell a lot about a nation's mediocrity index by learning that they invented synchronized swimming. Even more by the fact that they're proud of it.

But ever since George W. Bush's reelection, news accounts have been rolling in that disillusioned Americans are running for the border in protest. This prompts the thought that it may be time to stop treating Our Canadian Problem with such cavalier disregard. In fact, largely as a result of Bush and his foreign policy, what was once a polite rivalry has become a poisoned well of hurt feelings and recriminations.

These days, Canadian publications are chockablock with surveys showing that Canadians see themselves as something akin to a superior race. The prime ministers of what was once a reliable ally that ponied up in times of war have treated us like traffic-light squeegee men when we've stopped at their corner asking for assistance with our latest military adventure. They have spurned our missile defense shield out of spite, even knowing it would save their Canadian bacon. Their legislators have publicly called us "bastards" and stomped on our president in effigy. Their citizens have booed our children at pee-wee hockey games.

Being bloodthirsty Americans, we have naturally fired a few warning volleys in lieu of slapping them with a restraining order. A few years ago, my friend Jonah Goldberg from *National Review* wrote a piece elegantly titled "Bomb Canada," encouraging us to smack Soviet Canuckistan, as Pat Buchanan calls it, "out of its shame-spiral" since "that's what big brothers do." Canadians responded as Canadians always will when faced with overt aggression. They wrote inordinate numbers of letters of concern, exercising what Canadian writer Douglas Coupland calls their "almost universal editorial-page need to make disapproving clucks."

Equal outrage was caused when Conan O'Brien showed up to help boost tourism after the SARS crisis. Along for the ride came a Conan staple, Triumph the Insult Comic Dog, who in dog-on-the-street interviews relentlessly mocked French Canadians. When one pudgy Quebecer admitted he was a separatist, Triumph suggested he might want to "separate himself from doughnuts for a while."

Canadians seethed—though polls show they pride themselves on being much funnier than Americans (don't ask me why, when they're responsible for Dan Aykroyd, John Candy, and Alan Thicke). One MP from the socialist New Democratic party called the show "vile and vicious," and said it was tantamount to hatemongering. Historians believe this to be the first time a member of parliament has so categorically denounced a hand puppet.

With the reelection of Bush, however, this poor man's cold war may be swinging Canada's way. Trend spotters on both sides of the 49th parallel have taken note of "the Bush refugee," the American progressive who has decided to flee to Canada after growing heartsick at the soul-crushing death knell of liberalism that pundits declared after the president's two-point victory.

A cottage industry was born. Anti-American/pro-Canadian blogs proliferated, as blogs unfortunately do. Websites like canadianalterna tive.com are open for business, trying to entice emotionally vulnerable Americans to turn their backs on family, friends, and country with boasts that Canada has signed the Kyoto Protocol, legalized gay marriage in six provinces, and seen its Senate recommend legalizing marijuana. Vancouver immigration lawyer Rudi Kischer took a whole team, complete with realtors and money managers, to recruit in American cities, helping potential defectors overcome immigration concerns, such as how to pass Canada's elitist skilled-worker test for entry (Give us your affluent, your overeducated, your Unitarian masses yearning for socialized medicine).

Dejected Americans, most of whom already live in progressive enclaves, began sounding off to reporters, vowing to check out of the Red-American wasteland before true misfortune befell them. In footage of a Kischer seminar in San Francisco that I obtained from a Canadian documentary film crew (working title of the piece: "Escaping America"), one attendee who looked like a lost Gabor sister but with more plastic surgery said, "I really can't stand George Bush. I can't stand this culture, which is very selfish, aggressive, and mean, violent I think." After going to Canada for just half an hour from Buffalo, she concluded, "It was like a completely different country. . . . The people seemed more internationally aware, not so isolated and unilateral. There was less evidence of commercialism and corporations. People were friendly."

It sounded like such an idyllic Rainbowland that I had to see it for myself. So I flew to Vancouver in late January to get a closer look and to meet up with several already-arrived and soon-to-be American expatriates. Taking a day or so to get acclimated, I threw myself into this unspoiled Eden by going to the multinational Virgin Megastore to purchase some Joni Mitchell and Leonard Cohen CDs (buy Canadian!). I also looked for Canada's greatest (only?) contribution to world cuisine, Tim Hortons doughnuts, which is owned by the American fast-food behemoth Wendy's.

With nothing but a Lonely Planet map and a thirst for knowledge, I sought out Vancouver's landmarks—the Gastown clock, which lets out steam and whistle-toots every fifteen minutes, Brandi's Exotic Nightclub, where Ben Affleck fraternizes with strippers when in town, and the New Amsterdam Cafe, where potheads openly smoke the potent BC bud, taunting tobacco users, who are confined to a glass cage like common criminals. (The tokers snack on "jones soda" and "chronic candy" and other foodstuffs so cutely named it could make even the most maniacal libertarian cheer for mandatory minimums.)

To see Canadian progressivism in action, though, I trekked down to the East Side, Vancouver's Compton, where the storefront Supervised Injection Site caters to junkies on the government teat. With the surrounding streets hosting an open-air drug market, the Site was conceived as a way to rid the neighborhood of discarded drug paraphernalia and promote "safe" drug-taking practices. In typical Canadian fashion, it's a long way around the barn to get rid of litter.

If the Site has in fact encouraged addicts to do their drugs off the streets, they still buy them right outside. To reach the place, I have to pass through a herd of about a hundred junkies over a four-block radius. They offer to sell me all manner of substances my company won't let me expense. When I make it inside the Site, along with several itchy, twitchy customers in search of free cookers and needles and a clean booth to shoot themselves silly, an attendant tells me that unless I'm there to take drugs, I can't stay without a media relations escort. "What we do here is important, so we try to keep a low profile," he says, perhaps oblivious to the hypodermic needle that's embossed on the door.

The staffers aren't rude, however, and retrieve for me a helpful government brochure called "The Safer Fix" that has made me something of an expert on the proper way to tie off. Though it's a bit mind-blowing to a law-and-order American, this is actually pretty small beer compared with a new Canadian government-funded study called the North American Opiate Medication Initiative. While the Supervised Injection Site is strictly a bring-your-own-smack affair, the new experiment will study the effects of giving half of the drug-addicted research subjects heroin, while the other half get methadone. As a female attendant describes it to me, we agree that it must really suck for the methadoners. But for the other side? "Dude!" she says, stating the obvious, "free drugs for a year!"

Rudi Kischer, the immigration lawyer who went trolling for clients south of the border, has probably done more than any single person besides George Bush to induce Americans to become former Americans. At the top of a high-rise building overlooking Coal Harbor, where seaplanes land in steady succession, Kischer invites me into his office. He is tall, with the bland good looks of a soap opera extra. By way of an icebreaker, I tell him I flunked the skilled-worker test and so became a journalist. He says not to worry. Up until a few years ago, lawyers were completely banned from immigrating, the first fact I've heard that recommends his country.

While numbers are hard to come by, it is generally thought that some thousands of Americans are poised to change countries, making them the largest influx Canada has seen since our draft dodgers came this way during Vietnam—much less since Brit-loving Loyalists were shown the door to what was then New France by American revolutionaries. Whether or not this is true, Kischer has plenty of horror stories from interested clients: concerned parents who are moving so their children won't be drafted into Bush's war machine, the rich guy who lives on a yacht and would rather pay exorbitant Canadian taxes than bear the shame of flashing his imperialist American passport when sailing into foreign ports.

I tell Kischer it's a bit much to swallow that so many Americans are being persecuted for disagreeing with the president, since we live in what most regard as a fly-your-freak-flag country. Take me. I wasn't keen on the war in Iraq, and I work in the belly of the neocon beast that gets partial credit for hatching it, yet I've never felt a lick of persecution for offering dissent. Kischer studied briefly at Duke (former basketball great Danny Ferry was in his poli sci class, he says excitedly), so when I ask him if he ever felt oppressed in America, he laughs as if I've asked a ridiculous question. Of course not, he says, "but it depends on personality types, too. I'm a lawyer, so I've had worse things said to me by better people, right?"

When in America, he blended seamlessly, he says, with everyone else who shops at the same khaki shorts store. People didn't really suspect he was Canadian, since Canada's not on the radar. "I read one article about Canada in four months," he adds. "It said the socialists are about to take over the government. From the American viewpoint, maybe they already have." Kischer voices a typical concern. Canadians are traditionally so insecure about the lack of attention we pay them that their government has even paid American universities $300,000 to study them. One of the foremost Canadian Studies programs in the country is at Duke. A professor in the program has said, "We're the most important university to make a serious effort to study Canada. That's like being the best hockey team in Zimbabwe."

My first interview with an American comes not in Canada, but in Bellingham, Washington, about ninety minutes from Vancouver. I drive south and clear the Peace Arch border faster than I could a McDonald's drive-thru line (note to Homeland Security), and meet up with Christopher Key in his middle-class rambler with a FOR SALE sign in the yard. Key is still a patriot, but he hopes to soon be an expatriate. He's descended from "Star Spangled Banner" writer Francis Scott Key, who he admits "wasn't much of a poet."

He has become a minor celebrity of sorts, profiled by everyone from the Canadian Broadcasting Corporation to the *New York Times* (whose reporter flies in the day after me). The silver-haired Key looks like a Chamber of Commerce burgher. He likes to point out he's not some stereotypical longhair, having just left his editor's gig at a failing business magazine. He's had several other career incarnations too: everything from art gallery owner to charter boat skipper.

But Key's weirdest job was in the military, when he served in Vietnam. "They called it 'press liaison,' I think, but I was a news censor," he says. As a wet-behind-the-ears nineteen-year-old, he was supposed to tell media big shots like Ed Bradley what they could and could not cover. They all ignored him. "My take," he says, "is that while I had an odious job, I managed to do it very poorly."

Key caught shrapnel on one mission, and later was ambushed in the Central Highlands. While running to his truck, he felt a stitch in his side. The wound took out a good bit of his right kidney, and served as his ticket home.

Though Key wasn't bullish on the war when he was drafted, he never thought of fleeing to Canada to beat it. He comes from a long military line, and running isn't what his family does. But since Bush was elected in 2000, he says he's watched the country go into a tailspin, becoming less tolerant, more mean-spirited, more judgmental. In the past, Key waited out Nixon and Reagan. "I voted for Dukakis," he says. "I'm used to losing." But the war in Iraq pushed him closer to the edge, and at about 3:00 A.M. the day after the election, he made his decision to eject. "All the voices of moderation—Colin Powell— were going to be replaced by yes-people like Condoleezza Rice. It's going to get worse."

He says that when satellite trucks first started showing up in his driveway, the neighbors were atwitter. He loves his neighbors, a healthy mix of Republicans and Democrats. They regularly get together for barbecues, and come see him perform in community theater. As a Universal Life Church minister—he secured his ordination certificate off the Internet for twenty-five bucks—he's performed their weddings and funerals. But they couldn't talk him into staying, even though his adult daughter lives next door with her family, and her former twin sister, now her twin brother, lives in Seattle. How could he stay in a place that would frown on his performing the wedding of his own daughter/son?

"Come again?" I ask.

"This gets confusing," he apologizes. His second daughter, Bonnie, it seems, "who became my son, was a lesbian before he went transgender," making him heterosexual. The twins are actually scheduled to go on *Oprah* to discuss this. I think I understand, but ask for a flow chart to make sure. "Listen, it won't help. It looks like an explosion in a spaghetti factory," he says. "I can't keep up—how the hell can you?"

While Key puts a premium on Canadian tolerance, he's spent long enough in the country to understand it's not Canaan. A part-time blogger, he's even written pieces with titles like "The Canadian Identity Crisis," in which he tweaks his future compatriots for being America-fixated ninnies, and for coasting on their reputation for politeness. While Canadians don't exhibit road rage, he says, they are carpool lane cheaters and worse: "Victoria dumps its untreated sewage into the waters off Vancouver Island. How impolite can you get?"

Still, Key is leaving his homeland, and he's sick of hearing from talk show types who say good riddance on the one hand and he should stay and fight on the other. "Shouldn't you?" I ask, picking up the latter sentiment. After all, he gets along beautifully even with his Republican neighbors, and nobody except a few journalists has questioned his patriotism. So how bad, really, is the alleged cauldron of intolerance known as America? Isn't he boxing with Sean Hannity's shadow, responding not to the America he actually knows but to the polarized version of it that lives in his cable box?

Besides, I suggest in a windy disquisition (I've had wine with lunch) after hearing at length how he once marched for civil rights and against Vietnam, even if this ugly America is as pervasive as he says, isn't it our duty as Americans to get in on the debate, to jump into the sandbox and hit somebody on the head with a shovel while no one's looking? It's what made our country great. Our forefathers may have quit their home countries once upon a time, but they came here to build a better one.

He isn't buying. "I'm fucking tired," he says, "and I don't need to rebuild the country. There's a perfectly good one thirty miles away."

Just how perfectly good a country Canada is, is a matter of dispute. The expats I eventually meet buy into Canadian self-mythologizing without so much as giving the tires a kick. Yet even some Canadians gag on the constant stream of virtue-proclaiming advertorials that are, for lack of a better word, a crock. This is self-evident in the pathological Canadian claims of modesty and politeness.

Will Ferguson is a cockeyed nationalist and brilliant satirist, who calls his country "a nation of associate professors." In his book *Why I Hate Canadians,* he writes that his countrymen even boast about their Great Canadian Inferiority Complex. While it's difficult to go five minutes without hearing how collectively nice Canadians are, Ferguson says, "what we fail to realize is that self-conscious niceness is not niceness at all; it is a form of smugness. Is there anything more insufferable than someone saying, 'Gosh, I sure am a sweet person, don'tcha think?'"

This strain of nails-on-the-blackboard nationalism is most evident in the recent bestseller *Fire and Ice,* an Americans-are-from-Mars, Canadians-are-from-Venus study of the two countries' values by Canadian sociologist Michael Adams. Based on three head-to-head values surveys done over a decade, it shows Americans coming up short on matters from militarism to materialism. This is hardly news. But Adams pushes his luck, giving conventional wisdom a twirl by advancing that it is the Americans who are actually the slavish followers of an established order, while Canadians are rugged individualists and autonomous free thinkers.

Give Adams points for cheek. His is, after all, a country that didn't bother to draft its own constitution until 1982, that kept

"God Save the Queen" as its national anthem until 1980, and that still enshrines its former master's monarch as its head of state. Her Canadian title is "Elizabeth the Second, by the Grace of God, of the United Kingdom, Canada and Her other Realms and Territories Queen (breath), Head of the Commonwealth, Defender of the Faith." Maybe they should change their national anthem again, to Britney Spears's "I'm a Slave 4 U."

After suffering through Adams's book, I decided two can practice snake-oil sociology. So I spent three days on Nexis kicking up every comparison survey and statistic I could find on American/Canadian values. I became so gripped with the subject I could have been mistaken for a Canadian.

This unscientific research quickly confirmed that Canadians are bizarrely obsessed with us, binge-eating out of our cultural trough, then pretending it tastes bad. Plainly the two things Canada needs most are a mirror and a good psychiatrist.

Though they don't know who they are, they know they're not us (roughly nine out of ten comparison surveys are done by Canadians), so they bang that drum until their hands bleed. Still, it seems there is almost nothing Canadian that isn't informed in some way by America. When the late Canadian radio host Peter Gzowski had a competition to come up with a phrase comparable to "American as apple pie," the winner was "As Canadian as possible, under the circumstances." In 1996, when Canadians were asked to name both the greatest living and the all-time greatest Canadian, 76 percent said "no one comes to mind." Another survey showed them to believe that the most famous Canadian was Pamela Anderson, star of America's *Baywatch*. When Canadians were asked to name their favorite song, they settled on one by a good Canadian band, the Guess Who. The song: "American Woman."

Several years ago, Molson beer aired a commercial featuring Joe Canadian, a regular beer-drinking Joe who went on a rant aboot what Canadians are and aren't (not fur traders or dog sledders; they pronounce it "about," not "aboot"). He became a media darling and a national mascot. Then the actor who played Joe moved to Hollywood to find work. When he returned, tail tucked between legs, even he admitted, "I think, yeah, it is a little sad that Canadians draw their identity not so much from 'I am Canadian' as 'I am not American.'"

While Canadians pride themselves on knowing more about us

than we do about them (undoubtedly true), the problem—captured in a survey done for Canada Day in 2000—is that even historically challenged Americans know more about ourselves than Canadians do about themselves. In parallel ten-question quizzes on everything from our first president/prime minister to the words of our respective national anthems, 63 percent of Americans scored five or more right answers. Only 39 percent of Canadians did. One Canadian television critic expressed disbelief, writing, "Average Americans appear to be in worse shape—judging by the evidence on TV, anyway." She would know, since at the time of her comment, 92 percent of the comedies and 85 percent of the dramas on Canadian television were made elsewhere, mainly in America.

Where Canada fails is no big secret. Most of us know that its universal health care is a great thing, if you don't mind waiting, say, nine months for an MRI on your spinal cord injury. We all know Canadians are overregulated, to the point that Canadian rocker Bryan Adams was denied "Canadian content status" for cowriting an album with a British producer, limiting the play his songs could receive on the radio (a policy that's supposed to encourage Canadian talent but that, in Adams's words, "encourage[s] mediocrity. People don't have to compete in the real world. . . . Fucking absurd").

We all know the Canadian military has become a shadow of itself. Things have gotten so dire that a Queen's University study (titled "Canada Without Armed Forces?") predicted the imminent extinction of the air force. This unpreparedness has become such a joke that Ferguson says their military ranks just above Tonga's, which consists of nothing more than "a tape-recorded message yelling 'I surrender!' in thirty-two languages."

What many don't consider is how much Canada has oversold itself in the areas where it purportedly does succeed. While it's true that the government has been much friendlier than ours to gay marriage, only 39 percent of Canadians decidedly support it. While Canada is supposedly more environment-friendly, it has been cited for producing more waste per person than any other country. While Canada is supposedly safer, a 1996 study showed that its banks had the highest stickup rate of any industrialized nation (one in every six was robbed). And while a great deal is made of Americans' passion for firearms, the *Edmonton Sun,* citing Statistics Canada, reported that Canada has a higher crime rate than we do.

Canadians are supposedly less greedy than Americans, yet they lead the world in telemarketing fraud, and most of their victims are Americans. Are they more generous? Not by a long shot. The Vancouver-based Fraser Institute publishes a Generosity Index, which shows that more Americans give to charity, and give more when they do.

Is the Canadian "mosaic" more successful than the American "melting pot," a distinction they constantly make? You be the judge. Imagine every decade or so America's Spanish-speaking southwesterners holding a referendum over whether to secede. It's happened twice since 1980 among the Francophones of Quebec, and some say it's going to happen again. While America has figurative language police on its college campuses, Quebec has literal ones—"tongue troopers," the locals call them—who ruthlessly enforce absurd language laws requiring, for example, that restaurant trash cans feature the word "push" on their lids in French instead of English.

Apart from the Anglo/Franco teeter-totter that Canada can't ever seem to get off, are Canadians less racist, as many of them claim? Well, like America, they saw both slavery and segregation. If Canadians today are less racist, someone ought to tell their aboriginal peoples, who've spent centuries getting their land annexed and being generally mistreated (as of 2000 in Nova Scotia, there was still a law on the books offering hunters a bounty for Indian scalps).

Recent polling shows 35 percent of Canada's "visible minorities" (such as blacks and Asians) have experienced discrimination in the last five years. Another poll showed 54 percent of Canadians believe anti-Semitism is a serious problem in Canadian society today. It certainly was yesterday. Around World War II, a few Jews did manage to squeak in—despite the policy summed up by Canada's director of immigration as "None is too many." Will Ferguson points out that more Nazi war criminals are thought to have found sanctuary in Canada than refugees fleeing the Holocaust.

But even when Canada succeeds, it carries the whiff of failure. For nearly a decade, the country sat atop the United Nations quality-of-life index, a fact that Canadian schoolchildren could parrot in their sleep. When Canada dropped to eighth, just behind the United States, its collective psyche took a beating. The next year, Canada shot past us again, but not back to the top. The headline in Ontario's *Windsor Star* tells you all you need to know about Canadian triumphalism: "Cheers to Us, We're No. 4."

In a sense, Canada is the perfect place for American quitters, as it evidences self-loathing masquerading as self-congratulation. This I learn over dinner in Vancouver. A delightful realtor named Elizabeth McQueen has enticed me with a promise any American boy likes to hear—that we'd be dining with "two very attractive lesbians." She didn't lie. One of them could make a killing as a Courteney Cox celebrity impersonator. Besides, they're psychotherapists from San Francisco. They ask me to change their names to Cocoa and Satchi since their patients don't yet know they're leaving America.

They've come to Vancouver to look for real estate, having gotten married on an earlier trip to Canada. They were politically active back home. They wrote letters to the editor for every cause: "Save the whales, save the trees, save the lesbians," says Cocoa. They hate the war and the Patriot Act and the results of the gay marriage resolutions. They hate the conservative agenda and fundamentalist crackers and all the other usual suspects. They hate it that Karl Rove, in Cocoa's words, helped to elect "an alcoholic butthead who can't put two sentences together, cocaine addict, married to a frigid drunk-driver-murderer-Martha-Stewart-wannabe."

But beneath all her gracious sentiments is something else: a loss of faith. When describing how she feels traveling abroad, Cocoa sounds like the old joke about how Canadians apologize when you step on their shoes: "I felt ashamed as I was going everywhere with my American passport. It was just like, 'I'm so sorry.' . . . After the last election, I kind of lost faith in what we Americans are doing in our country."

Even many Canadians recognize that theirs is a faithless country compared with America. Not just in terms of religious belief—though they are much less fervent. As *National Post* columnist Andrew Coyne recently wrote in a piece chiding his countrymen for regarding American patriotism as cheap sentiment, "You see, in Canada we gave up believing years ago: in religion, in ideals, in much of anything, really. Secure as we were under the American defense umbrella, we were infantilized; having no need to defend ourselves, we could not understand why anyone else would have more. Or perhaps it was this: having renounced even the wish to defend ourselves, having absorbed the notion that the country could be destroyed at any moment by a vote of half the population of one province [Quebec], what was left to believe?"

There are some American expats, however, who are of more robust stock. I journey out to a hippie-leftover, New Agey enclave on British Columbia's far western shore, Quadra Island, where I actually smell spliffy smoke on the ferry ride over. At the island's edge lies the Heriot Bay Inn, owned by American Lorraine Wright. She bought it last year after moving north a while ago, partly for business opportunities, partly because of the political climate back home.

On this island, natural beauty surrounds us. Nick, her boat captain (she also owns a whale- and grizzly-watching adventure tours business) takes me out through choppy coastal sounds to deliver explosives to a remote construction site, since he doubles as a water taxi in the off-season. We look for sea lions and seals, which the locals call "rock sausages." They often serve as finger food for transient killer whales.

One night in Wright's wood-paneled, maritime-themed bar, I meet her cast of regulars. There's the bar curmudgeon Bruce, who shakes hands with one that has lost a finger to a circular saw. He seems to like being on my tab, but spends most of the night whispering anti-Americanisms in my ear. There's oyster farmer Brian, whose border collie lolls between the tables. He offers to call up a Vietnam draft dodger friend who might make a good interview, though the friend's not home, just as he wasn't when his country called.

Lorraine, who has a large personality and a barbed wit, blows in like a northerly in an orange Arc'teryx jacket. We tuck into a discreet corner where the barmaid keeps finding us with a steady supply of my whiskeys (bourbon, not Canadian—drink American!) and her cosmopolitans. For the next four hours, I and this former surfer girl from California, born to a Republican family before she became a bleeding heart, go at it like two drunks in a bar fight, which come to think of it, we half resemble.

She calls herself a "compassionate capitalist" and clowns on my old Clinton-bashing pieces, which she's pulled off the Internet. I try my level best to make her feel like Benedict Arnold, who lost the fight when we invaded Quebec during the Revolution, before he slunk off to England. Instant friends, with similar sensibilities, we throw flurries of rabbit and kidney punches. But just when I think my roundhouse is going to drop her like a sack of potatoes—after I posit that real Americans, whatever their political persuasion, are fighters, not runners—Wright clocks me with this:

"America is built on people leaving places. We're a country of people who've left. Constitutionally, the pursuit of happiness is something we not only honor, but something we legally protect. This ain't Russia. I don't have to stay. This ain't Cuba. I can leave.

"In fact, find me one American who would make me stay and fight. They'd say no, go, do what's right for you. I found happiness here. I'll be in BC the rest of my life. I pray to God that I don't die somewhere else, that I'm not vacationing somewhere when I die, because that would bum me out. . . .

"Pursue your happiness. We were the first country to do it. And we live for that, the fact that people have personal rights. Go where you want. Do what you want. The fact that I chose Canada is almost a bigger embodiment of the American dream. . . . I still love America."

"So you're saying being unpatriotic is an act of patriotism?" I counter, though my heart is no longer in it.

"I've had too many cocktails for that one," Wright says.

I settle the tab, and the next morning I'm off, promising that someday I'll come back to visit with my family. By then, with any luck, she'll have had a chance to explain America to her new countrymen.

END OF THE ROGUE

The Pirate Kingfish Savors
His Last Taste of Freedom

I am standing in the kitchen of the one they call the Pirate Kingfish. It's two weeks before the verdict will be delivered in Edwin Edwards's corruption trial, and after nagging entreaties, the former Democratic governor of Louisiana has permitted a peek into what could be his last days as a free man ("Get on down hee-ahh," he grudgingly acceded over the phone).

Edwards is late for our afternoon appointment, so I'm grilling George, his cook, a liberally tattooed ex-con. As George sings the guv'nah's hosannas while stabbing a strawberry piecrust with a fork, a haggard Edwards walks in, tossing his keys on the counter. Back from a third day of jury deliberations, he looks unhappy to have a visitor. I don't wait for an introduction before presumptuously making chummy. I inform Edwards that George, here, has allowed me to rifle through Edwards's underwear drawers. Edwards does not offer a courtesy smile, and instead fixes me with a stare through those possumlike orbs that served him so well during governor's mansion poker games. "It don't both-ahhh me none," he shrugs. "Everybody else does."

In Louisiana, there have always been three truisms: (A) No matter how ugly a truth you visit upon a native (the state's obesity and syphilis rates are among the nation's highest, while livability and literacy rates are the lowest), they'll still give thanks to the Lord for creating Mississippi; (B) If one finds oneself at a fine dining establishment and is tempted to rely on the "How to Eat Crawfish" instruction poster, one better stick to shrimp, in the interest of avoiding ridicule; and (C) If one is in the employ of the U.S. Attorney's office, one will be regarded as too sluggish, too stupid, or too unlucky to catch Edwin Edwards.

Or so it seemed—until Tuesday. That's when Edwards sat impassively in the Russell B. Long federal courthouse, where a portrait of the son of Huey Long (the original Kingfish) keeps sentry over the lobby. There, a jury convicted Edwards, the only person to ever serve four terms as governor of Louisiana, of seventeen counts of racketeering, money laundering, conspiracy, and extortion. It's ironic perhaps that the man often likened to a riverboat gambler (who has slipped the feds in nearly two dozen investigations, as well as two corruption trials in the 1980s) is finally headed up the river for attempting to rig the disbursement of state riverboat casino licenses.

On the courthouse steps, Edwards looked the part of the vanquished gladiator as he stood stoically with his wife, Candy, herself looking glum in an otherwise festive pink pantsuit. Only four years ago at the building's ribbon-cutting, then-Governor Edwards joked that the ceremony was "my first invitation to a federal courthouse not delivered by U.S. marshals." It was a typical Edwards line: no fat, black-humored, enhanced by his velveteen Cajun accent. A political Houdini, Edwards has always had a knack for making use of his worst liability (the perception that he's crooked) and wrestling it into submission in a sort of rhetorical aikido: he absorbs the momentum of the suspicion, then flips it to his advantage.

The perception has given him ample opportunity to employ his wit, which amuses even his enemies—a large segment of his audience. In 1983, in the course of a single campaign against the vanilla incumbent Dave Treen, Edwards pulled a hat trick, formulating the three most entertaining lines ever uttered by an American politician. The deliberative Treen, he said, was so slow, "he takes an hour and a half to watch *60 Minutes.*" While Treen had surmised that if Edwards won, he'd be up to his armpits in the public cookie jar, Edwards rejoined that if voters reelected the ineffectual Treen, "there'll be nothing left to steal." Then, after it became apparent he would steamroll Treen, Edwards boasted that the only way he could lose was "if I get caught in bed with a dead girl or a live boy."

After the verdict, however, it was hard to tell if Edwards was joking. "I have lived seventy-two years of my life within the system," he said of the decision, "and I will live the rest of my life within the system." If Edwards isn't in peak comic form, it's certainly understandable. For a devoted gambler who has reaped millions rolling lucky numbers down the fast felt of Las Vegas craps tables, Edwards faced a series of daunting numbers that didn't hold much promise. A two-year FBI investigation, complete with surveillance tapes and wiretaps, yielded twenty-six thousand recorded conversations, five thousand of which involved Edwards. This resulted in a thirty-three-count indictment against Edwards and six codefendants (including his son Stephen), involving six extortion schemes in connection with fifteen riverboat casino licenses.

The four-and-a-half-month trial featured sixty-six prosecution witnesses, three of whom turned state's evidence against Edwards. Only one of those witnesses (Eddie DeBartolo Jr., former owner of the San Francisco 49ers), could directly link Edwards to an extortion attempt, and even then it was somewhat ambiguous, since in Louisiana, one man's graft is another's "consulting fee." DeBartolo testified that Edwards, by then out of office, scribbled a number—$400,000— on a piece of paper in a Radisson hotel bar, indicating what it would take for him to wield his influence with the state Gaming Control Board to approve DeBartolo's casino license. The feds failed to record this conversation, but they were willing to take the word of DeBartolo—which Edwards says isn't good for much. Edwards is heard on tape grousing that DeBartolo skipped out on a half-million-dollar gambling debt, a dishonorable act to a former governor who paid his casino tabs with suitcases of cash—a habit that did not go unnoticed by investigators.

But the numbers that really mattered were those returned by the jury: two defendants acquitted, the other five guilty (including Edwards's son). Edwards himself was convicted on seventeen of twenty-six counts, for a potential maximum sentence of 250 years. To frame that horror in Edwardsian terms: if it were possible for the seventy-two-year-old Edwards to outlive the sentence, his thirty-five-year-old wife, Candy, would no longer be less than half his age, as is commonly emphasized, but nine-tenths of it. Not that he has any intention of letting that happen. Edwards has always been a realist, and figures he has only six to ten years left of "biblically allotted time."

Local handicappers aren't yet making book on Edwards's chances for appeal, but if ever there was a case filled with irregularities, this was it. While most defendants are convicted by twelve angry jurors, Edwards had only eleven, since Juror No. 68 (as he was known under the judge's anonymity order) was bounced in the middle of deliberations after a three-day logjam of sealed notes and closed-door huddles. The local media had a field day speculating why—everything from the juror being a piney-woods pew-jumper whose religious beliefs prevented him from judging others, to his being ostracized by his fellow jurors for refusing to deliberate. Whatever the reason, everyone generally agrees he was kindly predisposed toward Edwards, and one dissenting voice is all it takes to hang a jury.

Another possible reason for appeal concerns the impetuses for wiretapping Edwards in the first place. The original order came as a result of tips to the feds by Michael and Patrick Graham, two brothers who'd been investigated for everything from phony real estate development schemes to forgery. In their new line of work as FBI informants, one of the brothers admitted that they'd been given immunity for more crimes than they could remember committing. The wiretaps were allowed to continue largely because, an FBI agent conceded in testimony, he wrongly established in affidavits that Edwards had bribed five members of the Gaming Control Board. "I cannot say Edwin Edwards passed money to anyone," said the agent. That's hardly surprising. Most veteran Edwards watchers will tell you the former governor is way too greedy to pass along a bribe.

From there, all manner of baroque absurdities abounded. Almost every transaction under investigation involved large amounts of cash hidden in strange places. There was cash carried in briefcases and worn in money vests, stashed under Jacuzzis and frozen duck carcasses, and deposited for pickup in dumpsters and ash bins. In one cash-carrying point of contention, an Edwards attorney argued that his client couldn't have worn a money belt filled with $400,000 of DeBartolo's money while walking through the San Francisco airport, since he'd have been stopped for looking "like the Michelin Man."

Edwards on tape is as clipped and cagey as ever, leaving many of the schemes open to interpretation. But some of his alleged bagmen had verbal tendencies that seemed to cast a shadow on the rectitude of their "consulting" arrangements. At one point his son Stephen can be heard wondering of a prospective business acquaintance, "You don't think that motherfucker could be wired?" And Bobby Johnson, another Edwards crony, employed similar subtlety when informing a casino applicant that he'd be requiring 12.5 percent ownership to make the deal happen: "I ain't being an iron ass, but I mean, I want a piece of that."

Johnson, a self-made cement magnate who used to live in a

cardboard box under a bridge, was not the sharpest Ginsu in the knife block. His own attorney called him a "buffoon." When Johnson begged out in the middle of the trial so that he could have quintuple bypass surgery, the crotchety Judge Frank Polozola (not-so-affectionately nicknamed "Ayatollah" after threatening to jail squabbling attorneys and barking at reporters for tromping through courthouse flowerbeds) was rebuffed when he offered to let Johnson communicate with the court through an Internet hookup. Impossible, Johnson's attorney said, because Johnson could neither read nor write.

For someone as dim as Johnson, it would seem a formidable task to locate a jury of his peers. But the court managed. When deliberations began, one juror asked the judge for a dictionary to determine the meaning of "extortion." Another jury note inquired, "Do you become a part of a conspiracy if you except [sic] extortion money along with others?"

But if jurors weren't easily educated, neither were they easily charmed. Edwards tried, tossing off snappy rejoinders on the stand, such as when he was asked if he'd been lying throughout his testimony. "No," he replied, "and if I were, you've got to assume I wouldn't be telling you."

Many longtime Edwards watchers, including his biographer John Maginnis, say Edwards's shtick is now shopworn. It lacks the spark and imagination of, say, his mideighties courtroom performances, when he was on trial (and eventually acquitted) for profiting off state hospital contracts. Back then, Edwards rolled up to court in a horse-drawn buggy in order to illustrate the slow wheels of justice. And a younger, sprier Edwards fearlessly taunted his tormentor, U.S. Attorney John Volz, once rising to his feet for a toast in a French Quarter bar while trilling, "When my moods are over, and my time has come to pass, I hope they bury me upside down, so Volz can kiss my ass."

It's perhaps a measure of his fading potency that even his mortal enemies sound a tad nostalgic after his conviction. "It's good for the state," says Volz, who suffered a heart attack and lost two judgeships in the fallout after losing to Edwards in federal court. "Still," adds Volz, "we're seeing the end of an era. There'll never be another Edwin Edwards in our generation."

Even David Duke, whom Edwards felt a certain camaraderie with, as they were "both wizards under the sheets," passes up the obvious gloat. Edwards trounced Duke in the 1991 gubernatorial election as skeptical voters rallied behind the bumper sticker VOTE FOR THE CROOK, IT'S IMPORTANT. Duke's political career has waned ever since, but he says, "As much as I dislike Edwards, I think I dislike the wiretapping federal government a lot worse."

Times-Picayune readers seemed to agree. When, during the trial, the paper polled its readership in an Edwards referendum that ran right next to a question about banning silly string from parade routes, readers came back three to one in Edwards's defense. Such tolerance of Edwards is born not only of his considerable contributions to Louisiana civic life (rewriting the constitution, instituting open primaries, funding patronage jobs and services on the backs of once-booming oil companies) but also for his sensibility. For while every discount A. J. Liebling who parachutes into the state likes to establish that Louisiana is ruled by scampish Cajun kings, tin-pot Napoleons, and back-slapping, nut-cutting populists of the Long stripe, it is a stereotype that historically has been, well, sort of true.

Novelist Walker Percy, a native, best explained the effects of cross-cultural corruption in the port city of New Orleans: "Unfortunately and all too often, the Latins learned Anglo-Saxon racial morality and the Americans learned Latin political morality. The fruit of such a mismatch is something to behold: Baptist governors and state legislators who loot the state with Catholic gaiety and Protestant industry." Edwards, unlike Huey and Earl Long, was never a Baptist (he's a nondenominational churchgoer, by way of Catholicism, by way of the Nazarenes, which is to say, he's covered his bases).

It's no small wonder why most pre-verdict discussions of Edwards's guilt or innocence, outside the courtroom, were purely academic. Much more important than "Did he do it?" was "Would he get caught?" As one of his trial-lawyer boosters snorted when I inquired what he thought of Edwards's guilt, "Hell yeah, he's a crook, but what's that got to do with anything?"

The electorate's collective yawn over such matters has historically meant a teeter-totter between Long-style populists and their less entertaining reformer counterparts. But even the latter camp, in Louisiana, can sometimes use peculiar methods. Liebling once related how Cousin Horace, his pseudonymous source, was so overcome with disgust for Long's corruption that in a flare-up of civic consciousness, he joined like-minded reformers to raise funds to bribe the legislature to impeach him. Louisiana is probably one of the few places in the country where Potch Didier, a sheriff from Edwards's native Avoyelles Parish, could win reelection while serving a sentence in his own jail. Likewise, the last three insurance commissioners have been indicted, including Jim Brown, the current one, who, as luck would have it, is a codefendant with Edwards in an upcoming state insurance corruption trial—yet another jurisprudence nightmare on Edwards's horizon.

Everywhere one turns, it seems, a whiff of larceny permeates. You sense it in the thirty-four-story state capital building in Baton Rouge, where Long fell either to an assassin's bullet or to his bodyguards' return fire—or, if the woman standing next to me fingering the bullet holes in the wall is to be believed, by agents of Franklin D. Roosevelt, who was concerned the Kingfish would take over the world as he had Louisiana. Throughout the edifice, inmates from the Dixon Correctional Institute swab the floors, while future inmates populate the legislative chambers (forty-eight public officials were indicted in 1998 alone).

You also sense it pushing to the outskirts of the city, to Edwards's home in a gated golf course community that also boasts as residents Master P, C-Murder, and other felonious rappers from the No Limit empire, with whom Edwards has not yet had occasion to barbecue. Inside the tastefully decorated house, George the cook, a former governor's mansion trusty whom Edwards pardoned for his role in a robbery, holds down the kitchen.

George is whipping up strawberry and lemon icebox pies for that evening's "defendant's sup-pahhh," a regular ritual the accused and their attorneys engage in while waiting for the verdict. Andrew Martin, one of Edwards's codefendants, who like Edwards will shortly be convicted on multiple counts of racketeering, is also mulling about the kitchen, assuring me that though I'm not invited to stay, all I'll be missing is crab roti, shrimp as thick as a midget's forearms, and people "getting drunk, singing, and telling dirty jokes—the usual routine."

As Edwards and I retreat to his living room and sink into his chenille sofa, my eyes pass over the built-in shelves which hold beautiful leather-bound books, the spines of which appear to have never been cracked. There's *A Stillness at Appomattox, Catch-22,* and *All the King's Men*—the story of a gifted populist Southern governor who gains the love of the people, but who suffers a fall when reverting to bribery and intimidation in the service of his selfish ambitions.

Edwards takes a while to warm up, since Judge Ayatollah has everybody spooked with his restrictive gag order prohibiting the trial's players from talking to the media. "You have to understand," Edwards says, "I can't say a damn thing." But after assuring Edwards that I won't publish until after the verdict, he relaxes, as he's never been too great a stickler for other people's rules. Of the wiretaps, which ultimately did him in, Edwards tries to take lemons and make lemon icebox pie. "Fortunately," he says, "there was nothing derogatory towards anybody—no use of racial slurs, or threats of violence, or references to drug trafficking or anything like that." Regarding the betrayals of old friends who flipped for the state, Edwards tries to remain a forgiving Christian, though he suggests their motivation to testify was dictated by something other than veracity. "There's no telling how much money [the feds] could have gotten out of [Eddie DeBartolo]." Edwards says. "He's worth four hundred to five hundred million dollars, but only had to pay a fine which is the equivalent of you paying twenty-five dollars. They gave him probation and no jail time, so what the hell? I'm not prepared to say I wouldn't do it myself if I was in that situation."

When discussing other incidentals that don't bode particularly well for him, he employs the Socratic method. Of the allegations that he made plans to profiteer while still governor, with payments deferred until he got out of office, he is incredulous: "You think if I was the kind of person who wanted to take a bribe, I'd do it on the *installment* basis?" Maintaining that he was being paid consulting fees from casino applicants, Edwards notes that in some cases, he was actually paid more money than he allegedly extorted. "If a person kidnaps your child and sends a note for a $2 million ransom," he says, "do you send him $2.2 million?"

Of payoffs being left in dumpsters, Edwards bristles with contempt. "Nobody's gonna put one hundred thousand dollars in a paper bag in an ash dumpster and not wait around to see who picks it up. Do *you* believe that?"

I ask Edwards if the stress of the trial has caused him to lose any sleep. "Hell no," he says. "I sleep like a baby." Though he wouldn't make a prediction as to the outcome of his case ("I don't want to look like some stupid ass") he had not made much preparation to go to prison: "Not financially, not psychologically, not nothing."

We talk a bit of politics, specifically about some of the good-government reformers on the ascent of late. "[They] are all passing fancies," Edwards dismisses. "They sound good. They look good in the press. But they accomplish nothing." Edwards realizes the media no longer rewards politicians for flamboyance and eccentric individualism. He indicates that the new climate would suffocate Huey Long or Uncle Earl or maybe even a young Edwin Edwards. "I'll draw the last breath of a dying breed of populist governor," he sighs.

As for the charge that Edwards spent most of his time on the stand committing perjury, he says doing so to escape prison wouldn't be worth "condemning my soul to some never-ending hell of pain and agony and torture for lying under oath." When I suggest Edwards should become a Baptist, like the Longs, whose beliefs would not dictate that one is banished from the Kingdom for fibbing in a courtroom, Edwards scoffs. "If you're one of those once-in-grace-always-in-grace Baptists, maybe you could get away with it," he says. "But I don't know if I could ever get to the grace, so that wouldn't do me any good."

If there is one thing that Edwards the gladiator and gambler does not seem to cotton to, it's all these weak sisters taking pity on him. "Everybody was surrounding me patting me on the shoulder saying, 'I'm sorry you have to go through all this,'" he says of his days on the stand. "Hell, I'm having fun. The adrenaline flows. It's the clash of minds—the challenge. Why did Hillary climb Mount Everest—because it's there. I'd rather spend my time doing something else, but if I've got to spend my time doing this, let's have at it."

While I'm expected to leave before the "defendant's sup-pahh," I catch up with Edwards in court the next day. When we reconvene in the courthouse cafeteria, we're joined by his adult spitfire daughters, Victoria and Anna. Anna playfully shakes me down, telling me if I intend to interview her father, I ought to pay for breakfast. Edwards doesn't seem concerned. He's too busy working the roomful of reporters, who eagerly serve as punch-line fodder when he inquires how they got through security or whether they intend to find respectable employment.

As he sits down at a Formica table, forking a Styrofoam plateful of bacon, eggs, and grits, Edwards grows paranoid. The cafeteria is crawling with prosecutors, and he's at least trying to observe the spirit of the Ayatollah's gag order, if not the letter. "I can't be seen talking to you while you're writing," he says, prompting me to drop my notebook under the table.

To be safe, we take it outside, and as we walk down the courthouse steps, Edwards looks longingly at the microphoned media corral. He has been forbidden by the Ayatollah to play to the cameras, where he's always done his best work. If it wasn't for the gag order, he says, "I'd be having a press conference every day." Though Edwards hasn't been of much use to the media lately, one reporter takes a shot anyway. "Governor," he yells, "how have you been spending your time?"

"Miserably," says Edwards, pointing to me. "Look who I'm spending it with."

We adjourn to the parking lot, along with Edwards's daughters. The four of us chat in Victoria's Dodge Durango, well out of earshot of nettlesome prosecutors. "Daddy, why don't we take a ride?" Victoria offers. As we briefly tool around downtown, Victoria points nonchalantly: "That's where I used to live."

There's a fence around the grounds now, though there wasn't when Edwards was governor. He and his daughters say that during his tenure, the house was filled with an endless stream of legislators and supplicants who had all-access passes to the governor. Sometimes they'd be lined up in the anterooms, sipping iced tea while waiting. One might even run into uninvited voters, who would sometimes knock on the mansion door and be invited to stay for lunch. But it's different now—with the fence and Edwards's successor, Mike Foster, a millionaire sugar heir and self-proclaimed reformer, whose campaign ads touted that he wasn't just another pretty face. "He sure isn't," quips Victoria.

Before I leave Baton Rouge, there is one more mission to carry out with Edwin Edwards. It involves the Caesar matter. If there was any doubt that the fates have decided to kick in Fast Eddie's slats, Caesar is barely living proof. It seems that on the last day of closing arguments, George the cook brought the Edwards's seven-year-old yellow Lab, Caesar, down to their lawyers' quarters to eat lunch with Edwin and Candy. But on the walk back to the courthouse, a vehicle plowed into the dog, then fled the scene (nobody knows who was driving, but some have suggested overzealous prosecutors). The car launched poor Caesar airborne, and when he hit the ground, he suffered everything from a scleral hemorrhage in his eye to a broken hip.

For a week, Caesar has been laid up at the LSU veterinary medical clinic, and now we're off to bring him home. But Edwin informs me at his house that we'll be taking separate vehicles, as he must run an undisclosed errand. To make the most use of my interview time, I suggest Candy ride with me. Edwin consents, but looks pained, as one suspects many younger men would like to part her from his company. If Candy were a refreshing beverage, she'd be sweet tea. She's all blonde drawl and tanned legs, and today she is sporting linen shorts and an aquamarine shirt knotted over her taut midriff.

As Candy takes the wheel of my rental car so I can take notes, our heads pop like dashboard ornaments while she acclimates herself to my brakes. Edwin has warned her not to talk about the trial on account of the Ayatollah. So she doesn't. Instead, she talks about his prostate gland. It seems Edwin's errand involves going to give blood for a PSA test. "He doesn't have prostate cancer or anything," assures Candy. But, she says, searching for the correct medical terminology, "It's *large*. Most older men have enlarged prostates."

The Edwardses have been married for six years (they met when Candy was twenty-five). During that time, she has endured all manner of obloquy concerning her husband—from the unsubstantiated charges that he removed expensive furnishings from the governor's mansion, to tales of his unrepentant womanizing (he reportedly used to cruise LSU's sorority row in the governor's limo). But that, Candy says, was all "B.C.," their shorthand for Before Candy. "Since the day I've met him," she says, "he's been wonderful."

While Candy is not one to dwell on the specter of Edwin's going to prison (she had a jitterbug band all picked out for the post-verdict victory party), she does say Edwin told her that if he was incarcerated, "'You're going to need to go on with your life,'" she says, recoiling. "Like go on and find somebody else! As soon as he tells me that, I'm crushed. I just immediately break down."

When we arrive at the veterinary clinic, Caesar is in bad shape— a shaved, stitched heap of surgical screws and hip plates. He looks fairly despondent. Then he sees Candy. She immediately sets about rubbing his rose petal ears, showering him in baby talk ("You're my baby," "How's my baby?," etc.), which he seems to enjoy—and who wouldn't?

A while later, Edwin walks through the door and Candy's sugary drawl goes up an octave when she peppers Caesar with, "Wanna see Poppy?" The dog's brush-thumping tail indicates that he does. But when Edwin approaches the cage, he is all manly vinegar.

"Git up," he barks, half mockingly.

"Look," Candy says to Edwin, displaying the purple LSU kerchief around Caesar's neck, "a keepsake."

"I'll have a keepsake," Edwards cracks dryly, "a canceled check."

For Caesar to walk out to the car, a nurse has to hammock a towel around his groin area while pulling up on both ends, providing support. As we hobble through the waiting room, an old woman tending her cat cries out to Edwards, "Give 'em hell, Guv'nah."

Once outside, Caesar slowly limps over to a patch of grass and sniffs the ground in anticipation of urination, though his schwantz is aimed a bit too easterly from the pressure of the towel against it. While Edwards conspires with Candy about how to get Caesar into the vehicle, an onlooker approaches Edwards and offers her support. "I admire you," she says. "I'm one of your fans. You're going to beat the whole damn bunch of them."

Edwards neither smiles, nor does he hold his characteristic poker face. Instead, he wheels around, eyes afire, and thunders to his amen corner, "Let me tell you what, in America, nobody should be subjected to what I've been subjected to unless you're suspected of murdahh or espionage."

"People are out to get you," the woman concurs.

"They've been after it for a long time," Edwards says, permitting a slight grin.

As the woman departs, Edwards falls into preoccupied silence. He might be thinking about the well-being of his young wife, or the realities of imprisonment, or his prostate slowly growing to the size of a tangelo. Or maybe he's not thinking at all, as he watches Caesar, a creaky old yellow dog, trying to gain his balance in the weeds without squirting down his leg.

ARNOLD ÜBER ALLES

The Wild, Final Days of the Schwarzenegger Campaign

San Diego, California

It seems like only yesterday that I was jetting around California with Arnold Schwarzenegger, enjoying one-on-one access, eating Arnold's food, laughing at Arnold's jokes, choking on Arnold's cigar smoke. In fact, it was a year ago, when Arnold was campaigning for his ballot initiative promoting after-school activities. Back then, he was running a modest little jobs program for former Pete Wilson aides. Now, five days before the 2003 recall election, at the kickoff of his home-stretch bus tour at the San Diego Convention Center, it's apparent that Schwarzenegger has gone Hollywood. There are so many staffers on the ground that it's hard to know who to suck up to.

I start with a woman standing by a velvet rope, behind which sit two hundred journalists' suitcases. It's a bad call. "I'm just the luggage lady," she says. "I'm a hanger-on. I used to be with [former candidate] Bill Simon." I have better luck with Rob Gluck, a Troy Aikman doppelganger who describes Schwarzenegger's warp-speed, two-month campaign for governor of California as having to "lay track full speed ahead as fast as we can, trying to get to the Pacific before the train does." Gluck is part of a small but all-powerful clique within the campaign known as the Murphy Mafia. It's a reference to their leader, Mike Murphy, the evil genius behind John McCain's presidential bid. Three years ago, Murphy launched McCain's Straight Talk Express, the rolling cocktail party in which journalists engaged in back-slapping, glad-handing, and finally tearful goodbyes with the candidate. Now, Murphy has launched what will be nicknamed the No Talk Express—in which he invites hundreds of access-starved journos along for the ride, then essentially tells them to piss off.

It's not a dumb strategy, considering the circumstances. There are some days in the campaign business when it would be easiest for an aide to wake up, put on her best dress, then step in front of a bus. Today in Arnold World is one of those days. The morning sees charges that Schwarzenegger is an ass-grabbing lout. By evening, he'll stand accused of loving Adolf Hitler. As one colleague puts it, "Any day spent on the trail talking about Adolf Hitler is not a good day."

The *Los Angeles Times* kicks things off with a morning story in which six different women allege Arnold's nonconsensual touching. While four of the six remain unnamed, and none has filed legal action, the *Times* claims that even if their story smells like a ninth-inning political black-bag job, none of Schwarzenegger's opponents helped the paper find the women. The charges involve several breast grabs, a hand-under-the-skirt buttock clinch, an elevator groping, a simulated sex act, and several mature-language propositions too clinical to replicate here. These charges, and some that follow them, are enough to convince me—someone who likes Arnold, thinks he's utterly charming, deceptively smart, and a charismatic leader—to rethink my drink. Now I'm quite prepared to believe that despite his good qualities, he's additionally a big creep, to borrow a coinage.

But critical thinking isn't in evidence at the convention center during Schwarzenegger's final-swing kickoff rally. Outside the building, Christian schoolgirls who say they're slightly troubled that Arnold is "pro-abortion" still squeal like he's the lost Backstreet Boy and wear pro-Arnold bumper stickers on the perky derrieres of their jeans (not a visual the campaign desires today). When I charge into a cluster of stageside Arnold supporters, some of whom are holding REMARKABLE WOMEN JOIN ARNOLD signs, and ask them about the charges, they are uniformly dismissive: "It's just the usual dirt they dredge up before an election. . . . It's a bunch of hooey. . . . You got to do something while you're in an elevator. . . . The Hollywood agenda is just different than what we're used to."

Schwarzenegger takes the stage to raucous applause. Even at his age (fifty-six), his face and body look chiseled from Sheetrock, never mind that the hair and overly taut skin are a tint not found in nature, the color of an apricot Fruit Roll-Up. He sounds all his usual campaign themes about rescinding the car tax and reforming workers' compensation. He delivers his money lines: "Gray Davis has terminated jobs! Gray Davis has terminated opportunities! Now it is time that we terminate him!" And he delivers the money lines of others:

"We are mad as hell and we're not going to take it anymore!" Of the morning papers, he says that "the people of Cal-eee-for-nee-ah can see through this trash politics."

But then he admits that it is true he has "behaved badly" sometimes. The crowd titters, expecting him to let himself off the hook, possibly with one of his corny movie one-liners, like "Game ov-ahhh" or "Milk is for babies." But instead, he goes earnest, saying that on movie sets, he may have done things that he thought then were "playful," but that "now I recognize that I offended people." To them, he says, "I'm deeply sorry about dat, and I apologize." If elected, "I will be a champion for da women. I hope dat dey will give me the chance to prove dat."

It's a remarkable moment, even by the standards of the Remarkable Women for Arnold. Except it serves as a Rorschach test. To Arnold supporters, it's a heartfelt apology, a tidy way to put an end to something ugly before it begins. To journalists, it's waving the red cape. With a general apology, he has tacitly admitted specifics, meaning that Topic A for the rest of the election won't be the economy, or offshore drilling, or other things we couldn't care less about.

He concludes the speech with his signature "I'll be back," which makes little sense in this context but pleases the crowd anyway. Then Arnold's tour bus, which looks like it was spray-painted by Leni Riefenstahl, as the entire side bears Arnold's oversize Aryan mug looking off beatifically into the middle distance, drives up behind the stage. The crowd nearly keels over from excitement. As the arena is filled with his theme song, Twisted Sister's "We're Not Gonna Take It," Arnold boards the bus, hangs out the door, and shoots thumbs-up to everyone. The bus does a racetrack pattern around the now stampeding crowd before taking off out the back of the arena.

Reporters take off after him, hurriedly mounting our buses. All the buses on the tour are named after Arnold movies. His own tricked-out coach is "The Running Man," while his slightly less elaborate VIP bus is "Total Recall" (get it?). The wags in Arnold's press shop titled the media buses "Predator 1–4." But we get the last laugh. In light of the new allegations, we call them "Sexual Predator 1–4."

I'm initially assigned to Bus 2, which in the social pecking order ranks behind Bus 1 (TV anchors, big-circulation print reporters, favored California press) and ahead of Buses 3 and 4 (technical people and leftover foreign press, respectively). Bus 4, Gluck tells me, "is like that room in *Animal House* where all the uncool kids kept getting steered." Foreign reporters, the campaign constantly reminds us, won't get Arnold any votes in California.

My bus is initially acceptable. Our "bus captain," Patrick Dorinson, a former flack for a failing energy company, does a flawless Arianna Huffington impression, which he regularly treats us to over the PA system: "Oooo, sir! That's such a good idea. Let's have a hand for ze man vith ze good idea! I'm going to put that idea in my new constitution." I take a seat next to some Japanese TV people, who do their best to communicate with me in Godzilla-movie English. An Asahi TV producer tells me Arnold is big in Japan, where he does Cup O' Noodles soup and energy-drink commercials. He says they call him "Schwa-Chan," which loosely translates as "childish boy." Since it is fairly clear early on that access to Arnold will be next to nil, journalists interview other journalists from foreign countries. When my seatmate's colleague starts interviewing the French documentary crew in front of me, the producer feels compelled to quickly get his face out of the shot. He dives into my lap, barking orders in Japanese which are muffled in my crotch. It leaves me with steely resolve to get off this bus and make it onto Sexual Predator 1.

At the next stop, the Orange County Fairgrounds, it's a homer conservative crowd. But still, the freaks are out in force at presidential campaign levels of weirdness. A man with two gold teeth in an otherwise toothless mouth stalks the grounds yelling "Free Tommy Chong!" An elderly Vietnamese albino in a flowing ceremonial robe walks around pumping a pro-Arnold sign but speaks no English. I fall in with Alan Schwartz, an audio-visual technician in a Triumph motorcycle jacket.

He's a Democrat who has come to torment Arnold over the allegations, though even he admits he probably couldn't stomach voting for Gray Davis again. Schwartz holds a visually complicated magic marker sign that says GOP, OUI—that last bit being a reference to an ancient *Oui* magazine article in which Arnold explained his dabbling in group sex. Between the *G* and the first *O*, Schwartz inserted a small *r*, and after the *P* he added a small *e*—making it "GrOPe" to the eagle-eyed. As Arnold stumps, Schwartz gets a cool reception. Arnold supporters yell at him to take down his sign and to "sit on it," and tell him his "penmanship sucks." Schwartz is convinced he's drawing extra heat because "Oui" is French, and this is a freedom-fries-eating crowd. So he subtly mocks them back. When one befuddled woman reads his sign, Schwartz says, "It's French and subliminal." Yeah, she says, catching on, "it means, 'You're a jackass.'"

As Arnold crescendos, telling the crowd how much more they are paying in car taxes for each specific make and model, Schwartz winces, yelling, "How much is a burger at Planet Hollywood [a restaurant chain in which Arnold once owned an interest]?" But then Schwartz gets upstaged by the big finish. "Let me show you exactly what we are going to do to de car tax when we get to Sacramento," says Arnold. He points to an empty parking lot near the crowd, where a lonely Oldsmobile sits, inscribed with the words CAR TAX. A crane right next to the car crushes it with a wrecking ball. Schwartz is struck dumb.

It's part of the intended effect. Mike Murphy tells me that when he initially talked to Arnold's pyro people about the stunt, the campaign advance guys thought it was "the scariest thing in the world. But to Hollywood stunt guys, blowing up a car is like going to Mc-Donald's. They said, 'What kind of car?' and 'Do you want anybody in it when it blows up?'" Murphy determined an explosion posed too many safety risks, and "though it broke my heart," he settled for the wrecking ball.

Impressive as it is, however, Hollywood spectacle can't completely inoculate the campaign. On the far end of the parking lot, a media feeding frenzy is under way. A new woman has materialized, claiming that back in 1978 one of Arnold's friends picked her up and pinned her against a wall while Arnold yelled from his vehicle that he was going to rape her, after which she managed to run away. As we labor to get the details, Schwarzenegger staffers yell that "the buses are leaving." Immediately, they go into debunk mode, and in this case, it's relatively easy, since the woman showed up with a bunch of other women in matching WORKING WOMEN VOTE T-shirts. They are affiliated with a union that has vowed to defeat the recall. Whether or not her story is true (the campaign denies this one categorically) we don't have time to tell. The buses are leaving. And our Quiznos sandwiches are getting cold.

In a strange way, the new allegations are a good break for the campaign. It allows them to perfect their elegantly simple defense strategy: Whatever happens, blame Gray Davis or the *Los Angeles Times*. It is a strategy they will employ with nearly every allegation (fifteen women will come forward in all). The campaign will try out any number of combinations: Blame the *Los Angeles Times* for opening a can of worms too close to the election, blame Gray Davis for unleashing his Democratic henchmen, who doubtless supplied the tips to the *Los Angeles Times* (this is never proven), blame the *Times* for not spending enough time blaming Gray Davis (they never, for instance, gave wide play to the *New Times*'s charges that temper-tantrum-throwing Davis physically attacks members of his own staff, women included). The campaign does everything, in fact, but blame Gray Davis for reading the *Los Angeles Times*. And this, it turns out, is a devastatingly effective strategy for two reasons: (a) Voters hate the media, and (b) If there's anything Californians hate more than the media, it's Gray Davis.

The next stop, at Riley Elementary School in San Bernardino, gives them a chance to put their plan into action. The school provides the ideal scripted setting. Small people of color are everywhere, eager to meet the action star. The backdrop banner has prints of all their little hands, with an inscription thanking "Mr. Schwarzenegger" for promoting after-school programs. The busload of perpetually trailing alternative candidates, who've attempted to crash the scene in order to generate publicity for their own boutique issues such as limiting population growth and getting junk food out of public schools, have been cleared from the premises. Reporters wishing to talk to them must reach over a tall chain-link fence to shake their hands or receive their literature. It makes us all feel like extras in some sort of Turkish prison movie.

Former NFL player and star of the eighties detective show *Hunter* Fred Dryer comes off the VIP bus to warm up the kids by taking questions about Arnold. They ask if he's married, did he really play the Terminator, what time is this going to be over, and can he run for president? "No," says one child, of the Austrian actor, "he can't run for president, he's from Canada."

The kids love Arnold and Arnold loves the kids, and the staff loves Arnold with the kids because kids don't ask questions about women showing up in parking lots claiming that Arnold threatened to rape them. The same can't be said of the big kids on the press bus. The men who must deal with our queries, the conservative versions of *War Room*–era James Carville and George Stephanopoulos, are Arnold spokesmen Rob Stutzman and Todd Harris. They both do their work brilliantly, and if I ever run for office and get accused of being an ass-grabbing Nazi in the final stretch of a campaign, I will hire them without blinking. Stutzman wears white JOIN ARNOLD golf shirts and is witty, convivial, and downright jolly except when we confront him with new allegations. Then the mercury rises in his face, as he works up a full head of steam about the *L.A. Times*/Gray Davis nexus. He is slowly transformed from a thirty-five-year-old California political consultant into a professional wrestler who has gotten an unfair call and is about to send the pencil-necked referee careening into the turnbuckle.

Todd Harris, thirty-two, is the second highest ranking member of the Murphy Mafia (behind Murphy). He is rumpled and bleary-eyed, with cheese-grater growth and the thousand-yard stare of a campaign aide who has suffered too many box lunches. It doesn't dampen his laconic good humor. He gives his title alternately as "Minister of Truth and Enlightenment" and "First Piece of Meat."

It's in this latter capacity that he is interesting to the press. While we encircle him on the Riley Elementary playground, we ask him exactly zero questions about Arnold's after-school programs. Harris sets about decrying "puke politics," saying that these "ridiculous allegations" bear "the first Democratic fingerprints of union involvement and the Democratic Party." When reporters fall back on the morning paper's allegation, which Arnold has not categorically denied and in some ways has admitted, Harris insists that his boss is taking responsibility for what he has done, "in sharp contrast to the way Gray Davis has handled the budget crisis, the energy crisis, and the special-interest crisis." A reporter asks Harris what he thinks the headlines will be tomorrow. "Harris dazzles media with impromptu press conferences," he deadpans. The piranhas are circling and Harris is the chum bag, but he knows how to end a press conference. "There's beer on every bus and it should be cold," he loudly announces.

But by the time we get to our hotel in Los Angeles, ABC is moving news that a book proposal by *Pumping Iron* director George Butler has Arnold saying in a 1975 interview that he had admiration for Hitler as a public speaker. It doesn't help Arnold that his father was a Nazi, or that the *New York Times* simultaneously reported that Butler claimed in the proposal that he played "Nazi marching songs . . . frequently clicked his heels and pretended to be an SS officer." Arnold immediately went on *World News Tonight* to say he remembered none of this, and that he despised Hitler. But the campaign knows we won't be sated, so at the hotel, they arrange a conference call for us with a pool reporter who attended a fund-raiser where reporters were allowed to ask a few brief questions of Schwarzenegger.

Staffers and reporters crowd into a conference room to get the play-by-play from Joe Mathews of the *L.A. Times.* As we wait, someone asks Harris what was served at the fund-raiser. "I had a little bit more to do today than to worry about whether they served chicken or steak," he replies. Mathews relays both important and ancillary details: Arnold's wife Maria Shriver's expression was "businesslike" while Arnold's was "subdued," "Kenny G walked by," a security guard slammed Mathews's arm in the door, Arnold reported that he'd "misbehaved" and that he didn't "have memory" of many of the alleged incidents. So many incidents had now been alleged that reporters forgot the entire point of the pool—to ask Arnold about Hitler—so Rob Stutzman, Arnold's own staffer, had to ask him what he thought of the Führer. ("I always despised everything Hitler stood for," said Arnold.)

A very long day is winding down. In one corner, I hear a reporter relaying the day's events to his editor ("So then this chick says he threatened to rape her . . .") while in another corner, TV people are making all kinds of Nazi talk. As I exit the conference room, I overhear one more thing: an Arnold staffer saying "I want my mom."

The next day, at the L.A. Arboretum, Rob Stutzman tells us that their campaign has actually jumped a point or two in the polls, despite the allegations. It's insane, but apparently true. The way some of us figure, if Arnold can get on the trail and goose some Jewish women, they might not even need to have the election: Davis will be forced to concede. But my mind, quite honestly, is on more important things. Today, with Stutzman's help, I will leave behind the Japanese lap dancer on Bus 2, and I will make it all the way to Sexual Predator 1.

As I suspected, life is better on Bus 1. Snacks taste fresher, beer is colder. While I miss Patrick, the Arianna impersonator, Stutzman and Harris keep up a constant patter, spinning us silly. Harris even shares his best press-secretary-isms. "Okay, this one's my favorite," he says. "Off the record—'yes'; on the record—'no.'" He also provides complimentary air-sickness bags inscribed with a Ghostbusters crossbar through the words "puke politics." The bag contains a foam rubber Sacramento capital dome and a tin of a substance called "grip goo." I ask what the purpose of the latter is. "None," he says, "it's just fun."

The journos themselves are a lively crew. We receive regular updates from the *New York Post*'s David Li, who keeps us plugged into the latest Siegfried and Roy/white-tiger-mauling developments. ("Great news," says David, "Roy lives!") Our unofficial DJ is Adam Housley from Fox, a rangy former college baseball player who's secure enough in his masculinity to spin ABBA CDs on his laptop without buckling to ridicule.

But the bus's MVP has to be the reporter I spy when we cruise into Bakersfield. A crowd, mistaking us for Arnold's bus, greets us with the kind of enthusiasm Jesus would get if He were touring with the reunited Beatles. The reporter on our bus begins banging on the window with both hands, yelling back at them exultantly, "I'M THE MEDIA! YOU LOVE THE MEDIA!" I can't tell if the sinewy, leathered scribe with bandito facial hair is a former outlaw biker or a former pirate, since he looks like the bastard spawn of Sonny Barger and Jean Lafitte. I settle on the former. "What motorcycle magazine does he write for?" I ask one colleague. "The *New York Times*," they reply. "That's Charlie LeDuff."

Part Native American, part Cajun, LeDuff won a Pulitzer after spending a month in a North Carolina slaughterhouse. Before becoming a journalist at around the age of thirty, he did stints as a teacher, a tannery worker, and a bartender. But he seems to have taken to the sport. Like most good reporters, he inspires sources to perform for him because they like him, but also because he tips them off balance. Throughout the bus tour, Charlie keeps people honest. Once, at a Sacramento bar, he shakes up all the media/staffer chumminess by breaking an empty wineglass on his forehead. ("It's a trick," he tells me later, "the glass is thin up at the top.")

His antics are not only a news-gathering method, but a performance-commentary on the whole preposterous kabuki dance. A mystery woman turns up in Modesto, making vague claims against Arnold, before she is rushed off to a car by a campaign staffer. We all write down her license plate, and LeDuff indicates he's having the plates traced. A few minutes later, on the bus, he acts like he has news when he receives a call. "Here we go, listen," he says urgently, putting his cell phone on speaker. It's one of his friends relating the unspeakable acts he's performed on Schwarzenegger. "I better take this privately," says Charlie.

Another time, in front of the press corps, LeDuff jabs a recorder in Mike Murphy's face and asks, "If Arnold is elected governor, do you vow right now that he will not grope women?" (Murphy feigns choking.) Then there are his fashion choices: bandannas, shorts, and a rival *New York Post* cutoff baseball shirt. But the outfit for which he draws resounding cheers comes when he rolls a pair of pants up to his knees, then parades around as if it's normal. "Why did you do that?" a staffer asks him. "Because of all the bullshit I got to wade around in here," he replies.

It's guys like Charlie that keep Team Arnold rightly reticent to open up to pack questioning, or to give us print guys much chance to slice and dice and weigh Arnold's every word and gesture. When I complain yet again about lack of access, Murphy explains it thus: "You can't be the chef at Nobu, which in the magazine business is what you guys want to be."

For this reason, we are forced to work out extra hard on Arnold's punching bags, Todd Harris and Rob Stutzman, with often ridiculous results. Here is a typical exchange between a reporter and Stutzman, after we've watched Stutzman escort the Modesto mystery woman to her sister's car, then watched Stutzman get in a car himself and speed away:

Reporter: Describe what it was like getting in her sister's car.

Stutzman: I didn't get in her sister's car.

Reporter: Whose car was it and can you describe what it was like?

Stutzman: I got into a car with a staffer who drove me to Pleasanton. It smelled like McDonald's.

Because of the near total lack of access to the candidate—unless you're Tom Brokaw or *Entertainment Tonight*—reporters are forced to find their own entertainment. I find mine in Paul Walton, write-in candidate for governor of California. I stumble upon him one night at 1:00 A.M. as I'm walking through the parking lot of my Fresno hotel. He is holding court and mixing margaritas in a campaign bus as big as Arnold's. The back of his bus is emblazoned with WE'RE KICKING ASS, even though he's not. If he had the resources to poll this race, he'd be at zero percent and dropping like a rock.

But like every other candidate, Paul is an optimist. A telecommunications millionaire by the time he was thirty, he took eleven years off to see the world, then got back to work as a spa owner in Escondido. Paul is not unlike most of the suckerfish on the Arnold tour (the campaign hacks, the press hacks, the other freak candidates) who are trying to get over on Arnold's publicity. But Paul is more overt about it. His official campaign press badges, which he distributes liberally, display a photo of him and Arnold shoulder to shoulder in tuxedos. It was taken at one of the awards shows he weasels his way into. "I'm an awards show junkie," he says.

Paul is forty-seven years old, favors expensive double-breasted suits bought at a discount in Bogota, and has the white-bread looks and lulling speech of a midnight shift, easy-listening DJ. His three "security guys"—Dan, Achilles, and Andre—are all former military, and Andre used to bodyguard for MC Hammer. His bus driver, who pilots his "home on wheels," used to drive for R.E.M. When he shows me the twelve bunks in his fully outfitted bus, he says, "If these bunks could talk, they'd have said a lot more when R.E.M. was here."

On this night, however, Paul, who's single, and his crew, have some female companionship. Christina's and Crystal's skirts are as short as their hair is platinum, though they've come back to the bus only to give Paul a haircut. Christina, or maybe it was Crystal, works at the Cutting Edge in Bakersfield, and I compliment her on her handiwork. "It looks kind of boufy," she says modestly.

Like almost every alternative candidate I meet in this race, Paul is not a traditional freak. No sandwich boards, no fright wigs, no boring pamphlets about Mumia. Like others I meet who have real jobs as structural engineers or hazardous-waste removal experts, Paul is just a guy with a dream—someone who wants to live outside himself, to in a sense live Arnold's life. "I see it as a two-man race," he says guilelessly. "That's why I took out my picture with Schwarzenegger. Let the battle begin."

Paul has spent nearly fifty thousand dollars of his own money to keep this crew on the road, and he's not even officially on the ballot. Not wishing to see him cause himself any further financial harm, I tell him he ought to think about dropping out, since the only way he can score Arnold's name recognition is to shoot somebody famous, possibly Arnold. He knows he stands an outside chance of catching Arnold with just a few days remaining, and he doesn't really have much of a platform to speak of, besides spending less on incarceration and more on education (a line that comes in handy when I later watch him try to pick up a girl whose boyfriend is in jail for drunk driving). But one gets the feeling Paul is in it for the pure sense of adventure.

Paul likes to read his *USA Today*—"my Bible"—to find out what's happening not just today, but also tomorrow. Frequently, he flies all over the world to worm his way into important events such as the fall of the Berlin Wall or a peace summit in Jackson Hole. He also likes to read obituaries. "To some people, it sounds morbid," he says. "But for me, it's an uplifting thing to actually read that someone didn't make it through the day. It makes me happier that I'm alive. It trivializes any problem you have, including possibly losing for governor."

Before Paul became a rich guy, he used to teach high school civics. But he decided long ago that it was too boring. "How much more exciting to actually live history and be a part of it," he says. "That's an analogous sense of how I'm living my life. It's like catching the crest of the next wave, and you never know if it's going to take you all the way to shore, or if you're gonna come crashing down in the Banzai pipeline, losing life and limb."

It's hard work, living history, as Paul finds out in the next few days. Following Arnold all over the state, he'd planned to challenge him to a debate. (When I point out that Schwarzenegger won't even debate Davis, he responds that Arnold might think he'd lose to Davis, "but maybe he'll think he'll win against me.") Keeping one eye on Arnold, the other on Paul, I run into him again sitting on his bus at a Schwarzenegger rally in Modesto. I try to light a fire under him by telling him he needs to start working voters. There's plenty to work, since Arnold's turned out the crowds. Paul is shy, but he takes my advice and heads down to the rally. But just as it's getting under way, he demurs. He doesn't want to be seen "as some eccentric with a bullhorn. . . . I'll make my stand in Pleasanton," he promises.

In Pleasanton, I never see him. So I call him in between press gaggles on new Arnold bimbo eruptions. In "an ugly new low," Paul alleges, the California Highway Patrol diverted his bus when it came too close to Arnold's "Running Man." "At first, I thought they were giving me a police escort to the fairgrounds," he says naïvely. Then he learned the ugly truth. By the time he gets to Sacramento for Arnold's big-finish bus tour rally on the statehouse steps, he is hopping mad, pushing press releases about the incident to reporters, who mostly push them back.

As I set out to meet Paul on the morning of the mega-rally (it's nice to have access to some candidate), I make my way through our hotel lobby, where a National Federation of the Blind conference is adjourning. Throughout the hall, a flood of visually impaired types are bumping into furniture while probing with their sticks. "Kind of reminds you of voters," says one colleague. Paul first stops by the fringe candidates' microphone stand (over a hundred candidates, plus the write-ins, are supposed to share it), but there's no crowd around. So he decides to go campaign in the maw of Arnold madness.

For a Sunday morning political rally, it's quite the spectacle. A large black man runs down the street claiming he's been groped by Arnold. Behind the press risers, feminist groups and pro-lifers join forces against Schwarzenegger, proving that he's a uniter, not a divider. Stutzman is surveying the campaign staff's magnificent handiwork, but he doesn't seem to enjoy it. "Goddamn it," he says. "I'm going to get the bald-spot burn. Middle-life sucks." I decide to hit him up anyway. "Tell me something inside," I say. Stutzman eyes the stage with Dee Snider singing Arnold's theme song, "We're Not Gonna Take It" (a song we've heard so many times that LeDuff now sings "We can't fucking take it"). "Lip-synch," Stutzman nods.

It's loud as all get-out: the percussive Asian drums, the Chinese paper dragon snaking through the audience, the stylings of "Twisted Sist-ahhhh," as Arnold calls them. But there is one sound that stands out above all others: the sound of irony being lost on people. Every protesting lefty I encounter at the rally, who spent the entire nineties hibernating while the likes of Juanita Broaddrick and Kathleen Willey alleged that Bill Clinton had groped them and worse, thinks Arnold is a beast. Every conservative who spent the nineties playing moral scold, saying that behavior reveals character and that character counts, maintains that Arnold is a victim of dirty tricks and liberal media bias, and ignores charges for which he's apologized.

The Arnold supporters of course outnumber the Arnold detractors about 250 to 1. There are Ranchers for Arnold and Farmers for Arnold, Bikers for Arnold and Immigrants for Arnold. I approach an Arnold staffer, saying, "You guys dropped the ball—no Lepers or Hermaphrodites for Arnold." "No," he says, "but we have those," pointing to a sign that says IRANIAN AMERICAN REPUBLICAN COUNCIL FOR ARNOLD. LeDuff, who has taken to alternating his bike-messenger wear with crisp jackets and khakis to look more like Arnold's security guys ("I'm making it to the front line," he says giddily), comes and collects me. "C'mon!" he says. "They're going to let the foreign press look at Arnold's empty bus! We can talk our way on."

Two by two, reporters are shepherded through. One British crew actually shut themselves into his bathroom and report, "This is where Arnold takes his 'Terminator 2s.'" LeDuff is by now in full mockumentary mode, keeping up a running commentary to whoever will listen: "I need to see that toilet, I'm on east coast deadline. . . . I just want to look at it. . . . Do you think it's made of gold?" After forty minutes in line, it is my turn to walk the empty bus with a BBC camerawoman. But I'm stopped by Skip, Arnold's bus driver, who spies the Paul Walton/Arnold lammie that I've taken to wearing out of solidarity with Walton's lost cause. "You just shot yourself in the foot," Skip says. "You're not getting on the bus."

I spend election morning covering the race poolside at the Mondrian Hotel in Los Angeles. I tell my waitress, Mashia, that I should be working the polls, but I've had it with real people. "That's okay," she says, "there's not many of them left out here." I ask her whom she voted for. She says she hasn't and she's not going to, because she doesn't really know the issues, and she doesn't think ignorant people should vote. I want to hug her, and not just because she's hot and wearing a sarong.

That night, at the Century Plaza Hotel, the polls have not yet closed, but the celebration is already on. Arianna Impressionist in Chief Patrick Dorinson is viewing the night through the eyes of the Greek socialite and erstwhile gubernatorial candidate: "Vell, I think it's a lovely affair, there's just so many people in favor of the recall. I've changed my mind again." Todd Harris sits at a table drinking a light beer, jokingly recounting the path to victory: "It takes a confluence of incredible political skills, brilliant strategy, and pedestrian reporting."

LeDuff, wearing a black leather motorcycle vest and tie, approaches former candidate Bill Simon, who's telling a television crew what a "good family guy" Arnold is. Charlie points at Simon and asks, "Catholic?" Simon nods in assent. "Catholic," says LeDuff, pointing to himself. "Conservative?" asks LeDuff. Simon says yes. "Conservative," says LeDuff, again pointing to himself. So how is "snatching women" a family value? LeDuff asks Simon.

"There's a saying in our church that goes like this," says Simon. "Forgive the sinner, but not the sin." I pile on, asking Simon if he felt the same way about Clinton.

"Certainly," he says.

Whatever. Tired of being too far away from the action, I put on the staff bracelet that a campaign aide slipped me. I use it to get all the way up onstage during Arnold's acceptance speech, just to prove to myself that I still can. I stand in the hot lights, alongside Arnold and Maria and their supporters. There's director Ivan Reitman and comedian Jay Leno and actor Rob Lowe and professional nutjob Gary Busey. In such close proximity to all the Shrivers, my teeth feel smaller and my hair thinner.

I listen to Arnold thank his fahn-tas-teek wife, and watch them sweep into the wings to endure another grueling interview with *Access Hollywood*. I take in all the sights: the belching confetti cannons, the balloon drops, the stripper who hops up onstage and gets down to her thong before security practically dive-tackles her. But it feels like something's missing: I have no one to share this spectacularly surreal moment with. And that's when I bump into Paul Walton.

He is overjoyed to see me: "We are unstoppable!" he says. "It doesn't matter where in the world, we're there." I ask how he even got in, let alone all the way up to the stage, without the proper bracelet. He knows the hotel like the back of his hand, he tells me—he comes here for awards shows—and he slipped in with Darrell Issa, the congressman and publicity tapeworm/father-of-the-recall. "He was denied!" Paul says. "He couldn't even get in. He had to find his own way in through a service elevator. Woo-hoo!"

Paul is amped like I've never seen him amped, and he's brought company—a woman named Janet who identifies herself as "Paul's lover when he's in San Diego." He tells me that at the polls that morning, he found his name on the write-in list. It had been wadded up and thrown in the trash, but he got it out, and it "felt wonderful to finally see my name in print, even if it was on a crinkled piece of paper."

I'm ready to head back to press quarters at the bar, but Paul is not quite set to go. "Matt," he asks, "are you right-handed or left-handed?" I tell him I'm right-handed. "Then stand on this side of me," he says, aligning us shoulder to shoulder as we face the blinding lights of the camera crews using the stage for their nightly news backdrop. "One, two, three," he counts, "we're gonna wave." And we do. He then asks Janet to throw some fallen confetti on us, just for the full effect. I feel ridiculous, but not much more than I have all week. "That's what it's all about, I'm really enjoying this," he says, beaming. "If you can't win, at least you can feel like a winner."

AMONG THE PORNOGRAPHERS

Just look at them sitting together, luxuriating in one another's gazes like fat hounds in the sun: Over there, the First Amendment lawyers, with their chalkstripes and barrel cuffs and owlish widow's peaks. There's the professoriat, suited up in seat-cleaving Dockers and itchy tweeds or camouflaging guts in frowzy guayaberas. And here are the belles of the ball—the porn stars and starlets, in all manner of neoprene saris, split-to-the-cervix gowns, do-me pumps, reptile tattoos, and black banded shirts fastened with onyx studs like the ones favored by soft jazz saxophonists and effeminate magicians.

This odd assemblage has gathered for a four-day World Pornography Conference in the Universal Sheraton, amid the strip-mall sprawl of the San Fernando Valley, porn production capital of the world. The meeting is sponsored by the Center for Sex Research at California State University, Northridge—a sort of Left Coast Kinsey Institute.

Over five hundred academics—sociologists, anthropologists, sexologists, film and gender studies teachers, and interdisciplinary seekers from across the country—are attending under the guise of studying "Eroticism and the First Amendment." But the real aim is simpler: to celebrate pornography. As center founder and professor emeritus of history Vern Bullough says, speaking for the twelve-year-old in all of us, "We hope to get more [pornography] deposits from the industry—so we'll have the biggest porn collection in the country!"

The profs are hardly alone in their enthusiasm. Despite unmerited accusations of bluenosery from more thoroughly debauched Europeans, the fact is, Americans love porn. We spend $8 billion a year on it, more than on hot dogs or country music. Last year the industry released 7,970 porno flicks—thirty-five times the number of mainstream Hollywood features. With the nineties resurgence of Qiana-draped, seventies-era porn chic (*Boogie Nights,* Larry Flynt's deification, etc.), gone is the stigma that once forced smut enthusiasts to slink away to red-light strokehouses. Porn's pervasiveness on VHS and AOL and DVD and pay-per-view allows any midwestern pharmaceutical salesman on expense account to access *Sorority Slumber Sluts* in La Quinta Inn, queen-size solitude.

It is small surprise, then, that the same state system of higher education that harbored Mario Savio's Free Speech Movement and brought us Angela Davis's appointment as "professor of the history of consciousness" has seen fit to confer scholarly legitimacy on this once-closeted form of entertainment. Cal State Northridge has conducted other sex conferences—in 1995, the First International Congress on Gender, Cross-Dressing, and Sex Issues; in 1997, the International Conference on Prostitution—on the principle that they enhance "the university's service to the community." As media attractions, these spectacles tend to garner more coverage than discussions of the epidemiology of gonococcal infections.

But porn plenaries make for unorthodox encounters. Riding up to the opening session in a packed elevator, I watch fellow journalist Luke Ford come nose to nipple with a porn producer's statuesque companion. "I look at your wife with the utmost respect, a coequal partner in the search for truth," Luke booms in his Aussie accent.

Luke is from Cooranbong, outside Sydney. He's a kind of shaggy-haired, acid-washed Brad Pitt, the thirty-two-year-old son of a former Seventh Day Adventist evangelist. After a bout with atheism in his twenties, he converted to Judaism on hearing Dennis Prager, the Jewish radio theologian. Luke moved to Los Angeles and decided to write a book on either ethical living or pornography. He settled on porn, and his *A History of X* will be published next year. In the meantime, he serves as the industry's Matt Drudge, operating a porn-news website, where profiles of Wendy Whoppers and Max Hardcore are garnished with Torah references and discussion of whether Jewish porners keep kosher.

Loathed in the porn industry for aggressively reporting stories such as an HIV epidemic that has seen five stars test positive since January, Luke is forced to cadge a *Sydney Morning Herald* press pass to gain admittance to the conference. I ask him why he stays on this beat, and after feeble protestations about being the only critical observer in a racket filled with industry shills, he finally shrugs: "Good question—it's something I talk about weekly with my shrink. She's an orthodox Jew."

Like everyone else here, Luke discounts claims by feminists and fundamentalists that pornography leads to violence against women. But unlike anyone else here, he seems perplexed about porn, offering eloquent disquisitions on its corrosive effect and tendency to desensitize. Once able to abstain from watching the stuff, he has developed a taste for the roughest hardcore.

Luke breaks with the academics and porners who've adopted a chipper Rousseauian view of things: No impulse should be subjugated; porn is nothing but natural man expressing himself in the most natural of ways. He regards pornography as "inherently wild, nasty, and vicious." "The male animal is very bad news," he says, "and pornography exemplifies that. These people are divorced from the foundations of our civilization." As Luke sees it, "the best arguments against pornography are religious ones: that sex should be sacred, that the human being contains the image of God, that we should not act like animals but live in a more moral, elevated sense. I buy that," he says, "even if I don't live up to it."

Despite his inner conflict, Luke serves as my Sacagawea, guiding me through the alien biosphere that is this convocation, pointing out people I should meet. Because his name is recognized and reviled by industry regulars, Luke intermittently uses an alias, and I join in for sport. We introduce ourselves to potential sources as retired gay porn stars Dick Dundee and Jack Hammer.

My first introduction is to Ed Powers, whose soft-leather boots and head-to-toe black make him look like a Riviera pimp. The brains behind the ever-popular *Dirty Debutantes* series, Ed considers himself a true "innovator" and thinks the scholarly attention afforded by the organizers of this conference has been "a long time in coming—excuse the pun." Rare is the speaker who does not make at least one "no pun intended" or "so to speak" aside.

Luke points out Vanessa Del Rio, who once sucked milk out of a cow's udders on a magazine shoot. She's here to pick up a lifetime achievement award from the Free Speech Coalition, the conference cosponsor and porn industry trade association that has made a major bid for respectability. The coalition provides "talent" with health insurance, peer counseling, AIDS tests, and diagnostic information on scabies, syphilis, and venereal warts (the porner's carpal-tunnel syndrome). It also sends articulate porn stars like Juli Ashton out to lobby against sin taxes and zoning ordinances and to "educate" the world at large to see that "we're just normal, nice, moral people." (Juli has sex with a pair of circus clowns in *New Wave Hookers 4.*)

The opening ceremony will take place in a panoramic rooftop conference room. In the crowd milling around the cash bar, we run into a truly extraordinary apparition: Dr. Susan Block, who looks like Little Bo Peep on leave from a French bordello, in her layers of ruffled chiffon, peek-a-boo garters, and barely contained decolletage. Dr. Block graduated magna cum laude from Yale and earned her doctorate in philosophy at San Francisco State University. A sex therapist and bestselling author (*The 10 Commandments of Pleasure*), she hosts a syndicated cable talk show, where she dispenses advice on matters coital. After the show, which is broadcast from her home-studio "pleasure palace" in Beverly Hills, the guests and onlookers often dog-pile in some sort of living-room bacchanal.

Like many of the academics at this conference, Block has constructed her own discipline. She calls herself an "ethical hedonist." As we talk, she pulls me and Luke and a Canadian documentary film crew into the ladies' room, along with her lovely assistant LaVonne.

Unprompted, she removes a rubber phallus from her purse and hikes up LaVonne's dress, baring her derriere. Block paddles it and kisses it while LaVonne coos. Before she can return to explaining her philosophy, Block is seized by inspiration: "Wanna hear me tinkle?" The Canadian boom-mike operator eagerly nods.

Not much of a hedonist, I rejoin the scholars, now taking their seats in front of the stage for the first evening's proceedings. The profs are gawking, cotton-mouthed, at the bounty of stilettoed vixens; they burrow clammy hands in snug chinos pockets like nervous ethnographers dropped into an Amazon tribe of sexpot savages.

The entertainment, dubbed "Pornocopia, Our Body of Work," doesn't disappoint. Performance artist Annie Sprinkle, porn's Yoko Ono, asks the crowd how many of them have made pornography. Nearly half the people in the room raise their hands (including Luke, who sheepishly admits that he recently completed a pseudo-documentary, *What Women Want*). Sprinkle, so named for her practice of urinating on stage, slogs through a tortuously blue monologue, which elicits belly laughs from the hundreds of profs intent on proving they're in on the joke.

The headliner, though, is porn veteran Nina Hartley. She starred in the mainstream *Boogie Nights,* once lectured at Harvard, and is highly regarded for her script memorizing ability and educational fare like *Woodworking 101: Nina's Guide to Better Fellatio.*

Nina dances topless and virtually bottomless while lip-synching an old Alberta Hunter tune until her glutei glisten like the haunches of a slightly dimpled Clydesdale. When she finishes, Nina barely has time to slip into her floral dress before being stormed by inquisitive academics, including a white-whiskered educational psychologist who wants to talk about developing a program where porn stars work with the handicapped.

He wishes to remain anonymous, since he's affiliated with Los Angeles public schools. But I ask the good doctor what he has in mind. "I don't know, we haven't sat down and talked," he says, still glassy-eyed from Nina's performance. "This isn't the place. But I have lots of ideas; so does Nina. This whole world is new to me. I'm just exploring and seeing what I can do that's instructive. . . . There's a lot more I need to learn."

"About what?" I ask.

"About sex!" he says, exasperated.

Of course, many of us have been operating under the illusion that sex is a fairly straightforward proposition. Not so the academics. These professors have tripped upon a glorious discovery. It all started when the old canon was torched in the late sixties in favor of spot-scholarship on any given researcher's own personal interests, manias, viewing habits, and turn-ons.

This led to the proliferation of victim studies and human sexuality courses and, more important, to the advent of pop culture departments, whose prototype hatched at Ohio's Bowling Green State University in the early seventies. As Ray Browne, architect of that department, once noted, academics found respite from neuroscience and deepest Descartes to rejuvenate themselves at these "intellectual fat farms." Some took up tenured residence there and are bingeing still on postmodernist sweetmeats: All things are worthy of study. Any nugatory pastime should be seen as a "text," to be decoded by liberal-arts gnostics. In this way are new disciplines erected ("LesBiGay-Trans Film Studies"), a new lingo created ("patriarchal hegemony"). Papers are presented at conferences with titles like "Body Slam: Professional Wrestling as Greek Tragedy" and "1960s Spy Films as the Locus of Heteronormative Masculinity."

By now, "porn studies" is featured at several universities (the State

University of New York, New Paltz, for example, and the University of California campuses at Santa Cruz, Santa Barbara, and Berkeley), though the courses may hide under headings like "community studies." Getting paid for teaching porn is "a good gig if you can get it," says porn star Sharon Mitchell, who like Nina Hartley occasionally lectures in these classes (when not pursuing her goal of a Ph.D. in child development).

The porners, of course, love their new academic cachet. Most thought they were merely escaping lives rolling gorditas on Taco Bell assembly lines when they took up rutting strangers for money in badly acted films with poor production values. Only now are they realizing that what they do is worthy of study. The Cal State types have even taken to calling porners "adult entertainers," much as they call prostitutes "sex workers." As Luke loudly proclaims in the hotel lobby, aiming to reduce the toxic levels of pretension, "These are not whores and pimps and mafiosi! These are actors, directors, producers, and technicians, and journalists, and professors. We're not just wankers!"

They're all these things, and feminists as well. Not your classic, fang-baring Andrea Dworkin, Catherine MacKinnon, all-sex-is-rape feminist theoreticians incensed by pornography and harassment, but "sex-positive feminists," as Nina calls them. This is no less than a sea change. In the past, feminist politics—not conventional morality—has stood as the chief impediment to the open acceptance of pornography on campus: Pornography, preached the old feminists, objectifies women within oppressive power hierarchies.

But over the past decade, a spate of Nina Hartley types have given voice to the noble savage. Hartley is a brainy red-diaper baby and socialist who contributes essays such as "Frustrations of a Feminist Porn Star" to turgid anthologies, tossing off references to Newtonian and Einsteinian physics and correctly deploying words like "etiology." She talks about promoting "worker control of the means of production" to reclaim porn as the embodiment of female empowerment and sexual expression as originally envisioned by our foremothers during the sexual revolution.

Though MacKinnon and Dworkin—or "MacDworkin," as the sex positivists pejoratively call them—would have us believe that the women of the porn industry are victims of patriarchal hegemony, Hartley and company claim to do what they do for profit and pleasure. This is an egalitarian argument—and it can truly be said that porn women are just as autonomous, as morally bereft, and as capable of making bad decisions as porn men.

There's a certain seductive bonhomie among the positivists, as I learn traveling with Hartley and Sharon Mitchell to a sixty-five-dollar-a-head porn industry benefit to combat racism (an event not linked to the conference). I am riding in Nina's stretch limo, drinking Nina's bourbon, listening to Nina prattle on about the need for increased interaction between porners and profs and how, were she not so exhibitionistic, she'd like nothing better than "to retreat happily to the study of sex and books in a life of contemplation." Nina says all this while receiving a foot rub from Sharon, whose gazelle legs gape apart as she sits in the low-slung seat across from me. Sharon is wearing gold shoulder glitter and a stitch of a dress with no panties under it.

It is hard to imagine riding in a limo drinking bourbon with a pantyless MacDworkin. Harder still to imagine wanting to—and probably unnecessary, since MacDworkinism is increasingly marginalized by sane people everywhere. Even on campuses, the porn-positive feminists sunny up the business enough to lend it cover and discourage scrutiny of its bothersome aspects (AIDS, rampant drug use and suicide, miscellaneous violence—Sharon Mitchell was nearly killed by a fan who broke her larynx while biting her all over her body). Once the sex positivists gain the advantage, political unanimity prevails—everybody at the conference is a staunch libertarian—and the only remaining issue is aesthetic. No one here would dream of asking the question, What do we become by watching porn? Instead, the question is, What kind of porn should we watch?

Sociology professor James Elias, the conference host and director of the Cal State Northridge sex research center, says he tried to find someone to represent a countervailing view but was unsuccessful. MacDworkinites typically will not debate the merits of pornography. As for porn critics whose objection is religious, Elias says that "to take an evangelical person [and] put them up against one of the top defense attorneys in the country to debate—it would be an embarrassment for everyone."

He's referring to the American Civil Liberties Union's Nadine Strossen, who has come to the conference to defend the proposition, as the ACLU has for years, that engaging in all modes of depravity is a cherished and absolute American right. She told a roomful of porners "how essential" are their efforts to overcome "our puritanical heritage" and applauded their "vital contribution to First Amendment freedoms," adding, "Keep it up! So to speak!" One would think, listening to Strossen and her ilk, that Anthony Comstock were still screening our mail. The truth, as reported by the *Adult Video News,* is that there has been no better time in American history to be a pornographer. Obscenity prosecutions have slowed to near extinction under the Clinton administration, and adult industry output has doubled in the past five years. While autograph seekers congregate around Strossen, Al Goldstein, the corpulent vulgarian who is the editor of *Screw* magazine, stands next to her signing programs.

"Oy vey," says Luke. "Proverbs says the fear of the Lord is the beginning of wisdom. This conference will show you how incredibly stupid people get when they don't have a fear of God."

He's speaking of the professors, who slither through the halls ogling passing porn actresses and purchasing wares like the "Fleshlight—Man's New Best Friend," a lifelike molded-gel insert made from "Real Feel Super Skin™" and used for—well, for educational purposes. Also available is an array of catalogs from which to order classroom materials. Porn is now so mainstream that there are even blooper videos: Watch "P.J. break up her costars by passing a little gas."

When one views one's perversions with scholarly detachment, it seems, all things become permissible. The only genre denounced at the conference is child pornography—except at the child pornography panel. There, Harris Mirkin, a political scientist from the University of Missouri, Kansas City, asserts there is no real evidence that children are harmed by being photographed naked.

Meanwhile, David Sonenschein, formerly of the Kinsey Institute, illustrates the supposed ludicrousness of child pornography restrictions by showing us a photograph once forced out of an exhibition. In the picture, a cherubic, naked two-year-old grabs and explores the penis of the photographer, who is reclining naked on a bed.

I ask Vern Bullough, the center's founder, whether he is bothered by such a display, especially since the photographer wasn't the child's father. "I think it's one of those gray areas," Bullough says, adding that it is "very educational. . . . We ought to [let children] explore. When I had children, they explored me in the shower."

I ask Bullough whether anyone else's children explored him in the shower. "I don't think that's an appropriate question," interjects the conference's eavesdropping legal counsel. "People's relations have never been an issue at this conference. It is all based on the material we presented in a professional and scholarly manner."

Except, it turns out, at the "Night of the Stars," the Free Speech Coalition's awards dinner, which serves as something of a porn star prom night and is held during the conference at the same hotel. Luke can't attend, as he has to keep the Sabbath holy. Needing a new guide, I turn to Jena, an attractive twenty-five-year-old just off the bus from Orlando. She entered the business three weeks ago and has already starred in seven films—*Fresh Flesh* and six others she can't quite remember. Jena is fairly finicky by porn actress standards: There are varieties of sex she won't engage in on screen, including interracial—that is, until Mr. Marcus saunters up behind her.

Mr. Marcus, who looks like a tightly coiled anaconda with elephantiasis of the deltoids, is fresh from starring in *The World's Luckiest Black Man,* so titled because Mr. Marcus couples with 101 costars. He says the shoot took one day, though industry sources snit that it actually took three. Still, that's 33.6 women a day, and nobody's questioning his work ethic.

Though Jena has promised to take me to an after-party at a place called the Rubber Room, she disappears with Mr. Marcus. Ten minutes later, I find her in a meeting room where stragglers are eagerly congregating. She is on her knees pleasuring Mr. Marcus for the benefit of twenty or so onlookers. In the same room over the next hour, various awards-night attendees and industry shutterbugs view other impromptu live sex shows.

Two starlets lie on a table, licking each other like postage stamps as matter-of-factly as if they were exchanging business cards. Another barely coherent platinum-haired actress in a silver sequined cocktail dress spreads her hands against the wall to gain her balance. All hard bones and hollow eye sockets, her head involuntarily bobbing side to side like a spring-necked dashboard ornament, she lowers herself onto an empty Bud Light bottle. She is met with cheers from her carny-barker escort and from the sweaty spectators who have pressed around her like punters at a Balinese cockfight. As she sits sprawled on the floor, emitting alcohol-induced giggles, souvenir seekers take turns cozying up behind her to have their pictures taken.

Jena tells me such exhibitions are good for business. Only later do I learn that she has a husband who knows nothing of her extracurricular networking (her six-year-old daughter doesn't even know of her "acting" career). She begs me not to write about it, until I remind her that she fellated Mr. Marcus in front of a roomful of photographers. "All right," she relents, "go ahead."

Most of the panels, however, present no vexing dilemmas: Porn is good. Pantsuited porn starlets wax self-analytic at a session headlined "Victims or Visionaries?" Verdict: Visionaries! Against this consensus, panels explore the particulars of porn's artistic merits and cultural significance, harvesting insights so minute as to be barely detectable. At the "Role of Fetishism" panel, philosophy professor David Austin of North Carolina State University has determined through rigorous Internet study that the number of "necro[philia] enthusiasts is about three times that of [menstrual] period enthusiasts." The next speaker, Midori, a "FetishDiva" squeezed into a black rubber Emma Peel cat-suit with six-inch stiletto boots, shows us slides of nineteenth-century Austrian pumps that "render the wearer immobile and thrust the foot forward like an offering."

Over in "Cum Shots: History, Theory, and Research," Dr. Peter Sándor Gardos, a San Francisco clinical sexologist, explains his research on the ejaculatory "money shot," the genre's most sacred convention. Gardos recruits college sophomores to view porn movie clips of actors ejaculating on their female counterparts, then gauges whether they find the images degrading. His data have led him to conclude that "no pornographic image is interpretable outside of its historical and social context. Harm or degradation does not reside in the image itself." Bill Margold, who has starred in over four hundred films, begs to differ, asserting that such shots represent "vicarious re-venge exacted upon the cheerleader by X number of men who could not get that cheerleader."

Another panel deconstructs Ed Powers's *Dirty Debutantes* oeu-vre. Peter Lehman, a University of Arizona professor and Blake Edwards scholar, reads from a laborious treatise laced with allusions to Godard, the Lumière brothers, and Méliès. Powers's contribution: He displaces "the monotonous emphasis on the meat shot" and con-structs instead "a comic Woody Allen–like Jewish persona for himself, acknowledging insecurities such as worrying about his penis size." Lehman concedes to me that he and his colleagues "are legitimizing [porners] within the culture," but only in a way "that I think they deserve."

Academics, it seems, are the only people who can de-eroticize sex more completely than pornographers. The most striking instance comes when the University of California Irvine's Jay Lorenz delivers his presentation on the "gonzo" films of John Stagliano, aka Buttman, one of porn's top directors, a Cato Institute benefactor, and an unapologetic gluteus enthusiast.

Citing Stagliano's voyeuristic vérité travelogues, which begin as interviews and culminate in sex in public places, a straight-faced Lorenz launches a lengthy exegesis comparing Stagliano's persona to the late-nineteenth-century flaneur as described by Baudelaire. He illustrates with clips of *Buttman in Barcelona*. Lorenz's purpose? To expatiate on the "binary collapse" and "epistemological flippage" brought about by "the erosion of the once-secure border distinction between the private and public spheres."

Himself a panelist, Stagliano looks slightly embarrassed by the attention. "All I wanted to do was make videos that really turned me on," he mumbles, his shirt unbuttoned to mid-sternum. "Another idea I had was to make a video about, uh, my obsession, uh, with female butts."

Nobody laughs. But if anyone entertains lingering doubts about what fuels Stagliano's artistic vision, he need only walk to the back of the room, past the beard-tugging academics, past the beaded water pitchers, to the table that contains an advertisement for Stagliano's *Buttman* magazine. There, beneath a letter from the editor titled "From the Crack," is a picture of Stagliano: Auteur, Libertarian Champion, Toast of the Academy, Harbinger of Tomorrow's Canon. At least it looks like Stagliano. It's difficult to tell. His face is buried in some girl's fleshy keister.

A RAKE'S PROGRESS

Marion Barry Bares (Almost) All

Let me live in a house by the side of the road,
Where the race of men go by;
The men who are good and the men who are bad,
As good and as bad as I.

        —from Sam Walter Foss's "House by the Side of the Road,"
          the first poem Marion Barry recited in church as a boy

In most conceptions of Washington, D.C., the city operates on Eastern Standard Time. But those who pass through Marion Barry's orbit know there's another zone, which has nothing to do with the mean solar time of the seventy-fifth meridian west of the Greenwich Royal Observatory. It's called "Barry Time." The former four-term mayor of D.C. will show up for speeches, meetings, and civic events whenever he damn well pleases.

This translates into many minutes, even hours, of waiting for Barry to appear. So after being slated to hang out with Barry for several days, I am surprised to receive a call from his spokesperson, Natalie Williams, two days before we're supposed to meet.

"Mr. Barry wants to start early," Natalie informs me. "He wants you to come to church with him tomorrow."

"Great," I say. "What time does church start?"

"Eleven A.M.," she says.

"Okay. And what time should I meet him before church?" I ask.

"Eleven-thirty," she responds with complete seriousness.

Barry, now in his second postmayoral term as a councilman representing the city's poorest ward, is these days something less than a political powerhouse, but my interest had recently been rekindled in the man universally known as one of the two or three finest crack-smoking politicians our nation has ever produced. A 1990 FBI sting yielded grainy video of Barry holding a crack pipe to his lips that was broadcast around the world (launching a booming "bitch set me up" T-shirt industry), and his name became a late-night comic's rim shot, especially as he won one more mayoral term in 1994 after serving six months in jail.

Now, after a relatively dormant postmayoral period of local politicking, serial brushes with the law, health and taxman problems, with the occasional drug relapse, Barry seemed to be enjoying a renaissance for both good and bad reasons. The good, for him, has come in the form of a balanced, years-in-the-making documentary called *The Nine Lives of Marion Barry,* now in regular rotation on HBO. It traces Barry's arc from an idealistic, dashiki-wearing civil rights activist, through his rise and fall as mayor, to his current redemptive plateau period, a life that has made him the singular figure in the history of D.C.'s municipal politics.

The bad came this past Fourth of July weekend, when Barry was arrested for "stalking" his former girlfriend Donna Watts-Brighthaupt after an argument they'd had on the way to Rehoboth Beach. She changed her mind about the trip and returned to D.C., flagging down an officer when Barry was allegedly pursuing her in his car. The stalking charge looked like an honest lover's tiff, amounted to nothing, and was quickly dropped.

In typical Barry fashion, however, there were baroque touches that gave the story national oxygen. For instance, the Barry team called a late-night press conference to denounce Watts's psychiatric fitness, and she showed up in the middle of it, loudly denouncing their denunciation. Scribes at the *Washington City Paper,* who still enjoy riding Barry like the village Zipcar, detailed the knotty love triangle between Barry, Donna, and her ex-husband—whom Barry had had banished from the City Council building—and ran transcripts from leaked voice mail tapes of a lovesick Barry trying to woo Donna back. They did the same with a taped fight in which Donna proclaimed that Barry had booted her out of a Denver hotel room "'cause I wouldn't suck your dick," a quote that provided likely the most memorable cover line in *City Paper* history.

Still, this was just the entertainment portion of the program. The real trouble was Watts-Brighthaupt's employment arrangement with Barry, who had (legally) garnered nearly $1 million in earmarks for various nonprofits in his ward—which journalistic Nosy Neds discovered had all sorts of irregularities, such as outfits overseen by Barry's City Council staffers, contracts thrown to women he'd dated (not just

Watts-Brighthaupt), people being paid for do-nothing jobs, alleged forgeries, etc.

Nobody has yet alleged that Barry personally profited. For all the perceptions of Barry over the years as a dirty politician, he's been a remarkably clean one on the financial front. Having periodically teetered on the edge of personal insolvency, even as two of his deputy mayors went upriver for embezzlement and corruption in the 1980s, Barry has never been caught with his hand in the cookie jar, and not for lack of investigators trying.

Barry has audaciously proclaimed he's done nothing wrong—if you can't throw work to qualified girlfriends with City Council–approved taxpayer money, just who can you throw work to? Barry insists he wouldn't give a job to his mother if she wasn't qualified. Still, as Barry points out, "Old Man Daley gave his son the insurance contract, and was criticized for it. He said, 'If a father can't help his son, what the hell is he here for?'"

The whole messy business has resulted in the City Council's authorizing an ethics investigation of Barry by superlawyer Robert Bennett (something of an expert on ethically challenged politicians, having represented Bill Clinton). It has also reportedly piqued the more serious investigative interest of the feds, who've never lacked for zeal in building cases against Barry, having spent tens of millions doing so going all the way back to the FBI's 1967 file on "Marion S. Barry, Jr., Negro Militant."

When I ask a Barry staffer if her boss is spooked by the new attention, she says, "No. He never gets spooked. We get spooked." By the lights of longtime Barry aficionados, this latest doesn't rank very high on his scandal Richter scale. A ward boss throwing sketchy patronage jobs to friends? It could make a Barry connoisseur very sleepy. Plus, some Barry watchers think he might be losing a step. There wasn't even any cocaine involved.

Yet the scandal wasn't my reason for visiting hizzoner. Barry bashing has been a near ubiquitous sport, and approaching him in order to find holes in his stories is about as sporting as taking candy from a quadriplegic preemie. Rather, I was curious to take his measure as a human being, which many forget he still is, despite the caricatures and self-parodies. For seventy-three years, over forty of them in public life, Barry has kept rearing up like a plastic varmint in a Whac-a-Mole game. No matter how many times he's batted about the head with a mallet, he relentlessly reappears.

Like countless Maryland commuters, I drive past the turnoff to Marion Barry's house every time I go to the District without ever giving his Congress Heights neighborhood in southeast Washington a thought. The Suitland Parkway that runs past it doubles as the most common artery from the city to Andrews Air Force Base—Air Force One frequently casts shadows on your car as you drive it. The denizens of Ward 8 commonly refer to their locale as "east of the river"—by which they mean the Anacostia River, an 8.4-mile-long, meandering toxic soup that is about as clear as Swiss Miss and where up to 68 percent of the brown bullhead catfish have been found to have liver tumors. Flowing into the much more celebrated Potomac, it's the kind of river most people tend to forget, just as they do the ward that nestles it.

For decades, Ward 8 has been the crime and poverty and every-other-dubious-statistic headquarters of D.C. It is the land that the real estate bubble forgot. Amid the check-cashing places and screw-top liquor stores, it contains such tourist meccas as the reeking Blue Plains Wastewater Treatment Plant and St. Elizabeth's psychiatric hospital, where Ezra Pound sweated out his insanity plea for treason and John Hinckley Jr. can compose rock operas for Jodie Foster in peace. While only minutes from Capitol Hill and from the more prosperous black suburbs in Maryland's Prince George's County, Ward 8 might as well be in Burkina Faso to the commuting class. The only reason to pull off there is if you need to buy a quick fifth of Hennessey for the ride home, or possibly something less legal.

It is here, after cruising past street signs bearing the names MARTIN LUTHER KING and MALCOLM X, that I find Barry's house, a rented redbrick duplex. (He lives alone, as Cora Masters Barry, his fourth wife, left him in 2002, without going through the formality of getting a divorce.) The window shades are yellowed and drawn. There is bird splat on the bricks. A Metro bus-stop pole is posted right in front of it, meaning Barry sometimes has a chance to involuntarily meet constituents, as some end up waiting for their ride on his barren concrete porch.

I knock on the door—the doorbell's missing—even though I'm a good half hour early. I don't want to make Barry late for being late to church. "Come in!" he yells. And as I do, I find him sitting on the couch, wearing track pants and a loose workout shirt, eating a greasy, four-course IHOP take-out breakfast on a TV tray in front of his big-screen. He looks both gaunter and more appealing than during the glory years, when the drugging and boozing often swelled him up like a sweating, smirking sausage. His skin is smooth—he believes in the healing balm of moisturizer—and the lines on his face make him look more avuncular and settled.

The furniture is no-frills—the dining-room table is pushed against the wall, and some chairs still have the plastic on them. There is no vanity wall of past glories. Décor is minimalist, besides the Afrocentric statuary and Barack Obama's beatific mug on a commemorative "From Slavery to the White House" blanket draped over his couch. The coffee table is littered with books of the self-improvement variety: the Bible, M. Scott Peck's *The Road Less Traveled,* Gary Chapman's *The Five Love Languages: How to Express Heartfelt Commitment to Your Mate.*

Most jarring is the end table littered with prescriptions—thirteen bottles in all—and syringes. It looks like Elvis's medicine cabinet, circa 1977. At first I think maybe I have the wrong day and have walked into a Vista Hotel scene redux (the location of his 1990 crack bust). But I'm looking instead at all the meds he takes after a February kidney transplant. The syringes, he explains, are for "taking my sugar," which he has to do as a longtime diabetic. Barry has other health issues too. He has hypertension. His cancerous prostate is a distant memory, the surgery for which caused some incontinence issues. He keeps a urinal next to his bed for middle-of-the-night emergencies. It's not the most ideal arrangement for a legendary Romeo, but, as he points out, "the alternative is worse."

Barry speaks in a mumbly whisper ("I'll talk louder," he repeatedly promises when I keep checking my tape recorder for pickup), but seems in fine spirits. He's used to dodging bullets. With varying success, as he reminds me of the time in 1977 when Muslim terrorists took hostages in the District Building when Barry was a council member. It was shortly before his first mayoral run, and he caught a bullet in the chest. "Do you have a scar?" I ask. "Let's see," he says, lifting up his shirt, so that within ten minutes of arriving, I'm eyeball to areola with Barry's left nipple. It's a move that's very Barry. Most times, he reveals nothing at all. Then he reveals too much.

After about thirty seconds of examination, we can't decide if what we're looking at is a fading gunshot wound or a skin blemish. But for Barry's seminakedness, he's still adept at showing less than everything. The point I shouldn't miss, one of the reasons he wants to bring me to church, is that "I go through this time and time again, when if it weren't for God, I wouldn't be here." He catalogs various dramatic happenings in his life: making it out of Mississippi as the son of sharecroppers, near misses during his SNCC-organizer days in the civil rights movement, the Vista Hotel.

I wasn't even going to bring up the latter until our second date, as it's generally bad manners to mention your host's crack bust straightaway. But since he mentions it, I pursue a bit, asking him how he felt when he realized he'd been stung. "I didn't realize what happened," he says. "It happened so fast. And so my instinct was, as I said, 'This bitch set me up.'"

"She kinda did," I offer, an objectively indisputable point.

"Not kinda—she did!" he reiterates of Rasheeda Moore, the former model and Barry paramour. While Barry admits to using cocaine "recreationally" beforehand (several witnesses at his trial said he "recreated" habitually), he says he had not smoked crack before (also at odds with the testimony of witnesses), claiming he even needed to go to the bathroom to practice holding the pipe, so as not to look like an amateur in front of Moore. In the video, Barry is seen asking her multiple times how to do it and brushing off her initial invites. But, he adds, "Rasheeda could talk an Eskimo into buying a refrigerator."

One of the more underappreciated, pathos-laden aspects of the video is how the main impetus for Barry's being present "was sex," as he freely admits, and he repeatedly grovels to Rasheeda on the video. I mention that I recall him grabbing her breast. "Tried to," he readily agrees. "The manly instincts took over . . . I guess what was probably in my mind—first time I thought about it—was if I took a hit, maybe she would change her mind about sex."

"So your motives were pure," I note.

His cell phone rings, as it incessantly does, and he answers it. "I'm gettin' ready to go to church, let me call you back." He hangs up, saying, "I'm glad you're interested in all that. Very few people ask me."

Of his own culpability in the matter, Barry's a little less forthright. He says he's thankful to God, as it "could've turned out another way." I point out that the incident and resulting trial turned out pretty badly: serial humiliation, his third wife leaving him, and eventually six months in jail (not, actually, from the Vista incident, but from another misdemeanor possession that was part of the fourteen-count indictment). "People assume there was crack cocaine in there. The jurors didn't believe it," he says.

Some pro-Barry jurors did speculate that the pipe was filled with baking soda. But he at least assumed there was crack in it, I assert. "How do you know?" he asks, now defensive. Well that's what most people assume is in a crack pipe, I proffer, hence the name "crack pipe."

"I don't know," he says, completely straight-faced. "I didn't think about it. Who knows what the FBI put in there? I know this: They tried to kill me. That's for sure."

We are joined for church by a slew of younger women, many roughly half his age, in their Sunday finery. Barry gives off the whiff of a black Hugh Hefner: old enough to seem a fatherly elder that younger women like to mother-hen, lusty enough that you're never sure which of his female relations goes beyond platonic. There's Natalie Williams, his spokesperson, and her friend in from Los Angeles, who is a dead ringer for the actress Robin Givens. There's Chenille Spencer, Barry's sometime companion and personal assistant, and her nine-year-old-son, Fats, who is Barry's godson. (Barry has five godsons, as he says it's important for the kids around his ward, often raised by single mothers, to have "positive male role models.")

Barry is often circumspect about whom he has seen romantically. Though when I point out to him that he's entitled to see whomever he wants, he agrees: "That's right. I'm free, black, and twenty-one." There is Kim Dickens, though, whom Barry admits he "takes out" sometimes and who was kind enough to donate a kidney to Barry after his renal failure. She basically saved his life, but makes no great to-do about it. I ask Kim if she misses her kidney. "I do have separation anxiety," she says. "But I visit him enough. So the kidneys see each other."

There is also a CW network cameraman along for the morning, collecting B-reel for a two-part series on Barry. The star goes upstairs to get suited up, right down to his silver wraparound cuff links. "A professor told me if you want to be a millionaire, look like a millionaire," explains Barry. We finally gather ourselves to go to church, about forty-five minutes after the opening bell. Kim waves off our lateness. "Marion likes to get there to hear the Word," she says. "They'll still be praising the Lord, honey."

Before we go, Barry huddles everyone in the center of his cramped living room and instructs us to grab hands for prayer. I join in, but we decide I should fall out, as the praying white reporter kind of confuses the cameraman's visual. Barry lifts his voice to the heavens, which is still mumbly, so my tape doesn't pick up the particulars. But I am struck by two things while listening to him:

The man prays with the familiarity of someone who regularly talks to God.

Who prays in front of a cameraman and *before* they go to church?

We arrive in a blue Cadillac with a missing hubcap (a loaner, since his 2000 BMW is in the shop). The ushers at the Temple of Praise in southeast show Barry a deference due a visiting dignitary, though it has been his home church for some years. The congregants are in the full throes of Holy Ghost power when we arrive. The percussion from both the band and all the stomping comes up through the floor, rattling the soles of your shoes. Rookies would do well to wear a mouthguard, as they might catch a stray elbow, as I did, from rapturous church ladies performing the Pentecostal shake. At one point during a song, I watch a beefy elder onstage square his shoulders, tuck his head, and dash down the steps like a fullback hitting a hole, then into a breakaway open-field sprint around the sanctuary. Natalie asks if I'm okay. "Sure," I tell her, "this is just like my church."

My vantage point is excellent, since even though we arrived an hour late, the front pew is cleared out for Barry and his entourage. He has a standing reservation whenever he wants it. Bishop Glen Staples, a silky prosperity-gospeler, welcomes "our dear mayor-for-life. We are thankful that he is here." Staples alludes to Barry's recent troubles, saying, "I love him because he's taught me how to get back up."

Staples finds the old rhetorical rhythms, as congregants whoop on the rests. "You got to learn how to get up. [*Whoop.*] Because everybody in this life, if you are alive and breathing, that is the one thing you can be sure of, making mistakes. [*Whoop.*] When you fall down 'cause of mistakes, get back up, dust yo'self off, and start over again. [*Whoop.*]" Staples instructs us to grab one person and tell them "I know you're going to make it!" The audience obliges, and whoops some more, as Barry is called to the stage over pumping, orgasmic organ.

"Praise the Lord!" Barry says. "Hallelujah!" He is echoed by the audience. "Whenever you see me, I'm going to praise the Lord, because with all that I've been through. [*Whoop.*] You understand." The thought doesn't need to be finished. They understand.

Barry says the media have tried to demonize him, "but y'all know how much I care. [*Whoop.*] There are a lot of people who don't like what I do. [*Whoop.*] Lookin' out for black people. [*Whoop.*] Lookin' out for black people. [*Whoop.*] Standin' up for black people. [*Whoop.*] They don't like it, and so I'm constantly attacked. But because of God's mercy and grace and power. [*Whoop. Whoop. Whoop.*]"

Again, he doesn't need to finish. The crowd is all about extending however much forgiveness he needs, even if he doesn't feel he needs any, and it was never asked for. "So I want to thank this congregation and the bishop for your prayers," Barry continues. "Thank you, Temple of Praise. You love me, and I love you!"

Bishop Staples retakes the pulpit and whips the crowd into a frenzy with a hell-for-leather sing-songy sermon that is half T. D. Jakes, half Otis Redding. Only amateurs wait for the altar call. Most just come up front during the sermon, wailing and whooping and feeling the electric surge of Holy Ghost power hitting in jolts like the Staples-punctuating organ.

Staples laces the sermon with plenty of Barry references. But the main subject is Paul and his thorn of the flesh, which God wouldn't remove. Instead, Staples says, God told Paul, "'I'm gonna leave it right there, to keep you humble.' You better believe that everybody in here got a thorn in yo' flesh. But God said the prescription that I'm gonna give you for your malady of being a human being is called grace."

Barry is by now transported himself. He gets up and joins the mosh pit of ululators, swinging his arms like a child readying himself for the standing broad jump at a school track meet. When asked afterward what part of the sermon spoke to him most, he says, "All of it," then starts throwing some Bible himself. "It says, 'Greater is He that is in us than he that is in the world,'" Barry says, adding his own interpretation: "Greater than devils, and evil-doers, and haters. Barry critics."

It's a tad ironic that while all but emperor-for-life in Ward 8, Barry didn't make his bones as mayor by standing up for "the last, the least, and the lost," as he has spent the post-Vista half of his career rebranding himself in these parts. While his signature summer-jobs program for youth ensured that you can swing a cat in a local black neighborhood and hit five adults for whom Barry provided their first gig, his primary accomplishment was riding eighties-era real estate boom market forces.

Barry threw the city open to development the likes of which D.C. hadn't seen before. He was so proactive that old staffers tell how, early in his mayoral tenure, he used to have weekly brainstorming brown-bag lunches with architects and developers and would fast-track formerly glacial construction approval processes with Post-it notes saying "Good idea, do it!" When he assumed office in 1979, whole quadrants of the city were ghost towns, and there were streets untouched since they were torched in the '68 riots.

During Barry's first term, seventy new buildings were either started or completed, and millions of new square feet of downtown office space were added. Even Republicans, after rolling through their mental rolodex of Chris Rock crack-smoking jokes or using Barry as a handy excuse to deny D.C. statehood, sometimes recall the eighties-era Barry with fondness. Even if there were accusations of untoward cronyism, he was a mayor you could do business with. "The one thing Barry fundamentally understood is that nobody—not the city, not the private sector—profits off a weed-strewn lot. In that way, he was a supply-sider," says one.

In other ways, though, he was a raging redistributionist. "Some call it socialistic, some call it democratic," Barry tells me. "I don't go by labels, they don't mean shit to me." Figuring if the Poles and Italians could feather nests in Chicago and the Irish could dominate Boston, Barry ruthlessly insisted that all of his departments meet minority set-aside contracting quotas, up to 30 percent. At the same time, his knack for creating patronage jobs would've left Huey Long gaping in awe. At one point in the late eighties, the city didn't even know how many employees it had on its own payroll (an independent commission estimated there was one city worker for every thirteen residents). By the end of Barry's third term, shortly before the Vista bust, the size of the municipal payroll had swelled to 52,000— that's 14,000 more taxpayer-funded jobs than Los Angeles, a city five times the size of D.C.

Barry, always intent on buffing the scratches out of his legacy, tells me that he didn't just foster a black middle class in D.C., but also in neighboring Prince George's County. He's more right than he'd like to be. For much of the newly created black wealth fled the city, as they had a much better chance of enjoying their spoils without getting shot in the suburbs.

Barry's early electoral success was also partly attributable to lily-white affluent do-godniks, enamored by the exotic former black radical taking on the establishment. He was championed by the *Washington Post*, which endorsed him in three out of his four runs for mayor, though the *Post*'s editors later publicly wished they could rescind the last one. But his consistent racial polarization and claims of martyrdom when running into various ethical and personal lapses eventually cost him that goodwill.

In the late eighties, most of the poor black wards became drug-ravaged killing fields, and it was their voters that saved Barry's hide in subsequent elections. (Barry's talents as a political Machiavelli are grossly underrated—he's lost only one election ever, for an at-large council seat right after his trial. "I had to get that out of my system," he jokes. "Even then, I got fifty thousand votes.") Some of these circumstances were far beyond Barry's control. But then, some of them weren't. As Harry Jaffe and Tom Sherwood detailed in their 1994 book *Dream City*, D.C. became an inefficient, pothole-ridden sinkhole, and even Barry himself admits that he'd lost all energy by the third term (1987–91). "I was getting tireder and tireder," he tells me, "because the job was so damn hard."

Most of the talent that had graced his first administration had left through attrition and indictment. The schools ranked as some of the worst in the nation. The hobbled police force was literally outgunned by homegrown drug-dealers and their imported Jamaican rivals. Barry was distracted, disconnected, and partying like he was getting paid by the gram of whatever he ingested. As *Dream City* suggested, some of his more suspicious hospital visits for things like "hiatal hernia" were likely cocaine related.

Things grew so bleak that the liberal *Washington Monthly* even ran a piece in 1989 that jeopardized Detroit's civic pride, with a detailed house-of-horrors portrait titled "The Worst City Government in America—Washington, D.C."

But here at the Temple of Praise, people don't break out the scales and stack Barry's good deeds versus his bad ones. His popularity here transcends such minutiae. Supporting him, in spite of his struggles—even because of them—is almost a symbolic sacrament. Plus, he does something few other politicians in the District, even the city's later black mayors, do: he shows up.

Over the course of my time with him, he shows up to senior centers, where he gives twenty bucks to the oldest doll in attendance, which often takes some sorting out, what with senility. He shows up to the planning of the Labor Day picnic that he throws out of his own budget, overseeing details down to the hot dogs and what go-go bands are hired. The fact that he regularly gets raked over the coals by newspapers—which Barry tells me Ward 8ers largely don't read—for tax evasion and traffic arrests and addiction issues and many of the pathologies that plague their community in such numbers might help him rather than hurt him.

One morning, Barry hauls me to a "Ward 8 Leadership Council" breakfast at the gleaming new IHOP—considered a Ward 8 development triumph, which Barry helped champion. I find out that there isn't technically a "Ward 8 Leadership Council." Barry has merely assembled seventeen people in a back room—everyone from activists to ministers to community leaders to a Giant store manager (the first grocery chain to do business in the ward in a decade). There's even a white real estate developer named Jeff Epperson, who has a Texan accent, used to work for the National Republican Senatorial Committee, and speaks from experience that "politicians and perfect behavior should never be mentioned in the same sentence."

They tell me of Barry's tireless devotion to the ward, of how "he remembers people that don't have no title, no nothing," of how after forty years of public life he will "stand at the gate" for Ward 8 "and knows every crook and cranny in City Hall, he knows exactly where the money is at, where the dead bodies are," and can therefore put people with resources.

They tell me how the ward is finally moving in the right direction (Epperson's company is investing there), even if Bishop C. Matthew Hudson of Matthews Memorial Baptist says he's preaching two funerals that week—one for a gunned-down eighteen-year-old, the other for a seventy-six-year-old man beaten by a group of teenagers on Malcolm X Boulevard. (One afternoon, when tracking home with Barry, we get out of the car to see a dozen squad cars at the Congress Heights Metro station, as a young man in a wife-beater is being cuffed and put into one of them while the woman he just assaulted, and who dropped her baby in the melee, lies crying on the ground. "In Ward 8," Barry tells me, "if it ain't one thing, it's another. But it's always something.")

The IHOP convocation is a Barry-engineered Potemkin exhibit, to be sure. But the intensity of their possessiveness is no put-up job, and is similar to what I encounter all over the ward. When I interview Barry standing on Alabama Avenue, a random car pulls up and a woman yells out the window, "Are they pickin' on you again?" The

IHOP amen corner pisses blood over the way their man has been pil-
loried for behavior that's conveniently forgotten when it comes to the
likes of Bill Clinton or Ted Kennedy.

As James Coates, senior minister of Bethlehem Baptist Church,
says, "He understands our path—stony the road we trod. So when
someone attacks Mr. Barry, they attack all of us." I push back, and ask
the ministers and others what it would take for Barry to lose their
support. Would they still support him if he killed somebody? "Yes I
would," says Coates without blinking, then breaks into laughter. The
ministers then give biblical murder precedents—Moses killed, David
killed Bathsheba's husband, etc. "I'm coming to your church next
week," says Epperson.

When I visit Barry's constituency office one day in the ward,
conveniently located a few floors above the local welfare office, the intensity of this devotion is put quite explicitly to me by a woman who
mans Barry's phones and who's been volunteering for him for years.
She wears a matching African-print gown and head wrap, and she is
called "Mother Boone." She says she came to D.C. decades ago, when
her husband was laid up overseas in a hospital after getting injured in
the war—she doesn't remember which war.

"It started with a 'K,'" she says, her spotty memory failing her.

"Korea?" I ask.

"Maybe," she says.

After arriving from St. Louis, she lived in her car with her baby.
"The front seat was my living room, the back was my bedroom." Who
gave her shoes and milk for her baby? "Mr. Barry!" Boone says. Who
found her a place to live? "Mr. Barry!" When she was shot in the
stomach after getting carjacked, she got a special room at the hospital
with extra flowers and nightgowns and the works. "Guess who was
there with me?" Mother Boone intones, practically grabbing my lapels. "Gawwwd, and Jesus, and *Mr. Barry!*"

A few minutes later, I ask Barry if she in fact got shot when she
was carjacked. He shrugs, and says, "I don't know." Mother Boone
"goes in and out," a staffer explains. In some parts of the city, Barry
can't buy credit for things he's legitimately done. In Ward 8, he gets
credit even for the things he hasn't.

After church, Barry is famished. If you participate in a Temple of
Praise service, your cardio requirement is fulfilled for the day. Barry

insists on taking me and the Barry Angels to the pricey Old Ebbitt Grill downtown, since the only sit-down restaurants in Ward 8 are the IHOP and a former topless bar, the Players Lounge, where Barry likes to order the liver and onions and occasionally takes the stage to sing his theme song, T-Bone Walker's "Stormy Monday."

Before we go, however, we have to deposit "what little money I have" in his account so his debit card can cover it. The Caddy rolls up to a Safeway grocery store in neighboring Ward 7, which contains a SunTrust bank counter that sits behind bulletproof glass. Barry and I go in, and he spies the long line. "Oh my god, I gotta cut that," he says. So he heads to the front of the line and negotiates with a woman, telling her he's with a reporter, and he's in a hurry (after cutting, he'll later work every person in the line, as he's a perpetual campaigner).

While I wait behind him, a woman with a neck tattoo and bandanna-covered head approaches, assuming I'm a Barry staffer. Her name is Vicki Mitchell, and she's on the phone with her son, Lejeevan Toudle, who's currently in lockup for armed robbery. Telling her son Mayor Barry just walked in, she tells me, "My son said to tell you D.C. jail ain't got no air. You wanna speak to him?"

I grab the phone, and Lejeevan proceeds to tell me how it's 110 degrees in his cell. Not only that, "the canteen is messed up, they don't give us what we ordered." Spying my notebook, his mother adds, "put that on the list." I ask Lejeevan if he wants to speak with the mayor, who's technically a city councilman. He does. I hand the phone to Barry. "Yeah, what's happenin'?" Barry says, hearing his complaints. "All right," says Barry. "I can deal with that tomorrow, can't deal with that today." Barry gives me Lejeevan's phone number to write down, but is a digit short. No matter. He never asks me for it anyway.

Back in the car outside the Safeway, a booty-shaking lass walks by, giving Barry the eye. Kim, the kidney donor, offers play-by-play from the backseat: "We call it grinnin' and skinnin'."

"Y'all leave her alone, now," says Barry, adding, "I'm glad I'm in the car."

"We glad you are too," says Kim, "or you'd be out there another fifteen minutes."

"God gave me the gift of being gregarious," Barry explains. "I'm a touchy-feely kind of person." I offer that that's gotten him in a spot of trouble in the past. "A little bit," says Kim, caustically. "Everybody has some trouble sometimes," Barry assents. Another Safeway patron extends well wishes through the car window. "I don't care what no-body says. You my man!" he says. "I can't come in here," Barry says to me. "If I were to shop, I wouldn't be out of here till three hours later."

Arriving at Old Ebbitt, we are seated in a side room in the front of the restaurant ("the slave quarters," one of the girls calls it). Barry orders his favorite, the trout parmesan, and shows a sign of aging, as he occasionally does, when asking the waiter where his spinach and mashed potatoes are—they're under his fish.

I order a post-church bourbon, and Barry joins me by order-ing a white zinfandel, having sworn off the cognac—along with the cocaine, he insists—that used to cause him so many problems. If he bothers ordering any, he stops at one glass of wine during the many meals we have together. Still, I'm pretty sure that's not in the program of the AA meetings he's attended for years. Isn't even one glass of wine bad for his sobriety?

"No, it's bad for my kidney," he says, telling me everybody deals with addiction differently. "I do it my way," he says. "Oh no," says his spokeswoman, Natalie, sitting beside him.

I hadn't visited Barry to put him on the rack. But his responses to addiction issues, along with a host of his other troubles, practically dictate that any self-respecting reporter play prosecuting attorney. Barry is gentlemanly, never malicious, but he's also eternally argu-mentative. Anything you preface with "I read in the *City Paper* or *Washington Post*" will immediately elicit an objection. So that if, for instance, you told him you'd read that he loved his mother, he'd have to insist he didn't.

It's understandable, perhaps, that a man who is constantly under attack tends toward the defensive. But Barry frequently loses track of his own narrative, contradicts his former public utterances, and shows a less-than-straightforward hold on the truth. Over the entirety of our time together, we incessantly play cat-and-mouse. At various times, he insists he never really had an alcohol or serious drug problem—that his post-Vista trip to Hazelden was a "tactical move" for the upcom-ing trial. Then later he'll admit that alcohol is his only real addiction.

When I ask Barry how a seventy-three-year-old man can still find so much trouble, he says, "I don't get into trouble. People *get* me in trouble." But he does have a knack for getting into more trouble even when he's seemingly in more trouble than he could already be in. For instance, when already in prison, he was transferred to another facility after witnesses reported seeing him receive oral gratification from a female admirer in the visitation room. (He denies it to this day.) And after failing to pay his taxes for roughly seven years, repeatedly getting hauled before judges for his negligence, and having his pay garnished for roughly $3,050 per month (he says it was due to "procrastination"), Barry was put on probation by a judge and subsequently failed a drug test in 2006. Barry insists it was an unfortunate relapse. As with most of his problems, "a woman was involved," he admits.

Yet he swears that despite persistent rumors and even public declarations by his friends calling for him to take his sobriety more seriously, he did not use drugs from the time of his 1990 arrest until the 2006 relapse. When I bring up a 2002 incident, when police found a five-dollar rock in his car and claimed Barry had white powder on his face (they didn't charge him, saying they were trace amounts), Barry insists it was a frame-up. "It's really not consistent," he says. "If I'm smoking crack, I don't have powder on my face." He decided not to run for City Council afterward, and his fourth wife left him two weeks later, but he insists none of this was related.

I mention to Barry that his real addiction seems to be women. And in fact, in the early nineties, he confessed to sex addiction. "I never said that," he insists. Yes he did, I inform him. I had just read the clip the night before. He said it on an episode of *Sally Jessy Raphael*. "No, that's bullshit," he says. "We made a tactical mistake. We were trying to get our story out about what happened at the Vista, and she put me on with a sexually addicted person. We corrected that." I recheck the *Washington Post* clip later. Headline: "Marion Barry, Airing His Vices; on Sally Jessy Raphael, the Ex-Mayor Tells of Sex Addiction."

So naturally defensive is Barry that at one point, when driving around Ward 8, I ask him what pisses him off most about what he sees. "Some things don't piss me off, some things make me angry."

That's the same thing, I tell him. Natalie laughs and shakes her head, as though I'm seeing what she's up against.

"Nah, nah, there's a difference," he says.

"You argue about everything!" I tell him.

"I have to!"

Barry feels like he's been in a fight his entire life. Born to Mississippi sharecroppers (his mother used to carry him around in a cotton sack in the fields), Barry and his sisters were eight when their mother split for Memphis with them, leaving his father behind. Barry never saw him again. "I used to be ashamed of that," says Barry. "So in my bio, I used to say he died. 'Cause I was ashamed that I didn't have a natural father."

Growing up, he says, "I was very insecure. Didn't like my name. It was a lady's name. Didn't like my looks. Didn't like anything about myself." Kids would tease him about his name, and "I'd pop 'em in the mouth, damn right I would. Then I got to the point where I said what the hell. That's what God gave me. That's how I was born. This is how I look. To hell with them. Though I wasn't cussin' back then."

Sure, Barry has taken a beating over the years. "But I'm not supposed to be here," he tells me. When he was in high school, he'd never even heard of college, didn't know what it was. "In fact," he says, "my sixth-grade teacher told me, 'Marion Barry, you not gonna be anything. You're not gonna be anywhere.' I went home and cried to my mother. She said, 'Now don't listen to that stuff. You can do anything you want to do.' Here's a woman with a fourth-grade education talkin' about what I could do."

"I felt depressed for a couple days, then I said I'm not gonna buy that in my own mind." He became an achiever. He consistently made the honor roll. He was an Eagle Scout. He recited poems in church. He went to college and stopped one year short of getting his doctorate in chemistry, quitting to join the civil rights movement. "In chemistry, there's order," he says wistfully. "In politics, there's disorder. The rules change just about every other day."

I mention to Barry that for all his biblical invocations, the Bible teaches us to be humble, a trait he doesn't often display. "But there's a time to be humble, and a time not to be humble."

"When's the time not to be?" I ask.

"In front of your enemies," he says. "Because if they're trying to break your spirit, even if your spirit is broken, you can't let them know it. God gave me a strong spirit. People expect me to come in with my head down and out. Not me. I'm not doing it. I hold my head up. High."

Barry's spirit is sung home to me by longtime Barry watcher and critic Mark Plotkin, a political analyst for WTOP radio. In 1986, Plotkin unsuccessfully ran for City Council, and in the midst of his campaign he went to see Barry, who shared some advice. "I don't remember anything else he said," says Plotkin. "But the one thing that sticks in my mind twenty-three years later, which sums him up, is he told me, 'My whole life, people have told me what I can't do. And I'm not going to abide by that.'

"I think that's what motivates him more than anything," says Plotkin. He remembers talking to Barry right before sentencing in the income tax case. "I said, 'How do you feel about this?' He said, 'Well, you never know how these things turn out.' He was majorly calm. I'd be a sweating wreck. He was literally flirting with the clerk who announced the verdict. Talk about chutzpah."

After lunch at the Old Ebbitt, the check comes. I offer to split it, but Barry waves me off and throws down his debit card. The waitress disappears, then returns apologetically, informing Barry that his card's been rejected. I throw my credit card instead, and Barry's spokesperson, Natalie, panics, saying she should pay so I won't write about it. I tell her I will anyway, so she might as well let it ride.

A symposium commences at the table on the journalistic pros and cons of what just happened. The only person who doesn't care in the least? Marion Barry. "It just shows I'm human," he says. "Millions of Americans go through this every day. Think they got the bank thing straight, don't have it straight. Come on. We make mistakes. We have frailties." It turns out Barry has a big wad of bills in his pocket, which we notice when he tips the valet outside. "You could've paid for lunch," observes Natalie. "I had it," says Barry. "But whenever the *Weekly Standard* offers to pay, I'm takin' it."

"Welcome to the family," Natalie says with a grimace.

A few days later, Barry wants to return the favor, taking me and Natalie to lunch at Acadiana, a New Orleans–style eatery where he'll have the fried catfish and watermelon salad. First, though, he has to go to a downtown SunTrust and see what's what with his card and his retirement check, which seems to be missing from direct deposit.

"Who do I see about a problem with my card?" he says, once in the bank. As Barry cools his heels, customers, both white and black, come up to make small talk and take cell phone pictures. The branch manager, Yolette Olufemi, sits down with Barry and checks the damage. She looks a little sheepish about what she's discovered and gingerly informs him that Thrifty Car Rental has billed his card for $1,353.10, which has caused him to be overdrawn and to be assessed an additional penalty.

Barry mutters that the police impounded his car during the stalking charge episode, and, though they didn't press charges, "The police had my car. For a week. Illegally." He must've forgotten to pay for the rental car he needed in the meantime. He tells her apologetically that he should have his paycheck soon and can cover the shortfall. She sees me taking notes and seems somewhat embarrassed for him, telling Barry she waited on him six years ago and thanked him then, because he was responsible for her first summer job when she was a high school student. "Those lifetime experiences helped to put me where I am today. So I always say, 'Kudos Mr. Barry,'" she adds with somewhat strained cheer, offering to reduce his overdrawn penalty.

Marion Barry was, is, and will always be a ladies' man. We talk about women plenty. When I chat up one of his supporters, commenting on the fake gemstones glued to her eyelashes, Barry leans over my shoulder and says, "Don't hit on those women. That's my job."

One of the women he won't talk about much is Donna Watts-Brighthaupt, the central character in his current troubles. But when I ask him what the biggest regret of his life is, he has only one woman on his mind: "Effi."

He's referring to the late Effi Barry, his third wife and mother of his son, Christopher. Effi was an elegant former model with an aristocratic bearing, best known for sitting by Barry every day during the six-week Vista trial, hooking a rug in supportive silence, while a parade of witnesses detailed sex 'n' drug specifics that would've caused any normal wife to have a stroke.

She stuck with Barry for a while longer, then left him before he went to prison. They remained close, however. And he says that in the years before she died of myeloid leukemia in 2007, they even talked about getting remarried. The depth of his affection for her was evidenced from what he said at her funeral at National Cathedral: "I was not late, this time, Effi. I was on time."

One afternoon, in Barry's City Council office, after a vigorous interrogation, he says, "Wanna go to lunch? I ain't got no money. Card's still messed up." Before we do, however, he walks over to a framed photo of him with a laughing Effi at a Chamber of Commerce dinner. "Come look at this over here. Look how fine she looks. Yeah, my God." I ask if he misses her. "Absolutely," he says. "I do. I miss her. For about the last ten years or so, I didn't dream. After my transplant,

I started dreaming again. I dream in color. The toxins are out of my body. Two or three nights ago, I dreamed about her."

I ask what he dreamed. "I don't want to get into that," Barry says, as he often does about subjects he brings up.

Later that day, she comes up again. Barry has insisted we visit Linda Greene, his "fine" former chief of staff and decades-long friend, at her beautiful restored Victorian at the foot of a national parkland hill in Anacostia, atop which sits Frederick Douglass's old house.

Inside Linda's living room, the television is on, showing the "beer summit" between Obama, Skip Gates, and the Cambridge cop who arrested him. Barry and I both agree the spectacle of Obama and Co. pretending they're just regular guys having a brew is preposterous. When I suggest it might be useful for him to have a beer summit with the police, he grunts: "They'd probably poison my beer."

Barry sinks back on his shoulders into Linda's luxurious couch while eating pineapple and cheese slices from an hors d'oeuvres tray. She takes a seat on the arm of the couch beside him. They flirt, they reminisce, she fusses over his tie, telling him she doesn't like it much. They seem like an affectionate old married couple. I ask if they've ever been romantic. They both insist not, though Linda says her ex-husband still asks her if they ever got it on.

Linda was one of Effi's best friends and was with her at the end, so she and Barry start trading off, giving me the blow-by-blow of Effi's last days. Barry had seen Effi shortly before, in what ended up being her deathbed in Annapolis. "Even then," he recalls, "she said, 'Marion, I'm getting tired. I'm getting tired.' I said, 'You're not getting tired. It's gonna be all right. You're gonna make it through this. We've gone through worse than this.'"

Shortly thereafter, he left for Memphis to see his ailing mother. Linda called him while he was there and told him this was it. He knew he couldn't get back in time. "About ten minutes later," Barry says, "Linda called back again and said she's gone." His face pinches when he says this, his lip starts quivering. He shuts his eyes tight and tears stream from them, which he quickly covers with his hand, so nobody can see.

He eventually lightens the mood, looking at Linda. "Linda complains about me sometimes. But Effi willed me to you. So I'm stuck."

Both Barry and Linda talk freely about how much he cared for Effi, which prompts me to ask how he could put her through what he did: the infidelity, the public humiliation. Linda covers for him: "He's not doing it out of disrespect, or less love for the person he's committed to at that time."

Barry takes this in, meditatively chewing on a pineapple slice. "I haven't thought about it much," he confesses. "First of all, I love people. Attractive women. They're all attractive to me if they're female." We laugh.

"No, really," he insists. "But I guess part of what happens in life is you are what you see. Growing up without a natural father, I didn't see these one-on-one relationships. I'm just thinking about it for the first time, quite frankly. I mean I've thought about it, but not in this depth. I think there ought to be fidelity between a man and a woman. But you are what you see. And when I was growing up, I didn't see men who were one-woman men. So I guess it sort of got caught in my personality. I'm not rationalizing it. It is what it is."

We're ready to leave Linda's. We go out to the car, and on the floor of the backseat is a Häagen-Dazs cup filled with melted butter-pecan ice cream. Natalie had bought Barry a cone when she was driving us around D.C., as Barry showed me his mayoral-era development triumphs. But the cone started dripping all over his suit. I suggested throwing it out the window, but this is Barry's city. He adamantly refused. He might run afoul of the law every now and then, but he's not some kind of litterbug. So instead, he quickly ate it while letting the rest drip into the cup.

When he slides into the car at Linda's, he reaches down, drinks the melted ice cream, then hands the empty cup to Linda. "Oh thanks," she says. "Now I'm the trash woman."

Several days later, I follow Barry to New York for the premiere of *The Nine Lives of Marion Barry*. He is in his glory, disembarking from a stretch limo with his Angels for a screening high atop the HBO building, which overlooks the yoganauts and Ping-Pong players of Bryant Park. He sings a few bars of the old gospel hymn "Victory Is Mine" when he takes the microphone after the screening (I told Satan to get thee behind / Victory today is mine). He accepts well wishes from statuesque blondes, who are aroused at the sight of a young, militant Barry in a leopard-print dashiki. "You're a beautiful man, I just want to put that out there," says one.

At a reception buffet line, I run into Jim Vance, a tall, well-dressed, barrel-chested African American news anchor from

D.C.—half of the longest-running anchor team in Washington—who has known and covered Barry since the late sixties. Vance too was addicted to cocaine for seven years back in the eighties.

Around Barry, Vance is all hugs and smiles. But I ask him to give me his straight-up assessment of Barry. He raises his eyes to the ceiling, thinks a bit, then says, "There were so many of us who had so much hope for Marion. I don't know too many people that were more blessed or that had more skills than Marion had, nor too many people who were a bigger disappointment, quite frankly."

Vance's own addiction "snuck up on me": "It was a pattern of behavior that was nobody's fault but my own. I think the same applied to Marion. A pattern of behavior began that Marion couldn't blame anybody, or anything, except Marion for. There comes a point for most of us who are addicts, that today, I'm either gonna live, or gonna die. And you begin the process of living, or continue the process of dying. I don't know that Marion's got to that point yet."

After the screening, Barry and the Angels and I load into the limo and head uptown for chicken 'n' waffles, fried catfish, and shrimp étouffée. It's supposed to be the last of our time together, but he insists on breakfast the next morning, to clear a few things up. Just as he'll do when he calls me a few days later, unbidden, at home.

The specifics of what he says turn out not to be that important. But it feels as though he is addressing some advice I'd given him when catching him at the screening. Earlier that afternoon, from my hotel, I'd watched him tussle with an MSNBC anchor while promoting the film, Barry insisting yet again that he'd done nothing wrong at the Vista. I suggested to him that if he didn't insult people's intelligence regarding the things they already know about him, he might get a fairer hearing regarding the things they don't know.

So, for instance, at breakfast the following morning, Barry offers, "When I told you about recreational use, I don't want you to think I'm trying to minimize it. It was a serious problem, yeah. But the good news is, look at me now!" Of course, such rare moments of honest disclosure come between hours and hours of amnesia, revisionism, suspect self-justification, airbrushing, and legacy buffing.

But that's okay. It felt, over the time I was with him, as if there were several moments where Marion Barry was trying to tell me something. Maybe even the truth. If he can't quite always get there, it's still a commendable effort. After all, he hasn't had much practice.

GOODBYE, BABYLON

Jesus Bleeds on Satan's Music

When I was a kid, my parents found Jesus, took to Him like otters to water, and left the more traditional churches of their upbringing to enlist as full-fledged evangelicals. Depending on where my military officer father's assignments took us, we did turns in all kinds of nearly indistinguishable denominations, from Evangelical Free to Bible churches. But we spent the bulk of our time with the Southern Baptists. I liked the SBs, as we called ourselves. We were steady and without pretense and highly egalitarian, yet still earthy enough to kick dirt on our charismatic, Pentecostal brothers, what with all their emotive pew-jumping and tongues-speaking. If we wanted people carrying on from the pulpit in languages we didn't understand, the SBs reasoned, we'd have become Catholics.

In the one-dimensional world of easy secular stereotypes, many mistakenly think that most Baptists have a bit of the snake handler in them. But the only time I saw a rattler at church—behind the education building—one of the deacons killed it with a shovel. Being Baptist was actually much less dramatic than getting bitten by poisonous snakes. The articles of faith were easy to keep track of. Baptists generally believed that faith in Christ and His redeeming sacrifice earned you salvation, that you would evidence this faith by climbing into a baptismal one time in your life to get dunked by a preacher in fishing waders, that you were to religiously attend potlucks to which you'd never bring a store-bought sheet cake, and finally—and this one was open to some interpretation—that you would refrain from drinking, dancing, and especially drinking while dancing. If you lapsed, and did either or both, you could still ask forgiveness and were in no danger of getting your name scrubbed from the Book of Life. But you were taking your chances in gossip circles—gossiping being Baptists' official sport outside of church, and often inside of it.

The no-drinking-and-dancing planks never bothered me much.

Though I've since made up for lost time with the former, I still cite the no-dancing rule, not for moral reasons, but because it keeps me from getting dragged onto the floor at wedding receptions during The Electric Slide. What did bother me, however, was when my moderate parents briefly fell sway to peer pressure, as the youth minister called it. A fire-breathing band of aspiring church splitters (splitting churches between quarreling factions also being a favorite Baptist pastime), decided rock 'n' roll was Satan's theme music. Unlike other zealots of that time, they didn't conduct any record-burning bonfires in the church parking lot, or listen to Zeppelin albums backward to hear Robert Plant pledge fealty to the Prince of Darkness. What the records said forward was bad enough for them.

This wasn't good news for me. In addition to suffering through the pop offerings of the day—from rock gods like Toto and Michael "She's a Maniac" Sembello—I also regularly dipped into my dad's old soul records, enjoying a 101 course in everything from the Motown sound to Ray Charles to funkier stuff like War and the Jimmy Castor Bunch. When my parents decided it would be best to lock this vinyl gold away, I was forced, like thousands of Christian kids before me, to cop my music fix in the artistic wasteland known as contemporary Christian music (CCM). The moratorium lasted about three years, and it was a dark time for all.

Since the CCM world didn't offer enough selection to be truly discriminating, my friends and I tended to gravitate toward those who'd made their bones in the secular world—closer to what we actually wanted to be listening to. It was our sincere hope that though they were singing for Jesus now, our new idols had once snorted their weight in cocaine and boinked arenasful of groupies. It was bad for the soul, we reasoned, but good for the music. We liked Kerry Livgren because he'd cofounded the group Kansas, Joe English because he'd been a drummer for Wings, and Leon Patillo because he'd played keyboards for Santana. Never mind that I hated both Kansas and Wings, or that the Santana résumé-sweetener was nothing to brag about (considering they had sixteen lineup changes from 1966 to 1984 alone, it's quite possible that I played keyboards for Santana, and just don't remember).

With some exceptions, the music tended to be too on-the-nose—saccharine and over melodic—all light and no shadows, all gaiety and no grit. And when Christian artists tried to dirty themselves up, it was often painful to watch, such as when the hair metal band Stryper came around in the mideighties (their name, they said, was an acronym for "Salvation Through Redemption Yielding Peace Encouragement and Righteousness"). Stryper released albums like *To Hell with the Devil.* They wore matching yellow-and-black spandex, making them look like bumblebees with Farrah-hair. They didn't scare anybody. Except maybe when they'd play bars, where they'd try to have it both ways by chucking Bibles at patrons from the stage, making the more pragmatic among us wonder how you're supposed to win people to Christ when you're making them spill their drinks.

I had to get out. So I went to my folks with all the theological profundity a fourteen-year-old could muster, asking them: How could a God who doesn't appreciate the beauty of the "yeah-yeah" echo in Sam Cooke's "Bring It On Home to Me," or the Saturday-morning horns in Curtis Mayfield's "So in Love," be a God worth serving? My parents, being reasonable people, didn't think God had bad taste. So we resolved to serve Him, and go back on the hard stuff. They took to listening to all the soft-rock hits of the sixties, seventies, and eighties. I became the eclectic paragon of musical refinement that I remain to this day.

But I take the long way around the barn to pose the question that has haunted Christians for centuries. Proto–Jesus rocker Larry Norman actually crystallized it in song once, asking "Why Should the Devil Have All the Good Music?"—a question that purportedly dated back at least to the time of Martin Luther, who asked it concerning his own hymnody when he was attacked for appropriating tavern songs. The going understanding of both Christian and heathen alike has been that when God banished Satan and carved up their respective fiefdoms, He kept all the key stuff: the clouds, the mansions, the streets paved with gold. But as a sop for assigning Lucifer to an eternity in fiery darkness, he gave him most of the good music. Therefore, Satan got the Rolling Stones and Robert Johnson. God kept Debby Boone and George Beverly Shea. Most people think that God got screwed.

But the new six-CD boxed set, *Goodbye, Babylon,* shows that God may have been slyer than originally thought—having held in reserve long-forgotten and recently discovered gems that have been dusted off by Lance Ledbetter, a twenty-seven-year-old Atlanta software installer and former DJ. Having become obsessed with sacred music from the early part of last century, Ledbetter, over a five-year period, scoured the bins and collections of knowledgeable musicologists, enlisting help from everyone he could lay hands on, including his father, who pulled appropriate Scripture passages as companion notes for songs. He financed this labor of love on his credit cards.

What he came up with is 135 songs and 25 sermons—the largest collection of sacred music ever assembled. Instead of relinquishing control to some major label (which, with *Goodbye Babylon*'s critical success, will hopefully inspire knockoffs), Ledbetter put the whole thing out on his own start-up label, Dust-to-Digital. It's an appropriate name for the time-consuming process of finding, cleaning up, and finally transferring source material from the scratchy, hissing records. As Charles Wolfe, one of the many invaluable liner note contributors, writes, the records, which predated mixing or multiple microphones, often cut in makeshift studios, were carried everywhere from coal camps to railroad yards to juke joints. But for the love of a few obsessive custodians, the music would've been lost forever, as most of the records were "worn out, broken, thrown away, made into ashtrays, used as target practice for local carnival-ball throwing contests, plowed into landfills, or donated to scrap shellac drives during World War II."

What these salvagers have preserved is a gospel hodgepodge, everything from Sacred Harp singing to hillbilly romps to field holler/prison chants to front-porch blues to jubilee quartets to old-timey country to Sanctified congregational singing to Pentecostal rave-ups. They all come down in a rain of clamoring tambourines and bottleneck slide guitars, clawhammer banjo picking, booming jug band blowing and barrelhouse piano rolls. The songs come from many traditions, though the overwhelming influence comes from both the black and white strains of Holiness music—which resulted from the merger of the Fire Baptized Holiness Church and Pentecostal Holiness Church in 1911. This came five years after the 1906 Azusa Street revival, in which the black holiness evangelist William Joseph Seymour sparked a movement that church historians say resulted in thousands receiving the "Pentecostal baptism with the Holy Ghost with the apostolic sign of speaking with other tongues."

Pentecostals had spent the first years of the twentieth century breaking away from the Methodists and Baptists from which they sprang, who just weren't cutting it worship-wise. Some Baptists would eventually catch up—Thomas A. Dorsey, an African American secular musician who became the "Father of Gospel," was a Baptist—as was Mahalia Jackson. But Pentecostals rejected the starchy hymns, nonrhythmic accompaniment, and nonimprovisational singing of these established denominations.

Those who became Pentecostals were a largely hardscrabble lot accustomed to having cosmic bricks dropped on their heads. This formed both their musical vernacular (derived from everything from mountain music to old spirituals) and their perception of God (many blacks were still around who had lived through slavery). When it came to worship, Holiness types didn't play around. In both song and sermon, they portrayed a fierce God—one of redemption, but also of vengeance—not the simplistic elbow-patched grandpa or open-armed hippie Jesus of the modern superchurch soundtrack. In a 1930 song called "Memphis Flu," Elder David R. Curry, pastor of the Oakley Street Church of God in Christ, and his congregation sing over barrelhouse piano runs, hand claps, and interjections of "Praise Jesus!": "Yes, He killed the rich and poor / And He's going to kill more / If you don't turn away from your shame."

Referring to the gift of tongues—central to their theology—the Holiness types spoke of being "baptized with fire"—as opposed to their gentler cousins the Baptists, who stuck with water. And while there's no tongues-speaking on *Goodbye, Babylon,* it would be difficult for anyone listening to the holy roar of Reverend Sister Mary Nelson on the tune "Judgment" to tell the difference. ("Well, all you hypocrite members / You wasting your time away / My God's calling for work-mens / And you had better obey.")

All of this strange and wondrous music comes in a package that itself lessens the pain of the hundred-dollar outlay required to own it (it would be a bargain at twice the price). I've had it for a week, and already it is among my most indispensable possessions—right up there with my *Complete Hank Williams* box, my *Stax Singles,* or my *'70s Soul Experience* set, itself ingeniously encased in something resembling an old eight-track tape holder. The packaging is as beautiful as anything I've seen. It comes in a slide-off wood box slightly smaller than the family Bibles salesmen used to peddle door to door. (Ledbetter contracted with a wine box manufacturer). The cover is adorned with a Gustave Doré Tower of Babel etching from the late 1800s called *Confusion of Tongues.*

Open the box, and you are met with the smell of cedar, as if from an old dresser drawer full of lost treasures. It is packed not only with six CDs and a two-hundred-page booklet intended to represent an old hymnal, but also with raw cotton, which Ledbetter, if he's not putting me on, told me was "handpicked from Alabama—my uncle's brother helped us out with it." The cotton is not intended to keep the box's contents from rattling around inside, but rather, as a note says, "This set is dedicated to all the artists who wanted their message to be heard. The cotton is a reminder of the struggle, strife and sorrow that so many of them endured."

By now, the figure of the ethnomusicologist has nearly become one of sport—the earnest white guy in search of The Source of All Things Authentic—looking for some gnarled old black man held together with nothing but epoxy or suspenders, missing half his teeth and all his wits, preferably sitting on a porch, ready to throw down with a self-taught instrument, exhibiting his primitive genius. These sleuths follow in the footsteps of John and Alan Lomax, who scoured the plantations and prisons of the south for Library of Congress field recordings, or those of Harry Smith, whose 1952 *Anthology of American Folk Music* is considered the genre's seminal work. Neal Pollack, in his recent novel *Never Mind the Pollacks,* nicely lampoons the phenomenon, as his protagonist, a pretentious rock critic, is on a holy quest to locate "Clambone Jefferson," a bluesman who was raised in a three-room outhouse, who sings songs like "The Devil Bit My Ass in Two," who went to jail for disemboweling his uncle with a tuning fork, and who was "the horrible essence of American music. He is my god."

Ledbetter escapes this fate by concentrating on sacred music exclusively—which has been neglected by all but the most rabid collectors. Instead of the telegraphed blues clichés we've become accustomed to as one collection after another rolls down the remastered assembly line (one servicing one's big-legged woman, one dusting one's broom, one selling one's soul to dicey characters one meets at crossroads in Mississippi), Ledbetter's set has all the rawness and vitality of the blues masters. But lyrically, the artists he collects—many of whom were secular stalwarts who dabbled in or switched full-time to gospel music—are playing for much higher stakes.

There are all sorts of grand themes running through *Goodbye, Babylon:* deliverance and judgment, mortal expiration and eternal salvation. Many secular critics haven't quite gotten past the buckets of blood, alluded to in songs like the one by Da Costa Woltz's Southern Broadcasters, a 1920s string band, who ask, "Are You Washed in the Blood of the Lamb?" Or there's the number by Ernest V. Stoneman—Thomas Edison's favorite hillbilly artist—who, along with his Dixie Mountaineers, sings, "Oh, the blood of Calvary's brow / I can see it flowing now." But to the church-steeped whose ears are already acclimated, it's standard Sunday-morning viscera.

The more striking leitmotif is the blindness. The collection boasts Blind Lemon Jefferson, Blind Roger Hays, Blind Benny Paris and his blind wife, Blind Alfred Reed, Blind Joe Taggart, Blind Mamie Forehand, and no fewer than four Blind Willies (Davis, Harris, McTell, and Johnson)—the last of whom was blinded when his stepmother threw lye in his eyes during a fight with his father. And that's just the artists with "blind" monikers. There's also blind Roosevelt Graves and Brother (his brother wasn't blind but had only one eye), and blind Jimmie Strothers (found by John Lomax in a Virginia state prison, where he presumably came to Jesus after murdering his wife with an ax). So fashionable was it to be a blind gospeler, that it is said Blind Joe Taggart wasn't even blind, he just had cataracts. And then there was blind Arizona Juanita Dranes, an influential gospel singer who once traveled from Chicago to Texas with a note of introduction that read, "Since she is deprived of her natural sight, the Lord has given her a spiritual sight." Even nonbelievers have to give God points for consistency: He sticks with His blind people.

Such physical impairments are a keen reminder that this is hard music made by hard people—singers to whom grace did not come cheaply, and who are not big proponents of today's prosperity-gospel, *Prayer of Jabez* type rhetoric. In a song recorded at the Parchman State Penitentiary in 1940s Mississippi, a prisoner named Jimpson sings "No More My Lord," his rhythm section nothing more than the sound of splitters thudding against wood on his work gang (at one point during the recording, a wood chip actually hits the microphone). Then there's Elder Effie Hall and Congregation, who did their version of Thomas A. Dorsey's "Take My Hand, Precious Lord." Dorsey was a jazz and blues sideman who decided to stick on the Gospel Highway after composing his most famous song, which he wrote after locking himself in a room for three days after the death of his wife and son during childbirth. These are the songs of people who had accepted their lot, and weren't holding out for a much better deal—at least not in this life. ("Precious Lord, take my hand / Lead me on, let me stand / I am tired, I am weak, I am old.")

While much contemporary Christian music strives not to even mention the J-word—favoring double entendres that could serve, depending on the listener, as either sacred music or generic love songs, these were singers who took their Jesus straight, without chasers or apologies. While plenty of the artists of *Goodbye, Babylon* are famous—Mahalia Jackson, Bill Monroe, Skip James—just as many are one-offers who, in addition to being coal miners or migrant farmers, were sisters and elders, deacons and reverends. Not viewing the church as a springboard to popular success as so many legions of R&B stars have through the years, they sang with conviction and without embarrassment, maintaining that the believer conformed to the belief system, not the other way around. They were direct and raucous; in short, they put the "fun" back in fundamentalism.

They were groups like the Jubilee Gospel Team, who sang in 1928 that "Jesus will be your lawyer / He'll be your lawyer all the way." They were singers like Mother McCollum, who sang, over her own slide guitar in "Jesus Is My Air-o-plane," "Reeling and rocking, you can hide no sin / Jesus coming in His air-o-plane." They were stiff-necked dogmatists like Sister O. M. Terrell—a street minister from the Fire Baptized Holiness Church of God—who, with a wink, put everyone from adulterers to "snuff dippers" on notice, singing: "You know the Bible right / Somebody wrong / God knows / You're wrong." They are people whose God often seems to have failed them, but who believe anyway—whose songs and wails and murmurs are often defiant affirmations. Death does not make them blanch, or intimidate them from tending the pressing business of "getting right," which explains sermons like Reverend J. M. Gates's 1926 Christmas pick-me-up "Death Might Be Your Santa Claus," followed by "Will the Coffin Be Your Santa Claus?" and the capper, "Will Hell Be Your Santa Claus?"

As musicians and vocal stylists, they took a backseat to no secular artists of the day—and often, they doubled as the secular artists of the day. Legendary blues guitarist Blind Lemon Jefferson, of Primitive Baptist stock, went so far as to record religious material under the pseudonym "Deacon L. J. Bates" to conceal his secular identity. They were singers like Brother Claude Ely, who, in the Kentucky Holiness tradition, sings and plays the perennial Church of God in Christ shout, "There Ain't No Grave Gonna Hold My Body Down," with a ferocity that suggests he was getting sawed in half while performing.

There are tracks of mysterious beauty, without equivalent in any of today's gospel, blues, R&B, or country idioms. In a 1927 cut, Washington Phillips, in his laid-back Pops Staples–like way, sings, matter-of-factly, "Oh lift him up, that's all / Lift Him up in His word / If you tell the name of Jesus everywhere / If you'll keep His name a'ringin' everywhere that you go / He will draw men unto Him." Phillips, whose demise was long thought to have come in a mental institution, was found only recently by researcher Michael Corcoran to instead have passed on from head injuries sustained in a tumble down a flight of stairs at a welfare office in Teague, Texas. The otherworldly instrument he played is also a source of scholarly debate. Some think it is a dolceola—a portable baby grand piano–like instrument, of which only fifty are thought to exist today. Others who knew him said it was a zitherlike instrument of his own creation. In any case, it sounds like a ghostly calliope from some half-remembered dream.

Then there are songs like "O Day" by Bessie Jones and the Sea Island Singers—as satisfying as music gets. Sung typically as a Christmas and New Year's shout after an all-night worship service, this version, recorded by Alan Lomax in St. Simons Island, Georgia, in 1960, features voices twinning, yet not quite harmonizing. They overlap and swirl and loop around each other over a guitar, syncopated varying-tempo hand clapping, and a fife that threatens to derail the entire process like a fluttering wheel on a runaway shopping cart, but instead provides the perfect tension that holds it all together. It is infectious Holiness music, that when I play it—over and over and over again—sees my one- and four-year-old boys bounding through my office door, clapping and dancing as if in some tent-meeting trance. I'd probably join them, if I hadn't been raised Southern Baptist. The lyrics, simple and repetitive, pretty much sum up the whole ball of wax, redemption-wise: "Yonder come day, I heard him say / Yonder come day, it's a dying day / Yonder come day, it's a burying day / Yonder come day, I was on my knees / Yonder come day, when I heard him say / Yonder come day, that's a New Year's Day / Day done broke into my soul / Yonder come day, well, come on, child / Yonder come day, Jordan roll."

In a recent piece for the *Washington Post*, Eddie Dean, one of the great chroniclers of lost America—which isn't a crowded field—interviewed Dick Spottswood, who, at Ledbetter's behest, served as both music and liner notes wrangler on much of the *Goodbye, Babylon* set. Spottswood, himself a Washington, D.C., institution as host of the local public radio station's invaluable *Obsolete Music Hour,* is no holy-rolling Bible thumper. But he perfectly nailed the difference between the old and new sacred music: "It's not like contemporary Christian songs, which are all praising Jesus, with nothing about sin or guilt. They've turned Jesus into a very cheap, off-the-shelf, one-size-fits-all Jesus. There's nothing of substance left, and the music reflects this sort of mindless cheerfulness. With the old-time gospel songs, like [the Monroe Brothers'] 'Sinner You Better Get Ready,' there are dark clouds and tragedy and death and all the unpleasantries you have to go through before you can stand in line at the redemption counter."

As a kid, I would get chills when we used to sing the old 1899 Lewis E. Jones hymn "There Is Power in the Blood." The women, trying to out-falsetto one another, would sing, "There is power, power, wonder working power in the blood, of the Lamb." The men would double-time, walking a steady bass line underneath, with "There is power, power, power, power, wonder-working power." And there is, in fact, power, listening to Jesus bleed into the Devil's music.

It's a sensation I get over and over again, watching secular artists reach up to address the sacred. The great ones often seem to get greater (the Rolling Stones singing "I Just Want to See His Face" and "Shine a Light"). The not-so-great acts often achieve greatness doing the same (the closing flourish of Lionel Richie and the Commodores' much-overlooked 1981 song "Jesus Is Love" is one of the most pristine acts ever committed in a studio).

I was reminded of this during a recent re-viewing of *The Last Waltz,* the universally acclaimed 1978 film in which the Band took a final bow by inviting tons of more famous guest stars like Eric Clapton and Bob Dylan to turn them into a backing band at their own farewell concert. In between all the high-wattage stage performances, which made the soundtrack, came a quiet moment tucked in the middle which has been all but forgotten. It is one of my favorite moments in the Band's history, and, by extension, one of my favorite moments in music. At some flophouse, the Band, looking desiccated and debauched from Lord-knows-how-many years on the road, was enjoying one of their last moments of total camaraderie. Keyboardist

Richard Manuel sat in a chair, while Robbie Robertson and Rick Danko sat on an adjoining couch.

They seemed blissfully unaware that their best years were soon to be behind them. Manuel, less than a decade later, would hang himself in a motel room. And Danko, who played the loose bass lines and sang the yearning, desperate harmonies that crystallized their sound, looked beautifully doomed as always. (He would later lose a son, and die prematurely himself.) Monkeying around for director Martin Scorsese, Manuel suggests the boys strike up "'Old Time Religion' for the folks." Robertson and Danko oblige. Robertson strums his guitar, while Danko, not even bothering to lift his fiddle to his shoulder, saws off the opening notes. Robertson sings it straight—*give me that old time religion . . . it's good enough for my grandpa . . . it's good enough for me . . .* while Danko, still fiddling, lays down some percussion, kicking tables and stomping floors as he echoes Robertson, while improvising "good enough" interjections around the song's nub. The whole moment is ragged and off-the-cuff and lasts only about forty-five seconds. But somehow, it is perfect. At its conclusion, with the spell broken, Robertson takes a drag off his cigarette and offers, ironically, "It's not like it used to be."

Indeed, it isn't. Which is why we should study and cherish collections like *Goodbye, Babylon*. There is something ennobling about watching fallible man—tired and weak and old, in Thomas Dorsey's words—stumbling around to find God in the dark. Vicariously, we take their ride, as men and women who knew difficulty hope that the best parts of themselves cross the goal line—that they, in the words of cataract-addled Blind Joe Taggart, get to the "great camp meeting on the other side of the shore." Meanwhile, we are left with the documentation of their struggle, the bottleneck slides and jug blows and hand claps of those who left the next best part of themselves behind on scratchy vinyl, pointing the way for the rest of us, still stumbling around in the dark.

HITTING HEATHENS WITH CHAIRS

George South, Evangelical Wrestler

Concord, North Carolina

Every now and then, one encounters a man who is not afraid to face the darkness, to lock eyes with the devil, to climb inside the squared circle, and to hit somebody in the head with a chair for Jesus. George South is such a man.

At first glance, South seems like nothing special: He has twenty-inch biceps for arms, and a mean-*muchacho* mustache. He wears his banana-hammock shorts high and tight, and when his shoulder-length ponytail becomes unslicked, it frizzes into an angry mane. Many of his colleagues share these traits, with one notable exception: the John 3:16 scripture on the seat of his trunks. For upon second glance, George South is the oddest of ducks—he's a Christian professional wrestler.

Christianity and athletics have commingled since the mid-nineteenth century. It was then that the "Muscular Christianity" movement (which promoted character-building through sport) took root in British schools, as exemplified in Thomas Hughes's 1857 novel *Tom Brown's School Days.* Making its way across the Atlantic, Muscular Christianity found adherents among the likes of gospeler Billy Sunday, an ex–baseball player who sounded like a pro wrestler when he denounced sinners as "beetle-browed, hog-jowled, peanut-brained, weasel-eyed four flushers." Since then, enough Jocks for Jesus tomes and Christian athletic associations have proliferated to keep faith-professing athletes booked on the church banquet tour in perpetuity.

Professional wrestling, however, has remained a godless province, watched by thirty-four million viewers—fakery be damned—who catch national broadcasts six nights a week. Wrestling script-writers used to conjure up ritualized battles between good (the babyfaces) and evil (the heels). But today's wrestlers, says Dave Meltzer, of the

Wrestling Observer Newsletter, all inhabit the same moral wasteland, no longer breaking down into faces and heels, but into "badasses and badder asses." Consequently, groups like the Parents Television Council release studies finding that the World Wrestling Federation's *Smackdown!* show alone accounted for over 11 percent of the combined sex, profanity, and violence on television in 1999. Where wrestling fans used to be treated to milk-drinking babyfaces and mustache-twirling foreign menaces, they now witness subplots incorporating everything from rape to transvestites.

Needless to say, the sport isn't noted for religious iconography, though there has been some. In the eighties, scores of Bible-belt youth were scared witless by wrestler Kevin Sullivan, who pledged solemn devotion to Lucifer. On the Christian side of the ledger, most characters working religious angles were objects of scorn or heels in disguise. There was snake-oil salesman Brother Love, and Ernest Angel, a heel manager out of Memphis who used to clock the opposition with Bibles. A few years back, the WWF tried to launch the Sisters of Mercy, a nun tag team consisting of Sister Angelica and Mother Smucker—an idea that met its just demise after one outing.

In recent years, there's been a slew of ex-wrestlers who have joined the ministry: everyone from Tully Blanchard to "The Million Dollar Man" Ted DiBiase. But they are just that—ex-wrestlers who have forsaken the profession that corrupted them. This year, in Texas, the Christian Wrestling Federation was founded by Robert "Jesus Freak" Vaughn, a Sunday School teacher and former football player who put together an evangelical wrestling road show. But none of the talent has ever actually wrestled professionally. Of that rather narrow demographic—the preaching, active-duty professional wrestler—there is, by my count, only one man who still prizes his faith and his work, and who has never forsaken either: George South.

I first meet South in a strip mall parking lot in Concord, North Carolina, which lies just a few miles east of the Charlotte Motor Speedway. Here, in a converted grocery warehouse that sits behind a hair replacement shop and a Mexican mart, he runs a wrestling school. South bellows a hearty "Hey, Buddy!"—his favorite salutation—as he emerges from his GMC van in Converse All Stars, an "I love Jesus" cutoff tank top, and shorts slit to accommodate his quadriceps.

A twenty-year veteran of the business, the thirty-seven-year-old

South used to wrestle as "Gorgeous George"—a moniker he's dropped because "it's false advertising," he says, pointing to the furrowed scars on his forehead. Now, he is "Mr. Number One," which is not a boast, but an homage to Paul Jones, the former National Wrestling Alliance champ and South's boyhood idol, who used to wrestle under the same. Jones now runs a garage in Charlotte and has contracted cancer, affording South the opportunity to witness to him and pray with him weekly—a dream come true that South says could be rivaled only by "him beating me with an Indian deathlock."

South was born in the foothills of the Smoky Mountains in Sugar Grove, North Carolina. Both of his parents died in a car accident when he was six, scattering George and his thirteen siblings and forcing them to rely on the charity of townspeople. Early on, South discovered his two animating influences: Christianity and "rasslin." When he was thirteen, his brother Bill helped out with the former, informing George that everyone was on their way to heaven or hell. When curious George inquired how you arrived at each destination, Bill replied, "Well, to get to hell, you ain't got to do much. You're headed there anyway." George opted for heaven, and was relieved when Bill told him the plan of salvation wasn't much more complicated: "Just ask Jesus into your heart, and ask the Lord to forgive you your sins."

South was introduced to wrestling a short time later, when "The Nanny," an elderly woman who took George in for nine years until he graduated from high school, turned him on to television matches. From there, he started frequenting the Monday-night bouts at the old Charlotte Park Center, rooting for Paul Jones as if his life depended on it. The first time South attended, "I spent fifteen minutes just sniffin' the popcorn," he says. "When I saw that ring, I thought I'd start crying; I was in heaven."

South became what the pros call a "mark for the business," believing every last staged "spot" (the wrestlers' preplanned moves). After high school, he got a job driving a truck at a textile mill. But his calling beckoned when he saw an ad to "Fulfill your dreams—be a wrestler." South showed up for the casting call in his work clothes. "It was like a movie," he says, recalling how he opened the creaky door of an old building in Charlotte to see a Samoan, an old man, a woman, and a midget, who invited him into the ring. "I was so stupid, I said okay," recalls South. "They took turns. The old guy, Rusty Roberts, tied me in knots. The woman hurt me worse than the rest of them. The midget kicked me in the ribs as hard as he could. They tore my work pants. I was bleeding. They about killed me." George was hooked for life.

South spent the next five years or so wrestling on the Carolina circuit (which he says is to professional wrestling what the "little shriner circus is to Ringling Brothers"). From there, he hooked up with the league that would become—Ted Turner bought them out—World Championship Wrestling. South simultaneously wriggled into Vince McMahon's World Wrestling Federation.

Though he called himself Mr. Number One, his ranking stood much lower. South was an "underneath guy" or "jobber"—a stooge paid to sacrifice his body and lose matches, which he calls "a lost art" now that everybody wants to be a main event guy. Of the four thousand professional matches South estimates he's fought, he says he's won "about a hundred." In his dated highlights reel, you can see him getting stomped by the best. From "Nature Boy" Ric Flair to "Dirty" Dick Slater, every match seems to end with the words that were music to Mr. Number One's ears: "That'll be the end of George South."

While South was never a contract player, he saw plenty of TV time—until he mixed his faith with his wrestling persona. South had always passed out tracts in the locker room. But in the midnineties, he finally decided to work his faith into his wrestling gimmick during a Georgia Championship Wrestling broadcast on Turner's TBS Superstation. Determined to debut his John 3:16 rasslin' britches during a match with "Heavy Metal" Van Hammer, George was pulled aside by Grizzly Smith, the federation's road manager, and was told Ted Turner wouldn't stand for overt displays of religiosity. If South did not remove his trunks, he would not be paid. "I could go out there with a woman half-nekkid or cuss on the microphone, and that's okay," says an incredulous South, who notes that "Stone Cold" Steve Austin now sports the blasphemous "Austin 3:16" on his trunks. "I wasn't goin' out there to preach, I was goin' out there to get my tail kicked like I always do." After holding up the broadcast for thirty minutes, South relented and wore his drawers inside out. Afterward, "I apologized to the Lord," says South. "I didn't do TV after that. I could've gone back, but it was with that stipulation."

Instead, South has returned to the hardscrabble independent circuit. After two decades in the business, he has witnessed just about everything. There was Brutus "the Barber" Beefcake, who shaved South's head four weeks in a row at the WWF. ("You'd make a hundred fifty bucks for rasslin'," says South, "plus three hundred bucks for lettin' 'em cut your hair—plus afterwards, you get trimmed up by the WWF beautician.") There was Rattlesnake Westbrooks, who used to eat dog food and cockroaches backstage ("his dressing room shows were better than his matches"). Then there was The Convict, who ended up getting busted for boosting the checkbook of the National Guard Armory where they were wrestling. "That guy lived his gimmick, buddy," South says.

South has taken his encyclopedic wrestling know-how and put it to good use. His Exodus Wrestling Alliance stages full-service dustups, after which George takes to the center of the ring, coated in enough sweat to make him look like a glazed doughnut, and shares the undiluted gospel. And on the indie circuit—where witnessing can be a tougher proposition as one dodges flying cups of tobacco juice—George still wears his scripture britches and passes out tracts and Bibles at intermission.

Behind the strip mall in Concord, South's wrestling school is a no-frills cinderblock edifice with a ring, fifty metal folding chairs, an open-faced fan, and nothing else. If trainees complain about the lack of air-conditioning, George tells them to come back in the winter, when they can wrestle with icicles hanging from their nose. This is not the WWF's training center, "The Power Plant," which George derisively dismisses as an antiseptic, climate-controlled fantasy, the equivalent of "singing in the shower." Here, he allows wrestlers to learn how to work a hostile crowd of paying customers, while he trains them in "the old-school style—when the wrestlers really worked."

The "school" doesn't even bear a sign. Advertising, he complains, typically attracts every beer-gutted bus driver who ordered wrestling boots out of a catalog and thinks he is owed a WWF contract. George mostly shoos them off or makes them take so many consecutive "bumps" (or falls) that they expire from exhaustion. "They'll quit before I ever touch them," he says. "Most of them can't get off the couch and walk to the refrigerator without being out of breath." For those who stay, George charges three thousand dollars—though he rarely, if ever, sees all the money. He often settles for wampum—such as a new pair of wrestling boots.

On a sweltering summer night, George is prepping for one of his training shows, where his charges will dazzle a local Baptist youth group. George runs a broom over the floor and sets the radio to a classic rock station while swilling mouthwash—a professional courtesy for the tight clinches, he says. One by one, the wrestlers straggle in. There's John and Andy Adcox—two coal-eyed squirts from George's church whom South has informally adopted since their father died in a car accident a few years ago. Andy wrestles as The Little Package, while John says he is Superstar, which causes him to roll his eyes, as he hates the assigned name, preferring Maddog. There's The Carolina Dreamer (inexplicably introduced as hailing from Tampa, Florida), who shows up in shower shoes eating chicken fingers, while hauling the Dr. Perky grape soda that will serve as that night's concession. In the corner, oiling himself up is Shogun, the Sexy Samurai, who is not an Asian warrior but a tree surgeon with blonde-surfer locks.

As his wrestlers take warm-up bumps and South yells instructions, the Baptist youth file in, their senses overwhelmed. The mat-splatting bodies sound like sacks of potatoes getting dropped on trash can lids. When the matches start, one little girl begins to cry. But two chubby adolescent boys—not youth group regulars, but wrestling aficionados—grab ringside seats and start heckling. They give the business to everybody. They place a chair in the ring to help expedite the demise of The Little Package. They ridicule the guest referee, their own youth pastor, who splits his pants in the middle of the bout. "Your moon is shining," says one.

While South keeps his junk-talking to a minimum during the match, even when they mock his receding hairline, he takes a microphone to the middle of the ring afterward to scare the little heathens into the kingdom. Practiced from years of microphone work in wrestling broadcasts, and from teaching Sunday School at Reedy Creek Baptist Church, George tells the kids that nothing in this life matters—not even wrestling. He says they can ignore the eternal verities as long as time permits—but they can't know when their time will expire. He tells them that they have heard the plan of salvation from this "dumb rassler" in this "ol' ugly building," and if they ignore it, they do so at their own peril. He offers a stripped-down version of Pascal's wager: "When it's all over and the smoke clears," George says, if he's wrong, then "I haven't lost anything but peace of mind. But if we find out I'm right and you're wrong—look what you've lost."

Nobody comes forward for George's altar call. But a few weeks earlier, after his teenage sons, George Jr. and Brock (also aspiring wrestlers), had spit water on the crowd and thrown each other through tables, George preached a similar sermon, and three people came forward to accept Christ—including the referee whom George had love-tapped during an earlier match. South, who also runs side ministries such as delivering food to the homeless, says church crowds can be the toughest. "Some of the meanest people I know are Baptist preachers. They'd make excellent heels."

The next day, I visit South's house, the front porch of which contains turnbuckles and ropes and all manner of wrestling debris. "Welcome to the Addams Family, buddy," says South. During the week, he plays Mr. Mom to his five children and a black cat named Dog. His wife works "a real job" at a downtown brokerage, and George is grateful for the benefits, as he says it's terribly difficult to take out insurance as a professional wrestler.

South's converted garage is a wrestling museum, a grappler's Cooperstown—with all manner of board games and action figures, fight marquees, and photographs. Many of the photos are of his friends, and many of them are dead. There's "Hot Stuff" Eddie Gilbert, whom George says he discussed God with just a few days before his "heart exploded" in Puerto Rico—from drugs, George thinks. And there's "The Juicer," Art Barr, whom George fought shortly before he expired. South's roll call of dead friends—there are many others—lends his ministry an added urgency, and he has no patience for genteel types who say the gospel doesn't belong in a wrestling ring. "Jesus didn't go to the people who were well," South says. "Well people don't need a doctor. Sick people do."

That afternoon, we are off to Wentworth, North Carolina, a small town outside Greensboro where George has been wrestling for the past several weekends under the imprimatur of the Renegade American Wrestling Alliance, one of North Carolina's best indie federations, headed by Chris Nelson, aka Slim Jim Bolen. When we get to "the arena" (a converted Bingo hall), Slim Jim is in full meltdown, as the ring he just bought from a South Carolina wrestler named High Performance is anything but. The ring's center spring keeps popping out from under the metal girders, and when George gets there, he is forced to jerry-rig the coil so that they don't have to rassle in the parking lot—which George has seen happen elsewhere. "Easy on the ring tonight," Slim Jim tells his troupe, "it's just for show."

202 of MATT LABASH

Backstage, it is a Star Wars bar of oddities. Slutty-looking valets—perhaps on furlough from their Dairy Queen shifts—preen about in high heels. A member of the Daulton Boys—a black-dustered cowboy outfit—carefully conceals a metal weight in his ranch-hand glove. Vern the referee, who will change costumes and double as V-Jak, a hard-core wrestler, shows me the blade he will use to cut his forehead open during a six-man tag team trash can match. The United Nations of Devastation tag team—consisting of Hubie the Canadian and Drake the Swede—will draw some of the most serious heat of the night, as the crowd, deprived of Cold War Russians and Oil Embargo Arabs, is still starved for foreign-born heels. When I ask Drake what Sweden could have possibly done to incur such wrath (price-gouging at IKEA?), he refuses to break character, telling me in a perfect West Virginia accent how much he hates Americans.

As he suits up, George ignores the coquettish valets. Slim Jim says that tonight, the wrestlers are generally curtailing their swearing, "out of respect for George." As he checks his Food Lion bag full of Bibles, which he will distribute at intermission, George talks over the night's spots with Little George—a slight twenty-one-year-old playing George's son. To match Big George, Little George is forced to wear an "I Love Jesus" T-shirt, which South finds amusing, since L.G. is currently trying to chat up some of the looser-looking arena rats.

The Georges are matched against the Southside Players—two black gentlemen who in civilian life are a health care facility worker and a Hardee's manager. The Georges and the Players talk over spots before leaving the dressing room, wish each other safety, and the Players even bow their heads in silent prayer. While South is supposed to be a heel, there's no chance two dice-shooting brothers are going to go over with the redneck audience, who delight in taunting them in Ebonics (causing one of the Players to flip a heckler off). Throughout the match, George is tepid, reluctant to "leave my feet" against two dilettantes. Instead he quietly tells them to keep their heads up in the clinches (to avoid accidental head-butts). The Georges make short work of the Players: As Big George distracts the ref, Little George hammers them with a foreign object pulled from his pants.

We leave the arena after midnight, and on the way home George is critiquing the show like a fussy mother. He is incensed that one wrestler kicked another "in the goo-loos" right in front of the ref, who jeopardized his credibility by not disqualifying him—"that's in the fake rule book," says George. He is scandalized at the indiscriminate violence—all payoff with no buildup—that younger wrestlers favor. Before the bell even rang, it seems, Slim Jim had hit one opponent with a crutch, a cookie sheet, a trash can, and a wet-paint sign. "Where do you go from there?" asks George. But above all, George can't wait to turn heel on his faux son, Little George, who he says has all the enthusiasm of "a knot on a log."

In wrestling's minor leagues, there will be lots of nights like this. Still, it wasn't a total loss. George passed out his Bibles. And though he wasn't permitted to preach, a fan told George at intermission that he'd memorized John 3:16 after seeing it advertised weekly on George's trunks. "Most people think if we don't get called to [be a missionary in] Africa, God ain't gonna call us," explains George. "But He might. He might call you to do just what you do every day. Like in Wentworth, Carolina, tonight, buddy."

A YEAR OF FIRSTS AND LASTS

Edlene LaFrance Remembers Her Husband, Murdered by Mohamed Atta

Bronx, New York

I met Edlene LaFrance on the worst day of her life. Or maybe it was the second worst, or the fifth, there are so many to choose from now. Two days after the Twin Towers fell, her forty-three-year-old husband, Alan, lay buried at the bottom of one of them. Though the city was awash in acts of unparalleled selflessness, I'd spent that morning thinking selfishly, walking the ash-caked streets of lower Manhattan, trolling for battle-scarred humanity to fill my notebooks before deadline.

On a bum tip, I rushed to the Chelsea Piers, where ambulances full of recovered wounded were rumored to be arriving. When I got there, a bystander scoffed at my naïveté. "There aren't any more wounded," he said, letting the thought finish itself. Another reporter suggested the action had moved crosstown to the National Guard Armory on Lexington, and indeed it had. The street outside the building looked like a third-world bazaar. Except instead of merchants peddling trinkets, family members were holding "Missing" posters, begging for whereabouts and clues, as if their loved ones had gone down to the corner for a pack of cigarettes, then had forgotten the way home.

The media were supposedly barred, but I slipped inside the building. In all the chaos, it was about as difficult as crashing Penn Station. Hundreds of family members sat in rows, their bodies racked with tension and slicked with sweat in the unair-conditioned hall. Amid this grimness, I scouted for the most approachable faces, which belonged to Edlene, her son, Jody, and his wife, Camille.

I asked if I could follow their family through this process, and they graciously assented. Edlene clutched a photo of her husband in his white wedding tuxedo. Their twenty-first anniversary was in two weeks, and on the morning of September 11, for some reason, she'd come close to giving him his biggest present early—a new wedding ring.

We made polite chat over grief counselors' incessant offerings of sandwiches and Sprite. Edlene quipped that she could use some tranquilizers instead. She answered all my questions dutifully, but her eyes kept drifting to the archway at the front of the room. It was there, down a staircase, that twenty people at a time were being taken to scour two lists—the first indicating that their loved one had turned up hospitalized, the second that they'd turned up dead.

When it was the LaFrance family's turn, we went downstairs. A Red Cross volunteer offered to look for Alan's name. Edlene, a portrait of poise a few minutes earlier, simply laid her head down on a table while her son sat beside her, stroking her hair. Alan didn't turn up on the deceased list, but he wasn't on the hospitalized list either. A deductive silence enveloped us—the sound of someone's life coming undone.

A year later, as journalists and grief groupies again jostle for a piece of 9/11, it's tempting to sit back and chortle at excesses and opportunism. God knows the past year has seen enough of them: American Paper Optics issuing "Images of 9-11 in 3-D," the commemorative cigarette lighter with a flame flickering right over a picture of a burning World Trade Center, the "9/11: 24/7" mock tribute album from drag queen Tina C. featuring songs like "Stranger on the Stairwell" and "Kleenex to the World."

Still, as we congratulate ourselves on how life goes on in all its wretched excess, there are thousands like Edlene. Her life actually has changed, and will remain that way beyond any news cycle.

I catch up with her at an apartment building that sits next to a noisy highway in the Bronx. A landlord's letter posted in the lobby cautions residents not to let their pets urinate in the stairwell. She welcomes me at the door, and says that she has lost some weight and some hair since we last spoke, but she is just as I remembered: diminutive and dignified, her warm voice accented with a steel that suggests she is being brave by necessity, if not by nature. Her rent is $709 per month, and it seems a bit steep for the two rooms she inhabits. They're the same rooms she lived in with Alan. And in a way, that $709 is what got him killed.

An audio/visual technician, Alan freelanced all over the city—
primarily doing conferences at a New York public library and at the
Windows on the World restaurant on the 106th floor of the World
Trade Center's North Tower. Edlene could always tell to which job
her husband was headed by what he was wearing. If he was off to the
library, he'd wear casual clothes. If it was the World Trade Center,
he'd put on a black suit. The library gig was more lucrative, but his
employer took too long to pay (six to eight weeks).

Though usually Alan just worked nights at the World Trade Center, he sometimes needed money to make rent. So the morning of
September 11, he went there to set up a breakfast conference. Edlene
can't remember her last words to her husband, but for days after the
towers went down, she tricked herself into recalling that he hadn't
been wearing his black suit.

From the testimonials of his friends and relatives, it is clear Alan
was the kind of guy you'd want to be around. He liked his breakfasts
big and greasy at a nearby diner, and he loved to play drums. At his
Jehovah's Witness congregation's cookouts, he always assumed the
role of grillmaster, perhaps because even at 6'4", he was such a suspect
basketball player that friends mockingly called him "Jump Shot." He
took his grandmother shopping almost weekly. He liked to work on
cars, but not for money. Often, Edlene would gaze out the window
at busy Bruckner Boulevard and see a stranded motorist. She'd shoot
her husband a help-those-poor-people look. He'd grumble a little,
then grab his tools and ride to the rescue.

Now, the first face Edlene sees in the morning is Mohamed
Atta's. She keeps a *New York Post* cover photo of the man who killed
her husband on the floor next to her bed. Every morning when she
wakes up, she steps on his face. It is a small, desperate gesture, but it's
the only revenge she'll ever get. When asked why she'd keep a picture
of this murderer in her bedroom (she never calls him a "terrorist" or
"hijacker," always a "murderer"), she says, "A lot of times when I don't
think it's real, I just turn over and there's his face. Then I know it's
real."

It wouldn't seem she'd need any more reminders. Her husband,
who had no life insurance, handled the finances, and within the first
few weeks after he died—her mind scrambled and her heart literally
palpitating—she couldn't even locate her checkbook. Unable to keep
track of the bills, she had to get an extension after an eviction notice.

Though some charity has found her (BlackAmericaWebRelief ended up footing her rent through August), most of the thirty thousand dollars or so she's received from victim's assistance funds has gone to offset her son Jody's expenses, since he frequently has to fly back with his family from Chattanooga, Tennessee, to help his mom navigate mounds of paperwork and other disasters.

A typical one occurred when Alan's old Volvo had to be retrieved from an impound lot where it was towed from the train station after sitting there for weeks (Alan had the only key). Likewise, her telephone was nearly cut off, but with her nursing job in a "clinic in a bad neighborhood," she has managed to keep it paid up, along with Alan's cell phone account. She doesn't have the cell phone—Alan had it with him when he died—but by keeping the account open, she can still call his messages to hear his voice. "They never found remains," she explains. "It's all we have left of him."

Edlene LaFrance is not a whiner, though she could be forgiven if she were one. She hasn't told her overburdened son that her doctors are worried she has breast cancer. Having switched nursing jobs earlier this year, she has told no one at work besides her boss that she lost her husband on 9/11. Even her own mother, who is senile and whom Edlene doesn't wish to traumatize, has no idea her daughter is now a widow. "When she asks where Alan is," Edlene says, "I tell her he's at work."

I ask her if she blames God for any of this. "Why would I?" she asks, out of conviction or convenience or both. "He didn't do it." She says she's been hitting the Scriptures pretty hard lately—not Job, as you might expect, but all the widows 'n' orphans passages. There are a lot more of them than she had noticed before, and she says they present a compelling body of evidence that God won't let her fall through the cracks. So far, she says, He hasn't.

The thing that's changed the most for her is time. She no longer measures it in weeks and months, but in firsts and lasts—the last time she did something with Alan, the first time she must do it without him. She doesn't cry much anymore, but the day before my visit, a lightbulb burned out in her hallway. She ended up in a heap on the kitchen floor for twenty minutes. It was a thousand-hour bulb that Alan had last changed. She has not replaced it.

There are long lists of firsts she is avoiding. She will not go on vacation, and chooses not to go to the movies, since that was Alan's favorite pastime. When she goes to their favorite diner for breakfast, she sits at the counter, since she and Alan used to sit at a booth. She knows she must get over this, and it will be easier to, she reasons, after September 11. Right now, she dreads that date the most. Though she'll be surrounded by extended family, all she really wants to do, she says, "is take some sleeping pills and wake up on September 12th."

After hours of conversation, we set off for the train station on foot, strolling through her neighborhood in a late summer half light. Another thirty minutes, she says, and she wouldn't be out on these streets. At first, I think she means because they're crime-ridden. But no. "That was the time me and Alan always walked together," she explains. As she says this, I nod understandingly. But I can't understand. Not really. We have all grown rather possessive of September 11, taking it out, reexamining it when it suits us, making it mean what we want it to mean. Edlene doesn't have that luxury. I want to make it easier for her, but that can't be done, so I hold my tongue. She thanks me for listening, and I nod some more, as she puts me on a train that will take me back to my wife and son.

MAKING IT

A Run for the Iraqi Border
with Christopher Hitchens

Safwan, Iraq

It is essential, during times of war, to be in good company. And to that end, fellowship prospects improved markedly last week around the Kuwait City Hilton—known to hotel warriors as central command. After thirty-six sleepless hours, I had just stolen three or four when my phone rang. "Hello, Matt," said the voice on the other end. "It's Christopher Hitchens. I'm here. Did I wake you?" Yes, you did, I told him, though I wasn't about to turn down a social call from one of our finest magazine scribblers and seekers of truth. "Good," he said. "I'll give you five minutes to put your teeth in, then I'll be right over."

You can tell how at ease a man is in the world from the scarcity of possessions he lugs around with him. When I came here, it was with large backpacks and overstuffed duffels, extraneous tote bags, pouches, and carry-ons. But Hitchens showed up at my door with nothing more than a firm handshake and a half-smoked pack of Rothmans. As he stood there, rumpled and slightly jet-lagged in blue jeans and a black leather jacket, he looked sort of like the Fonz—if the Fonz had been a British former socialist who could pinch large swaths of Auden from memory.

We plopped down in the living room, and I asked him why he hadn't brought his gas mask, chem suit, and Kevlar. "I wore Kevlar in the Balkans once," he said, "but it made me feel like a counterfeit, so I ditched it." Despite this cavalier disregard for safety, I was so grateful for the company that I offered him a Welcome-to-Kuwait shot of "Listerine" (as it is known by Kuwaiti customs officials). "I don't usually start this early," said Hitchens with feigned reluctance, "but holding yourself to a drinking schedule is always the first sign of alcoholism."

As I briefed Hitchens on the difficulties and dangers of getting into Iraq as an unembedded reporter, his eyes betrayed a wild impatience. "I have to get to Iraq," he told me. "You and everybody else," I replied, adding that the line started around the block. No, he said, I didn't understand. *Vanity Fair* had paid his freight, and he had only a short time. If his boots did not touch Iraqi soil, the mission would be a failure. Luckily, my best Kuwaiti contact called. The Kuwait Red Crescent Society was going into southern Iraq on a humanitarian drop. "Can you be downtown at the Sheraton by 1:00 P.M.?" she asked. It was 12:55, and we were in my car before she hung up.

When we got there, the convoy was pulling out and we weren't in it. "This can't be happening," Hitchens said, as if not getting in-country three hours after his plane touched down was an utter professional failure. The next day, the Red Crescent made another run, so we got to the Sheraton at dawn's crack to make sure we were on board. At the hotel press center, staffed by Kuwaiti Ministry of Information officials, an overflow crowd of journalists scurried about, all trying to cut deals to gain passage.

With hundreds of journalists waiting anxiously, like theater majors hoping for a speaking part in the school play, the list was finally posted. Hitchens and I were on it. I looked around to celebrate, but he was out having a smoke. When I finally spotted him, I broke the good news. I asked him if we should capture this celebratory moment with my disposable camera. "No," he said, exhaling a cloud of smoke. "Save it for the bloated corpses. Don't say anything," he said, "or something bad will happen."

Hitchens told me that outside the hotel, he'd just run into P. J. O'Rourke. P.J. was riding in a caravan with ABC radio, and he'd asked Hitchens to join him. "They only had one seat," said Hitchens, "so I declined." (Like the Marines, Hitchens never leaves a comrade behind.) I ran into the gift shop to fill up my bag with gifts for the Iraqis. I already had Matchbox cars and Tic Tacs, so I grabbed several cartons of Marlboro Reds. When I came back out, Hitchens was having a smoke, and O'Rourke had rejoined him.

As I sidled up to them, O'Rourke, here for the *Atlantic Monthly*, congratulated me, telling me I was probably the only person here serving a smaller readership than he was. I showed both of them the contents of my swag bag, from which I intended to pass out gifts like GI Johnny from some bad World War II movie. "What?" said

O'Rourke. "No chewing gum?" O'Rourke is an old hand in these parts, having gotten a book out of the first Gulf War (*Give War a Chance*). And so he was holding forth with mock bravado, telling us we hadn't seen anything. During 1991, he said, Scuds were coming down like rain. "The worst part was, the Saudis didn't know how to respond. They'd be driving like this [turning the wheel wildly] while looking out the window up into the sky. You stood a lot less chance of getting killed by a Scud than you did by an unguided Chevy Caprice."

Suddenly, we were barked at by a scratchy bullhorn, held by a Ministry of Information official named Yacoub. "Get on the bus," he said, though with the poor amplification quality it sounded like "Let up the truss." We got the gist and were eager to get gone. I took a middle seat between Hitchens and a network TV producer friend I'll call Gabe.

Just as we were about to pull off, we heard two deafening booms overhead. They were missiles of some sort—either being intercepted or landing—that made a sound like God doing a can-opener off heaven's own high dive. Hitchens turned to me worriedly. "You know what this means," he said. "That we're going to be injured or die?" I offered. "No," he said, "the trip's off." We all flocked out of the bus, looking to the outskirts of the city, where it seemed the sounds were headed. I ran up to a hotel employee and asked him what we'd just witnessed. "Sir," he said, smiling the smile of someone practiced in the slow-rolling of information, "this is Kuwait. We won't know that until a week from now."

Yacoub jumped back on the bullhorn, sounding like Charlie Brown's marble-mouthed teacher. "The clip has a manifold," he mumbled. "Huh, what?" we asked. He said it again: "The clip has a manifold." Still unable to make it out, I walked up in front of him, stopping two feet away. "What did you say?" I asked. "We can't understand you." He raised the bullhorn again so that it was just inches from my face. "THE TRIP HAS BEEN CANCELED!" Why? I asked. "Due to weather and instability," he said.

Hitchens looked at me in disbelief, and something about his face had changed. His skin had tightened, and his eyes looked backlit with fire. He was a man with too much momentum to be stopped by bureaucrats with scratchy bullhorns. We were going to Iraq this very afternoon, he informed me, just as the block-red letters on our press passes deigned us—as "unilaterals." In the lobby of the

Sheraton, Gabe the producer introduced us to one of his network's many drivers. The driver had a Syrian uncle who worked at the French embassy. Hitchens asked him how much it would cost for him to shuttle us around the checkpoints, into Iraq. "Make him an offer," said Gabe. "What is this, the souk?" said Hitchens. "No Hitchens has ever haggled. Tell him to tell me what he's worth."

The nephew settled on five hundred dollars—a fair price, it seemed, to risk his life and ours. I was feeling a little jumpy about the whole endeavor. Numerous colleagues had told me that about the nuttiest thing that can be done in a war zone is to hook up with journalists of the British or French persuasion. Now I was headed for Iraq with a driver from the French embassy and a Brit whose idea of planning ahead, provisions-wise, was to dig into the humanitarian food stash once we got in-country.

While we waited for our driver to get there, we went upstairs to Gabe's hotel room. He poured us two shots of liquid courage out of an Apollinaris water bottle. I thanked Hitchens in advance for getting me killed. "It'll be fine, really," he assured me. "I totally trust Massoud"—our driver. "You've never even met Massoud," Gabe pointed out. "He's from the French embassy," Hitchens responded, as if that eliminated all doubt about his qualifications. I asked Gabe to ride with us. The more sane people on the trip, I figured, the better. I dialed P. J. O'Rourke as well, and told him we'd love to have him along. "Can't," he said. He had to be on the air with ABC radio shortly. "Plus," he added knowingly, "you'll never get past the first checkpoint."

He had obviously never met Massoud.

We went downstairs. Before Massoud pulled up, I suggested we pick up provisions in case we got stranded. Hitchens waved it off as unnecessary. "We'll be back by tonight," he said. Then his eyes grew saucerlike, as if he'd forgotten something. "Bananas!" he said. "We need bananas—it's the easiest way to carry food—plus, they're good for you." He disappeared somewhere and came back with a couple of bananas and cheese sandwich platters. If we ran into surly Baath Party types, we could create a diversion by offering them our pickles.

Massoud's first idea was to switch to my SUV. Our driver, it seemed, didn't want to get his car dirty. We hopped into my truck, and Massoud took the wheel. He appeared to be a good enough driver. He stayed in his lane, and always signaled when turning. But the reason we hired him was to go off-road around checkpoints, so judgment was reserved. He spoke pretty good English, and told us all about the Iraqi occupation in 1990—how he'd had friends who'd been raped, had their cars stolen, and been shot in the head—the usual stuff. Hitchens seemed to be breathing easier. "It's so good not to be in a convoy," he sighed. "Convoys are an insult to journalism, I think."

As we reached the Matla Pass, about fifteen miles northwest of Kuwait City, we rolled into the first checkpoint. A young British Royal Air Force policeman was standing sentry with a rifle and helmet that looked so oversize, you could've fit a bowl of soup in it and still had enough room for his head. The soldier told us we needed a special pass to get through. Hitchens replied that we'd already been issued two press passes—one from the Americans and one from the Kuwaitis. "What are these good for then?" he asked. "I haven't got a clue," said the Brit. He added that he couldn't let us go through for security reasons. "Security is only a word," protested Hitchens. "But it's not a reason, is it?"

Massoud pulled the car over, and Hitchens was on slow burn. "They're trying to protect us," he said indignantly. "Well, I didn't ask to be protected." We exited the car and walked up to a sentry booth to haggle with the Kuwaiti official in charge. He wore a khaki uniform, had a squirrelly mustache, and resembled an Arab version of Mario from the old Donkey Kong video game. He wore a dust mask, since the air quality in a Kuwait sandstorm is like pre-EPA Youngstown, Ohio. When we asked again if we could pass, he said no. Even if he said yes, he pointed out, others would say no at numerous successive checkpoints. While many of us pop off about personal liberties, Hitchens tends to view them as something other than polite abstractions. "We are asking for one thing," he said emphatically. "To travel freely in a free country!" The Kuwaiti still said no. Seeing that Hitchens's give-us-liberty speech didn't cut much ice, I took the Kuwaiti aside and tried to offer him a bribe. Noticing that he wore some extravagant, salmon-tinted Gucci glasses, I told him, "In my country, we have Gucci glasses on every drugstore rack. I will buy many, and send them back to you." Despite my generous offer and slow-motion English, he wagged his finger at me disapprovingly, prompting me to cut off negotiations.

When we got back in the truck, I was now as distraught as Hitchens. What kind of Middle Eastern country is it when you can't even bribe your way through a checkpoint? Massoud pulled away to drive back to Kuwait City, so we asked him what happened to all our off-road plans. We could've gotten turned back at a checkpoint by ourselves—and paid a lot less for the pleasure. Massoud shook his head. "Too dangerous," he said; if the Kuwaitis catch us running checkpoints, "they will shoot us in the back."

We paid off Massoud—one hundred dollars instead of five hundred, due to breach of contract—and waited for our luck to turn. The next morning it did. The Red Crescent had another humanitarian run into Safwan. The convoy had grown by at least ten buses from the day before. Once in it, we took our seats behind a Red Crescent volunteer and local journalist/fixer who asked that I change his name to Najeef. A Palestinian from Jerusalem and a graduate of Texas Southern University, Najeef offered pointers on how to identify the bad apples in Iraq. "The people who are for Saddam," he said, "I can tell from their physical appearance. The way they stand. The way they act." He said they throw the equivalent of gang signs—with a forefinger and middle finger extended, and with the thumb aiming out. Their facial expressions are also distinct, he said, pointing to his own and struggling to locate the correct English terminology. "Their glands are very sharp."

He told us that before the first war, the best way to bribe Iraqi officials was to offer them chocolate ice cream and bananas. "Even Saddam loves bananas," said Najeef. "If you gave bananas to Saddam, he'd probably let you [have relations with] him." Perhaps Hitchens was a better trip coordinator than I originally thought.

Najeef told us how wired he was in Kuwait. If we chose to hire him as a fixer, he could translate; he could get us into the yacht parties of decadent young Kuwaitis. He is close—personal friends—with a nephew of the emir, who he said heads something called the Kuwait Bowling Federation. If we needed to get in any bowling while covering the war, Najeef was our man. He warned us that despite many forward-thinking Kuwaitis, like those in the Bowling Federation, there are others, like those in the Ministry of Public Relations and Moral Guidance, who are restrictive.

"They stop the boys from teasing the girls," he said. "They want you to go for prayer, to not listen to music—music is wicked. They don't want you to look at a girl or [have relations with] her." Though, Najeef reasoned, since the penalty in the afterlife is supposedly the same for each infraction, "it is better to [have relations with] her any-way." Generally speaking, Najeef said of the Islamic fundamentalists, "they kill all good things, all good activities. Live your life, let others live theirs. They live to fuck your life up. They don't like to see any-body happy."

Our bus caravan rolled on down the Highway of Death—which earned its nickname during the Gulf War, after Americans obliter-ated fleeing Iraqis in what was widely considered a turkey shoot. As death-related interstates go, this is a fairly nice one: It is wide, comes with rumble strips, and has fewer potholes than your average Wash-ington, D.C., thoroughfare. Along the way we passed long convoys of U.S. military vehicles: Humvees and bulldozers and flatbed trucks stacked with fresh lumber. We passed soldiers, many of them looking baked and caked from the months spent in this forbidding landscape of scorched, featureless flatness that could very well pass for West Texas.

Numerous times, we were pulled over and forced to cool out at checkpoints for no apparent reason. After going about forty miles in four hours, we were all a bit on edge. At one checkpoint, a group of soldiers sat around a Humvee, eating their MREs. Bored journal-ists gathered around them clicking pictures, as if they were one of the Seven Wonders. We asked a Sergeant Eric Jones from Knoxville, Tennessee, what he was eating. He warily eyed the plastic bag out of which he was shoveling chow. "It says chicken and noodles," he said, "but we still can't verify. They may convince a jury of their peers to believe it, but we don't."

Back on the buses, the Kuwaitis—lovers of bureaucracy and pro-cess—asked all the journalists to again sign their names and affilia-tions on a circulating roster. "Who wants to know?" Hitchens asked. He pointed out a journalist to me. "Look at him, reading the list upside down. Do you sign anything they put in front of you? You've got to push back hard or you'll get too used to being pushed around. What are they going to do with the list?" he inquired loudly. "Sell it to telemarketers," another couldn't-be-bothered reporter yawned.

Hitchens was right, there did seem to be more needless delay. "It's nearly midday," he said, "and we've been at this since 5:00 A.M." He reminded our driver that this was supposed to be a trip to assist the hungry. As we watched the Red Crescent volunteers waiting to get their forward-march order, while lollygagging outside their trucks in red, white, and blue Evel Knievel–style jumpsuits, Najeef concurred. By the time we got there, he said, "The starving people of Iraq will eat us as well."

Our convoy finally crossed into the DMZ, and we were stopped one last time. Our bus perched right on the border. Before we could get moving, some sort of mortar or shell landed on a hillside about a mile away. We heard the boom and saw a large plume of smoke ascend. We had no idea if it was from enemies or friendlies, but nobody seemed too pressed. It was just close enough to spook us, but far enough to make us want to go on, like Moses on Mount Nebo, ready to taste Canaan.

Miraculously, the Kuwaitis let us go on. We pushed forward to Iraq, into the tiny border town of Safwan. As we did so, skinny children ran alongside us, sprinting past fall-down mud-brick houses, some of them without roofs. The recent fighting had knocked out the town's electricity and water. The locals were smiling, but wanly, desperately, many of them trying to wave the humanitarian trucks up to their houses, as if special deliveries were an option. The Red Crescent's eighteen-wheeler stopped on a dirt road, and the word had already gone forth. People swarmed the rig from every direction, with their feet mud-caked and cracked, walking briskly with the panther steps of those used to not owning shoes. The journos tumbled out of their buses and watched a mosh pit form behind the back of the trailer truck.

Red Crescent workers screamed frantically for order, but there was none to be had. They initially refused to open the doors and throw out the boxed provisions, which just made everyone struggle harder. It was degrading to watch, and Hitchens, trying not to sound like some bleeding-heart humanitarian, said, "If they'd have been a bit more British about it, and formed a polite queue, they'd have all gotten a package."

Instead, the strong bulled their way in, elbowing and jostling like power forwards clearing the boards in an inner-city pickup game. Everyone had to wait until they got tired of hoarding. Hitchens and I hovered on the periphery, trying to grab people for interviews. Some spoke a little English, and if they didn't, we nabbed Arabic journalists or relief workers to do some quick translating. One Arabic journalist led me to an Iraqi and asked, "What do you want to ask him?" I tried to keep the question simple. "Americans and British," I said, "good or bad?" "Not bad," he answered. "Does that mean good?" I followed up. The Iraqi spoke before being asked. "It means—not bad," my translator reiterated.

The body language of the crowd told you as much as their stunted English. While little boys approached us, chanting "Booooosh, yes!" the village teenagers had the damaged air of the older kids at the adoption agency who never got picked. I gave one of them some cigarettes, and shot him a corny thumbs-up sign. He shot one back, but mockingly, elbowing his buddy, who flashed the hand gesture that Najeef had described as the Baath party gang sign. At the back of the line, we hit my swag bag pretty hard, trying to earn goodwill. I passed out Tic Tacs and Matchbox cars to the little ones, who rolled the wheels against their hands. Then I dispensed cigarettes to Iraqis of all ages. (Hitchens went even further, giving them a light.)

As I did this, a small boy ran up to me with a blank piece of paper. He motioned for me to scribble on it, but I had no idea what he wanted—a picture, an autograph? I reached down and made a nonsensical doodle. He nodded appreciatively, then bolted for the truck. "He thinks you wrote him out a food ration," one of the relief workers explained. While working the crowd, trying to make connections with Iraqis, I felt a slight tug at my back. When I turned around, no one was there. But off to the side stood a young boy who had just been there a moment before. He held up my water bottle, smiling sheepishly, as if to ask, "Permission to steal?" Permission granted.

The young ones coveted cigarettes as much as their older brothers and fathers. When I offered a choice of orange or white Tic Tacs, they responded with a chorus of "smoke, meester, smoke" while tapping fingers to their lips. I would give them smokes, they would palm them, then ask for more. Occasionally, I held a pack out, allowing a self-serve situation. With the older ones, there was no gratitude, none of the recognition one typically expects between supplicant and benefactor. There was just an urgency and desperation, a savage grab to take possession of something before it could be taken back.

It was hard to know exactly what they were thinking. Based on the translations I received, I don't think many of them knew either. They spoke in a rush of conflicting words and emotions. Coaxing out coherent answers was like conducting a telephone survey in a hurricane. The same person in the same sentence would often express distrust of Saddam, as well as of Saddam's invaders. After talking to one Iraqi man, Najeef translated: "They are not sure if this is liberation or occupation. They will wait till it's all over."

The people of Safwan are used to being disappointed. They have suffered greatly under the rule of Saddam and, more directly, under his Kurd-slaughtering henchman, Chemical Ali, who'd been given charge of the region. Back in '91, several miles north in Basra, the Americans had encouraged a Shiite uprising against Saddam, then, when it went off, pulled out prematurely. The Iraqi rebels were crushed, and Safwan became a temporary haven for refugees. In order to survive, many were forced to eat boiled leaves with salt, and had to draw their water from mud puddles.

It is understandable, then, if their actions and emotions aren't easily classified—if they don't look too happy at all these journalists piling off buses like Great White Santas on safari. They love the help, and hate that they need it. While I passed out candy and toys to children, on more than one occasion an adult stepped in and waved me off. One shot me an assassin's glare and offered a stern admonition. When I asked a relief worker what was said, he explained, "He is ashamed of his shit conditions. They are proud. This is not who they are. They do not want outsiders coming here and seeing them this way."

I temporarily refrained from emptying out my goody bag, but I couldn't stop. Especially not with Jasim standing on my arm. The boy, one of the most handsome kids I have ever seen, shadowed me through the crowd. He couldn't have been more than seven, only four years older than my oldest son. He tried to speak English and smiled a lot, while standing shoeless beside me. I watched him bleed from his ankle. It was not the kind of blood that comes from a bite or a picked scab, but the kind that flows from an incision. He didn't nurse it or even favor it—he just forgot it—as he stood by my side, continuously cadging cigarettes.

I will likely go to hell for all the cigarettes that I doled out to children this day. But it seemed the only pleasure they'd been granted for God knows how long. The Campaign for Tobacco-Free Kids will doubtless bristle, but then, if these kids lived long enough to contract lung cancer, they'd be doing rather well. "Smoke? Meester," Jasim said, smiling infectiously, while the blood trickled down his leg. I gave him Marlboro Reds, first one, then a couple, then an entire pack of

"20 Class A Cigarettes," as it says on the box. I'd have given him the carton if I didn't think he'd get beat up for it.

"Quite a burg, isn't it?" said Hitchens, as we made our way out. When our buses pulled away, the food truck followed, and we witnessed crazed teenagers throwing open its doors, pushing themselves up inside, and tossing boxed provisions into the road until they licked the trailer clean. Later, I would learn that Muna Khalil, a journalist from Dubai, had a knife pulled on her after an Iraqi adolescent climbed on her bus, so desperate for food and water. He didn't want to hurt her, he said, he just wanted sustenance. She prayed for him aloud, a prayer that translates roughly as "God bless your mother and father, just like you," she said. The boy was both startled and grateful, and said, "Oh yes, you know this prayer too? Okay, bye-bye."

Back over the border on the Kuwaiti side, Yacoub delayed us again, saying we needed to wait for other buses to arrive so that we could convoy home in the interest of "safety." "We're in Kuwait," Hitchens said, incredulous. "How are six more buses going to make us safer?" Yacoub exploded, and told Hitchens that he was taking his press passes. Hitchens gladly obliged, and told Yacoub he didn't want them anyway, since they didn't seem to get him anywhere. (He did express regret that he had to relinquish the one that said "unilateral.") Playing Powell to Hitchens's Rumsfeld, I got off the bus and tried to smooth things over with Yacoub, who had had a long day himself.

After cooling off, Yacoub decided to make nice, somewhat, by wordlessly giving Hitchens back his press passes. But Hitchens, still smarting from having his freedoms trampled, accepted the American one and handed the Kuwaiti one back. Insulted and red in the face, Yacoub screamed, "I will use my power! You will leave Kuwait tonight!" (Hitchens didn't get tossed that night—thanks to connections he had above Yacoub's pay grade.)

In a show of collegiality that typifies the press corps these days, another reporter snapped at Hitchens, taking management's side. "And you wonder why people think we're arrogant and rude," he thundered.

"They don't have to wonder in my case," Hitchens calmly replied.

I exited the bus and joined Hitchens outside, where as usual, he was having a smoke. I tried to console him, but he didn't seem to need it. "Remember my golden rule," he said defiantly. "Do something every day against Bastards HQ." An Indian journalist sidled up, playing the part of Hitchens's sole additional sympathizer. "We are the hollow men. We are the stuffed men," he said quietly, causing Hitchens to smile broadly.

"You see," Hitchens said. "Only in India do people really bother with English literature anymore." It seemed the perfect pull—these lines from T. S. Eliot's "The Hollow Men"—to describe life at this moment, on this side of the border. And, as a bonus, there were still a few lines left over, to fit the place and the moment we had just left behind on the other side: "Our dried voices, when / We whisper together / Are quiet and meaningless / As wind in dry grass / Or rats' feet over broken glass / In our dry cellar / Shape without form, shade without color / Paralyzed force, gesture without motion."

RIDING WITH THE KOSSACKS

The Daily Kos Celebrates
Someone It Loves—Itself

Las Vegas

Whoa! Did you just feel that? Did you just feel the earth stop spinning on its axis, then reverse its rotation? Did you feel the moon enter into its Seventh House, and Jupiter align with Mars? Did you feel Jesus stomp off in a snit, as He was replaced at the right hand of God by Markos Moulitsas Zúniga, aka Kos? As in the eponymous blog Daily Kos? As in the four-year-old progressive website that is galvanizing the netroots and igniting the People-Powered Movement? As in the site that is reshaping the political landscape, uprooting the old order, and, in Kos's words, relegating those who'd stand in the movement's way "to the dustbin of history"? Oh—and which is also a place where people blog about themselves?

Well, if you didn't feel that, it's probably because you weren't here at the Riviera Hotel on June 8–11, for the first YearlyKos Convention. Not to rub it in, but you missed out. Not to brag, but I was there. Sure, there were times throughout the proceedings when I wished I was elsewhere. Maybe during some of the jibber-jabbery panels and roundtables and caucuses and workshops. Maybe during the "Sustainable Energy—Energize America" panel with Governor Bill Richardson. I mean no offense, Bill. Maybe America does need other kinds of energy besides People Power. But do I really want to sit around a dingy conference room talking about renewable fuels when I'm in Sin City?

Maybe I'd have liked to be at the blackjack tables, or to see a Danny Gans show, or to hang out at the Palms Hotel pool, where all the women have brand-new breasts and all the meatheads keep feeling their triceps every few minutes to make sure they haven't shrunk since the last inspection. Maybe there were panels that made me cry out for my mom, like "MetaKos," moderated by Kos, which caused blogger Skippy the Bush Kangaroo to describe his dispatch from the conference as "blogging about people talking about people blogging about blogs. Did your head explode yet?" Maybe I yearned to be down the street at Gilley's at the Frontier casino, which promises "Cold Beer, Dirty Girls, Mud Wrestling Live, Bikini Bull Riding." I mean, after all, we People-Powered types cannot live on Kos alone.

But I stayed at YearlyKos, and I stayed because I had a little laminated rectangle around my neck that said "YearlyKos Convention," but that might as well have read "Press Pass to History." Because if you'd had ringsiders to watch Hammurabi inscribe his Code in black diorite, or Luther tack his Ninety-five Theses to the door in Wittenberg, you wouldn't have played hookie at the Frontier, watching dirty girls mud-wrestle bull riders.

No sir, you'd watch history get made. Because before history becomes history, it has to be a moment in time. And if I could cast the convention into song, I might very well make it Whitney Houston's "One Moment in Time." Or maybe one of Kos's selections, since he's also a piano composer. Maybe his 1996 track titled "Solipsistic Affirmations." Either Whitney Houston or Kos—maybe I'd have Whitney Houston sing, with Kos accompanying her on piano.

You could read about this history being made too. But not in some jive, dead-tree history book. I read about it in real-time pixels—what we in the People-Powered community call "live blogging." It means blogging something as it's happening, rather than after it happens—or even before it happens, which one blogger told me is called "predictive blogging." I read about the history that was being made in all-star blogger SusanG's Daily Kos diary. She wrote it in the middle of the convention, in a post she titled "Yearly Kos: The Magic of People Power Made Manifest."

"We are hungry," she wrote, "hungry for each other in person." Easy, SusanG, the World's Fare Buffet is just down past the Capri room. (Sorry, we netroots types like to kid each other.) She went on to call it "pure magic," saying, "We are here. We are at the gates. We will no longer remain passive and meek in order to court favor. We, the people, are coming to power slowly and indefatigably, here in Vegas, and here on the blog. We have arrived."

And they have too, as evidenced by the massive media turnout. There were tons of them. You couldn't tell where the netroots ended and the media began. Sometimes, if you were a journalist, and you were trying to interview someone in the hall, you'd have to first give them the once over to see if their netroots were showing. Otherwise, you might end up accidentally interviewing Maureen Dowd. It's like SusanG wrote: "It seems like every fourth person you run into is here covering the phenomenon of . . . us. We're worth it, too. We are something else."

You tell them, SusanG. You tell them why the politicians from Barbara Boxer to Wes Clark are turning the Riviera into a giant kissing booth. You tell them why prospective Democratic presidential candidate Mark Warner rented out the observation tower of the Stratosphere Hotel to toast you with sushi and "Kosmopolitans" and chocolate fountains and Blues Brothers and Elvis impersonators and laptop-shaped ice sculptures. You tell them why the *New York Times* sent six people and the *Weekly Standard* sent two (flood the zone!). Never mind, SusanG, I'll tell them. I'll tell them that it's because the Kossacks, as they call themselves, are happening now. They are so of the moment that a moment ago, when I wrote that they were happening now, I was sort of predictive blogging. But that was then, this is now. So don't blink or you'll miss it, because it's happening.

Okay, not all of them are happening now. Not all the ones wearing Howard Dean T-shirts, for instance. Not all the ones hanging on former Dean consigliere Joe Trippi's every word in the "Using the Blogosphere Workshop." Not all the ones who are memorizing the Democracy for America handout, which contains tips from Zephyr Teachout, Dean's former online guru, who dispenses advice like "Draft drunk, edit sober" and "People like stories and poems and songs—they like DJs—you're the DJ for this effort." These people were happening now about three years ago. They're yesterday's now. But now, they're ready to be today's now.

Don't misunderstand—the thousand or so conferees aren't all Deaniacs. A lot of them are just good, honest-to-God activist bloggers who like their politics progressive and their sandals with low heels. Now, see, that was a stereotype. And Kos warns the Kossacks about stereotypes. He's always getting stereotyped, in fact. The media are always trying to turn him into the leader of some creepy cult, because the media are unfair to Kossacks. Just like they are to the Moonies and the Scientologists.

Kos doesn't even like being the L. Ron Hubbard of the progressive blogosphere, which everybody just assumes he is because it's his face front and center in a Ned Lamont Democratic primary commercial against Joe Lieberman, or because he term-limits his all-star bloggers (or "frontpagers"), or because it's his name on the website, and the conference, and the tote bags, and the beanies, and the hoodies, and the organic sustainable cotton T-shirts.

I mean, sure, some cynics—I didn't meet any at YearlyKos, but I'm sure they're out there—would say this is a hype, like Internet IPOs or Vanilla Coke or Ross Perot. There are guys like *Daily Standard* contributor Dean Barnett, who've reported that Daily Kos, which everybody assumes is growing by leaps and bounds, actually went from twenty-three million visitors in one month last fall to sixteen million in May. There's evidence like the recent Gallup poll that shows that blog reader growth was "somewhere between nil and negative in the past year," that reading blogs ranks at the bottom of online activities, and that only 15 percent of the public reads blogs, even though there are over forty million of them, meaning a lot of bloggers are talking to themselves. But Kos wants you to know this is a real, enduring movement not centered around his cult of personality. It's about nonhierarchical netroots, it's about "the volunteers." Just like it was in the Reform Party, a vibrant, healthy organization that, even after Ross Perot left it, still dominates American politics to this day.

Kos doesn't even like doing media. When you see him chatting with the *New York Times* (which reported he had a media coach) or going on *Meet the Press* or doing a photo shoot in the halls of the Riviera, sure, he looks like he's kind of enjoying it. But reluctantly. He said as much on his blog the other day. He said, "The media glare is not something I crave." And I think he means it. After all, he said it in a diary entry that was facetiously titled "It's All About Me." It was 1,100 words long, painstakingly analyzed his media coverage, and was all about him.

But that's the media for you. Unfair, unbalanced, and afraid of their own obsolescence. Because that's what the dead-tree media do. They have their stories written before they get off the plane. They need to fit your round peg into their square hole, if I may work blue since we're here in Vegas. Take the Kossacks, for instance. I mean yeah, okay, they're bloggers. They live and die by the blog. They blogged in between panels and during panels and some even while they were moderating panels. The hallways were clotted with people sitting on the floor, click-clacking laptops in a blogging bacchanal. They were blogging every which way: one-handed blogging, blogging their brains out, blogging from behind.

But other than that, the stereotypes don't hold. "What is amazing about us in the flesh is our diversity," wrote SusanG. And she's right, it's evident. Like at Pastor Dan's Interfaith Service on Sunday morning, which featured "greetings from faith traditions." They had a Christian, a Jew, a Buddhist, a pagan, a Unitarian, and an atheist. And it wasn't the setup to a joke! They didn't walk into a bar or anything! An atheist! At an interfaith service! That's diversity!

I mean, sure, almost everyone at the conference was white. But they were different shades of white. Some were conference-room clammy white. Others were liquid-crystal-display blueish white. But there were both white men, and white women. Loads of 'em. And they weren't all nineteen years old and wearing pajamas and fresh from Dungeons & Dragons matches in their mothers' basements. The average age looked to be about forty to forty-five. These are people with lives and families and jobs, even if some of those jobs have titles like "pro bono philosopher."

And after moving among the netroots for three and a half days, I can say with some confidence that they're not Dungeons & Dragons players. That's so eighties, and so unfair. They're better than that. They're more World of Warcraft types, the kind of Night Elves who aren't afraid to descend the holy mountain of Hyjal to wield their mystical powers in the fight for the survival of Azeroth. So much for stereotypes.

Sometimes the only way to get around the media is to go through them. That can be hard for bloggers. Take away their narcissism, their lust for attention, and their ravenous appetite for self-congratulation (Daily Kos's Hunter recently wrote about the "absolute brilliance of some of the voices we've got as leading lights of the progressive blogosphere") and they're a meek lot. Many of them have faces made for the blogosphere. Still, their public is calling. "I'd rather not be on TV, but I don't think I can avoid it," said one blogger.

So it was good to see the netroots get forced out of their blogger shells at the Pundit Project Training, which was run by the Center for American Progress and led by [name redacted] and [name redacted]. As I came into the room and took a seat next to *National Review*'s

Byron York (or, as some of the conventioneers liked to call us, "the Enemy"), a volunteer came over and told us that we really shouldn't even be in the workshop, but that if we stayed, we couldn't use names or quotes or descriptions or any of the things that the corporate media like to use for those things they do called "stories."

We talked [gender redacted] out of it, for the most part, until this nameless, sexless person agreed that we could quote people and describe them, just not use names or identifiers. Because that's what the netroots are about, ultimately. They're about transparency, about honesty, about going on background instead of off the record.

It can be easy to forget in the middle of a People-Powered Movement, a revolution if you will, that sometimes the revolution will be televised. And not just on YouTube or your grubby little website either. Sometimes, you need to go on Chris Matthews and knock a few heads. And when you do, there are things you should know, according to the workshop handout.

You should ask the booker, "Will it be acceptable to interrupt the host?" Never get angry or strident—that's a tough one for the netroots. Guys, blue shirts look best, and accept makeup if the studio offers it. Ladies, don't dress like Ann Coulter. Cover up, for God's sake, preferably with a neutral-colored jacket and a bright shirt.

When the bloggers take turns role-playing on camera, they seem almost apologetic about their bloggerishness. "I have dimples, you can't see them—I have so much facial hair," says one. But the workshop wasn't just about constructive criticism: Smile, keep your hands out of the box, look at the camera, not the monitor. It was also about constructive celebration, celebrating oneself, one's own netrootedness, one's own bloggerhood.

After going two or three minutes without hearing bloggers praised as a species, one blogger in blogger glasses asks the trainers if there's anything that bloggers naturally do right that "attracts producers to them." Yes, say the trainers. It turns out bloggers become experts on everything, they are not afraid to "speak directly." Also, they tend not to be evasive and are generally comfortable with conflict. Also, they're truth-tellers. Also, says one trainer, they have "the irreverence, the wit, the research, and a certain kind of attitude that is greatly needed on the progressive side." It's important, therefore, for them to be who they are. "You're like the new cool kids on the block," says one trainer. "You should leverage that."

It is a pretty heady time for bloggers. Take Ellie Perelli, a seventy-eight-year-old woman who used to be a "lurker" (a reader only) but who has become a full-fledged Kossack, having just posted her first diary under "momster." She's now an unofficial mascot of the site. Ellie didn't even know how to blog. But shortly after our Mother Talkers Caucus the other day, headed by Kos's wife, who runs mothertalkers.com, a website featuring "rants and raves on modern motherhood," a woman named Shannon "took me upstairs and showed me how to do it." I ask Ellie what it felt like to blog for the first time, upstairs with Shannon. She laughs naughtily. "Satisfying," she says. "Exciting. Like I just opened a Christmas present and it was everything you wished for."

In these circles, there's lots of pressure to blog, to say something, anything, and to say it loudly and often. Take my new friend Alex Barrio, whom I met when he headed the Student Caucus I attended. He called the meeting to order by saying, "Before we get started, let's all grab the hand of the person next to you." Then he said he was just kidding—he was trying to scare the reporter. I wanted to hug him at that moment. I've been to lots of these gatherings over the years, and holding hands is some of the lighter physical contact I've been asked to participate in.

One day, in the hallway, Alex offers a confession: "I've read the blogs. But I'm a lurker." He says this with some shame, as if he's just admitted that he hands out porn at preschool bus stops. He's decided, however, that it's time to get more directly involved, so he registered as a user with Daily Kos. He's immediately allowed to comment on other people's diaries, but there's a one-week waiting period before he can write a diary of his own. (It's kind of like buying a handgun.) So instead, he borrows the handle of Luke McSweeney, a twenty-eight-year-old nuclear safety engineer who posts under "Cream Puff."

We take a seat at a table near the registration desk, and Alex agrees to let me watch him get his blog cherry popped. He pulls some notes he's scrawled out of a pocket, and focuses on the screen before him with laserlike intensity. He is oblivious to noise and the color commentary I'm providing to my tape recorder.

He is uninterested when Jodi Leib, an attractive woman from my Abortion Roundtable meeting, stops by to bend my ear about how we need to "create healthy sexual attitudes" and about how men need to "love their sperm, love their bodies." He doesn't pay any mind when she shares with me the lyrics to a song she wrote, "Love is Mystical": "Love, love, love / All our love is mystical / Love, love, love / Sexual is mystical." "Love your sperm!" I say to Alex, trying to get him to join in the love-fest. "I'm looking forward to my vasectomy," he says, without looking away from the computer.

Alex has some unfinished thoughts about the need for more students at the Student Caucus, and he's got to get them out. He is a student at the University of Central Florida, but it seems like he was one of the only students in his caucus. The rest were pros from places like the DNC and the Progressive Patriots Fund, trolling for young voters like online predators, because they've heard the kids are really hep to this thing called the Information Superhighway.

Alex is no top-of-the-brainpan blowhard. He labors. He crafts. He edits and reedits and then passes the computer to Cream Puff and another friend who blogs under "Shlomo Boudreaux, the Cajun Jew" for more copyediting. "What are you going to title it?" I ask Alex. "Student Caucus," he says. "Doesn't exactly grab you by the lapels. Doesn't say 'revolution,'" I helpfully offer, being in the words business myself. He goes instead with "YearlyKos Student Caucus—Students Needed!" Much better.

He hits "send." We sit and intently watch the feedback line as if we are waiting for a red light to change. It says "0 comments." Sometimes that big doughnut just lies there and mocks you, makes you feel as though you're spitting in the wind, as if your voice isn't being heard. But then it changes to "1 comment." It's from "jlove1982," who says she would've loved to have "networked with people" and that hopefully next year's convention will be "somewhere closer to the east coast. But good work." Success! Validation! People Power!

But all the Kossacks aren't as deliberative or scrupulous as Alex. Take Pontificator. I don't know him, but I've read his work online. He recently did a predictive blog about a subject I know a little something about—me. He wrote about my piece, this piece, a week before it came out. His diary was titled "Prepare for the Matt Labash Year-lyKos Hatchet Job Article."

That hurts, Pontificator. Why do you have to prejudge? Hear me now, Pontificator, if that's your real name: WORDS CAN WOUND. He and the sixty-nine commenters on his post purported to know everything about my piece, along with my comings and goings at the convention, without knowing much of anything. They didn't know that I get it. That I understand it. That I plug into People Power. That I too am People and have Power within me.

But how would Pontificator know that? He just posts from his digital masturbatorium. He called me "that scowling unshaven frat boy some of you may have seen skulking around the convention grounds." Not true, you lying sack of pontification. I wasn't skulking, I was practically skipping, as you would if you were headed to the "Hot Topic of the Day featuring a panel of top bloggers" discussion. Plus, I was never in a frat. Plus, I shaved every single morning with my Schick Quattro, which is designed "for the guy who wants everything . . . except irritation."

The commenters were even worse. Circle said that I "smelled like judgment." No I didn't, I smelled like Acqua di Parma, a symbol of Italian elegance favored by Humphrey Bogart and Cary Grant. Shayera said that I was sitting at her table at the Valerie Plame panel, that I got up in the middle and left for twenty minutes, returning with a *USA Today* that I read for the rest of the panel. "I saw that too," wrote Buzzer. "What a fucking jerk," said Sally in SF. Except for one problem: I was at that panel for only about five minutes, left, and never came back inside. Nor did I ever have a *USA Today*. Must've been a different Matt Labash. Hey, Shayera, good thing the blogosphere is here to check our facts.

Then there were the buttercups from my Abortion Roundtable. They practically stoned me after forcing me to admit I was pro-life. Some were rude enough that other people at the roundtable later apologized to me on their behalf. But somehow, I was the jerk for answering their questions. In a comment, Elise called me a "jackass" and said I "coughed rudely throughout the discussion (without covering his mouth!)."

Faboo claimed I threw a "tantrum about not being able to record the abortion roundtable." But nothing remotely close to that ever happened. I never asked to record, I was never asked not to record, and I did in fact record. Annrose, who runs abortionclinicsonline. com, and who moderated the roundtable, says I "blushed in that slimy way" when I was asked if I always use contraception when I don't want to procreate, and that I couldn't say yes. Actually, after stammering because of the presumptuousness of the question, I did say yes. The reason I was blushing, Annrose, is that you told me I was "too cute to be pro-life." Twice. (Call me, Sweet Cheeks.)

To be fair, the commenters reacting to Pontificator's post did get around to more important topics, like Byron York's cell phone. "For the record, Byron York's cellphone rang during the Plame panel," said QuickSilver. Shayera said it rang either "two or three times. And I'm sure about that." QuickSilver just had to know if York checked his caller ID before he answered it. He did, says Shayera of the man she called Byron "big hair" York. "I was two tables back and to the right, so I had a perfect view."

QuickSilver, Shayera, we salute your reporting. Stellar stuff. Thanks for showing us the way. Thanks for not just working it out in workshop, where the words disappear into the ether. But for putting it down, in black and white, where it can be read forever by the netroots, who need something to read while "Crashing the Gate," as Kos put it. And we can talk about this and so much else on Daily Kos. About the netroots and People Power and Byron York's Byronic locks and cell phone habits. And we can talk, and talk, and talk some more, even when we've run out of things to say.

TRUMP ON THE STUMP

Los Angeles

Of all the bizarre twists Campaign 2000 has taken, there is none so strange as the one that finds us on the rooftop of L'Ermitage hotel in Beverly Hills. The media have come to explore the possible presidential candidacy of Donald Trump, who has himself formed an exploratory committee, blanketed the talk shows, and threatened to spend $100 million to win not just the Reform Party nomination but "the whole megillah."

L'Ermitage is a magnet for studio junkets and celebrities convalescing after rhinoplasty. The hotel's suites run up to $3,800 per night, so demanding guests can expect amenities like personalized cell phones and eighty-eight-inch pool towels. It's what The Donald would call a "class facility," and he knows of what he speaks. Not only is Trump, in his own demure phraseology, "the biggest developer in the hottest city in the world," but his very pores emit class. In fact, he uses the word frequently—as an adjective, not a noun. Thus, everything associated with him is classy, even unauthorized biographies, like *The Really, Really Classy Donald Trump Quiz Book.*

Standing on the panoramic rooftop next to the classy pool, reporters anticipate Trump's arrival for a press conference. While waiting, we help ourselves to the Purel hand sanitizers that Trump aides have kindly set out in a fishbowl. The Donald thinks shaking hands is "barbaric" and unhygienic. Politics, however, is about compromise. Twenty yards away, a television crew sets up for an interview with actress Whoopi Goldberg. I have spent so much time talking to Trump's aides over the past week that I feel qualified to speak not only for them, but *like* them. So I approach the Goldberg camp, informing no one in particular that "Mr. Trump doesn't like to share the spotlight."

"Whoopi doesn't either," snaps a Goldberg lackey, "and she's a *real* celebrity." The Trump camp tries unsuccessfully to get the Goldberg camp to relocate. So instead of conducting the press conference by the shaded pool, the Trump press conference moves to a sun-scorched section of the terrace, making The Donald squint even more than usual.

As he takes the podium, Trump's entire entourage is present. There's Roger Stone, his political consigliere, who is, as always, immaculately and ornately haberdashed in café au lait suede shoes and a gangster boldstripe suit. "I haven't bought off the rack since I was seventeen," says Stone. There is Trump's bodyguard, all muscle and menace. His name is Matt Calamari, so we immediately start calling him "Matty the Squid," though not to his face. Most important, there is Melania Knauss, Trump's twenty-six-year-old supermodel girlfriend, who is four years removed from her native Slovenia. *Melania*. Her name is like a song. Her skirt is short, her heels are high. Her legs are so long that her torso seems an afterthought. She'd make a class First Lady.

Trump tells us that he will be forgoing individual interviews because of the crush of media present. There are only ten of us, and three of us are from German television; The Donald would have time to do interviews, close a deal, and still take Melania shopping before his next engagement. But no matter. Though he will ultimately decide on running for president after "going by my gut," he says his internal "polling has been amazing." He will not tell us the name of his pollster. Nor will he tell us the names of the economists he consulted for his debt-reduction plan, which calls for a one-time 14.5 percent tax on the entire net worth of the richest Americans (and Trump calls Bill Bradley a socialist). Trump quickly wraps up the press conference, promising us more later, and disappears with Melania and the Squid. He does not shake our Purel-coated hands.

Stone immediately swoops in for spin, assuring us that the polling, which Trump seemed suspiciously vague about, is concerned with issues, not the horse race. Stone says they are smoking Pat Buchanan in polls of Reform Party members, but have not polled the general election. This seems an odd claim, in light of Trump's "whole megillah" strategy. But we are quickly on to more important things, like how Stone is able to achieve a perfect double dimple below his tie knot. Stone insists I remove my tie, and as we document his every move, he puts on a double-dimple clinic. "It takes a while to learn," he says. "We're gonna have to work on it."

With Trump off-limits until that evening, Stone sets up a media availability with Melania. Next to a lobby anteroom where Melania sits, Whoopi Goldberg waltzes by. I ask her if she'd support a Trump candidacy. "What does he stand for?" she asks. "Donald Trump," deadpans another reporter. Melania is getting used to this sort of cynicism, and she is not easy pickings for interrogators. I ask her if she considers herself a supermodel, or just a really swell model. "I'm a person first," she says in her Slovenian accent, "and then I have a great career." (*Good answer: Decisive. Evasive. Conveys confidence without conceit.*) When asked whether, as First Lady, she would have a pet initiative like Barbara Bush's literacy or Betty Ford's alcoholism, she responds, "Yes, I love children." (*Textbook: When in doubt, invoke children.*) When asked if she is creeped out by Trump's germ phobia, she says, "You know, there are a lot of germs from colds and flu, and nobody is really talking about this." (*What a pro.*)

That night, we follow Trump to a taping of the Jay Leno show in Burbank. As Trump cools his heels in the dressing room before the show, Leno pops in for a visit, and sees Stone in his Bugsy Siegel rig. "Hey Donald," cracks Leno, "you brought your bookie." We journalists are briefly permitted into the studio to watch the preshow festivities. Warm-up comic Bob Perlow plies the crowd with stale jokes and show tunes. Then, spotting Melania in the audience, he insists she come up to the stage, where she is asked to dance seductively while throwing souvenir T-shirts into the audience. *Tonight Show* staffers claim this is a pregame tradition, but one suspects they invented it as an excuse to watch Melania gyrate.

She is supremely uncomfortable and refuses to comply, darting back to her seat, which is a piano wire's width away from Matty the Squid's. Wisely, Perlow does not persist. Stone comes out and stands next to me. He is concerned for Melania's well-being. But mostly, he is concerned about my newly double-dimpled tie. "No good," he says, shaking his head disapprovingly.

Back in the green room, after the show begins, we munch melon wedges and finger sandwiches with singer Michael Bolton's entourage. A Leno staffer says we will not be permitted into Trump's dressing room after the show. I protest to Stone, who, like any Trump devotee, tries to make a deal. He'll get us access, "but you'll refrain from making fun of Mr. Trump's hair again." Stone is referring to an article I wrote some months ago in which I charged that Mr. Trump's coif resembled an abandoned nest. Having now seen Trump's hair up close, I make no promises.

Though Leno mercilessly rags Trump, alleging at one point that he caught a sexually transmitted disease—from himself, Trump has the audience eating from his antiseptic palm. Of the women of the Clinton scandal, he says, "You have some beauties in that deal." Of his competition, Pat Buchanan, he says, "He's obviously been having a love affair with Adolf Hitler." One of Trump's loudest applause lines, which works everywhere he goes, is "I don't drink, I don't smoke, I've never had a cup of coffee." It comes as a surprise, but tea drinkers may be the soccer moms of the 2000 election.

In Trump's dressing room after the show, five reporters and a *60 Minutes* camera crew are chatting with The Donald. Leno stops by, holding a copy of Trump's upcoming campaign manifesto. Unable to obtain a review copy less than a month before publication, I ask Leno to see it. He passes the book, but it will not open. "It's a dummy copy," quips Leno, "[the book] hasn't been written yet." Trump asserts to skeptical reporters that his flirtation with the presidency isn't just a publicity drive for his book. The revenue the book generates, he says, will pay for his "airplane fuel to go back and forth from California." Besides, he repeats several times in the same conversation, he's already had three number-one bestsellers. Likewise, he is "running the biggest real estate empire in the world" and he's "very competent and very rich," though "I don't want to toot my own horn." It's not his way.

Trump invites us back to L'Ermitage for a reception with about a hundred Reform Party activists who pack The Donald's cavernous Governor's Suite, two floors below the Presidential Suite. He serves them goat cheese on black olive ciabatta and good Merlot, not the boxed Zinfandel they are accustomed to. The California crowd is stylish by Reform standards, but there are still a fair number of double-knit suits and visible nose hairs. As Trump takes the podium, Melania stands at his side, her Piaget watch refracting light as she shifts restlessly on her sinewy, tanned stilts. Trump takes questions from the audience, warning, "The camera is *60 Minutes,* don't worry about them. It's this little program on television . . . so don't worry about embarrassing ourselves with questions."

Trump, it seems, is a bit sensitive to the media perception of the Reform Party, which falls somewhere between comic relief and sad joke. This was reinforced yet again when eight Reform Party presidential "candidates," including Pat Buchanan, met on December 3 for a debate. At the Portland, Oregon, Marriott, about a hundred people assembled to hear the views of several crackpot prospects, while a microphone stand repeatedly toppled over, one candidate's name was misspelled, and Buchanan's speech was overshadowed by a Native American dance ceremony in the neighboring ballroom. A week before this California swing, I asked a Trump aide why Trump wouldn't be attending this debate. "What debate?" he asked, convincingly pretending ignorance.

Holding court in his suite, Trump answers Reformer concerns. He casts aspersions on the WTO and the U.S. trade representative. "Where does she come from?" he asks. "Has *she* made billions of dollars?" He rubs turpentine in the wounds of black-helicopter types, saying that he believes in the United Nations so strongly that "I'm building a ninety-story building right next to it." Though some hecklers ding him for dumping on other Reformers, Trump tears into Pat Buchanan and his new ally, the radical Lenora Fulani. "We have the ultraright and a Communist, you can have that party," Trump says. When one gentleman asks Trump if he'll support the party platform, Trump says, "Nobody knows what the platform is." Someone brings him a copy. Trump says he'll read it, but leaves it on the podium when the Q&A session ends.

It's a virtuoso performance. Trump has disagreed with, chided, and even insulted his constituency, and yet they mob him afterward, won over by either his Merlot or his candor. As Melania disappears into a back room to avoid getting pawed by the double-knits, Trump lunges into the throng, shaking hands—shaking hands!—and signing campaign literature. He looks my way, beaming. Holding up a picture of himself, he asks, "Isn't he handsome?"

A few hours after the reception, a small group of reporters are off to The Ivy. The Ivy is one of those insider Hollywood restaurants where out-of-towners come to experience the epicenter of cool, though since we know about it, it's likely on the verge of extinction. We are shunted off to a lonely patio corner with an obstructed view. Trump's fellow *Tonight Show* guest, Michael Bolton, sits at the next table, temporarily unaware of our existence. After about ten minutes, the Trump entourage, having already eaten, emerges from an inner sanctum where they've been chatting up Rod Stewart. Seeing us in the corner, Trump walks over and says to Bolton, in a voice loud enough for the entire restaurant to hear, "Watch out for these guys, they rule the world." Trump then vanishes into his limo, but the very molecular structure of the patio changes around us. Food tastes better. Wine flows freer. Strange women strike up conversations with us from distant tables. Michael Bolton rises to his feet and starts sucking up profusely to Adam Nagourney of the *New York Times*. We are, thanks to the Donald, what Matty the Squid might call "made men."

Bolton bores us with earnest accounts of how he's campaigning for Hillary Clinton. But he strikes pay dirt when he tells us how, after Trump once broke up with former wife Marla Maples, Bolton began dating her. It made Trump so jealous that he took her back. But then, "when he could have her," says Bolton, "he didn't want her anymore." As his presidential campaign seems to suggest, Trump is most attracted to things he can't have. Just two months after the death of Princess Di, for example, he expressed profound sadness to *Dateline*. "I would have loved to have had a shot to date her," he told Stone Phillips, "because she was an absolutely wonderful woman."

"Do you think you would have had a shot?" asked Phillips. "I think so, yeah," responded The Donald. "I always have a shot." Classy.

The next day, we rise at dawn to follow Trump to the Simon Wiesenthal Center's Museum of Tolerance, which bills itself, in Trumpian fashion, as a "world-class human rights laboratory." Trump says he was asked to come here, though Rabbi Abraham Cooper of the center tells us Trump made the request. Whatever: It's a natural photo op for Trump, who may wind up running against a man who's having "a love affair with Adolf Hitler." The Donald, Melania, and the media scrum follow Cooper through exhibits like the "Point of View Dinner," and a film montage depicting atrocities throughout the world. The Donald gazes intently, brow knitted, his lips fixed in puckered protrusion. In profile, he looks like a distressed mallard.

As we walk through the museum, he and Melania occasionally lock fingers, while Trump tries to impress the Rabbi by dropping the names of Jewish friends. "Do you know Nelson Peltz?" he asks. "Fantastic guy." We walk through the Holocaust section, where there are re-creations of everything from the Warsaw Ghetto to Auschwitz. Throughout the trip, Trump keeps saying things like "Good job, Rabbi" and "Great location," as if he is assessing one of his Atlantic City properties.

At the end of the tour, I approach Roger Stone, who is wearing "Nixon Is the One" cuff links, to ask if Trump will make news. "Is that what you want?" asks Stone, handing me a press release in which Trump will again denounce Buchanan. Trump gives a modified version of the statement in the museum atrium, praising the center but omitting the Buchanan references. By the end of the Q&A, however, he's again fitted Buchanan in brownshirt and jackboots. After the press conference, I try to talk about the speech with Stone, but his mind is on other things. He's looking me straight in the cravat.

"Your knot needs work," he says.

From the Wiesenthal Center, we board Trump's 727 at LAX for the fifteen-minute ride to Long Beach, where Trump will make $100,000 for twenty minutes' work addressing 21,000 people at self-help guru Tony Robbins's seminar. In a word, the plane is classy. Everything is fashioned from mahogany and teak. Crystal bar glasses and decanters line the cabinets (though The Donald doesn't drink), and priceless works of art hang throughout the cabin (the art, Trump says, is "off the record" for security reasons). With all these mangy journalists in tow, Trump has several mild panic attacks: "Don't put the glass on the table"; "Watch the paintings, fellas." But he quickly settles into boys-club gregariousness, punching reporters in the arm, talking about hot supermodels, and fielding compliments about Melania. "Pretty incredible, right?" he asks. "She's a beauty, and it's not just here," he says, pointing to his face. "It's the inner beauty too."

I catch up with Trump in his kitchenette as he tears into a bag of Lay's potato chips. Still curious about the Wiesenthal tour, which one could categorize as pretty cynical political theater, I ask if Donald Trump is good for the Jews. "Yes," he says immediately.

"How?" I ask.

"Not now," he says, crunching into a chip, "I gotta think about my fuckin' speech."

At the Long Beach Airport, we deplane and board a chartered bus, appropriately titled "A Touch of Class." We head to Arrowhead Pond arena, home of the Anaheim Mighty Ducks hockey team, which is filled with Tony Robbins seminarians who've spent hundreds of dollars to glean success secrets from celebrity guests like Larry King (*marry eight times, ask softball questions*).

Onstage, Robbins dons a headset mike and dances like an epileptic to a mega-mix version of "Real Wild One." Middle managers are instructed to knead each other's necks. "It's okay for guys to rub guys!" Robbins exclaims. Backstage, Trump has a case of nerves, skittishly pacing and shaking his legs to the beat. I tell him to picture his audience naked, and he seems to accept my counsel, wiggling his bushy brows as a female Robbins staffer walks by in a tank top that threatens her circulation.

Robbins introduces Trump to a receptive crowd, and Trump enters to two stageside explosions that nearly ignite his hair. Trump is not opposed to the nerf platitudes of self-help gurus; he and his first wife, Ivana, were married by Mr. Positive Thinking himself, Norman Vincent Peale. But today Trump offers a different kind of success recipe, one that sounds like a song-of-the-street beatitude uttered by Frank Sinatra and transcribed by Jilly Rizzo. Commandment One: "People tend to be very vicious; as the boxers say, 'Keep the left up.'" Commandment Two: "Get even. When somebody screws you, screw 'em back, but a lot harder." Commandment Three: "Always have a prenup." The crowd is ecstatic. Robbins is embarrassed. "It's not exactly my values," he says offstage. After the Prenup Commandment, I watch Melania. She forces a smile. But the lovelight momentarily flickers out in her eyes.

In a VIP tent after his performance, Trump faces a select group of tortellini-eating businessmen who've paid additional sums to ask questions of the celebrities. Ever the charmer, Trump chooses his interrogators by identifying their salient physical characteristics: "the bald guy in the suit" or "the beautiful woman in the semi-blouse." Of a Yorba Linda resident seeking Trump's advice about running for city council, Trump asks, "Are you a Reform candidate?"

"Yes," the man says.

"Lotsa luck," Trump replies.

Another woman asks how she can create capital "when all I have is my knowledge and training." Trump thinks a moment, then says, "Meet a wealthy guy." He distills his political philosophy into a very simple formula: "In business and in life, people want to hear straight talk. We're tired of being bullshitted by these moron politicians." The crowd is nearly speaking in tongues.

After the event, Stone enters our bus: "I'm here, who needs to be spun?" I ask how The Donald expects to sustain support when he so frequently expresses obvious contempt for everyone but himself. "You piss 50 percent of the people off no matter what you say," says Stone.

By his reckoning, Trump needs "only" 35 to 40 percent of the vote in a three-way election. That seems like a lot. Could that many Americans possibly want Donald Trump to be their president? You wouldn't think so. On the other hand, at the Tony Robbins seminar, twenty-one thousand people have just paid $270 apiece to derive wisdom from Billy Blanks, the founder of Tae Bo.

Before boarding the plane with reporters for a return ride back to Manhattan (the hottest city with the biggest developer), Trump is still discussing the Robbins "love fest" in colorful terms: "Did you see that one woman? She had an amazing body, but a schoolmarm's face." Wisely, he decides to go off the record for the rest of the flight, so we "can relax and have fun."

"Who wants to take up the plane?" he asks, allowing reporters to sit in the cockpit. The in-flight movie choice is *Midnight Express* or *The Godfather.* Trump picks the former, though Matty the Squid looks disappointed. Melania has shed her Blahnik pumps and pads barefoot around the cabin like an exotic cat. "We have pizza," she purrs. For the next six hours, we share locker-room banter that if transcribed could put an end to several careers. Trump's candor makes John McCain look Nixonian by comparison. As the adventure ends, Trump repeatedly taunts reporters, wondering how we'll ever go back to covering Al Gore and flying coach. It seems a sensible question.

Here's hoping The Donald runs.

REV GOTTA EAT

Al Sharpton's Hungry for a Place at the Table

Columbia, South Carolina

While many reporters like to cover frontrunner campaigns, I've always favored no-hopers. Losers are more vulnerable, accessible, and desperate, meaning they reveal rather than conceal. Plus, it is always perverse fun to watch a man's id hit the end of its leash, just to see how far it snaps back.

That's how I found myself in South Carolina in early February, for what many were billing as Al Sharpton's Last Stand, or, to be more precise, his First Stand, since stand-wise, he hadn't made any. Sharpton runs on his own clock, the time zone of which remains a mystery to his revolving-door schedulers. "Rev," as his staffers call him, has missed a plane to a televised presidential debate, never showed up to a confab in which he was supposed to net some rare endorsements, and even kept the Dalai Lama cooling his heels. So at majority-black Dreher High School, where Sharpton is set to launch Black History Month, smart reporters observe what could be called the Hour Rule: At any scheduled Sharpton event, it is wise to show up sixty minutes late. Doing so gives you time to arrange your news-gathering utensils, to acclimate yourself, and perhaps to get a snack before Sharpton himself shows up thirty minutes later. With Sharpton true to form today, I have time to fall in with a group of fourteen-year-olds. They don't seem to mind Rev's tardiness, on account of its helping them blow through algebra and physical science, though if he costs them a third period, it would be lunch, and fourteen-year-olds have their limits.

As I talk to them, it becomes clear that, though they know he's running for president and he's famous, they have no idea why. They missed the Reverend Al Horror Show of the late eighties and early nineties: the Tawana Brawley hoax, the Crown Heights and Freddy's

Fashion Mart violence that Sharpton egged on, the undignified ap-
pearances on *The Morton Downey Jr. Show*, such as the night when
the once-tubby Sharpton, at the height of his shiny tracksuit and
Cowardly Lion hair phase, was rolled off the stage like a bocci ball
after a fistfight erupted with another guest.

But that was many makeovers ago. That was before he slimmed
down in a Puerto Rican jail, protesting a U.S. naval bombing range
there. It was before his Senate and mayoral runs, where he played the
spoiler, swinging votes away from New York Democrats who now give
him the high hat. It was before he started getting tailored by the guy
who outfits television lawyers on *The Practice*. It was before he started
hijacking presidential debates, proving that even though he has stalled
at single digits in the polls, he is the only candidate who can turn a
phrase. And most important, it was before Jesse Jackson, his onetime
friend and mentor, was found to have been carrying some illegitimate
fruit on his family tree and became increasingly irrelevant. Before, in
other words, the media started taking applications for what Sharpton's
kitchen cabinet adviser Cornel West dismissively calls "HNIC—
Head Negro In Charge."

When asked who Sharpton is, the kids seem stumped. One
thinks he's a motivational speaker. Another thinks he "has something to do with the NAACP." A third ninth-grader offers, "He's
a reverend, right? He's named 'Reverend Al.' Gotta be preaching
somewhere." For most candidates, potential voters (or future voters,
in the children's case) not knowing who you are is a disadvantage.
For a Sharpton constituency, amnesia is one of the most desirable attributes. It allows the candidate to make a fresh start, which he needs
even among this group. I assume, stereotypically, that these kids will
be easy pickings for Sharpton. I couldn't be more wrong. An African
American teenager named Jerrod, wearing a "Dirty South" football
jersey, says, "He needs to think about improving America as a whole
instead of just one minority." A boy named Kamil seconds, "He's too
strong, he's always attacking something."

"Truthfully," Jerrod says, "I don't think America is ready for a
black president." Kamil takes it even further. "I don't think black
people are ready for a black president," he says, catching an elbow
from the girl sitting next to him. As if on cue, Sharpton pads down
the aisle, right on time, if we're going by his internal clock. He walks
at least four inches taller than his allotted five feet seven. He looks

buttery-smooth in an elegantly draped three-button suit, garnished with a white linen pocket square so immaculately fluffed, it could've been laid in his breast pocket by God or Adam Clayton Powell, the latter of whom holds pretty-close-to-equal standing with the former in Sharpton's estimation.

It is apparent, rather quickly, that Sharpton's makeover isn't merely sartorial. Over the years, I've witnessed—many times—Sharpton bullying and race-baiting like any two-bit bullhorn hustler. But from the look of things, a leopard can change his shiny tracksuit. At times, it almost seems that if he had a high-pitched whine and unnaturally long fingers, he could be Alan Keyes instead of Al Sharpton. He tells the students that acting like a thug or some debauched gangster rapper is not a "black thing—the black thing is to reach high, no matter how low you are." He asserts that using racism as an excuse for not making progress—even when it's the culprit—is unacceptable. "If I step off this platform and knock you off your seat, that's on me," he says. "But if I come back next Friday, and you still on the flo', that's on you." Acting disengaged and uninterested in the world at large, he says, is a way to permanently hamstring yourself. "Most old bums start out as young bums," he says. "They cut school, they hung out . . . until one day they were gray-headed, no teeth in their mouth, and the young guy that everybody thought was cool was just an old bum on his way to old bumblehood." The kids titter, while Sharpton looks over at their principal. "That's a new word. Trust me. Write that down."

Standing before the kids as a successfully unsuccessful presidential candidate, he proudly says, "I decided I wasn't going to let anybody tell me what I could be. I encourage you to do the same." He preaches the transforming power of vanity: "Be the chairman of your own fan club. Every mornin', I get up, I have a meeting of the Al Sharpton fan club. I'm the president, secretary, treasurer, and sometimes, I'm the whole membership. But it doesn't matter. Because if I'm on my side, it doesn't matter who's against me."

Out in a foyer press conference afterward, Tom Llamas, MSNBC's embed on the campaign, rifles one to Sharpton: NBC has him dropping to fifth place in South Carolina, a state in which it's generally believed he needs to finish at least third in order to prove he has any swat among black voters. "If I worried about an NBC poll," shoots back Sharpton, "I'd never get out of bed in the morning. They would poll that I'm going to sleep all day." Back inside, the students I'd been talking to, after standing up and cheering wildly during the speech, are now back to being dispassionate. "He proved my point," says Jerrod, "it was totally directed toward black people." A girl named Katherine tells me the speech was good, but "I'm already inspired by myself." When I snag a white kid walking by, sixteen-year-old Drew who dresses like an Abercrombie model, he is still smiling. The speech, he says, was "excellent—I was really inspired." Drew's is a sentiment that I encounter over and over again in South Carolina—often, and especially, among white voters—the gist of which goes: Al Sharpton, he's not that bad.

The nominal slugline on Sharpton's homestretch traipse through South Carolina is the "Take a Stand Tour." The campaign, says Andre Johnson, Sharpton's press secretary, even has a theme song—Bob Marley's "Get Up, Stand Up," though in typical Sharpton campaign fashion, nobody thinks to play it at any of the stops. Someone—all right, me—gives it another name: the "Rev Gotta Eat Tour." The name is minted when, at a stop at Columbia's Benedict College, Sharpton is running his characteristic hour and a half late. Llamas goes into the cafeteria and orders the last batch of chicken wings. They are cold, and as he gives them back to the cafeteria worker to heat up, Andre arrives. Andre then orders chicken wings for Sharpton, commandeering some of Llamas's. When Llamas protests, Andre offers no apologies: "Rev gotta eat," he says.

The phrase becomes a salutation, benediction, and all-purpose affirmation—as when Marines say "oorah." Whenever someone wonders where Sharpton is, another person responds with "Rev gotta eat." Some, instead of answering their cell phones with "hello," switch to "Rev gotta eat." Others even consider the metaphysical implications of the phrase: "What appetite, exactly, is the Rev feeding when he gotta eat?" What does Sharpton want? On his campaign website, which regularly posts news from three weeks earlier, he lists his top ten reasons for running—none of which seems particularly compelling. Most of his issues—universal health care, for instance—are already being addressed by other candidates. Making sure support for affirmative action stays in the Democratic platform doesn't seem worth the trouble, since it was in the platform last time anyone read it, which few people do. And increasing "political consciousness" hardly seems worth gallivanting around the country for—even if you are staying in five-star hotels, as Sharpton tends to do—when, according to your last filing, you're carrying nearly $400,000 worth of debt with only $8,000 cash on hand.

Sharpton outlines a delegate strategy, knowing full well he's going to lose, but reasoning if he wrangles enough delegates in mostly urban areas, he will get—in keeping with the Rev Gotta Eat theme—"a seat at the table" during the convention and beyond. At the moment, he won't need a very big table. As of this writing, Sharpton has 12 delegates out of a potential 4,321. To compare that to Jesse Jackson's first 1984 presidential run—as Sharpton himself habitually does—Jackson won four states, the District of Columbia, and 465.5 delegates.

How Sharpton plans to get there—even though he does regularly out-perform his poll numbers—confounds many. In South Carolina, the only place he bothered with a ground game, his organization is more like a dis-organization. His staffers give wrong addresses, then ask reporters for directions to campaign stops. His field director is Deves Toon, a churchless reverend. I stop by the ragtag campaign headquarters, which sports one of the only Sharpton signs I see during the entire week ("Signs are expensive," says campaign manager Charles Halloran). When Toon is asked how Sharpton will do, he says, "How am I supposed to know—I ain't got no crystal ball," before he steps into a closet with the only other volunteer present for a "strategy session."

Local activist/writer Kevin Gray, Sharpton's South Carolina coordinator who also worked on Jackson's two presidential runs, left the campaign last fall after not getting paid. Sharpton says part of the goal is to start a Rainbow Coalition–style movement that will last as a permanent progressive alternative to the DLC, but Gray seems skeptical that Sharpton could organize a dinner party. "People keep saying the campaign's in disarray," says Gray. "It's not. To be in disarray, you have to be in array first. . . . He's running a publicity campaign. If you get these delegates, what are you gonna promote? Antiwar? Five out of the nine candidates were antiwar. Reparations? I doubt it. I like Al—he's a likable fella. But I just believe politics ought to have a focus beyond establishing who's the Head Negro in Charge."

When I submit to Gray that I find Sharpton to be more talented than Jackson in nearly every way—smarter, more likable, a better communicator—Gray, who's worked for both, says Sharpton's missing the most important attribute: "campaign discipline—Jesse had it." (Indeed, in 1988, Jackson won 30 percent of the total vote and 1,218.5 delegates.)

Roger Stone couldn't disagree more. An unofficial Sharpton adviser, Miami-based Stone is a Republican who cut his teeth working as a Nixon-era dirty trickster, and has been regarded as a controversialist ever since (Stone once found a steak knife sticking in his caricature at the Palm). In numerous recent articles, Stone has been accused of everything from aligning with Sharpton just to sabotage the Democratic primary, to actually keeping the campaign afloat with byzantine financial arrangements. Of the conspiracy charges, he says, "My name is Roger Stone, not Oliver Stone." And while some have suggested that Stone and Sharpton have one thing in common—they both hate the Democratic Party—Stone says his motivation is much simpler. He likes Sharpton, finds him to be a "charming rogue," and besides, he says, "I like the game." While this is a believable explanation knowing Roger Stone, his friends suggest that Stone cares as much about solidifying support in the black community in New York, where he frequently makes electoral trouble. When I ask Charles Halloran, Sharpton's campaign manager, what Stone's game is, he smiles and says, "If Roger found some ants in an anthill that he thought he could divide and get pissed off with each other, he'd be in his backyard right now with a magnifying glass."

Stone says people misunderstand his candidate's lineage. "Sharpton's not MLK, he's ACP," says Stone, referring to Adam Clayton Powell, the flamboyant and often hilariously abrasive congressman/pastor of the Abyssinian Baptist Church. "He's a showman, a performer. He does the big speech. He knocks everybody dead. He says what everyone is too timid to say." As for Sharpton's organizational deficiencies, Stone waves them off: "He is the organization." After the Michigan primary, in which Sharpton picks up seven delegates, Stone tells me, "The guy went into Detroit penniless, and he waged a one-man free media blitz. Between black radio and local cable, the guy dominated the news for four days—and it's all him, his performance. He's not a glad-hander. He's a rock star. Have you seen his church performance? It's electrifying."

On this count, Stone couldn't be more correct. Two days before the primary, we see Sharpton as everybody should see Sharpton at least once—working a black church on a Sunday morning. The day starts off with a slight disappointment. The first church he preaches is in Aiken—James Brown's hometown. A week earlier, Stone had suggested that the campaign was working on a cameo by "a certain hardest-working man in show business." But then Brown was arrested and released for pushing his wife down and threatening to hit her with a chair. It was enough to keep him off the trail, even if Sharpton did bring along Brown's daughter and his former cook, who Sharpton says "makes the best banana pudding in South Carolina."

If Sharpton's life were a bad sitcom, which it sometimes is, it would be *My Two Dads*, with Jesse Jackson and James Brown, the Godfather of Soul, playing the fathers. They are his two poles, the bumpers between which he ricochets. Jesse, he tells me, raised him in "politics and civil rights," but James raised him "personally—manhood stuff—we could talk about everything from dating to saving money to adversity to real estate."

Sharpton made a name as a wonderboy preacher in Holiness churches from the age of four (in first grade, he actually signed his name "Reverend Al Sharpton"). After his real father split to have an affair with his half-sister, plunging the rest of his comfortably middle class family into poverty, and after Brown's real son was killed in a car accident, the two found each other. When Sharpton graduated from high school, he toured with Brown, his job literally being to hold the bag. Seeing as how Brown didn't like credit cards or checks, the bag was often filled with as much as $100,000 cash.

When I ask Sharpton to distill his preaching style, I expect him to mention preaching greats like C. L. Franklin (Aretha's father). Instead, he says he learned many of his techniques from Brown. "When you see a James Brown show, and I've seen about a million, he does this thing where he identifies somebody in the audience who's heartbroken and hurt, and he sings to them. . . . When he sings 'I Feel Good,' he thinks about somebody that didn't have no job—we've talked about that. When I preach, the reason I'm animated and dramatic is I try to identify with the people in the audience."

Having grown up in a tradition where church and community were indistinguishable, where a put-upon janitor could get a self-esteem jolt by becoming a deacon, Sharpton says, "People come to church, particularly in the black community—some of them are trying to get from one Sunday to the next. I don't give them some detached oration. I try to give them real hope, because I go back in my mind to when I needed somebody just to get me to the next Sunday. I learned from James how to identify with the guy in the audience, and say what he feels, and then bring him to where you want him to go."

Sharpton likes to joke on the stump that he's a natural to deal with a budget deficit since "I've been broke all my life. . . . I was born in a deficit." Indeed, he has been overcoming deficits his entire life—financial deficits, a credibility deficit, and, currently, a vote deficit. As a friend of his tells me, "He continuously sabotages himself mostly because he's only capable of fighting off his back. He's an adrenaline junkie. He needs to live on the cusp of failure and humiliation or he can't fully function." This worldview seems to spill over into his preaching. On the Sunday I catch him, he prepares the crowd at Second Baptist Church in Aiken by first getting them good and hostile.

Slated to preach the 7:45 A.M. service, Sharpton doesn't show until nearly 9:30. After stalling with announcements and songs like "Ain't No Party Like a Holy Ghost Party," it's preaching time, so the unprepared host is actually forced to give an off-the-cuff thirty-minute sermon, which he takes out on Sharpton ("Al's coming when he's coming. Even though he's LATE! But when Jesus comes back—He ain't gonna be late!"). Sharpton finally arrives, and pads across the stage imperiously without offering an apology or an explanation. One can almost feel the room turning into John Edwards voters.

Sharpton takes the lectern and leads with an overtly political spiel, explaining that everybody says he's going to lose, but he has a little secret to share: "There are seven running, six of 'em gonna lose." ("C'mon, Rev—c'mon now!" the crowd echoes back, turning his way.) It's their choice, he tells them: Vote for a winner who will ignore them, another loser who will gain them nothing, or vote for him, and earn some delegates who will sit at the table and make sometimes impolite conversation. For too long, he tells them, the Democratic Party's been selling out the base to appeal to swing voters. "And you know if you married, you can go out swingin' all you want. Doesn't mean your wife gonna be there when you get back."

He builds to a sing-songish crescendo in which he relates how his abandoned mother was suspected of harboring a man in the house by a social worker, since they looked so well put together. He was mad, but his mom told him the woman was right, and here he falls into what the pros call the "whooping style," rasping: "I know a man / I know a ma-ANNN / He'll set you free / He'll make a way-AYYY." He then turns to the house reverend with apologies. "Oh," Sharpton says, "you preached already." The crowd is ecstatic. As common-man stump stories go, his takes John Edwards's tired son-of-a-millworker bit, spanks it, and sends it to bed without any supper.

But it's at the next church, behind a truck stop near the Georgia line, that Sharpton proves judging his speaking ability from the presidential debates is akin to assessing Michael Jordan's athletic prowess from watching him play baseball. Half political, half religious, Sharpton takes as his text the Passover passage from Exodus. He starts slowly, turns it up to simmer, then builds to the Full Al, his throaty gurgle rising to a boil until it sounds like he's going to cook his own vocal chords. He grooves like some old-timey gravel-voiced gospel shouter, and by the time he relates how the Lord is "gonna let the death angel riiiiiide tonight," the crowd is ready to hoist the black flag and begin smiting Egyptians.

Notes-free, as always, he runs through a feverish twenty-minute call-and-response, met with choruses of "Uhh-huhhs" and "Bring its." He shout-sings about everything from having decided to follow Jesus, to a saint being a sinner who falls down and gets back up, to his dad leaving him as a ten-year-old, to his bouts with government cheese in the long brown box, to his momma knowing a man who will make a way. "Do you know Him / Get on up." (Here you expect him to look over his shoulder and tell Maceo to take him to the bridge.) He shuffles from foot to foot like he's got a slight case of the trots, dips up and down like a firing piston, and caps it with two full rotations. He sticks the dismount, landing with his mouth perfectly squared in front of the mike, before dropping into a chair with I-can't-do-no-more resignation. The press corps—hard-bitten types paid to hate things for a living—stand in gape-mouthed awe. "Did he just do a 360?" I ask CBS's Ben Ferguson in disbelief. "I think it was a 720," Ferguson replies. For today anyway, Sharpton is neither politician nor preacher. He's quite simply an artist.

Not every day can be as easy as Sunday morning, however. Two nights later, Sharpton makes his way into a dingy Sheraton ballroom studded with interlopers from a funeral directors' conference. He valiantly tries to portray his third-place finish—in which he got only 10 percent of the vote and, worse, only one-fifth of the black vote and no delegates—as some kind of resounding triumph. As he grabs a cell phone, I hear him telling a mutual friend, in logic too tortured to replicate here, "I think the real loser tonight is our friend Reverend Jackson."

Later, I ask him about this. He smiles devilishly, telling me I wasn't supposed to hear that. But then I remind him that the last time I interviewed him in his Harlem headquarters in 2000, he actually had a Jesse Jackson videotape cued and ready to show me. "No offense, Al," I say, "but do you think you might be obsessed?" He smiles and asks, without sounding defensive, who a guy like him is supposed to use as a realistic gauge of success. "If I watch films of Jesse, you say I'm obsessed. If I was watching films of Doug Wilder, you'd say I was out of my mind." He compares it to Mike Tyson watching films of Muhammad Ali, and Ali watching films of Sugar Ray Robinson. "They study those who mastered their art before them."

Having known Jesse since Sharpton was a teenager (Jackson is thirteen years his senior, the same as MLK was to Jackson, Sharpton is fond of pointing out), Sharpton says you can't just say that their on-again, off-again relationship, which has fallen prey to rivalrous sniping and philosophical differences, is merely off-again—even though they currently don't speak.

"I grew up on him—it's more complex than that," says Sharpton. "I've outgrown it, I don't take it personal—but it does bother me." Sharpton, who's currently rereading *Thunder in America,* a book about Jesse's 1984 campaign, says he's not quite certain Jackson even regards him as a peer. "I think in his psychology, I'll always be a thirteen-year-old protege." The obsession, by the way, appears very mutual. Recent reports have both Sharpton's former campaign manager Frank Watkins (a longtime Jackson intimate) and Jesse Jackson Jr., who endorsed Howard Dean (Sharpton suspects with his old man's okay), gleefully circulating stories about Sharpton's involvement with Roger Stone.

Say this for Sharpton: He's more forthright than Jackson's ever been. When I suggest that his campaign is little more than an exercise in ego, he goes with it. "No one with a weak ego could run for president—'cause you're ultimately telling people you can run the Western world, and that you're better than anybody else to do it. So for somebody to say it isn't an exercise in ego is like saying water isn't wet." Having said that, he adds, "Does the exercise help or hurt a given cause? I think the cause of civil rights, human rights, workers' rights is helped by my exercise in ego."

Jackson, these days, gets romanticized in comparison to Sharpton.
People seem to forget that despite all Jesse's relative success in 1988,
it culminated in his founding a now moribund Rainbow Coalition
and receiving a plane to barnstorm the country for Michael Dukakis.
A man can be forgiven for having loftier goals than barnstorming
for Michael Dukakis. Jackson also attained something approaching
insider status, though it is here Sharpton ricochets back to the other
one of his two dads. He says the difference between where Jesse's
gone and where he'll end up is the "James Brown factor." Brown,
Sharpton says, "went everywhere, won every award. But he never became an insider in music. 'Cause he changed music from a 2/4 beat
to a 1/3 beat. I want to change the party, not join the party. I have
no problem going into areas they don't agree with. Because that's the
Brown in me. James never joined the Motown sound, never joined
the R&B sound. But twenty years later, rappers are imitating James.
He became the inside, he didn't join the inside. He redefined what
inside was."

TRAFICANT, CAN HE?

Of all the shots aimed at Rep. James Traficant (that he is a profane, ethically shaky, showboating vulgarian, for starters), there are none so cheap as those directed at his appearance. "It's tough being a fashion leader," the Youngstown Democrat admits. Knight Ridder said Traficant's hair bespeaks "terminal bedhead," while the *Los Angeles Times* settled on a "Planet of the Apes sort of hair helmet." *Washingtonian* said he resembled "a creature from Lake Erie before it was cleaned up," while *George* speculated that his wardrobe was his way of "subtly campaigning for a pay raise."

It hardly seems fair. So when I'm permitted by Traficant's chief of staff, Paul Marcone, to shadow the Ohio pol for a day ("Unless he gets sick of you—then he'll throw you out," Marcone warns), I resolve to look beyond cosmetics: to get past Traficant's kelly-green Dacron bell-bottoms, past the double-knit jacket that has held up so valiantly since its purchase during the Ford administration, past the coif that Traficant's hairdresser wife can't tame, as it makes a brisk ascent from his serrated bangs up his conical crown, stopping to rest in a Peppermint Patty–style nest of hair, which looks to be his own.

But it proves difficult extricating the man from the caricature, because, it seems, the man *is* the caricature. As I catch up with Traficant at the conclusion of his testimony before a Senate subcommittee, he shouts me down for being late, calls me "Kibosh" instead of "Labash," bellows to congressional passersby that I'm there to do a "castration job," and gives me a molar-rattling goombah-style smack in the face as he inquires, "Why would you want to do a piece on a jackass like me? Though I am at the zenith of my jackasshood, I want you to know."

Many would concur with that last sentiment, which is why Traficant, despite his high spirits, warns that "the buzzards are circling." With control of the House up for grabs this fall, it's not out of the question that Traficant—an unreliable Democrat who frequently sides with Republicans—could hold the balance of power. But the eight-term congressman, who rarely wins his general elections with less than 75 percent of the vote, had to slug his way out of a contentious multicandidate primary earlier this year. He suspects national Democrats plotted to vanquish him. And as if that weren't insult enough, he is now facing even more Democrats masquerading as independents in the general, who are trying to finish the job by, among other things, suggesting Traficant is crooked.

They have plenty of material to work with. In 1983, when Traficant was sheriff of Ohio's Mahoning County, he was tried for receiving mob bribes. He represented himself at trial and was acquitted after convincing a jury that he was conducting a one-man sting operation. (The IRS, unimpressed with his criminal exoneration, later dinged him civilly for not paying taxes on his take.) Instead of running campaign ads or sending direct mail to his constituents, Traficant has spent the better part of the year "preparing my electorate" by warning them he expects the U.S. attorney's office to indict him any day. What for, neither he nor prosecutors are saying. But the local press has speculated it will be an everything-and-the-kitchen-sinker—from sweetheart land deals to accepting illegal gifts, like free automobiles. Traficant insists he is innocent on all counts—whatever they may be. "They've got such a hard-on for me," he explains, "they" being the Justice Department, which he has long held is Satan's train-bearer.

Consequently, Traficant leveled a preemptive broadside in August against Attorney General Janet Reno. He has always been a sucker for a good conspiracy theory. But on Fox's *Hannity & Colmes*, Traficant out–Oliver Stoned himself, saying he had come across information that Reno was a lesbian drunk who'd been discovered in compromising positions with call girls, making her an ideal mob puppet when she became Dade County state's attorney. Her "blackmailibility," he added, later manifested itself in her failure to appoint an independent counsel to investigate the influence of Chinese money in our elections. The charges, which Reno denied ("Consider the source," she said), baffled even some of Traficant's friends. "What's that got to do with the price of watermelon?" asks Don Hanni Jr., Youngstown's legendary Democratic political boss and a renowned criminal defense attorney. Hanni—a close friend who tried to have Traficant committed for insanity when the two were political rivals in the early

eighties—has warned the congressman against foolishly antagoniz-
ing prosecutors. "I tell him to keep his goddamn mouth shut," says
Hanni, "but telling him what to do is like kicking a mule in the ass."

All of this would seem to be more than enough to relegate Traficant to Congress's fringes, but recently the opposite has happened.
Traficant has flirted with party-switching for years—he votes with
Republicans 70 percent of the time. This summer, however, he announced that he'd stay a Democrat ("Why should I let them drive
me out? I think they're fucked up") but would be voting for Denny
Hastert for speaker of the House. This set off a mild panic among
Democrats—who because of Traficant's apostasy will need to pick up
two extra seats if they plan to address "Speaker" Gephardt. Not only
that, grateful Republicans have actually taken to campaigning with
Traficant, rewarding him with a $25 million youth center in his im-
poverished district, and even coming to his defense. Ohio Republican
Steve LaTourette has said that if the latest investigation of Traficant
is a fishing expedition intended to cause political embarrassment, "I
will be happy to lead the charge to make sure everyone responsible in
the U.S. Attorney's Office loses their job."

Besides telegraphing his choice for speaker, Traficant does nothing to endear himself to his party's leadership. "I'm gonna do what's
best for America," he sniffs. "I wasn't elected to turn over a fucking
voting card to Dick Gephardt." One Democratic consultant says that
if Traficant makes it through the election and Democrats regain the
majority, "he'll be made chairman of the sub-subcommittee on public
restrooms." For now, though, they are praying he's bluffing, and no
one wants to risk further alienating him.

It's not the first time Traficant has found himself center stage.
Born in Youngstown, the fifty-nine-year-old was a star quarterback at
the University of Pittsburgh. After getting waived by the Pittsburgh
Steelers and Oakland Raiders, he ran a drug counseling program that
saw him named the Mahoning Valley's 1980 Citizen of the Year. His
model citizen credentials, however, would shortly be called into question.

As Youngstown has long served as a shuttlecock between the
Cleveland and Pittsburgh mafias, corruption infested the entire
Mahoning Valley. In the sixties, the *Saturday Evening Post* stuck
Youngstown with the unenviable laurel "Crimetown, U.S.A." And
the title was borne out in the years that followed. It became nearly

impossible for a civic-minded individual to avoid doing business with people bearing middle-name monikers like "Jeep" and "Beef." Enough car bombings occurred that they became known in FBI circles as "Youngstown tune-ups." Locals joked that so many public officials were on the take, they didn't fear imprisonment, but rather, being annexed by Louisiana.

In this climate, Traficant was elected sheriff in 1980, and in his own inimitable style, quickly made his mark. He set new records for drug busts, and once ran his cruiser through the front-yard fence of a motorcycle gang's home. Constantly accusing other public officials of corruption, he enjoyed such a contentious relationship with the local FBI that they reportedly considered shutting down their branch office, as they feared a shoot-out with the sheriff. At the same time, he endeared himself to the citizenry, doing a brief jail stint himself after refusing to sign off on home foreclosures during a time when the steel bust saw the region's unemployment rate rocket to over 20 percent.

But in 1983, after getting caught on audiotape admitting to having accepted more than $100,000 from the mob (as David Grann reported in the *New Republic,* he told Charlie "the Crab" Carabbia, "I am a loyal fucker"), Traficant was forced to stand trial. It may have been the most entertaining public-corruption spectacle in the history of the valley, which has seen its share. Discounting as fraudulent the confession that the feds said he signed, Traficant, who was not a laywer, elected to represent himself. During the course of the seven-week trial, which lawyer Don Hanni says was "some of the most brilliant defense work I've ever seen," Traficant cursed his way across the courtroom in short sleeves while munching cough drops, referred to himself as "my client," and asked the horrified judge for assistance in helping him muddle through procedural complexities, such as getting her removed from the bench.

After convincing the jury that he had pulled off "the most unorthodox sting in the history of Ohio politics," getting acquitted, and then demoting four of his deputies who had testified against him, Traficant, by now a local folk hero, won election to Congress in 1984, was elected president of his freshman class, and quickly solidified his image as the madman of the House when the IRS came after him for not paying taxes on his bribe. Conferring with his client, Traficant again decided to represent himself. As the IRS set about crushing him in court, Traficant conceded, "This stumbling jackass [the feds] may pull it off." They did. To this day, Traficant's $136,700 congres-sional salary is garnished, making his take-home pay, he says, about the same as a public school teacher's.

While remaining a good Rust Belt Democrat who attaches "Buy America" amendments to nearly every appropriations bill, Traficant harbors a deep and abiding mistrust of the IRS, the Justice Depart-ment, and nearly every other federal entity that has made him a con-servative darling. (Rush Limbaugh, whose visage adorns Traficant's congressional office lobby, calls him "my favorite Democrat.") Dur-ing his profanity-strewn one-minute speeches to the empty House chamber—a regular C-SPAN highlight; he is apt to pop off on any-thing from the topless "foxy ladies" of the Ohio State rugby team to Boris Yeltsin's alcoholism—Traficant regularly lays waste to his own party.

From the floor of the House, he says the "White House needs a lobotomy performed by a proctologist," and calls the Lincoln Bed-room the "Red Roof Inn." "If a dog urinates in a parking lot," he cries, "the EPA deems it a wetland." And OSHA should be shipped to Japan and China, so they can "screw those countries up." When a partial-birth abortion bill came up on the same day as a wildlife restoration bill, he fumed, "Unbelievable. Kill the babies, but save the trout and titmouse. Beam me up."

Review Traficant's one-minutes (which are available on his web-site, behind a glaring picture of him swinging a two-by-four with the inscription "Bangin' away in D.C."), and it's understandable why some Republicans find Traficant so appealing. He talks like they do, or the way they used to, before civility scolds and political expedi-ence relegated such rhetoric to Dark Ages Weekends and Rotary luncheons. This helps explain why House Republicans named Trafi-cant the "one-minute MVP," why they fast-tracked his taxpayer bill of rights, why they scatter puppy treats around his district when no other Democrats received projects in a $200 million emergency spending bill. It is why partisan Democrats like Barney Frank grouse, "I know we all want to show we like Traficant, but turning the House into eBay is a bad idea."

After spinning around the Capitol with Traficant, I can see why he is well liked. He is gregarious and courteous to a fault. In a per-mutation of Huey Long's credo, every security guard is "chairman," every elevator operator "chairwoman." But after several minutes of uneventfulness, he cannot help but play provocateur. As we ride a crowded elevator in the Rayburn Building, the married congressman declares straight-faced and loudly, as if answering a question that was never asked, "A lot of women hit on me. I take them on. I feel I have a responsibility to the American woman."

Back in his office, Traficant walks past the macrame plants and ten-pound dumbbell on his desk, and sinks into a blue leather chair that sits close to a tie rack teetering under a load of garish, skinny neckwear donated by his loyal C-SPAN following. The place feels kind of homey, and should, since he sleeps in his office to save money (he is, after all, on a subsistence salary). Traficant's lids look heavy through his auto-tint glasses, and one suspects the prosecutorial pressure is wearing on him, as over the past several months, numerous aides have been subpoenaed to testify before a grand jury. All this coming after Charles O'Nesti, his longtime (and now deceased) district director admitted that when he wasn't working for the congressman, he was moonlighting as a bagman for convicted racketeer Lenny Strollo.

When discussing his corruption trial, Traficant grows agitated. "I destroyed the fuckin' mob, and I'm very proud of that." (He seems to have missed a few, as the latest corruption sweep in the Mahoning Valley has netted seventy-eight indictments.) As for his pending indictment, which Traficant is certain will come, he says, "My attorney will discuss the case no further." "Your attorney being you?" I ask. "Well, yeah," he says. "The man that will represent me will be a man I completely trust, and he'll be a fucking bulldog."

Traficant rails against federal corruption, from the debacles at Waco and Ruby Ridge all the way back to J. Edgar Hoover. "The Chicago [mafia] had pictures of that transvestite in drag," he informs me. Inevitably, he gets around to his current obsession, Janet Reno. He has no evidence she's driving the investigation against him, though he claims an FBI informant nicknamed "Cheezl" told him there's a course offered at the FBI's Quantico training center on "how to get Traficant."

He says he has secret affidavits to prove his charges against Reno, though he's only in the preliminary stages of his investigation. I ask to see the affidavits, suggesting he blot out the names, but he demurs. "When you play poker, do you show your whole hand, Kibosh?" he asks. "Well, I don't either. Janet Reno is a fuckin' traitor." If he's mistaken, he says, "All she has to do is sue me. I would sue her if she called me a fuckin' traitor."

Like all good law-flouting demagogues, from Huey Long to Marion Barry to Edwin Edwards, Traficant has a special knack for eliciting sympathy from his constituents, turning his weakness into strength, and their distrust of government into trust in Jim Traficant. Though many of his allegations are daffy, he has likely headed off any pre-election indictment. Sources familiar with the investigation say the U.S. attorney's office is not anxious to get blowtorched by Traficant for affecting the outcome of his race. Not that it could. When I ask the Ohio state Democratic chairman, who can barely recall the names of Traficant's opponents, to handicap the election, he says confidently, "Traficant will win that district." And if he's indicted? "He'll probably win by a larger margin."

As Traficant works himself into a healthy froth, he abruptly stands up, commanding, "Now get out. You ain't gonna catch up with me no more. Don't call me again." He is not mad. I've been with the congressman for three hours, and his chief of staff says that if he dislikes someone, "He'll maybe give you five minutes before he throws you out." Traficant hands me a souvenir American flag as a parting gift, pointing an intent finger in summation. "I am a dangerous man. You know why? Because I've seen the other side of this fucking one-eyed jack. And I know that we have a Justice Department, an IRS, a Treasury Department—they're wagging the dog, man. No American should fear their government."

Perhaps Traficant should fear only half his government. After all, he still has his friends in the GOP. And when I ask a Republican leadership aide if he is at all concerned about Traficant's rants or legal woes, he laughs the satisfied laugh of one who does not have to claim ownership. "Of course not," he says. "He's a Democrat! We get all of the benefits and none of the downside." Besides, he adds, "Traficant's a good guy. We'll go out of our way to help him—so long as he doesn't end up in jail."

FORCED FUNTIVITIES

The Infantilization of Corporate America

Wilmington, Delaware

If you're a loyal employee like me, you occasionally check your company's Vision Statement to make sure all the *T*s in "empowerment" have
been crossed, and the *I*s in "mission" have been dotted. But if you come
across buzzwords like "excellence" and "leadership," you should know
that your corporate culture is sadly behind the curve—those terms are
as nineties as Reebok Pumps, Zima, and Total Quality Management.
There's a new core value on the loose, and it goes by the name of "fun."

Maybe you assumed the fun stopped when the tech bubble burst.
Or at least you hoped it did. After all, who could stand to read yet
another profile of the ubiquitous IPO-enriched dot-commissar, who'd
get the toe of his footie pajamas (which he wore in his nonhierarchical workspace) caught in the brake of his indoor Razor scooter,
causing him to bump into the Pachinko machine/copier, making him
spill his Tazoberry Crème Frappuccino all over the conference-room
foosball table? Ahhhh, the boyish hijinks of it all. With the benefit of
hindsight, we can all now agree that the real fun was watching dot-
com execs ride their Segways to the unemployment line.

But if you thought the fun stopped there, you're sadly mistaken.
Like a diseased appendix bursting and spreading infectious bacteria
throughout the abdomen, fun is insinuating itself everywhere, into
even the unhippest workplaces. Witness the August 2007 issue of *Inc.*
magazine, the self-declared "Handbook of the American Entrepre-
neur." Emblazoned on its cover was "Fun! It's the New Core Value."
Beneath that was a photo of Jonathan Bush, the CEO of athena-
health, which helps medical practices interact with insurers. Bush was
tearing his shirt apart to reveal a Batman costume underneath, the
same costume in which he gave a full presentation to a prospective
client after making a deal with one of his employees that if the latter

lost seventy pounds, the management team would dress as superheroes for a day.

But that's just the beginning. There are eighteen pages of similar stories to instruct and inspire employers to keep their employees happy at all costs, because happy employees make for happy customers. There are rubber chickens, Frisbee tosses, mustache-growing contests, pet psychics, interoffice memos alligator-clipped to toy cars, and ceremonies that honor employees for such accomplishments as having "the most animated hand gestures." Perks include on-campus wallyball courts, indoor soccer fields, air hockey, Ping-Pong, billiards, yoga and aerobics classes, company pools and hot tubs, and Native American themed nap rooms so that employees can sleep (sleep!) at work. And that's all at just one company—Aquascape, a supplier to pond builders based in St. Charles, Illinois.

The genius of the NBC television show *The Office* (and the original BBC show from which it derived) is that boss Michael Scott, manager of a failing paper-distribution branch in Scranton, goes well beyond the Dilbertesque stereotype of the dictator cracking the whip over his cubicle monkeys. Armed with nothing but business-book clichés and a desire to be loved (he is nearly incapable of firing a person, or "counseling them out," in the current parlance), Michael fancies himself a fun guy, an entertainer. His employees don't think he's the least bit funny, yet the Dunder Mifflin office is a stage, and Michael is its headliner.

So you get episodes like "Beach Games," in which Michael, wearing his Sandals Resorts T-shirt, insists that his employees all load up the "par-taayyyy bus" for a day at the beach. Except then he announces, to the displeasure of everyone but his suck-up henchman Dwight Schrute (whose most pressing concern is whether he's "assistant regional manager" or "assistant to the regional manager"), that "today, we are not just spending a day at the beach. We are all participating in mandatory fun activities. Funtivities!" Under the guise of fun, the employees will be subjected to Sumo wrestling contests and walking over a bed of hot coals to determine who will replace Michael. Dwight, pumping his fist as everyone else groans, says, "I knew it wasn't just a trip to the beach! I hope there will be management parables!" *The Office* is a sitcom, but it could easily be a reality show.

No slaves to fashion here at the *Weekly Standard*, where the clocks stopped around 1957, we have an office mercifully free of such managerial fads. About the closest our bosses come to official levity is the "inspirational" poster in the mailroom. A placid scene of rowers sculling on a glassy lake as their coxswain shouts instructions is disrupted by the caption: "Get to Work—You aren't being paid to believe in the power of your dreams." My nonjournalism friends aren't quite as fortunate.

As I contacted them for input to this story, their pain was evident. They are smart, competent, creative people with highly refined senses of humor—fully formed adults. Yet they're unable to escape the condescending infantilization of their workplaces, the coercive "fun," the forced march through the land of clenched-teeth joviality that so often takes place under the dreaded guise of "team building." One pal, who works for a large financial concern, tells me darkly, "My role here is largely 'gleetivities' oriented. We're actually planning a group event that will involve 'conference bikes.' It's a rickshaw-related transportation option focused on tourists. It's a bike with five seats in a circle. Should be completely ridiculous."

Another friend in the information technology sector lays it bare on background, since frowning on "funtivities" is considered very bad form by upper management. I'll let him have the floor. God knows he's earned it:

> Every typical corporate geek groans when we have to participate in these outings or events. I've done jet-pilots, geocaching, a lot of "war-gaming," all in the name of team building. The truth is, if they are done well they are a lot of fun, despite the pessimism that invariably precedes them. If they are done poorly, they are bad beyond your wildest journalistic dreams. I've had a few that have made me want to buy a VW bus and [hit the road]. There was one that was just canceled where we had to do jazz improvisation in support of team building. Everybody was groaning big-time on that one. Can you imagine standing up in front of seventy directors playing fucking bongo drums? It got canceled because of a firm reorg, not because it was ludicrous. But that was one where even the dumber people who actually enjoyed *Forrest Gump* were complaining about how gay it was.

Since the advent of modern management consulting, a chapter that arguably began with the founding of the industry's eight-hundred-pound gorilla, McKinsey & Company, in the 1920s, the business world has cleaved into two halves: those paid to work for a living, and those paid to come to your office, take lots of notes, run up expenses on your dime, and then file reports in impenetrable consultantese describing your shortcomings—how, for instance, you failed to incentivize your brand pyramid and now need to drill down on the granularity of your mind-share while on-ramping your knowledge-process outsourcing.

There is, of course, a consultant for everything these days. Professional consultant-basher Martin Kihn, who is himself a consultant, and who wrote *House of Lies: How Management Consultants Steal Your Watch and Then Tell You the Time,* writes of everything from flag consultants to compost consultants to Satanic consultants who don't actually worship Lucifer (consultants tend not to believe in anything). So it stands to reason that with the new core value of fun on the ascent, there would be fun consultants. They don't have a trade association yet, and they go by all sorts of different names, usually with "fun" as a prefix (funsultants, funcilitators, etc.). But if you had to distill what they do in one word, "fun" would be your best bet.

A considerable corpus of literature on their discipline is amassing. I use the word "literature" loosely, to mean a series of often ungrammatical double-spaced sentences put on paper, slapped between festively colored covers, and sold to mouth-readers with too much discretionary income. While most business books, according to Kihn, are written at about a seventh-grade level (there are exceptions like *Who Moved My Cheese? for Teens* that are written at a fifth-grade level), the funsultant literature regresses all the way back to primary school. Since we all forget to play as adults, as funsultants repeatedly tell us, they seem intent on speaking to us as though we're children.

Their books are thick with instances of how successful businessmen keep things loosey-goosey at work. Forget industriousness, talent, and know-how—the wellspring of employees' satisfaction, creativity, and prosperity is fun. In Mike Veeck's *Fun Is Good,* the co-founder of Hooters Restaurants reveals, "I don't know if we could've survived without humor," whereas to the untrained eye it looked like Buffalo Chicken Strips served with large sides of waitress's breasts were the secret to his success. Whatever. "Fun" is the cure-all for anything that ails your company.

If you thought there were only *301 Ways to Have Fun at Work,* as suggested by the smash book that's been translated into ten languages, then you're shortchanging yourself, because technically, there are 602 ways, according to the follow-up, *301 More Ways to Have*

Fun at Work. Using examples culled from real companies in real office parks throughout America, the authors suggest using fun as "an organizational strategy—a strategic weapon to achieve extraordinary results" by training your people to learn the "fun-damentals" so as "to create fun-atics" (most funsultants appear to be paid by the pun).

Here's an abbreviated list of the jollity that will ensue at your place of business if you follow their advice: "joy lists," koosh balls, office chair relay races, marshmallow fights, funny caption contests, job interviews conducted in Groucho glasses or pajamas, wacky Olympics, memos by Frisbee, voice mails in cartoon-character voices, rap songs to convey what's learned at leadership institutes, "breakathons," bunny teeth, and asking job prospects to bring show and tell items such as "a stuffed Tigger doll symbolizing the interviewee's energetic and upbeat attitude" or perhaps a "neon-pink mask and snorkel worn to demonstrate a sense of humor, self-deprecating nature, and sense of adventure."

In the interest of not appearing to be a killjoy, I should disclose that I am adamantly pro fun at work, if by "fun at work" you mean "sending tasteless e-mails to friends," "stockpiling office supplies," and "leaving early." And it is hard to argue with the salutary effects of enjoying yourself, even and especially at work. The medical literature, often brandished by funsultants, is unanimous on the health benefits of laughter (though nobody has yet looked into the possible detrimental effects of forced laughter brought on by leadership-institute raps).

Any Genesis subscriber knows that hard toil was originally conceived as a curse, God breaking the news to Adam that he'd be forced to stop lounging naked while snacking on fresh fruit, and that meals would now be served by the sweat of his brow. Mankind has pretty much looked for loopholes ever since. As you learn in Classics 101, the ancient Greek word for work was *ponos,* derived from the same root as the Latin *poena,* meaning "sorrow." Aristotle regarded work as a wasteful impediment to pursuing virtue. And the Romans were so work-averse that they outsourced all they could to slaves.

A good funsultant, however, doesn't bill fun at the office as a cessation of work, but rather, casts the two as halves of a whole, what Leslie Yerkes, author of *Fun Works: Creating Places Where People Love to Work,* calls a "Fun/Work Fusion." How necessary or advisable is it for employers to facilitate fun, and how fun could the fun possibly be that they are facilitating? After all, plenty of surveys show that people are pretty good at fostering their own fun at work and yet still remain a largely unsatisfied lot. (For all employer nods to serving as cruise directors on the Fun Ship Lollipop, a Conference Board survey reports that less than half of all Americans are satisfied with their jobs, down from 60 percent twenty years ago.)

A Microsoft survey of thirty-eight thousand people worldwide found that workers, by their own admission, average only three productive days per week. A Salary.com/America Online survey found the average worker admitting to squandering 2.09 hours of each eight-hour workday, excluding lunch and breaks, and other estimates have put the number as high as 40 percent of each day. A full 70 percent of Internet porn consumption takes place during office hours, and perhaps much of the rest of the time is dedicated to crafting Internet parodies, such as the following by one "Robert Moore," who apes the rhetoric of a funsultant, saying employers can make the workplace more fun by having "Tick Days" ("place ticks on the necks of your staff"). Writes Moore:

> There's gold in institutionally mandated humor. Humor, when used and managed effectively, can make your employees more productive cogs in your corporate machine. A laughing employee more quickly forgets the worthlessness of his existence and gets on to the daily drudgery. A smiling employee masks his discontent and horror from potential clients. The demons that gnaw achingly painful holes in his or her intestines are forgotten long enough to finalize that sales report.

There is a remedy for cynicism like Moore's: Hire a funsultant. As Alan Briskin, author of *The Stirring of Soul in the Workplace,* writes: "Sarcasm is one-sided fun. It is limited and non-universal." Fun isn't just about theory in books. It's about putting clown shoes on the ground.

So you might hire someone like Ronald Culberson, who heads FUNsulting, etc., "injecting humor into healthcare" (the *U*s in his logo are shaped like a smile). Not only does Ron understand the "intrinsic power of combining EXCELLENCE with humor," he's even set up a "humor injections" blog, giving cyberslackers a way to have good, clean, nonsarcastic fun.

Or you could hire "Energy Expert" Gail Hahn of Funcilitators, who can help you practice "Fun Shui" and conduct some "Out of the Box Olympics" for team building, and who is "authorized to lead laughter sessions sanctioned by the World Laughter Tour." Or perhaps Buford P. Fuddwhacker would be more to your liking. He dresses like a "backwoods, country nerd in red suspenders and polyester pants" and promises your employees some "high-octane country sunshine" with his "wacky inventions and crazy stories about kinfolk and farm animals. But there's always a point to be made, and he weaves valuable insights, motivational messages, and powerful teaching into his tall tales." Pass the 'shine, Buford!

For my money, however, if I was the kind of employer who was funhibited enough to have to hire a pro, I'd go with the Fun Department of Wilmington, Delaware, which endeavors to bring "recess to work." (Recess was always my best subject.) Last month, I went to see them in action.

I met one of their four principal partners for dinner—Jayla Boire. Her title is Marketing Maven (nobody in the company has a traditional title). She looks like a Marketing Maven too. She is bouncy, perky, tall, and blonde, with sculpted tan legs that start just above her ankles and end right below her clavicle. I wouldn't call them sexy— HR wouldn't approve—but they're fun to look at.

As I get the Montepulciano flowing (wine = fun), Jayla tells me about how she got into the "funnertainment" business. Once a freelance journalist whose favorite story ever was one she wrote on a local coffee shop named Brew Ha Ha, she had a host of marketing jobs before hanging out a shingle with her other straight-marketing company, The Right Idea. Jayla is a hard-core marketer. For fun, she often goes to Target to look at their innovative packaging.

Wilmington is a company town for DuPont, the world's second largest chemical company ("Uncle Dupey," as she calls it), and Jayla worked for them too. She thinks that's when the fun started. I ask her if she had a burning desire to further the cause of polyurethane. She didn't, she says, "though I thought nylon was pretty spiffy, and no woman would argue with Lycra." But having to make a chemical company seem interesting to outsiders—she wonders if "that wasn't the beginning of thinking about how you make work fun."

Even before they started the company, Jayla and her partner Nick Gianoulis, whose title is Godfather of Fun, had a reputation among their circle of friends as being fun people. "They'd say oh my gosh, here they come, it's the fun department." They might do something like stage suitcase races (racing down the street with suitcases) at a New Year's Eve party, and Jayla would always be on the picnic committee. An inveterate griller, Nick, who was a district manager in the electrical wholesaling business, was a member of the Circuit Club, which planned fun activities in their workplace.

But planning all that internal fun can be a real time goblin if you actually want to, well, work. So Jayla and Nick started thinking about providing a "turnkey solution" for companies who wanted to fun-up the workplace. They ended up joining forces with two other partners, Dave Raymond, the Emperor of Fun and Games, and Mark Doughty, Lord of the Deal, who would expertly translate fun theory into fun-filled games.

Dave and Mark also run their own successful mascot company— they are trainers and headhunters for furry creatures who perform at major and minor league baseball games. Raymond Entertainment Group shares office space with the Fun Department, and the Fun Department has its own mascot, a "purple party dude" named Reggie. But Jayla makes clear that the partners don't wish to have the mascot company used as a "brand identifier," even though Dave "knows fun from the inside out." From 1978 to 1993, he served as the Philadelphia Phillies mascot, the furry green bullhorn-beaked Phillie Phanatic. Thanks partly to Dave, the Phanatic is now in the Mascot Hall of Fame, even if Dave's father once called his son "a green transvestite."

The Fun Department is a full-service fun shop. They boast an impressive client roster, everyone from DuPont to AstraZeneca to QVC. Jayla says that they might be signing up American Standard, the toilet manufacturer, with whom they have a meeting on September 11 (tragic anniversaries = not fun; potty humor = fun).

The partners "take the work out of your fun" with a "turnkey fun infusion for your business." Services include everything from quick toy drops ("fun on the run") to staging Solid Gold danceoffs, paper airplane contests, silly string wars, human roulette, and a couple dozen other funtivities. They "create consistent, quick, at-work experiences that motivate and invigorate the work environment." They have "fun for fun's sake—while reducing tension, bolstering creativity, and building relationships." They have business cards featuring "Sparky," a smiling blue-faced logo with crazy, spinning goggle-eyes. "He's the face of fun," says Jayla. "Or of mental illness," I helpfully add.

Dave later tells me that at AstraZeneca, the pharmaceutical company, the Fun Department has even taken over the company's seldom-used lactation room, dressed it up as a doctor's office complete with a doctor character and a gum-cracking assistant, and wrote "prescriptions to play" while treating people "for terminal seriousness." AstraZeneca, it turns out, has a culture of fun, which makes the Fun Department's job easier. During their initial meeting, the head of HR told him that they'd just recently filled a coworker's office with packing peanuts on his birthday. "They get it," says Dave. "They understand."

Helping the Fun Department deliver all this levity are the Funsters, on-call hourly wagers, mostly college students who are fit and vital and look like beach lifeguards, and who wear zany tie-dyed shock-yellow-and-orange T-shirts with "Team Fun" inscribed on the back. I'm given a T-shirt—a medium instead of a large, since the large is "boxy"—and I'm wearing it as I write. It's cutting off my circulation. But I'm told snug 'n' sexy = fun.

The Funsters go through Dave's Fun Boot Camp and memorize the Funster training manual, where they learn the ins and outs of presenting fun, and also the no-no's. "No touching," says Jayla. "We have to be very careful. One of the things we've learned is, I'll be at an event, and some of my colleagues will be in that moment, because they're trained to be Funsters. So there's the CEO ripping his shirt off and swinging it over his head. And they're like, 'Oh my God, look at that guy!' And here's me [yelling] 'HR! HR!'"

The zaniness works, says Jayla, because "we're not their bosses." Still, she says, "We're crazy people. [But] we're completely irreverent respectfully, within the constraints of all the HR rules, because there are HR rules. No touching. Anything you think might be offensive." Consequently, the Fun Department deliberates over what games to play.

They reluctantly okayed Balloon Choo Choo, a race where people press balloons between their bodies, then chug away, moving as a team without dropping any. "We thought long and hard about adding that to our repertoire," says Jayla. "Say the balloon drops and somebody bumps into each other from behind. . . . We test every game. We think carefully about what body parts are involved." If Funsters see anything inappropriate, "they have to fill out a form" that would say, for instance: "Matt dropped his balloon and Jayla bumped into him in a way that might be construed as inappropriate." That way, if a concerned client calls, they can say, "Yes, we did notice that, and wrote it down. It happened at 12:05 P.M., and we talked to Matt and Jayla about it and they were okay with it."

Putting on my skeptic's hat, perhaps having never taken it off, I tell Jayla that it's well and good to have fun, but surely everybody doesn't subscribe to their brand of it. My office, for instance, would be a very tough sell. She looks at me wearily. She's dealt with Doubting Thomases before. "We can [bring the fun] for you too. You crotchety old curmudgeons." I tell her I just don't see it, though I would pay to watch her bolster Fred Barnes's morale with finger puppets. She indicates Fred would be an immediate target. "That's our job. We engage them," she says, adding with icy, assassin-like resolve. "Fred's a fun-killer. Our job is to eliminate the fun-killers."

Early the next morning, the Funsters are giddy with anticipation in preparation for a gig: getting loose, doing dance moves, engaging in lots of verbal towel-snapping. They are riding high, standing around a television set at a local gathering place/gym, high-fiving one another after having to wait through all the dreary news to watch CNN's Dr. Sanjay Gupta do an adulatory piece on their company (publicity = fun; Minneapolis bridge collapse = not fun). Also, the *Inc.* magazine fun issue has just come out, and even though they're not in it, Jayla says they consider it a "validation of concept."

Afterward, they shove off for nearby New Castle, Delaware, where they will bring the fun to HBCS, which stands for Hospital Billing & Collection Service. As a company that boasts of its value-added services utilizing advanced technology, whose experienced technical staff builds rugged interfaces that support financial efforts through the use of industry standards and web-based protocols, and who are proud as all get-out of their HIPAA (Health Insurance Portability and Accountability Act) compliance with government guidelines and requirements related to standard electronic transaction processes and integrity controls, they don't exactly scream: Barrel of Monkeys. But the Fun Department has come to do the company's second annual "playfair."

Housed in a nondescript brown-brick building, HBCS is surrounded by acre after acre of similarly anonymous looking office parks, places with seemingly identical topiary and opaque names that betray nothing about the kind of business actually being transacted. My pulse quickens as I spy the letters TA on one nearby building, since everyone knows T&A = fun. But a subhead on the signage reveals that they are merely WORLD LEADERS IN THERMAL ANALYSIS AND RHEOLOG. (Not fun.)

I make my way into HBCS to spy a look at their call center, where telephone operator after telephone operator sits in a drably lit matrix of cubicles, trying to cadge money from sick people and their families in eight-hour shifts, expected by management to hit quotas, as one automated call after another rolls in. It looks like a hard, monotonous job.

Several human-resources types collect around me and drape a visitor's badge around my neck as if I'm a creature from another planet. They proudly show off the place. They wear shorts and flip-flops and other casual wear, as it's something of a beach day for them. Since there's no beach or ocean nearby, however, funtivities will commence under the theme "Playfair Under the Sea." In the hospitality tent on a narrow spit of grass behind their building, there is lots of maritime décor: seashell fans, buckets of sand, plastic crabs, and starfish.

Inside are wan touches to cheer up the place: a glittery star hanging from the corkboard ceiling above the head of a top performer's cubicle here, a beach ball or a fish mobile there. Matt Sanders, a manager, sits in his office, a mini cowboy hat attached to a headband adorning his head. He has a helium tank on his desk, and is blowing up balloons that he then twists into hat shapes for coworkers. He says such displays let the employees see "our management group is actually human. They enjoy having fun. I think this day is actually critical. . . . Everybody's excited. People I never met before coming and saying, 'Hey, Matt, I want a hat.'" For some reason, this makes me want to cry.

On the call floor, Brian Wasilewski, vice president of operations, is crisply dressed, his plaid shorts and brown beach shirt looking as though they've been starched. He says though they've hired the Fun Department to fun up their company picnic, they try to keep it fun year-round. How so? I ask. Well, he says, during National Healthcare Compliance Week, "We did Compliance Jeopardy. Basically, we sent out a list of compliance-related questions at the beginning of the week, and anyone who scored a certain amount or higher got to play in the Compliance Jeopardy game." Winners went into the training room and played Compliance Jeopardy just like the real game show. Answers had to be in the form of questions. There were Daily Doubles. Gift certificates were awarded. But all the categories revolved around things like privacy information and patient claims. Says one vice president of human resources: "We try."

As the funtivities kick off, the Funsters form a dancing gauntlet around the back door, wearing swim caps and snorkels and other water-related funnery. They say cheery things like "Nice hat, girlfriend!" and

"Welcome to the fun!" while employees, blinking into the blinding sunlight, smile nervously, as a DJ booms "Takin' Care of Business" by Bachman-Turner Overdrive. Most head straight for the buffet line to feast on clams that are bound in mini fishing nets, which seem to be secured with Gordian knots. When one Funster asks a large black woman how the food is, she says, "I'll let you know if I can ever get to it."

There are "play stations" all over the grounds: an oversize inflated basketball hoop, a ring toss pit, a Yahtzee game with giant fuzzy dice, a "Deep Sea Fishing" station, which consists of two baby pools with children's fishing poles to fish out magnetic rubber duckies that can be redeemed for trinkets like finger puppets and wind-up toys. There are all sorts of relay games, like the aforementioned racy Balloon Choo Choo. I stand next to Mark Doughty, Lord of the Deal, watching the spectacle. He is wearing a referee's shirt, though he says, "I'm the referee just like in wrestling—the one who didn't see anything. It's not about playing by the rules. It's about them having fun."

As we watch a "Pass the Treasure Key" exercise, in which teams have to wrap yarn around their body parts, then string a key on it, passing the key all the way down the line in the fastest time, I ask Mark what the point of this is, expecting some sort of management parable. He thinks for a second, then says, "I got nuthin'. There's no lessons in this. If a moron asks you to tie yourself up with a rope and pass the key—don't do it." Unlike many other funsultants, to the Fun Department's credit, they go extremely light on the "OD," or organizational development—the cloying morals of the story that usually follow such team-building exercises. They think it's much more important to have "fun for fun's sake."

One of the most popular funtivities involves a manager's face-off, where the bosses must grab a partner and toss water-balloons back and forth to each other, wearing pirate patches on one eye to distort depth perception. They must also utter "Argghhhh" before each throw just to further humiliate themselves, cueing the hoi polloi that everyone has "permission to play."

One half of the managerial team that wins is Paul Kutney. I catch him cheating by flipping up his eye patch, and zero in on him afterward to blackmail some truth out of him. I suggest to Kutney that what the American worker really wants, more than anything, is to see his boss get hit with something. "If I got hit," he says, "I know people would be out there cheering."

I ask him how he feels about companies formalizing fun. He sees the upside of it, he says. Out here, he's relaxed, he's in shorts, he's eating Italian ice. And in there? I ask. "I'm a prick," he says without pause. "I've got seven people that have to process 1.7 million claims a year. So I have to be a prick." There's not a lot of time for fun and games in his world. "You have to break up the monotony somewhat," he says. So how do you do that now? I ask. "In my group, we don't," he says. "There's only so many hours in a day, and we've got to get so much work done. So everybody has to keep their heads down, and keep going."

The culminating funtivity is a cash grab on a Twister-like mat between two people, in which they stuff as much money into their various pockets, shirt fronts, and orifices as humanly possible. To find out who the lucky candidates are, the Funsters play "Hands Up/Hands Down." It's a variation on heads or tails, which the Funsters used to play by having everybody grab their heads or tails. But Mark says they had to modify it. "We had a client who was a little challenged by the political incorrectness," he explains. "[He said] we don't want our employees to put their hands on their tails, even if it's their own tails. We said we can play Heads or Hips. And they said 'no.' Sooooo— Hands Up, Hands Down."

One of the finalists in Hands Up/Hands Down is in a wheelchair. But after he incorrectly guesses "up" when the Funsters call "down," he is eliminated. You can sense a Funster sigh of relief (people grabbing as much cash as they can = fun; cripple flopping around on the ground trying to grab cash with his teeth = not fun).

The afternoon heat is sweltering, and by the end of the playfair, HBCS's CFO is in a magnanimous mood and lets everybody go home, though it's only 3:00 P.M. As a fun-killer, it'd bring me some pleasure to report nobody had any fun. But that wouldn't be true. People laughed, people lined the dance floor during the "Booty Call," people cleared out of the parking lot before the boss could finish his announcement. It was a good party (though "a little beer wouldn't hurt nobody," one Sprite-sipping woman told me), but not that good.

Still, there was a refreshing lack of management parables, and the Funsters, purists to the last, really did seem to want to bring the fun for fun's sake. Fishing rubber duckies out of a baby pool isn't my idea of fun, but I learned something. Call it a management parable, if you will: If you treat people like they're six years old, eventually they'll start responding in kind.

So who's to say the funsultants are worse than anything else that's happened to the American corporate drone over the decades? After all the paradigm-shifting and diversity training and outsourcing and TQMing and synergizing and empowering and value adding and globalizing and downsizing and full-frontal lobotomizing, maybe finger puppets are just the logical terminus.

As for the funsultants themselves, they're truly living the American dream. They've beat the system. As Lord of the Deal Mark Doughty explains, "I work very hard not to have a real job." Is that the work ethic that made America great? Probably not. But who am I to judge? I make a living writing about funsultants.

I turn to another old friend of mine, much more steeped in business culture than I am. He's my college buddy Don McKinney, a creative director/advertising hotshot responsible for campaigns like Nissan's "Shift." When I ask him what all this means, he strikes an optimistic note: "When you and I were born, there were two billion people in the world. Today there are six billion. Maybe there are only two billion real jobs and all the rest of us are being relegated to bullshit jobs, like fun coaches and creative directors. If we took away all the bullshit jobs, our economy would collapse."

On the other hand, he e-mails, "It occurs to me how completely spoiled we are as workers. I don't ever remember my dad or any of his friends having fun at work. Yet as soon as a job turns into an actual job (something my dad would actually call work), we start looking around for the next prettiest girl at the dance.

"'Coercive joviality,' as you put it, would have gotten your ass kicked in the machine shop, or at the very least it would have been seen as deviant. I would be willing to bet that, compared with the last generation, an overwhelming number of us would be considered support staff in a war. If you're in marketing, what do you actually do? You're not making anything. The best that can possibly be said about your output is that you've invented a bunch of new words that make your profession just esoteric enough that the lay person (the guy in the machine shop) will pay an extra quarter of a cent on every pack of Doublemint gum to 'double his pleasure and double his fun.'"

Don had some momentum, and I wanted to hear more. But he couldn't write anymore, he said. He had to go. Duty called: "I have an all-day meeting on metrics."

HUNTING BUBBA

Bagging White Men and Eating Deer Turds with Mudcat Saunders

Roanoke, Virginia

"You're slower than cream rising on shit. Haul ass down here so we can get this piece knocked out, brotha!" As I barrel down I-81 in Virginia's Blue Ridge country, Dave "Mudcat" Saunders is growling on the other end of the line. He first entered my consciousness in the summer of 2003, like some force of nature sent my way by the Color Gods of Feature Writing.

Back then, I was one of a group of short-straw reporters assigned to cover Bob Graham's "family vacation," a Winnebago caravan across Iowa that, in a lucky break for the Graham grandchildren, coincided with presidential campaign season. Stuck on a chaser pontoon on the Mississippi River for a fishing photo op, we watched Graham, on the lead boat, do what he did best throughout the campaign: aimlessly drift.

Mudcat (a childhood nickname earned by tireless bottom-fishing of the Roanoke River) was serving as Graham's "Bubba Coordinator." A couple of years earlier, Mudcat and his mentor, Steve Jarding, had become a hot ticket: They'd masterminded Mark Warner's ride to the governor's mansion in Virginia by figuring out how he could pick off the rural vote, a feat Democrats hadn't accomplished in the state in nearly a generation. Subsequently, the two formalized their partnership and hung out a shingle, calling the firm "Rural Renaissance." After a brief stint with John Edwards, whose campaign they fled over philosophical differences with other staffers, the pair signed on with Graham, who himself had entered the race so late that his poll numbers never stopped resembling those of Dennis Kucinich.

That morning on the Mississippi, Graham hands had imported Mudcat to give good quote, attempting to distract us from the candidate's inadequacies. But Mudcat too had to suffer the indignities of a tanking campaign. His hotel room had mistakenly been given away the night before, so he'd been forced to sleep at a truck stop, where he'd taken a three-dollar shower. He showed up on our pontoon boat Ivory-fresh and full of vinegar. He explained away Graham's lack of success as a fisherman by highlighting the candidate's unique catch-and-release system: "He releases them before he catches them." He told us that he suspected the Potomac River was the holiest in the world, since "you can take the dumbest sonofabitch and put him on the other side of that river and all of a sudden it becomes *Good Will Hunting*." When querulous reporters tried to kick his man's slats in, he didn't get nervous or defensive. Instead, he threatened to "Bobby Knight y'all's ass."

All told, it was a bravura performance. After a few captive hours under Mudcat's spell, listening to him spin how Graham could take the South, how he was knowledgeable enough to discuss "the gestation period of the Antarctic kiwi," how he could make the blind see and the lame walk, even the most hard-bitten among us thought Graham would last longer than another month and a half, which is actually all he had left. I also remember imagining that Mudcat would be even livelier without the encumbrance of a dead-weight candidate. I imagined right.

I decided to renew the acquaintance upon reading that he and Jarding had just signed with Simon & Schuster to do a book for mid–six figures, not bad for two campaign strategists whose candidate had finished way out of the money. Just try to conceive of anyone reading the political musings of John Kerry campaign manager Mary Beth Cahill, let alone paying for the privilege.

Foxes in the Henhouse is due to be released next spring. It is probably the first pox-on-both-parties manifesto to come with a companion CD. Mudcat, fifty-six, is a bluegrass fiend who hopes to get many of his friends in the music world to contribute to the disc. Bluegrass royalty like the Del McCoury clan and Ralph Stanley Jr. (whom he simply calls "Two") are his compadres. He's already working out the title song for the CD with bluegrass virtuoso Ronnie Bowman, who's cowritten, along with Music Row Democrats cofounder Don Cook, Brooks & Dunn's current chart-topping single. Mudcat guards the Foxes lyrics as if they were his daughter's chastity (though he's pretty generous in sharing his other verse via e-mail, including a favorite breakup poem he sent a girl, elegantly titled "Fuck you": I'm glad that you treated me rotten / I'm glad that you made me cry / Cause it's much, much easier to say "Fuck you" / Than it is to say "Good-bye").

The book itself, as Mudcat describes it, will "take a wire brush to Republicans" for peeling off traditional Democrats in southern and rural areas under false pretenses, first through Nixon's race-tinged Southern Strategy, then by suckering Reagan Democrats after preaching the gospel of limited government and heartland values while selling their jobs out to big business and socking the country with runaway deficits. But the screed is not only a prescription for how to bring those Democrats home on issues such as gays and guns. It's a stink bomb lobbed at fellow Democrats—or as Mudcat often calls them, "fuckin' Democrats," the northeastern liberals who he feels have contempt for his culture, and whom he dislikes more than he dislikes Republicans. (While the "foxes" in their tale are Republicans, Democratic leaders aren't so much hens as they are "possums—the ones who roll over and play dead.")

By now, it should be clear that Mudcat has a foul-language problem. It is the rare utterance that goes by without some similar indelicacy. But he doesn't curse for shock value so much as for percussion, working the blue words like a kick drum to help his sentences get off on time. "My vocabulary is less than two hundred words," he says by way of apology, asking at one point, as a favor to his aged mother, that I not quote him saying he no longer goes to "goddamn church." I accede. (What he actually said was "fucking church.")

Which is not to say the lifelong Baptist isn't big on Jesus. As a kid, he preached a youth service in which two congregants got saved. Unlike most political types, particularly of the Democratic persuasion, he is unabashed about his faith, to the point that he calls it "blasphemy" to employ it for political ends. He thinks the pulpit is no place for politics, and vice versa. It's part of the reason he quit attending.

"I got sick of preachers telling me how great Reagan was." (He voted for Reagan in 1980, though he now claims, "I was drunk.") "Jesus don't give endorsements," Mudcat thunders. "He don't give a damn about partisan politics. G-O-P, God's Only Party—that's bool-sheet. And it's bool-sheet that He's a Democrat—they'll tell you to doomsday about Him healing the sick and clothing the nekkid, as if that's proof. He's too big to get involved in partisan politics. I know this, because when I'm in politics, and pray about it, I don't get any answers. But when I pray about my heart, I get an answer right now."

After I check into the Hotel Roanoke, Mudcat picks me up in his SUV, wearing the usual: shorts, Motorcraft "Wood Brothers" ballcap, and a slack, all-purpose smile that could equally be saying "Welcome to Roanoke!" or "What the hell are you looking at?" He smokes like a Rust Belt factory. His dashboard features a pack of Winstons, his round-the-clock cigarette, as well as unfiltered Camels, which he uses to mainline nicotine when some restaurant or other nanny-state nuisance is about to make him go without.

As we drive off, he is already under the full sway of the religious tunes blaring from his stereo. He DJs furiously, as he will throughout my visit, both at home and in the car. During interviews, conversation halts and important points are lost as he leans over and says, "Listen to this, brotha," then strives with all his might to hit the high, lonesome notes. He plays his preselected "funeral song," Junior Sisk's version of "Purple Robe" (which Junior has already agreed to show up and sing, assuming Mudcat goes first).

He also blares the Bluegrass Brothers' version of "He Will Set Your Fields on Fire." In between croaking the chorus ("If you don't from sin retire / He will set your fields on fire"), he tells me about fulfilling his duties as Bubba Coordinator for various candidates.

For Graham, Mudcat tapped his contacts in the worlds of stock car racing, bluegrass, and Bubba-land generally, to turn out Dr. Ralph Stanley, Daytona champ Ward Burton, and Ben "Cooter" Jones from *The Dukes of Hazzard* for a single event. Scoff if you will, but in some pockets of rural Virginia, this lineup is tantamount to producing the Father, Son, and Holy Ghost.

When working with Mark Warner, he actually enlisted the Bluegrass Brothers to record Warner's campaign song. Mudcat had written the words in the shower, setting them to the music of "Dooley," which was originally sung by the Dillards of *The Andy Griffith Show*. This, on top of getting Jon Wood of the Wood Brothers racing dynasty to drive a MARK WARNER emblazoned Ford F-150 in NASCAR's Craftsman Truck Series.

With Mudcat overseeing the pyrotechnics and Jarding rolling out Warner's pro-rural policy initiatives, to give his message both substance and street cred, the pair pulled off a victory all the more eye-popping in that their candidate was far from the best on paper to execute the Bubba strategy. Their maneuvers helped Warner—a Connecticut-raised, Harvard Law–educated telecom millionaire—get over with southwestern Virginia voters, to the tune of picking up 101,000 votes. These came from the very same voters who'd given Democrats spankings for years, and who just twelve months before had rejected Democrat Chuck Robb against Republican George Allen for the Senate by roughly the same margin.

Even Republicans have to give the pair their due, sort of. While Mike Murphy, a Republican strategist, speculates that Mudcat and Jarding will "probably be ignored" by their party, he calls their line "one-third true, two-thirds hokum. It's a Carville-lite act with a NASCAR twist, aimed mostly at neurotic urban liberal reporters who love the southern fried two-fisted-damn-Democrat-'n'-proud-of-it noble savage shtick." Murphy adds that they "need to win a few more races before I (or Graham or Edwards) grant any big genius kudos. That said, I like Mudcat, and they do understand how to win governor's races in the South."

Considering that two southern governors are the only Democrats who've won the presidency in the past thirty-five years, it's nothing to sneeze at. Neither is Mudcat and Jarding's feel for southern white males, particularly rural ones, who used to be Democrats' most reliable constituency and now can't leave the party fast enough. These voters helped George W. Bush clean-sweep the South twice—the first time against Al Gore, a southern white Protestant. Even Bill Clinton, a southern white Protestant with more persuasive Bubba credentials, managed to carry only four southern states in each of his two victories. (By contrast, John Kennedy, a northeastern Catholic, garnered six.)

One of Mudcat's myriad cris de coeur (besides the lament that Democrats "have no testosterone" and are unable to "get through the culture" of the South) is that his party can't count. "Politics is about addition, that's all it is. It's not difficult," he says, giving me a primer on Mudcat math. "If I go get a white male," he asks, "how many votes do I get?" One, I reply. "No," he says impatiently, "I get two. Because I just took one away from Republicans."

It is the most elegantly simple precept, he says, one that could end the Democratic drought, and yet they don't see it because they think targeting Bubba males alienates their base and smacks of racism. "No it doesn't," he says. "My African American friends want to win as much as I do. . . . Democrats are insane. They say Republicans are insane, but they win. I don't see anything insane about winning."

Time after time, Mudcat says, he butts up against the intellectual condescension of the northeastern ruling elite in his party, who dismiss a counteroffensive out of hand.

When he and Jarding approached the Democratic National Committee about sponsoring a NASCAR truck decked out with fire-snorting donkey nostrils—as they'd done successfully with Warner, and as everyone from the NRA to the U.S. Navy has also done, as a way to start cracking the culture—he says they were rebuffed. "It wasn't the demographic they were going for." I ask what they were going for. "Fat women from New England," he snaps.

Or take John Kerry, he says, a prototypical modern Democrat, who when it comes to the South alternates between not trying at all and looking like he's trying too hard. At one campaign stop, Kerry forsook his classical guitar to break into some Johnny Cash. "I'll tell anyone who will listen how much I enjoy playing 'Ring of Fire,'" Kerry dorkishly told *Newsweek*.

Mudcat says that on the trail once, Kerry took him aside and told him that after the nomination was locked up, the campaign was headed south and Mudcat could "be there for the ride." A few weeks later, back home in New England, at Dartmouth, Kerry told an audience, "Everybody always makes the mistake of looking south," pointing out that Al Gore nearly became president without winning one southern state. "Now did you see Bush concede any state?" Mudcat asks rhetorically. "Hell no. The Democrats are a bunch of dumb-asses, is what they are." The way Mudcat sees it, Kerry telegraphed contempt for southerners, and in one fell swoop shot the bird to one-fourth of the country. "I'm not going to call him phony," says Mudcat, "but I am going to say he sprayed down my leg and told me it was raining."

Mudcat's house smacks up against the Blue Ridge foothills, with Back Creek snaking through a front lawn that is littered with deer feed and bow-hunting buck targets on which he scores lung shots, yawning, from fifty yards away. A moralist at heart, he won't shoot actual deer in his own yard.

It's an appropriate abode for a guy who's gotten so much mileage out of being a specialist in NASCAR Dads, though the term itself elicits an eruption of expletives. To his credit, he hates it. It has the ring of an election-year neologism (Security Moms, Office Park Dads, Duplicate Bridge Club Aunts) hatched by political consultants eager to keep up their chat show bookings by conning producers into thinking they've figured out a new wrinkle.

Mudcat prefers to call them "white males" or just "Bubbas," not only because it annoys the elites in his own party, but because NAS-CAR fandom itself is grossly misunderstood. Forty percent of the followers of stock car racing are women, and only 38 percent live in the South (a new track is opening in Staten Island). The advantages of slapping a candidate's name on a car, silly as it seems to some, are obvious, Mudcat says. NASCAR fans are fiercely loyal, and they are three times more likely than the average consumer to buy products advertised on their favorite driver's car. For a candidate who does this, it's just one weapon in his arsenal, he says. It won't win you a political race, but it can get you a hearing with voters who would otherwise be indifferent. "It's branding, brotha, just like Downy and Budweiser."

He jokes that I'll have him wearing a coonskin cap by the time I write the piece. But that would be only a slight exaggeration. Mudcat has made a nice chunk as a local real estate developer (politics largely being a hobbyhorse). He and his real estate partner, a regional publishing magnate named Richard Wells, are partly responsible for revitalizing downtown Roanoke. But his house is a modest converted migrant worker's shack with low ceilings and heart-pine floors. Twice divorced with two daughters who don't live with him, he inhabits a monument to southern bachelorhood and legal violence.

The big-screen in his living room features a constant loop of NASCAR races and hunting shows. The décor is Davy Crockett as told by Ted Nugent. A bobcat that met its end by Mudcat's hand serves as a valance over his living-room window. Antlers protrude on every side, and turkey beards and feet, used to make hat bands, junk up his refrigerator. In his study, where Mudcat's knocking out his section of the book, nine monster buck heads, mounted but not hung, sit on the floor in a semicircle around his computer stand, as if they were trying to spy a glance at what their liquidator is writing. Even his cat, named Kitty, is a stone-cold killer, preying on everything from rabbits to bats and regularly leaving gut-piles on Mudcat's porch.

When Howard Dean stepped in it, during the run-up to primary season 2004, by suggesting that his party needed to appeal to guys who have Confederate-flag decals on their pickup trucks, Mudcat was his target demographic. Mudcat's bedspread is a large Confederate flag, which he pedantically insists is the battle flag of the Army of Northern Virginia. The rest of the Confederacy appropriated it, he says, because it was Virginians like J. E. B. Stuart and Stonewall Jackson who "did most of the ass-kicking."

Since his own great-grandfather got his shoulder blown out by a yankee at Seven Pines, Mudcat is a proud member of the Sons of Confederate Veterans. But he wants it made absolutely clear that his celebration of heritage doesn't mean he's some racist—a common misconception, he says, which is why his fellow Democrats reacted to Dean as though he'd advocated electrocuting puppies.

Many of Mudcat's hunting buddies are black, and he points out that he hasn't shot any of them. In fact, he regularly pronounces against the racists who have tarnished his culture. He keeps a loaded shotgun set against a wall in his dining room, not only to "blast varmints," but also to warn any racists who've heard his taunts and want to stop by for an unfriendly debate. "I'd shoot one of them, and not feel a thing," he says.

Standing around his kitchen, he offers me a beer. I ask if he has anything stronger, and he looks at me like I'm in for it now. Rummaging through his freezer, past the bear slabs and deer burgers, rainbow trout and frog legs (much of which he will send home with me in a Styrofoam cooler), he pulls out a mason jar of purple stuff, a damson plum bobbing in it like a cork.

His house sits near the Franklin County line, which is the moonshine capital of the world. Everyone around here, a friend of his later tells me, has "either made it once, hauled it twice, or drank it a lot." Mudcat commands me to "hit some of this." I take a polite swallow and hand it back. Once a ferocious alcoholic, Mudcat hasn't had a drink in twenty-two years. He calls his sobriety "a gift from God." But he mocks my baby sip, saying, "Take a damn drink of likker, boy."

I take five successive gulps, and am amazed by its smooth, fruity finish. This is followed by a two-hundred-proof mule kick to the head, like drinking two double bourbons through a straw, fast. "There you go," he says approvingly. He screws the top back on, then hands me the jar. "Give some of this to Bill Kristol," he says, "I like him. Tell him I can make a run if he needs some pint bottles to give to his friends at Christmas."

"He's Jewish," I say.

"Well then tell him Happy Hanukkah from Mudcat," he responds.

Our revelry is interrupted by a rap at the door. One of Mudcat's neighbors has come over with a friend who wants to meet him. Seeing I'm a reporter, the neighbor introduces himself as Cravin Moorehead, a name I use all evening. Not until later when I'm transcribing my tapes, and sound out the name real slow, do I realize I've been had. His friend is Bobby the Eye Doctor. They are both deep into vodka tonics, which they've brought with them in plastic cups. They are celebrating Cravin's first kill of turkey season, which ends in only two days. "I've got the monkey off my back," Cravin says, after going twenty-seven straight mornings without pulling the trigger.

When Cravin tells Bobby I'm profiling Mudcat, Bobby asks if I work for a hunting magazine. He has no idea of Mudcat's political involvements. Bobby just wanted to meet him because Mudcat is something of a legendary hunter in the area. The winner of numerous "big buck" contests, Mudcat likes to spend every day of deer season up on the mountain, one of the reasons he says he honestly doesn't care if he ever touches another campaign. And he's known to scout the terrain months before the season opens. "Rednecks drink beer and watch their big-screens," says Mudcat. "Bubba scouts."

We adjourn to the porch and talk hunting for what seems like several hours while Mudcat encourages the boys to finish off the damson, "'cause after this story comes out, I can't have this shit in the house." After hearing about my magazine, Bobby identifies himself as a "fuckin' die-hard Republican. I love W. He's the man!" Mudcat settles in with his iced tea, and goes to work on Bobby's head. He drills him over the Contract with America, not because Mudcat disagrees with it, but because he says power-drunk, decadent Republicans have largely forsaken their principles and quit acting like Republicans.

Bobby takes strong issue, saying you can't blame Republicans for the deficit, since the economy is partly responsible. "Well they write the goddamned budget!" says Mudcat. "And the president is a Republican—who else do I blame?" Mudcat tells Bobby he may be a Democrat, but he's a fiscal conservative who believes in the sanctity of the Constitution and has a poor opinion of the Patriot Act. Furthermore, he tells Bobby that "there ain't fifty cents' difference in you and I politically." Sure, Bobby's a good Baptist who thinks gays have no right to get married, while Mudcat thinks it's a states-rights issue, and takes a more laissez faire attitude toward homosexuals, as long as he's not the object of their attentions.

But much as he did during the Warner campaign, when he and Jarding neutralized the NRA by forming their own pro-gun sportsmen's committees, Mudcat sings the glories of gun rights, and tells Bobby that as a sportsman he should be grievously offended that Bush relaxed standards on coal-fired generators. "They're throwing 3.2 percent more acid rain in our streams," he emphasizes. "They're killin' our fuckin' brook trout. They're gone!"

Bobby, who earlier said he didn't want to talk politics, by now is nodding furiously. Hitting an array of other cultural issues—mostly Democratic planks formulated in Bubba English—Mudcat's about ready to draw the net. He says that to keep their rural children home, they need to give them a reason to stay, through investment and better education. "We need to keep our culture," says Mudcat.

"Yeah," amens Bobby, and "what's the bullshit with the ban on Sunday hunting?"

"You're not a redneck," says Mudcat. "You're the spirit of Bubba, son. Just like Cravin sitting over there." He tells them that inside every rural Republican is a Democrat trying to get out. If a Democrat "would give you a reason to vote for him, you'd vote for him," promises Mudcat. "But they don't know how to shoot at Bubba."

He brings up Sportsmen for Kerry as an example, saying that the group's number one initiative was fully funding national parks. "Why the fuck do we want to fully fund parks we can't hunt?" screams Mudcat. Even Cravin, who's gone completely mellow in his vodka tonic stupor, but who periodically interrupts with outbursts in which he refers to himself in the third person, interjects, "Cravin Moorehead says that don't make any sense!"

By now, Mudcat is feeding off his audience. "I can take you down the road to Damascus in about four hours," he tells the boys.

"C'mon, Paul," says Bobby, "Bring it!"

"I can't make you vote for a Democrat," Mudcat continues, "but I can make you look at one." By the time we all take the fraternal leak in Mudcat's yard, Bobby the Eye Doctor, the former die-hard Republican, is ready to look, assuring Mudcat, "You know what? I vote for the person, not the party."

After hours of listening to Mudcat talk about how he hates foreign interventions but supports a robust military, about how he detests high taxes and profligate spending, about how he can't stand demonizing all rich people as greedheads, and how he's fervently pro–Second Amendment, I tell him he sounds an awful lot like an old-school Republican. Why not save some time and just become one? "Because since the beginning of time, the big sonofabitch has kicked the little sonofabitch's ass," he says. "Republicans are the big sonsofbitches. And I happen to like the little sonsofbitches. They're my people."

Over the next few days, Mudcat offers a crash course on "the Culture." He takes me to one of his many hunt clubs in the mountains, to pull rainbow trout out of a stocked pond. He wheels me over to Franklin County's Callaway USA, a legendary outlaw racetrack run by his good friend Whitey Taylor.

Whitey is a promotions genius who features attractions from school bus races to tracks hosed down with water on final laps for a little Slip 'n' Slide. Amateurs are encouraged to push their junkers to the limit, though Whitey gets mad when they hit the wall and catch fire. His fire extinguishers cost more than many of the cars. His philosophy: "Let it burn. It's part of the show, man."

The only things Whitey says you need at his track are a "seatbelt, a helmet, and no brains—nobody's been disqualified for the latter yet." When we pull up to the track, Mudcat doesn't stop in the parking lot, or even drive over to the infield. Instead, he guns it right onto the track proper, opening up his brand new Jeep Cherokee. He nearly flips us on the steep embankment of the first turn, while feathering us out of the high groove on the second. As I white-knuckle it, he lets out a rebel yell: "I'll show you a NASCAR Dad, brotha!" (We later found out he ruined his tires, but Whitey called to say we made the house record book for logging the fastest lap done by a late-model SUV "without us having to empty out your britches.")

Our best excursion, however, is a predawn turkey hunt on Bent Mountain. He's carrying heavy gear and I just a notebook, yet he seems to walk twice as fast as I can on the five-mile trek over hill and hollow. Mudcat moves through the brush like a shadow, while branches whack me in the face as I lag. "Sorry," he says, "didn't mean to Three Stooges you."

Boasting of his hunter's skill at bird calls, he says he can summon "a turkey egg up a hill." But despite his best efforts using a wooden Lynch Box, then a turkey diaphragm, a little rubber piece that he pops into his mouth (and which he says can also be used for contraception with "wild hillbilly women"), the turkeys seem to have gone into hiding. So instead we're left identifying animal droppings. "That's bear," he says, pointing to a pile that looks like a Wendy's double cheeseburger without the cheese. "And that's coyote; you can tell because of the hair in it." I'm impressed by his breadth of knowledge. He says, "Mudcat knows his shit."

He explains that deer droppings are vital to the expert hunter. If you pop a few in your mouth, you can tell if it's a buck or a doe that you're tracking. The buck's is bitter, the doe's sweeter because of her mammary glands. As we encounter some, I challenge him to chow down. "Not fresh enough to tell," he says.

The downtime allows me to get his biographical particulars. After college at Virginia Tech, he became a local sportswriter. Instead of going to the games as instructed by his editor, however, he'd often listen to the play-by-play on the radio at the Coffee Pot, a raucous roadhouse that featured the likes of Root Boy Slim, who used to vomit on stage after playing "Boogie 'Til You Puke."

Working at a paper in Newport News, Mudcat was briefly assigned to the Baltimore Colts, and relished all the free Schaefer's beer and crabcakes in the press box. But he didn't exactly cover himself in glory. In the locker room one day, Mudcat noticed Johnny Unitas's shower habits and asked him why he dried his balls before his head. He wasn't invited back. It was probably just as well. Mudcat had tired of dealing with "the egos of big men in short pants" and was ready for a change. After serial unemployment, and after developing an increasing problem with alcohol that resulted in lots of bar fights (he says his career record is 0–67), he got into the real estate game after cheating on the exam by buying old tests. "I didn't know what a deed of trust was, but I knew it was 'd' on the multiple choice."

He became one of the region's top salesmen, but when the market took a downturn in the early eighties, he nearly went bankrupt in every way, bottoming out with alcoholism and losing his family. He decided to blow his brains out on Sinking Creek Mountain. He rigged his rifle to make it look like a hunting accident, which would allow his relatives to collect some life insurance. But as he was about to pull the trigger, he stopped and prayed, saying, "God, if you're there, help me." He looked up and saw the bluest sky he'd ever seen. "I heard birds singing and shit," he says. "I wasn't like Oral Roberts.

I didn't see any seventy-five-story Jesus. But to me, hearing birds tweeting and seeing blue sky, it was a miracle. I started thinking things might be all right."

Afterward, he gave up booze, and remastered the real estate market. But he got itchy for some new action around 2001. His old DUI lawyer and friend Dickie Cranwell, then a powerhouse in the Virginia legislature, introduced him to the Warner campaign and Steve Jarding. Jarding had some unusual ideas about how to pick up rural voters, but needed someone with the contacts and touch to make it happen. The two have been a team since. "He's the hammer," Mudcat says of his partner. "I'm just a nail."

As we come off the mountain, we see a fresh, gleaming pile of deer droppings. "You gonna eat some?" he asks, since I had earlier promised to. "No chance," I tell him, "I thought you were kidding." He picks a few pellets up, and pops them in his mouth. After chewing them thoughtfully, he renders a verdict. "Buck," he declares. "What does it taste like?" I ask, now in medical shock. "Like shit," he says.

I meet Mudcat's partner at a restaurant in Old Town Alexandria. It is where Steve Jarding lives when not teaching up at Harvard's Kennedy School, a place that has provided the two with a pool of eager researchers for their book. They call the kids "The Dukes of Harvard" with gleeful irony, since Harvard is the very bastion of northeastern elitism they are decrying. "These kids haven't been ruined yet," says Mudcat.

Jarding is as reclusive as Mudcat is media-friendly. When I ask him to provide a photo because I've been unable to find one of him, he says, "Good. I hate photos." A prickly forty-seven-year-old who wears a "Deny Everything" ballcap, Jarding grew up in small towns across South Dakota, and, like Mudcat, is an avid hunter. He is the youngest of eight children, whose father died when he was four months old. His mom was a Nixon Republican but steadily grew more liberal, resenting the way Republicans soured voters against their government when, after all, it was the government that gave her a Social Security check to help make ends meet, and put all eight of her children through college when she had no money to send them.

Jarding is a purer partisan than Mudcat. In South Dakota, he was George McGovern's paper boy, and his first political gig came at ten years old, when he volunteered for Bobby Kennedy. On the morning after Kennedy was shot, his Hubert Humphrey–loving uncle broke the news. A gutfighter even then, Jarding says, "I was pissed. I asked him, 'Why did they kill Kennedy and not Humphrey?'"

After a series of local and state Democratic Party political jobs, he spent much of the nineties attached to former senator Bob Kerrey. When it became clear Kerrey wouldn't run for president in 2000, Jarding took over Warner's campaign and, as was his custom, checked in with Mark Gersh, an electoral numbers whiz at the National Committee for an Effective Congress. When Jarding told him he was working Warner, Gersh told Jarding that was too bad, because Warner couldn't win with just Virginia's traditional Democratic base.

Jarding insisted there were legions of untapped rural persuadables, and "Gersh lit up like a lamp," says Jarding. "He said, 'Not only do I believe it, I'll show you.'" Gersh told Jarding that all of his research indicated that there were more persuadable voters in rural areas than in the suburbs. The data suggested formerly Democratic rural voters were voting Republican out of habit, and largely on cultural issues, but they weren't necessarily satisfied customers. Jarding says twenty-five years after the Reagan Democrat phenomenon, "they said they hadn't gotten a damn thing for that vote. 'Our infrastructure is falling apart, we don't have any jobs here, we can't make a living.' According to Gersh's research, they were pissed off. Gersh said, 'They're voting Republican, but they're not Republican. You can get them back.' I said, 'How do I get them back?' He said, 'That's your job, I'm just telling you they're out there.'"

Jarding met Mudcat, launched their rural offensive, and the rest is election history. While Jarding is more of a traditional Democrat than Mudcat, he's just as peevish when it comes to recent Democratic behavior toward rural and southern voters: "If you say to them, 'You're voting against your own economic interest,' is that true? Damn right, it's true. But it sounds belittling. It sounds like you're saying, 'You're an idiot.' No, Democrats, you're the idiots. They're voting on their values. They're voting on something out there, because the other side gave them something to vote on. You've given them nothing, and while you're doing that, suicide rates are up. Unemployment rates are up. Wages are down—it's a terrible mess in rural America. And you've got the economic issues where you can go get 'em, but you've got to get through the culture and through to their values. Don't act like they don't exist. Democrats miss that point, and if they get that point, they're going to win a helluva lot of races."

When I ask Jarding why Democrats should necessarily concentrate on a demographic that's been hostile to them, since there's only a finite pie and limited resources, he grows increasingly animated: "I'd say let Republicans make that argument. Go to rural America and say, 'You're a finite pie, so screw you! All 21 percent of the country of you, all 60 million of you. You're a finite pie!'" Jarding, who nearly entered the priesthood before casting his lot in politics, says, "It's a moral argument. How morally right is it for our Democratic nominee for president to tell 60 million people, 'You don't matter to me'?"

Jarding says it's high time Democrats stopped worrying about appeasing the base, which isn't big enough to win national elections, and started making inroads into the approximately 35 percent of the country—the South—that they're ceding, by breaking it down into component pools.

He gives Louisiana as an example: Bush won the state last year by 283,413 votes. Using Mudcat math, that means the Dems would have to turn around 142,000 votes of the two million cast (pool one), while also courting the one million eligible voters who didn't vote (pool two). After hitting the one million or so hunters and sportsmen (pool three), the one-quarter of rural voters living below the poverty line (pool four), and active and retired military personnel (pool five), tailoring a pitch to each, all of a sudden winning 142,000 new votes seems rather manageable. Democrats, however, have written off these regions altogether, which Jarding can't understand. "This is not heavy math," he says. "That is how we did it in Virginia and won."

Back in Mudcat's Roanoke living room, the hour is late, and the political handicapping is under way. Surprisingly, Mudcat is rather bullish on Hillary Clinton's prospects, saying that while other Republicans and Democrats will "be banging on the left and right rails" throughout their primaries, it's in her interest to run down the center all the way through, meaning she'd have a leg up on the general election.

I ask him if she could make inroads with the Bubbas, since her "Sooey!" calls at Razorback football games when she was first lady of Arkansas probably won't cut much ice. Wouldn't Bubba rather hit her with rotten fruit than see her name on a stock car?

"But why couldn't she?" asks Mudcat. Bubba doesn't need to

know you're one of him, he just needs to know you appreciate him. She already swung enough in upstate New York to become senator. And after all, he says, Bubbas aren't just southerners. "What is Pennsylvania?" he asks. "It's Pittsburgh and Philadelphia, and it's Alabama in the middle."

It's time to start looking at things differently, just as he wants me to, when he abruptly pops out of his chair, saying, "I almost forgot your keepsake." He runs outside, then comes back in, flinging an empty box of Raisinets in my lap. Taped to the box on Waylon Jennings's old stationery (given to him by Jennings's widow, Jessi Colter, a personal friend) is an inscription from Mudcat that says, "One box of Mudcat's Deer Shit."

For half an hour or so, he glories in my humiliation. Then he turns things serious: "It's one of the most frustrating things for me in my life. I can make you believe I ate deer shit. But I can't get northeastern Democrats to believe they can get through the culture of the South."

AND THE BAND PLAYS ON . . .

The Music of New Orleans Is Still Alive, but Will the City Ever Recover?

New Orleans

To eat New Orleans raw, if you're into that sort of thing, it helps to be at the Maple Leaf Bar on Tuesdays around midnight. The Maple Leaf is a legendary watering-hole-in-the-wall. Its décor is of the scuffed-pool-table/Abita-beer-sign variety. It has worn plank floors and chipped crimson walls and pressed tin ceilings through which peek gaslight pipes from the days before the place went electric. Its music hall is about the length and width of three living rooms. It is here that almost every Tuesday night, on a rickety postage stamp of a stage, the best live band in America, the Rebirth Brass Band, makes its stand.

The band's leader and founder, Tuba Phil Frazier, describes their sound as not jazz, not funk, but "junk." But this "junk" is like mainlining the very soul of New Orleans—the sousafunky sounds of tuba and bass drum–driven percussion propelling call-to-war horns. It is the soundtrack of its streets and jazz funerals and "second-line" parades in which brass bands move through the city's black neighborhoods on Sunday afternoons during parade season. In keeping with the town's never-ending-party ethos—the reason New Orleans always seems three beers ahead of wherever you're from—the "season" lasts two-thirds of the year.

During it, brass bands take to the streets at the behest of the city's scores of social aid and pleasure clubs, collecting second-line dancers behind them as a coat collects lint. A tradition that predates jazz itself, it's serious business—like church without religion. Men will skip football for second lines, and women will buy outfits for them. Unlike the rest of America, accustomed to living in flat-screened isolation chambers, New Orleans people—or what's left of them after Katrina—like to go out into the street to see and be seen.

Though it is internationally renowned, now playing jazz festivals throughout the world, Rebirth still owns these streets. It developed its sound playing them ever since Frazier cofounded the band in 1983 with Kermit Ruffins (now solo). As high school kids in the Treme neighborhood, from where so many of the city's musicians come, they played the French Quarter for tips, using them to buy Popeyes chicken and beer for themselves, and lunchmeat for Frazier's poor family. "If there was any money leftover, our momma said buy some Kool-Aid—so you know we were ghetto," says Frazier's sister, Nicole James, an actress who works the door of her brother's show while pushing the T-shirts of her rapper/tax-accountant husband. (In these uncertain times, it pays to have a fallback gig.)

The band, as currently constituted, is nine players strong. They are mostly thirtysomething and all African American locals who came up in housing projects and some of the city's rougher neighborhoods, like the Ninth Ward and the Treme. They tend to stay a long time. Even Rebirth's rookies have six years under their belts, and some have been playing with the band since they were teenagers.

Like an army ready to advance, they take their places onstage in two straight lines. The back line is the foundation, as Phil calls it, that pushes the front. There is no set list or sheet music. Roughly half their songs are originals, but none are written down. Tuba Phil calls all the tunes by blowing the opening licks, from New Orleans traditionals to retooled R&B numbers by the likes of Marvin Gaye and Curtis Mayfield. If other players can't catch what he's doing from one of the five hundred or so songs in their repertoire, they're better off finding another band.

Joining Phil and his sonic boom of a sousaphone is Derrick "Big Sexy" Tabb, who plays with a viciousness that suggests he is skinning a cat, rather than hitting a snare drum. Mötley Crüe's Tommy Lee called him "one of the baddest drummers I've ever seen." Next to Big Sexy, strapped up to a parade bass drum, is Keith "Bass Drum Shorty" Frazier, Phil's younger brother and the only other original member of the band. Around town, he is known for a peculiar innovation. He plays his high-hat cymbal not with a coat hanger, as was the tradition before he changed it, but with a flathead screwdriver, since he likes the way it sounds: "like the swoop-splash of a rock hitting a lake."

Slathering all that bass in brass is the front line, who, standing six across in their wife-beater tank-tees, sports jerseys, and low-hanging jeans, look less like a horn section than like a hit squad of brass assassins. Each of them is a tight enough pocket player that he could hold the groove in the JB Horns (the Rebirth's heroes). But as a marksman, each is also dangerous enough to score a solo headshot from a hundred yards away.

On saxophones are Byron "Flea" Bernard, a social worker who also plays with his church band and who dearly wishes Rebirth would cut a gospel album, and Vincent Broussard, who looks like he should play with the Wailers with his back-length dreadlocks. On trombone is Lil' Herb Stevens, who is not lil' at all, and who sports Bible-themed tattoos all over his arms, patting Jesus on His head and apologizing if anyone says anything sacrilegious. Joining him is Stafford "Freaky Pete" Agee, so named for calling the ladies onstage and "freaking" them, though he is still a man of high principle: He refuses to play anything that's not grease-bucket funky.

Leading the charge are the band's slash-and-burn trumpet players. There's spark plug dynamo Derrick "Khabuki" Shezbie, whose cheeks turn into Dizzy Gillespie balloons when he blows (he often brackets one with his free fingers to get a tighter sound). A member of another brass band enviously tells me, "Khabuki could carry that band, and two others at the same time." Rounding the lineup out is Glen "The General" Andrews, who likes to head for the high registers like a runaway sherpa who's caught sight of the summit.

He is called "The General" because he, along with his cousin Big Sexy, likes to make sure everyone hits his parts (Khabuki, too, is a distant cousin). You'd never know that Andrews is self-taught and doesn't even read music. "Wynton Marsalis might say, 'What the hell are you doin'!'" he jokes. But as The General tells me with a gold-toothed grin, "I can go where he plays, but he can't come on our stage where we play. I play something I made up from my heart, y'know." It puts me in mind of something Louis Armstrong said of snooty Creole musicians when he and Kid Ory blew them off the street during a jazz funeral: "Any learned musician can read music, but they all can't swing."

And swing the Rebirth does, especially live. Not to take anything away from their thirteen fine recordings, but the difference between hearing them live and on disc is the difference between making love to a beautiful woman and having the experience described to you. Still, I haven't come to New Orleans to sign on as their roadie. I'm here on official business, to take a snapshot of their city a year and a half after Katrina nearly totaled it.

To that end, I bring to the Maple Leaf show one of my old guides to New Orleans, the pseudonymous Kingfish, of whom I've written in these pages twice before. When I first met him, as the waters were still rolling in after Katrina, New Orleans felt like a live adaptation of the Book of Revelation. People were dying in the streets, the desperate became more so, and the lawless were taking over. A good native son whose family goes back to the city's beginnings, Kingfish was one of the last men standing in his swank Uptown neighborhood. He let our visiting crew of journalists clean out his refrigerator and bathe in his pool, since the hotels had long since evacuated.

Before the gig, I stop by his house to collect him. His kids are snug in their beds, instead of in exile in Florida. And there is nobody sleeping on the couch with a shotgun, as was his looter-protection practice back during the flood. There is one remnant of those days, however. In his living room is a trophy case featuring a pair of beat-up Adidas sneakers. In between running humanitarian rescue missions during the storm, Kingfish lost patience with the looters. When he saw one coming out of a linen store with a swag bag—hardly a necessity unless the thief had to have cool fabrics for summer—Kingfish bore down on him with his shotgun. "Scared him clean out of his shoes," he says. "I just couldn't take it anymore."

As he fixes us some pregame Old Fashioneds, Mrs. Kingfish eyes his pressed khakis and Casual Friday chambray shirt disapprovingly. "You're going to the Maple Leaf," she says. "Don't you have a black T-shirt or something?" He shrugs his shoulders, in a what-do-you-want-from-me fashion. "I probably have a buttoned-down T-shirt somewhere," he says. While Kingfish plays at being the Uptown swell, like many whites in New Orleans who've benefited from three centuries of cultural cross-fertilization, he has more soul than he likes to let on.

We get to the bar before the Rebirth does, and Kingfish eyes the decrepitude approvingly. "You can't reproduce this," he says. "When you go to Joe's Crab Shack, this is what they try to do." The Meters play on the juke, while the bar is the kind of place where you can have enlightened debates as to who was the better piano player, Professor Longhair or James Booker (the late Booker usually wins, since he used to hold down Rebirth's Tuesday night gig). At the end of the bar is a photo of Everette Maddox, who was the Maple Leaf's "poet laureate" until he drank himself to death. Maple Leaf owner Hank Staples says that he's buried out back on the patio. At least half of him is. Seems there was a dispute among his friends, and the rest of his ashes were scattered in the Mississippi River. He died as he lived, and his tombstone testifies: "He was a mess."

It could be New Orleans's epitaph, and some would have it that way. But not tonight. Tonight the band takes the stage an hour and a half late (in the Big Easy, start times are mere suggestions). But the Rebirth makes up for it. The Frazier brothers lay down a thoracic cavity–thumping bass groove, and the rest of the band plays like their horns have caught fire and need blowing out. Empty beer bottles rattle on the speakers, while the band sings and spits and croaks out in frogman gurgles its burning-down-the-house anthem, "Rebirth Got Fire! Rebirth Got Fire!" Black and white and rich and poor and middle-aged and young bob violently like several hundred buoys on a gathering wave.

Talent buyer Stu Schayot of the Howlin' Wolf club sees a lot of great bands, but tells me there's none like Rebirth: "When those guys play, there's a feeling that there's no other spot on this planet where this moment is happening. And if you're from New Orleans, it's like you own it. It's such a New Orleans thing they've created. My philosophy is: If everybody saw Rebirth once a week, there'd be no crime in this city. You go to a show, and every walk is there. You could be standing next to a lawyer and a guy from the projects. No class, no race. All energy. Just people in unison, having a good time."

Close to me, I watch a freakishly nimble second-line dancer named Ron "The Busdriver" Horn, so monikered because he drives a bus. He moves as though his joints are made of Slinkys. He is black, but he wants me to meet Chocolate Swerve, his white sidekick and understudy. Swerve recently broke his ankle when the crowd got him over-pumped as he was dancing onstage during a Rebirth show at Tipitina's. ("In cowboy boots," Horn says with some embarrassment. "I laughed all the way to the hospital.")

Still, boasts Horn, "ain't nobody can deal with him," as Swerve replicates his moves. "We're brothers from another mother." Horn met Swerve after the former's house got washed out in the Ninth Ward. Swerve was a roofer from out of town—one of the rare ones who didn't try to cheat him. They became thick as thieves, and, well, now look, says Horn, like the beaming parent of an accomplished child.

I ask Horn if this stuff matters, in the grand scheme of the greater disaster that has become his city. He looks at me as if someone had jumped me with a stupid stick. "It's all that matters." After the storm, he says, he left "a wonderful lady" back in Atlanta "who I dealt with for eleven years" because he had to get back. "This," he says, pointing to the Rebirth, "is what makes the culture keep living. I came back for my kids and the culture." Now forty-one years old, he used to play trumpet in the same junior high band as Tuba Phil, and his son now plays trumpet in one of the best marching bands in New Orleans. "She's got the house now," he said, speaking of his woman. "But I came back for my culture. I told her if you ever need me, I'm there. But we're fighting here. Ain't gonna give up. I got to help rebuild."

I grab the Kingfish to introduce him, but the second he catches The Busdriver's eye, he exclaims, "Hey baby!" and they embrace. Years ago, Horn used to work for Kingfish. "This is New Orleans," Kingfish explains. "We all know each other." Kingfish doesn't tarry for long, however, as a pretty black girl innocently and wordlessly grabs his hand while the Rebirth plays "Feel Like Funkin' It Up." He spins her around the dance floor, or at least the two feet of it that are available to him. He smiles an isn't-this-place-great smile.

"Why do you think I put up with all the bullshit?" Kingfish says.

There are plenty who said New Orleans wouldn't come back after the storm. But it's back, all right—back as the murder and mayhem capital of the United States. According to one Tulane demographer, in 2006 there were ninety-six murders per hundred thousand people—68 percent more than in 2004. And 2007 is off to an auspicious start with thirty-seven murders as of mid-March. It's an impressive effort from the bad guys of New Orleans, who are putting up big numbers even though there are fewer people around to kill. The population has dwindled to 191,000 from its prestorm 467,000. With New Orleans's notoriously overstretched and feckless police force and DA, about two-thirds of the homicides are going unsolved. So many criminals have been released without charge that the term "misdemeanor murder" has gained wide currency.

While city spinmeisters would have it that the murder rate entails black-on-black drug-related killings—which is largely true—they're by no means all that's going on. In just one recent week, a female filmmaker and the Hot 8 Brass Band's Dinerral Shavers (who frequently sat in with Rebirth) were both killed in front of their own children, causing an outraged citizens' march on City Hall.

On some days, the *Times-Picayune* reads like good crime fiction with a southern gothic twist. There were the star-crossed lovers who met the night Katrina hit and who ended up cohabiting over a voodoo temple in the Quarter. They came to a bad end when he calmly strangled her, dismembered her, then jumped off the roof of the same hotel in which I'm staying, but not before leaving a suicide note that detailed his handiwork: Police found parts of her in a pot on the stove next to the chopped carrots and more in the oven on turkey-basting trays. "He may have in retrospect seemed a little troubled," said his landlord.

Then there was the bizarre murder allegedly committed by renowned radio talk show host Vincent Marinello, who police suspect shot his wife in the face twice, made it look like a robbery in a parking lot, then rode away on his bike. The tip-off was the to-do list found in his FEMA trailer, with checkmarks beside incriminating tasks like "mustache and beard" and a reminder to get rid of the weapon. He appears to have remembered everything except to throw away his list.

None of this, of course, even addresses the post-Katrina toll or the frustration New Orleanians feel with federal, state, and local officials. Even many of those who voted to reelect Mayor Ray Nagin have taken to calling him "the invisible mayor." And after George W. Bush rejected Louisiana's Baker Plan to help speed rebuilding, and failed to forgive the state the matching 10 percent it must pay for all federal disaster assistance as he did New York after 9/11, and neglected even to mention New Orleans in his State of the Union address, many New Orleanians were unclear during his recent visit, when Bush promised that they hadn't been forgotten, whether he was reminding them or himself.

At a Rebirth show at the Howlin' Wolf one night, I watch as trombonist Stafford Agee takes the mike and improvises a lament in which he name checks everyone from FEMA to the mayor to the president, with the sing-along refrain, "Fuck 'em all, fuck 'em all, fuck 'em all." The crowd joins in lustily. It doesn't feel like disaffected youth spoiling for a fight either. It's not angry, so much as weary: the song of a city that's given immeasurable joy to the rest of the country with its music and architecture and food, but that feels like it's getting erased.

The Katrina Index, put out jointly by the Greater New Orleans Community Data Center and the Brookings Institution, and which might as well be called the Misery Index, tells the story in numbers. Less than 1 percent of those who've applied for assistance through the state's Road Home Program have received their home repair grants. Public transportation has hardly improved in a year, with the city still at 17 percent of its buses. Though Orleans Parish schools were a disaster before the storm, with educational standards reportedly below those of Zimbabwe and Kenya, 56 percent of schools remain closed, and 69 percent of child care centers do as well. The mass exodus of doctors might have to do with the fact that only twelve of Orleans Parish's twenty-three state licensed hospitals are still in operation.

Then there are the things that statistics can't measure—the weirdness quotient. One afternoon, I take a spin around the city with another old friend, Joe Gendusa, a tour guide I met during Mardi Gras 2006. When he's not giving the Southern Comfort cocktail tour, he gives the Katrina Disaster tour for the Gray Line company three times a week. Gray Line is a bit of a disaster itself. Before the storm, it had sixty-five local full-time employees. Now it has four.

I took Gendusa's bus tour last year, but this year, as he drives me around in his car, I'm shocked at how little has changed in neighborhood after mostly abandoned neighborhood: Lakeview, Gentilly, the Ninth Ward, St. Bernard Parish, New Orleans East. The only appreciable difference is that most of the debris has been cleared and many of the houses gutted. Now the place has the eeriness of one of those Rapture movies evangelical youth ministers show their charges to scare them into the Kingdom. Except nobody's been called up to heaven. They're all in Baton Rouge or Houston or God knows where. Many old friends and neighbors still haven't found one another.

Tourists who travel only from the airport to the Quarter or the Garden District would never know anything's wrong. But the rest of the city? "It's a disaster, and will be for the rest of my lifetime," the sixty-six-year-old Gendusa says. "You're talking about rebuilding an entire city." As we drive down a boulevard in Lakeview that once boasted large houses and oak canopies, but that is now desolate and destroyed, the lifelong New Orleanian, whose Italian immigrant grandfather helped start the Gendusa bakery empire that invented po'boy bread, is gobsmacked. As he drives, here's a verbatim transcript of his reaction: "I don't recognize it. Oh my god! Look at this! Oh my god, look at this! Oh Jesus! Un-be-leeeev-able!" Keep in mind, he sees this wreckage nearly every day, since he is paid, in essence, to feed off the cadaver.

And yet it never ceases to shock him. Nor does the behavior of some of the citizenry. "They're looting FEMA trailers!" he says. "What a bunch of scumbuckets!" He tells a particularly galling story. One woman who'd recently had her mother cremated was saving the ashes until she could have a proper burial at one of the city's storm-damaged cemeteries. "Her trailer was broken into, looted, everything was stolen out of boxes," Gendusa says. "Guess what they stole? Her mother! These stupid asses looted the mother! She's on television crying, saying you can have whatever you want, just bring my mother home. We won't ask any questions, just put her on the steps."

We look at each other for a beat, then both start laughing uncontrollably. Sometimes, there's nothing else to do. I've always loved New Orleans, because life comes at you here faster and stranger and more darkly beautiful than it does in other places. Sherwood Anderson called it "the most civilized spot in America"—a place where there is "time for a play of the imagination over the facts of life." These days, however, the imagination can't keep up.

A swarm of African killer bees has been found in St. Bernard Parish. The city has turned into "the super bowl of sex" for hookers, say the police, since there are so many out-of-town construction contractors to service. For a while, a transvestite gang of shoplifters was terrorizing stores on Magazine Street. Researchers have now determined that parts of the city are sinking more than one inch per year. And as if that's not a bad enough omen, there's now irrefutable proof that New Orleans is reverting to third-world conditions: Squalor seekers Angelina Jolie and Brad Pitt just got a place in the Quarter. "No matter what happens, we'll always have better restaurants than Namibia," cracks my friend Danny Abel, an attorney and Creole chef.

Then there's the tornado. It hits overnight while I'm in town. My phone rings in the morning, and it's the Kingfish. "C'mon, let's go see the wreckage," he says. "It'll be like old times." We drive around, surveying the damage where the twister came across the Mississippi and took a path from Uptown to Pontchartrain Park, damaging hundreds of homes and killing an old woman who was living in a FEMA trailer in her front yard, just days away from moving back into her repaired house.

Kingfish spins me around to one home in particular. "That's my friend's," he says, of a once-beautiful place that's now seen its second-story porch completely collapse, so that it looks like a fence was erected across the front door. Snapped telephone lines hang from branches like Mardi Gras beads after a parade. There are tons of downed trees and out-of-commission stoplights and missing street signs, though that was already true before the tornado hit. It does feel like a nostalgia tour. In fact, it's sometimes hard to tell the new destruction from the old destruction. "Look for rust," Kingfish instructs. This city is starting to feel doomed, I tell him. "Yeah, but how 'bout them Saints," he deadpans.

The Kingfish loves this city as much as anyone who's still here—and very few people are still here by accident. But he's hardly a romantic. Since I saw him last year, he's hedged his bets by selling off 70 percent of his real estate. "I was scared," he explains. On our drive, he points out all the big chains that aren't coming back, one of which, Ruth's Chris Steakhouse, was born in New Orleans. Pointing at Ruth's old house next to the shuttered restaurant, he says, "She lived there till the day she died. The corporate people she sold it to won't reopen it. I used to go there every Sunday night."

The fundamental problem, he opines, is that no real help is on the way, and, simultaneously, the city is suffocating itself under paralyzed leadership that won't exclude any neighborhoods from redevelopment for fear of political blowback. They won't draw the net and stop pretending that they can support a footprint for six hundred thousand people when only a third of that is left. "We had more people here at the beginning of the last century. Where else has that happened besides Chernobyl?" Kingfish asks. Consequently, services are spread thin. The city is being repopulated helter-skelter as the result of hundreds of thousands of individual insurance transactions and private choices.

And on the rare occasion that you are made whole by your insurance company and can rebuild, what if your neighbors aren't and can't? As he points out random blocks where one person is back and three houses on either side of him aren't, he says, "You have the jack-o'-lantern effect all over the city." This will contribute to blight, and already has, as even his construction materials are frequently stolen from building sites. If there's one thing Kingfish learned from the storm, he says, it's that "police don't protect neighborhoods, neighbors protect neighborhoods."

In the midst of this reality, everything is becoming more difficult. He gives me an example. He owns a building worth $1.1 million in New Orleans, and recently bought another for the same price in Maine. The difference, he says, is that insurance "in New Orleans is forty grand, in Maine, it's four. What does that mean? There's less profit, the property's worth less, and I have to charge more rent." If you don't feel sorry for the Kingfish and his investment problems, keep in mind that his reality trickles all the way down to the poor. On average in this city, a lousy one-bedroom apartment that used to rent for $531 per month before the storm now goes for $836.

He points to an abandoned business. "How are we gonna support all this blight? What's gonna happen to this? Somebody will buy it at some price at some point. But who are his customers?" The market always corrects, he says, ever the capitalist. "But it's going to be ugly, and people are going to get screwed." He says the city should have taken its federal aid, bought out all the poor, low-lying areas like the Ninth Ward, made people whole, and given them the option to buy elsewhere, which would be less expensive than rebuilding it all. But now, individual residential renovations are already taking place, so a buyout would cost infinitely more. As he says, "It's too late now."

On my ride with Gendusa, he told me his brother had moved across the lake out of Orleans Parish and now mocks him for refusing to do the same. "This is my home," he said. "I walk the streets of the Quarter, and I feel my grandparents and my parents. I can still see my daddy, walkin'. He loved New Orleans. I can never turn my back on it, even if it hurts to see it bleed." When friends visit and remark that it is old and dirty, he tells them, "Go back to Disney World." He'd rather live in a diminished New Orleans than a thriving Orlando.

The Kingfish echoes the sentiment, as do nearly all the New Orleanians I speak to. He tells me still, even now, he's surrounded by beautiful architecture and brilliant music and world-class restaurants. "It's a unique place, great people," says Kingfish. "We have a very big soul here. But we have some fundamental flaws that are probably the opposite side of that coin. What makes us soulful also makes us sort of pitiful when it comes to fixing ourselves."

Yes, sometimes he gets jealous of friends who've fled to more stable places, where the headline of the day is that a new on-ramp will cut congestion, while the news here is "'Murders and Dismal Reality'—you just can't get away from it. . . . But you know what?" he adds defiantly. "I have friends leaving perfectly good cities to come back because they have survivor's guilt. They feel, 'I left my city, I gotta be in the game.' It's the biggest story to ever hit this town. So whaddya' gonna leave? Go live in Niceville?"

Two weeks after I've left, the Kingfish calls. He was coming home from the Louisiana Derby at the Fair Grounds racetrack, and in Mid-City he almost got caught in a drive-by murder. "We heard the *pop-pop*, and saw a bunch of thugs run past our car after the intersection was blocked. Had to back my car up to get out of there." He tells me to check the papers for the details. "Just make sure you get the right story. There were six shootings and three killings yesterday."

If New Orleans is not yet a Lost City, there is nobody in it who has not lost something. The Rebirth is no exception. During Katrina, over half the band members lost everything: their houses, their clothes, their instruments. Some won't even talk about it. Big Sexy Tabb, who had to hotwire a van to get his family and others to safety, is one of them. "If I could get hypnotized, I'd hope they'd say, 'You won't remember Katrina and all the shit it caused.' But you live it every day, man. Every day."

Even those from whom the floodwaters didn't take everything still have harrowing stories. Trumpet player Khabuki Shezbie, for instance, was on the fourth floor of his apartment building, so his place didn't get flooded. But when the water started rising over the second floor, he decided to swim for it. He swam almost a mile, "with my horn on my back—had to replace all the valves," he says. He saw dead animals and dead people. Parents tried to float their kids on mattresses. Though a boat finally rescued him, somebody broke into his place afterward and cleaned him out.

Sometimes, the loss manifests itself in the most innocent conversations. One day, I go see trombonist Stafford "Freaky Pete" Agee on his jobsite in a house that's being restored in the Lower Ninth Ward. He is one of two Rebirth musicians who also work civilian jobs (saxophonist Flea Bernard works in a welfare office and says after the storm, even six-figure lawyers were coming in for food stamps). Since Katrina hit, Agee has become an electrician, "just picked it up as I went." He wears a Lowe's apron, a white bandanna around his head, and his high school marching band sweatshirt, though the school no longer exists. We talk music instead of destruction, but then I ask him if he names his trombones. Yes, he says, he names them after old girlfriends. "I have a couple horns named Sandy—she came around twice," he says.

I ask if he's ever named one after his ex-wife. "If I had, I would destroy it," he says bitterly. Now fishing, I joke that she hurt him. "Yeah, she did," he says. She cheated on him with a friend, which he discovered during a Battle of the Bands in Houston. Rebirth was there to play "a down-home New Orleans dance party" for evacuees. Now his marriage is busted, and his kids live in Alabama with relatives since the public school waiting list is too long in New Orleans. So you see, he says, pointing to a socket that he's wiring, "I keep myself busy so I don't stay in my head."

The sadness is always there, he says. "But I take my frustrations out through my music. I use it to uplift myself. New Orleans right now is kind of a lost soul on standstill. The soul of it isn't here, because a lot of people that bring that soul are no longer here. It's not like it used to be." So right now, says Agee, in a sentiment that one band member after another expresses, "it's like the city's on our shoulders. It's taken on more importance. Where else in the world can you go and find a brass band parading in the street every Sunday, or have them come over to play for your party? We carryin' it, keepin' the spirit. When they think the feeling is gone, it brings people back home."

Rebirth has always played the small shows, on the theory that all the money adds up, even if sometimes, according to trombonist Herb Stevens, it costs him more to drive to the gig than he makes, once the check is split nine ways. But now the small gigs have taken on a missionary tint.

The Dirty Dozen Brass Band, which Tuba Phil idolizes and which revolutionized the sound of brass band music by incorporating contemporary R&B sounds (which the Rebirth has taken even further), has graduated from the street, sticking to the studio and big festivals. But Rebirth still lives off the land. They are truly the people's champion—not just a studio or festival band. They will play everything from baby showers to jazz funerals: As Shorty Frazier says, "When you're born and when you die and everything in between. 'Will you guys come play my bathroom while I take a bath?' Yeah, we'll do it. There's no gig too big or too small for Rebirth. It's good to stay plugged in."

In my ten days in New Orleans, I see them play everything from a second line in the Quarter, sponsored by a local sanitation company, to the Rock Bottom Lounge, where food consists of smoked pork chops you can order from a grill on the bed of a curbside pickup truck. It's a place where there's no stage, and the band is partly obscured by a brick column. When I ask the bartender for a receipt, Tuba Phil mocks me: "Ain't no receipts here. Boy, you in a real ghetto bar."

I watch Rebirth play a Jefferson Parish Mardi Gras ball at a senior center, where the gig has to be delayed for two and a half hours because some of the seniors are still getting their hair done and are out buying king cakes. And I miss a gig (after being told the wrong restaurant) where Rebirth plays a Hermes krewe party in an upper room at Antoine's, while strippers go at each other. "It was nice," Freaky Pete says grinning. "Excruciating and exuberating—there's no word that can describe it."

New Orleans, of course, had a lot of problems before the storm. And these, too, touched Rebirth. When I go to interview Tuba Phil at his Gentilly home, I notice a framed portrait of a rapper—the kind of severe *Scarface* art you often see on *MTV's Cribs*. It's his stepson, Soulja Slim, who was gunned down in Phil's front yard four years ago. And that's not all. Drummer Derrick Tabb was shot twice at his half-brother's funeral ("Still got a bullet in my shoulder," he says). Rebirth's late snare drummer, Kenny "Eyes" Austin, died from a blood clot after getting hit in the head by a frying pan while breaking up a bar fight.

I take a tour of the Treme one day with the wickedly talented trombone player and belter Glen David Andrews. He fronts a band called the Lazy Six, and can break your heart doing guts-on-the-floor renditions of standards like "Precious Lord, Take My Hand." He isn't in Rebirth, but Tabb is his half-brother, and trumpet player Glen Andrews is his cousin.

Just over Rampart Street from the Quarter, he gives me a crash course in the old neighborhood. There's no need to hunt for the roses or the thorns, they're all right in front of you. Drug deals go down around us as if we were invisible. And yet, music legends walk the streets that run between shotgun shacks and old Creole cottages.

You're just as likely to run into the Treme Brass Band's Uncle Benny Jones, or Henry Youngblood of "I Got a Big Fat Woman" fame, as you are some wino with cracked teeth muttering to himself in a drunken tongue.

That is changing, however. Big Sexy Tabb, Andrews's brother, tells me the "culture is dying." One mayor's office estimate said that only 10 percent of the city's musicians had returned full-time. In the Treme, the storm dispersed people (Andrews is now living in a broken-down FEMA trailer in Carrollton), and the institutional memory is drying up. There used to be so many musicians around that second lines were apt to break out at 3:00 A.M. Now, Andrews tells me, the Mexican laborers and white real estate opportunists who are snatching up damaged property as "timeshares" complain about the noise. It's killing the music, says Tabb. "To learn, you got to hang around the older cats that were in brass bands. But now, you don't have that community."

When Tabb was a kid growing up in the Treme, "if you played a horn, you wanted to get out there and shine." But the old musicians would box your ears, and make you wait your turn as you learned. The Olympia Brass Band's Milton Batiste made sure "you didn't play no funk till you learned the traditionals—you ain't never bigger than this here music. You might bring something new, but it's all been played before." Those who think the music will stay, even as its incubator is unplugged, are sadly mistaken. The continuum's been interrupted. If Tabb were a doctor, he says, "I don't go tomorrow, put on some scrubs, and do an operation. There's a process, going to work on somebody's body. And here, the whole process has been fucked up. You got to learn it. You got to feel it. You can't write what we do."

As Andrews walks me around the streets, he calls out to everyone he sees, "Where y'at, Uncle," and many of them actually are his uncles. (The Andrews clan makes the Marsalis family look feeble when it comes to breeding musicians, boasting everyone from James "Satchmo of the Ghetto" Andrews, to Revert "Peanut" Andrews of the Dirty Dozen, to Troy "Trombone Shorty" Andrews—the list goes on.)

Glen David Andrews shows me the Backstreet Cultural Museum—a monument to brass band musicians and Mardi Gras Indians housed in an old funeral home. He introduces me to many of the neighborhood characters, who like to hang out and drink on

Dumaine and Robertson. On this corner, Andrews's twenty-one-year-old cousin, Trombone Shorty, who's been praised by Wynton Marsalis and who has toured with Lenny Kravitz, later tells me some of the old men driven away by the storm still come back to hang out. So he goes to soak up their company while the soaking's good, "though most of them are drunk by the time I get there." Sometimes one of the codgers will hum a lick in his ear, which he'll end up using. "Everybody around there, in some way, is in touch with music even though they might not play," he says. "I'm afraid that's the last bunch of them. I try to get as much as I can."

As Andrews walks me through an intersection near Louis Armstrong Park, he grows morose. "Bittersweet place," he says. It's where his cousin Glen "The General" Andrews's mom was murdered. "I was about fifteen," The General tells me one day when we're sitting in the Candlelight Bar in the Treme, one of the last neighborhood bars left standing. "I was right down the street, saw the ambulance, and didn't know it was for her."

One afternoon, after the Rebirth has played an outdoor gig by the Mississippi, The General introduces me to his wife, Ingrid, and lets her tell tales out of school. She relates lively stories about everything from the jazz-funeral groupies to how he's always lying to her to go hang in the Treme. He walks a few paces ahead, clutching the hand of their six-year-old daughter. He periodically turns around, rolling his eyes and smiling like he's been trapped in a bad sitcom. "I got to go on a six-month tour," he jokes. Ingrid says she actually doesn't like the Rebirth's music (she prefers Mary J. Blige), but their girl already has it bad. She's taking trombone lessons and probably never had a fair chance, since The General, when Ingrid was pregnant, used to put his horn up to her stomach and blow Louis Armstrong tunes to his unborn daughter.

Ingrid tells me The General's a beautiful person who'll do anything for anyone, that he cares for her and is never mean, but that he's struggled with heroin addiction. When Katrina hit, he was doing a six-month prison hitch on a drug charge. She knows, she says, that it's his mom's death that did it—"he suppressed it with drugs"—though only the shrink knows what he's really thinking, since he won't talk about the murder with her.

Back at the Candlelight, I ask The General if he plays better when he's using. "Sometimes," he answers, "sometimes not." But he knows he doesn't need it, since the rest of the band doesn't touch it. I ask him to describe the music that comes out of him. "Lotta pain, sometimes," he says, taking a hit off his straight Hennessey. "I don't talk to people too much, so that's how I express myself. Through my horn."

One day, I ask bandleader Tuba Phil how he can handle the one-two punch of the Katrina aftermath, plus all the murder and mayhem. After all, his stepson was gunned down in his own front yard, also because he'd been involved in drugs. I love New Orleans too. But isn't he ever tempted to chuck it all and move to Tulsa?

"Look," he says, "New Orleans people are strong. The ones who came back, I got to pat them on the back. 'Cause it was a shithole [before Katrina], and it was a shithole after. But they believe, like I believe, that we can turn this thing around. I feel I owe this city. I love the music. I love the people. Everybody's so free-hearted. Then you got twenty-four-hour drinkin'," he says, belly laughing. "If I wasn't living in New Orleans, I probably wouldn't be doin' what I'm doin' now. A tuba player! Makin' a living playing tuba! I'm forty-one years old, never punched a clock. Making people happy, and they're making me happy."

"Other shit goes on," he says. "But when you come to our show, man, you forget about your problems, the mortgage, the insurance, the housing. You come, you release. The four *R*s: Rebirth, Relax, Relate, Release. Forget about all this other stuff. The music takes you to another level. You might go home to half a house, but you sleep better that night. That's what I hope our music does to people. That's our obligation. The bad and the good stand side by side. I have tragedy. But I'm a stronger person. I can take it. Keep on goin'. Try to make it better. When I play in New Orleans, I play like this is the last time I'm ever going to play again. What if the city really is sunk? I play like the hell with it. I play like I might never come back to this again. I play like it's my last year of livin'. That's how I play."

His brother, Keith "Bass Drum Shorty" Frazier, is less sanguine. One night at dinner at Tujague's in the Quarter, Keith tells me that what ails this place you can't "solve by blowing a trumpet or hitting a drum." After the levees broke, "I lost everything—it was gone. There's not enough money in the world to get me back here. I'll never come back [to live]. Never, ever." He evacuated to Dallas, where he's stayed.

Sure, he misses Two Sisters soul food restaurant, and the people.

And when they play New Orleans music to the diaspora (in Houston or Atlanta or wherever), he's physically moved. It's like bringing them a photo album that they thought had been destroyed. But the people who are still here are "walking wounded," he says. "They don't even know it. They think they're all right. Phil had a barber friend who committed suicide. Black people don't commit suicide. It just doesn't happen. Man, that shit is crazy. People think it's over, but it ain't gonna be over for a long, long time."

Besides, he's seen the future of this place—it'll be Disney World, or some dipsomaniac version of it. Donald Trump's already planning a residential and retail project on Poydras—the beginning of the end. His new home is cleaner and safer. He's a Cowboys fan anyway, and his daughter goes to a better school. "Everything's done by the book," Keith says. "You go to work, get off at five, eat dinner, go back to work. It's not as laid-back. It's very boring." When he's there, he doesn't even think about playing music, or the storm, or the things he's lost. He almost sounds convincing. Though sometimes, he admits, when he's walking around in this foreign environment, he does have one thought: "How the fuck did I end up in Dallas?"

I try to spend Mardi Gras Day like a good tourist—on Bourbon Street. But I am quickly fatigued by all the other tourists: fat and pink and naked and drunk. They pour out of karaoke bars and clip joints into the street, where the bottoms of their shoes will grow sticky with the residue of spilled drinks and body fluids. They will have fistfights over imaginary grievances, proving yet again that Jager shots and testosterone don't mix. They will applaud the gospeler who holds the I'M SORRY sign, apologizing for the other street preachers who are telling them they'll go to hell. It never occurs to them, however, that hell would be a redundancy under the circumstances. They're already on Bourbon Street.

For respite, I go back where I started—the Maple Leaf—for the Rebirth's Tuesday night gig. During a break between sets, I go up onstage to bid farewell to the musicians, who like to split right after the show. The General and I take a seat on a stage step, and something comes over me. I feel compelled to tell him that he's an exceptional talent, that he makes people happy, and that's better than most of us will ever do. Then I caution him not to waste himself, not to get enveloped in the darkness that surrounds him.

I prattle on in this vein for a while, and am, of course, way over the line. I half expect him to tell me to get bent, or to make a quick getaway to Smoker's Alley outside, but he doesn't. Instead, he tucks his head and nods intently. He claps my back, and repeatedly reaches to shake my hand, as if to signal me that though we both know I've overstepped my reporter/subject bounds, he appreciates the effort.

I go back to my place in the audience. It's a Fat Tuesday crowd, so there isn't room to breathe. The band likes to joke that the surest way to get Phil not to call a song is to request it. And all week long, I've been requesting "Blackbird Special," an old Dirty Dozen number that the Rebirth does better. When I do, Phil says to me, "I don't know what I'm gonna call. I gotta feel it in here," as he pounds his chest. Maybe he feels it now, or maybe he's just humoring me. But they play it.

The song is one of my near-and-dears. When my first son was just old enough to sit up, I used to plop him in front of the speakers and play it off Rebirth's *Live at the Maple Leaf* album—much like The General blowing his horn for his unborn daughter. My son would swing his arms wildly, and his hips would vibrate as the Frazier brothers' bassline rolled up his spine.

The band is cooking tonight—everybody doing his part. Phil bumps and pumps with his sousaphone, twisting sideways while simultaneously firing up and down like a piston. Bass Drum Shorty is throwing rocks in the lake, booming with his right hand while his left rides the high hat with a flathead. Big Sexy is banging like he's trying to bore a hole in the floor. The front line has hoisted the black flag; there will be no hostages taken this evening. Khabuki and The General, in particular, are on fire. Almost literally, in Khabuki's case. The room is so hot, even with the doors open in winter, that he has stripped to the waist and is slicked with sweat like a welterweight fighter doing twelve rounds on a heavy bag.

I watch The General, in his tank T-shirt and his blue Kangol hat, aim his horn toward the sky as he gets lost in the song. It feels like I'm watching New Orleans itself: raw and rude, bold and brilliant, improvisational and soulful and damaged. And maybe it can't save itself, but it's a grievous mistake to think it's not worth saving.

The crowd pitches and rolls and rattles and stomps. Humidity droplets form on the walls, while Rebirth's horns ricochet off the ceiling and out into the back courtyard/cemetery where the Maple

Leaf's poet laureate rests in peace—at least the part of him that hasn't washed out to the Gulf of Mexico. Amid the controlled chaos, I wonder what New Orleans will look like if I visit in fifteen years.

I strongly suspect I won't be seeing Rebirth at funky dives, standing next to gold-toothed second liners with names like The Busdriver and Chocolate Swerve. I suspect that if the city hasn't by then collapsed on itself, I'll be taking in "The New Orleans Experience" by monorail. Our tour guide (from Appleton, Wisconsin) will direct our attention to the overlit streets of the Treme, now studded with Banana Republics and Panera Breads. He will tell us how all the spirited black people used to march behind men with giant sousaphones, as we are served heavily breaded fried shrimp, harvested fresh from Ore-Ida bags, with a ketchup remoulade. The sound track on the speakers will be from *The Big Easy Tribute Album:* Josh Groban sings "Rebirth Got Fire"—with strings. I will be a good sport, and nod my head in time with the other tourists, as I die a little inside.

But those are tomorrow's worries. Because tonight, Tuba Phil has called my song. And some of the baddest men on the planet, the Rebirth Brass Band, are playing it. They play in a fever. They play loud and hard and fierce. They play like they're avenging a death.

And who knows? Maybe they are.

ACKNOWLEDGMENTS

I'm not, generally speaking, in the habit of acknowledging others' contributions to my work. Not that I have anything against it in principle. It's just that doing so takes away from valuable time in which I could be talking about myself. Still, in the interest of maintaining cordial relations with my family, friends, colleagues, supporters, and saboteurs, some thanks are owed:

I should start by thanking those whom I won't be thanking by name due to space, time, and national security concerns. A rather wide circle of friends, correspondents, and fishing advisers (that means you, Rick Boulin) helped me work through pieces in ways they can't conceive of, from their tossed-off e-mails to their midnight rambles. You never know where the next idea will come from or how the current idea will be fertilized. But often as not, it comes by accident through interaction with you, the unsung heroes. I suppose I could recite everyone, but then you'd lose your special unsung-hero status and would be just like the sung-hero riffraff. Personally, I think you're better than that.

There are any number of colleagues who must be thanked by name at the magazine where nearly all of these pieces were first published (*The Weekly Standard*). First and foremost, I should thank William Kristol, Fred Barnes, and John Podhoretz (who was responsible for hiring me as a young punk, so that I could ripen and mature into a middle-aged punk). Back in the midnineties, when dinosaurs roamed the earth, these three men did something heedless and dangerous that today would be considered unthinkable: they started a print magazine. We may never see their like again.

It's impossible to name all my key masthead mates, both current and past, but some of my longest-standing colleagues who have repeatedly lent a sympathetic ear or a piece of their mind, are, in alphabetical order: David Bass, Sonny Bunch (both have moved on, but are still missed), Christopher Caldwell, Philip Chalk, Matt Continetti,

Taybor Cook, Peter Dunn, Terry Eastland, Mike Goldfarb, Jonathan Last, Catherine Lowe, Vic Matus, David Skinner (gone/not forgotten), Nick Swezey, Phil Terzian, Carolyn Wimmer.

Most of the pieces in this book were first raked through by my trusty, gimlet-eyed editors: Richard Starr, Claudia Anderson, or Robert Messenger. You develop an attachment to people who unsplit your infinitives and undangle your participles. I owe each of them in different ways for guarding my flank and making my pieces better. Still, whatever mistakes are in this book, go ahead and blame them. They're the editors, the last line of defense. I'm just a lowly, undisciplined writer. They really should've been more careful.

A second helping of thanks is due Bill Kristol and Richard Starr. People think they know Bill Kristol from his public persona as some peacenik, dope-smoking hippie. And he is that, don't get me wrong. But even if you don't agree with his every political position, as I occasionally don't (Sarah Palin? Really?), he is without fail the best boss you could ever ask for—a man who is generous and good-humored and who regularly bestows a gift more valuable than money: the freedom to write the things you feel compelled to write (though money works too, Bill. Don't let me dissuade you).

The same could be said of my assignment editor, Richard Starr. More than any single individual, he makes my working life a pleasure, at least when I'm not being tormented by fruitless searches for the next kill. Good stories take time and aren't always inevitabilities. Richard cheers on my possibilities, even when those possibilities turn out to be impossibilities. Neither does he hold it against me when that happens. He also lends me the time and real estate within the magazine to do a story right, an editor's impulse that's in short supply if you've had a look around journalism lately.

Last, among my colleagues, I'd like to thank two others in no particular order. Stephen F. Hayes, my fellow senior writer, a dogged reporter, and my fourteenth best friend (with a bullet), has harassed me to write a book more than any person I know. He's written two of his own, I suspect, just to light a fire under me. Thanks for the pressure, Hayes. I know this is just a collection, but here's hoping it gets you off my back for a while so we can return to drinking in peace.

When I was a starry-eyed unemployed journalism graduate, I used to pour over old Andrew Ferguson pieces in the public library.

My style was nothing like his. But he seemed like something more than a good read. He seemed like a model for how to conduct yourself on the page. He obviously cared about what he was writing—not just the subject, but the music of words. He labored. He polished. But all the while, he made it look effortless. In his hands, difficult things became easy. Later, I became an intern at the magazine he then worked for. He held several doors open for me along the way, until I finally became his colleague, and eventually his hero and mentor. His wit and talent and munificence are still traits that young writers should strive to emulate, though good luck pulling off a convincing Andy Ferguson impression. Even old writers haven't managed.

While taking inventory in the early influences department, I should thank P.J. O'Rourke as well. When I was a college student reading his early books, it was evident that P.J. was the coolest man in the writing game. Getting to know him later—whether he was grilling steaks for me in his snow-covered driveway in New Hampshire or dodging unguided bar tabs in a Middle Eastern war zone—I'm pleased to report that my first impression of him was more right than I could've imagined.

On the publishing side, I thank my agent, Elyse Cheney—no relation to the man I fished with in this book. Though she's welcome to come out with us if we ever hit the Snake River again. Elyse doesn't fish, though I'm certain she'd have some useful suggestions for how Dick Cheney could craft a more profitable book proposal.

Random House's Brett Valley is one of the most patient, talented, and decent men in publishing. I owe him not only for his friendship, but for wanting me to write books for him even when nobody else was asking. So it stands to reason that he's pals with another of the most talented and decent men in publishing, Simon & Schuster's Colin Fox. Colin did do some asking. This book, in fact, would not have happened without his vision. Colin is interested in the world, much more so than in current fashions. Who has an appetite for long-form journalism anymore? Well, Colin does. If he likes to read it, he figures, it must be worth publishing. He is a champion and an enthusiast and refuses to let the thieves of wonder, as Nelson Bryant calls them, ruin his good time. He's also a budding fly fisherman. Which figures. Good men usually adhere to certain patterns of behavior.

My father, John Labash, was a thirty-year military officer and is still a gentleman. He's a great example and remains the most righteous, honest man I know. This suggests a paternity test might be in order. He's also the best publicist a guy could have, and I'd like to take this occasion to apologize to all his friends, who for years have had my pieces inflicted on them by him. My mom, Betty Labash, should just be called "The Glue" for short, as she is the unbreakable bonding agent that holds our family together with love and care and a ferocity of spirit. More important, she makes the meanest braciole on the planet. She is single-handedly responsible for my favorite compliment, one only a mother could execute, as it simultaneously inflates your head, then gently lets the air out: "I really loved your piece. It was concise."

My sister, Tamara, and her children Kari, Nick, and Zack, are a perpetual source of inspiration. I pray I'm half as tough as they are if I'm ever tested like they've been. I won't be surprised in the least if I'm reading one of their books someday.

My in-laws provide a second home. Sunday dinners wouldn't be the same without Laura, Eddie, Adria, and Nikki, and their assorted pets, boyfriends, and miscellaneous hangers-on. My father-in-law, Vic Peruzzi, perhaps more than any person, serves as an ideal test audience for unwritten stories. If I'm rewarded by his laughter, I know things might work out. My mother-in-law, Pat, faithfully collects all the finished products in laminated volumes. If my personal archives are ever consumed by fire or flood, her house will be my first stop. It often is anyway. Not only do I keep my kayaks there for year-around escapes down their creek, but Pat's compassion and selflessness are second to no one's.

There is only one man I ever considered to write the foreword to this book, but I figured Tom Wolfe was probably busy, so I asked my great friend Tucker Carlson to instead. Tucker started the same day at the magazine as I did in 1995, and his very first suggestion upon meeting was "let's go get a beer." (It was 10 A.M.) We talked for about four hours that afternoon and haven't stopped talking since. I've never had a brother. But I imagine that if I did, I wouldn't like him any more than I do Tucker. He's given me many gifts over the years, from striper-smiting flies to Joseph Mitchell collections. The best gift, however, has been providing ringside seats to his traveling circus. Like many of the characters in this book, Tucker lives a large life, is afraid of nothing, and gives you honest, wickedly entertaining takes on whatever comes his way. Unlike some of the characters in this book, he is generous and ferociously loyal, and he's interested in other people's lives besides his own. Whenever I finish a piece, the second person I send it to is my editor. The first person I send it to is Tucker Carlson.

Above all others, I want to thank the most graceful and engaging, easiest-to-laugh, and warmest woman I know, my wife, Alana. To detail all she's done for me would add another twenty pages to these acknowledgments and make people sick besides. But I'm most grateful for the two spirited hooligans she suckered me into having, Luke and Dean. Together, the three of them make me profoundly uneasy, as I harbor the suspicion that I have landed in more good fortune than any one man is due. Whatever miniadventures journalism affords, whatever interesting people enter my world, there's really nobody who keeps me more amused and invested in my own narrative than Alana, Luke, and Dino. They make me laugh ceaselessly. With them, even bad days are pretty passable ones.

Thanks is also due my big bear-dog, Moses, a majestic, beautiful beast. He's the only animal who could've filled the void left by the death of my beloved water dog, Levi. Dogs—they're more important than we give them credit for, though not in my acknowledgments.

Last, I want to thank the men and women who lent their lives to the stories in this book. Most of them have led large, untamed, and untidy existences. Some let me in during times of great flux and distress, some as the wheels were coming off, some as they were headed to prison. Some risked my unkindness, then suffered it graciously when I delivered. Some even became my friends afterward. Such is the stuff of life and interesting tales. Thanks for letting me tell yours.

Printed in the United States
By Bookmasters